Three Novels by
FLAUBERT

Three Novels by

FLAUBERT

A STUDY OF TECHNIQUES

R. J. SHERRINGTON

CLARENDON PRESS · OXFORD

1970

Oxford University Press, Ely House, London W.1

GLASGOW NEW YORK TORONTO MELBOURNE WELLINGTON
CAPE TOWN SALISBURY IBADAN NAIROBI DAR ES SALAAM LUSAKA ADDIS ABABA
BOMBAY CALCUTTA MADRAS KARACHI LAHORE DACCA
KUALA LUMPUR SINGAPORE HONG KONG TOKYO

MADE AND PRINTED IN GREAT BRITAIN
BY WILLIAM CLOWES AND SONS, LIMITED
LONDON AND BECCLES

PREFACE

Percy Lubbock's chapter on *Madame Bovary* in his *Craft of Fiction* provided the idea from which this study grew. One of the many appealing qualities of Lubbock's book is that it approaches the novel as a self-contained piece of work which invites examination because of its own excellence. This does not happen as often as one might wish; while the finished work is nearly always given precedence in theory, an enormous amount of critical attention is devoted to unpublished juvenilia, plans, manuscripts, letters, romances, obsessions, and laundry bills. These peripheral considerations can without doubt be valuable aids, so long as they are kept at a respectful distance; in Flaubert studies, they have frequently come close enough to be dangerous.

Lubbock studied a vital part of Flaubert's 'craft' which had been largely neglected, even by critics who did give due emphasis to the published novels. Many years later, some of his conclusions were taken up in an important article by Jean Rousset, who also indicated other equally promising ways of approaching *Madame Bovary*. But these two essays are very brief, and they examine only one novel. Some of their conclusions are incomplete, others are not quite correct; and they give a somewhat unbalanced picture of Flaubert's techniques.

The present study aims, in part, to verify and expand these two critics' appraisals of *Bovary*; it also tries to go much further. The techniques examined by Lubbock and Rousset, notably Flaubert's handling of point of view, can be related in a systematic way to his explicit artistic theories, and their development can be traced through his early works. I have tried to show how and why the restricted point of view came to take precedence over other modes of presentation, but without ever displacing them completely. In the three novels published by Flaubert, variations in the point of view seem to me to provide new insights into his methods of achieving two qualities which he regarded as essential—impersonality, and a unified structure—without ever abdicating his right to provide moral criticism. This is the main subject of my study.

Flaubert uses point of view in different ways in each novel, but he always uses it to the same ends. By the time he wrote *l'Education sentimentale*, he was using it in a way which was unusually subtle for a nineteenth-century novelist. Close study of his methods in this book suggests an interpretation of some parts of it which is both different from the one commonly accepted, and consistent with Flaubert's stated theories. The development of his novelistic technique up to 1869 is in part the development of his skill in weaving criticism of his created world into the fabric of the novel.

Flaubert's concern for methods of communicating his ideals did not end with *l'Education*, so perhaps I should explain why I have chosen to exclude from this study his three later works, *la Tentation de Saint Antoine*, *Trois Contes*, and *Bouvard et Pécuchet*. I am concerned with specifically novelistic techniques, and their relevance to the art of the novel as Flaubert conceived it. Flaubert published only three novels, and in them his method depends for its effect on following in detail the workings of a mind, and on inviting comparisons by the reader of this mind with others, or with itself. The method simultaneously penetrates a mind and remains aloof from it; it is patient and slow-working. Although the other three major works contain variations of it, and sometimes reflect very similar preoccupations, they cannot be approached in precisely the same way. In some respects their methods are very different, so that they would lead off on three separate tangents. They are not a tightly-knit group like the novels, nor does any one of them fit comfortably into the novel group. *Saint Antoine*, which in spite of its distinctive form is a turning-point in Flaubert's technique (it is his first book to look at the world through a single character's eyes while simultaneously indicating that character's delusions), has already been studied elsewhere.[1] The *Contes*, by the mere fact of being short

[1] See my article 'Illusion and Reality in *la Tentation de Saint Antoine*', *AUMLA*, xxiv (Nov. 1965), 272–89.

stories, contain differences in technique and intention which are
at least as significant as the similarities; since the novels depend
so little on events, but rather on minute analysis of reactions
to events through detailed descriptions and continual echoes,
their method just cannot be used to recount a life in fifty
pages.

   As for *Bouvard et Pécuchet*, a major reason for excluding it is
that it is unfinished. The techniques of the earlier novels are so
intimately connected with the form that their significance can
adequately be judged only if the book can be examined as a total
structure. Even Flaubert's intentions in *Bouvard et Pécuchet* remain
in doubt: a large part of the mass of critical writings on it is
devoted to arguments about possibilities. As it is frequently the
final few lines which give a book its perspective, such discussions
easily become sterile, and would in any case lead a long way
from the line I have followed in the present study. The presentation techniques of *Bouvard et Pécuchet* undoubtedly have their
roots in the methods of the earlier novels, but they are different
enough in orientation and development to warrant a separate
study. Its inclusion here would make this one very much more
complicated than it is already.

   All quotations from Flaubert's works are taken from the
Conard edition in twenty-six volumes (1910–54). To reduce
the number of footnotes, most of the page references to this
edition are given in brackets within the text. If no contrary
indication is given, such numbers refer to the book under immediate discussion. For convenience, I have numbered the
four volumes of the supplement to the *Correspondance* X, XI,
XII, XIII to follow on from the nine volumes of the main
edition.

   Quotations from the plans and notes published in *Flaubert et
ses projets inédits* follow Mme Durry in retaining Flaubert's frequently idiosyncratic spelling, punctuation, and accenting. In
all quotations from plans, whether from Durry or elsewhere,
square brackets indicate that the words enclosed by them were
not part of Flaubert's original draft, but were added by him
later.

My sincere thanks are due to the many people who have provided material and moral assistance of all kinds in the course of my work. I should particularly like to mention Professors Ross Chambers, John Davies, Pierre Moreau, and Lloyd Austin, Mrs. Joan Clare and Miss Lesley Marsland.

CONTENTS

I

THEORIES

Truth and Beauty

No work on Flaubert can avoid extensive reference to his correspondence: apart from its intrinsic value, the usefulness to critics of this collection of immensely entertaining letters seems almost unlimited. But its very wealth can be a disadvantage. To begin with, one finds difficulty in resisting the temptation to discover in it Flaubert's last word on almost any subject, to accept as revealed truth (blatant contradictions and the demands of common sense notwithstanding) the jumbled result of fifty years of hasty scrawling. As a sort of bible of Flaubert studies, it can be used to prove almost anything. All critics are aware, of course, of the devil lurking behind the faithful, even in the midst of their most pious occupations; but all too often a few introductory incantations (very like the present one) are taken to be sufficient to exorcize him. After which, one is free to go about the everyday business of criticism as if he did not exist.

Revealed truth is often considered sufficient truth. There is frequently an implicit assumption that the *Correspondance* contains all Flaubert had to say about literature, that it provides the key to his complete literary technique. There has resulted an unfortunate limitation of the subjects normally discussed by Flaubert specialists. Even those who do actually study his work in literary terms often do not go beyond analysing the application of theories and techniques mentioned in the *Correspondance*. That is only the beginning of the problem. Even an author's own discussions of his work, however exhaustive, inevitably leave a great deal unsaid—especially in letters. The only final statement of his aesthetic will be the works themselves. It is, indeed, one of the qualities of a work of art that it towers above any possible statement *about* it: they are always incomplete, the work is permanently complete.

Having said this, one must grant that at least the *Correspondance* is unlikely to be in direct conflict with the total aesthetic statement of the works. It is on this assumption that I shall refer to it initially. Since it is in fact largely silent on the technique which is the principal object of my study, it is important to begin by showing that the general orientation of Flaubert's thought does allow such a technique to develop easily and naturally.

My discussion of the *Correspondance* therefore makes no claim to be exhaustive. It mentions only the essential theories which recur frequently over a long period of time, those without which an adequate view of Flaubert's intentions and aspirations seems impossible. By its very nature the *Correspondance* demands to be treated with this degree of caution. It is the only way to avoid being taken in by certain striking and colourful statements (the eminently quotable sort) which on examination of the novels prove to be meaningless or incidental.

Most of the theories I shall mention are already well known individually, although some have in the past been insufficiently emphasized; and the total picture which they present is almost never used as a starting-point. It is the total picture which most needs to be stressed: Flaubert's assumptions are based on several closely interrelated elements, none of which is allowed to take precedence over the others. This is only another way of saying that Flaubert sought above all unity and harmony, the complete work of art.

Like many of his contemporaries, Flaubert had great faith in what was then called the scientific method in the humanities. He loses no opportunity to hold forth about scientific literary criticism, scientific religion, scientific philosophy, and even, in a fit of rhetoric, scientific government.[1] Not that he made a fetish of science: he was certainly aware of its limited usefulness

[1] e.g. *Correspondance*, III, 336–7, 360, 367–8; IV, 170, 361, 399; V, 110; VI, 33, 215, 228.

to a creative writer. What he admired about it was its basic attitude,[1] which he believed writers could profitably adopt. An author's first duty was to carry out a detailed observation of his subject—humanity—as of any other scientific specimen, taking care neither to admire nor to condemn:

> Il ne s'agit pas de déclamer sur telle ou telle forme, mais bien d'exposer en quoi elle existe, comment elle se rattache à une autre, et *par quoi* elle vit. ... Quand on aura, pendant quelque temps, traité l'âme humaine avec l'impartialité que l'on met dans les sciences physiques à étudier la matière, on aura fait un pas immense. ... C'est peut-être, comme pour les mathématiques, rien qu'une *méthode* à trouver. (*Cor.*, III, 367–8.)

And much later, in 1871:

> Pour que la France se relève, il faut qu'elle passe de l'inspiration à la Science, qu'elle abandonne toute métaphysique, qu'elle entre dans la critique, c'est-à-dire l'examen des choses.[2]

He emphatically does not believe that art should be like science in the sense that it starts out from a number of known facts and from these proves a new fact. Art, he knew, can prove nothing: it can be scientific only in that it impartially records, examines, and organizes facts already available.[3]

It is a direct result of his desire for impartial examination of facts that Flaubert believes no writer—and for that matter, no philosopher, religious or otherwise—can reach any significant permanent conclusion about human destiny. 'Ne pas conclure' is Flaubert's personal equivalent of the two slogans he so liked to quote: Montaigne's 'Que sais-je?' and Rabelais's 'Peut-être' (*Cor.*, I, 62). The reason for this belief is perfectly simple: we cannot reach any conclusions, because we have insufficient data. He objects to religious apologists trying to prove the existence

---

[1] For a contrast between Zola and Flaubert, see Thorlby: *Gustave Flaubert and the Art of Realism* (London, Bowes and Bowes, 1956), p. 9; also Digeon: *Le dernier visage de Flaubert* (Paris, Aubier, 1946), in the section dealing with Flaubert and Spencer, pp. 101 et seq., especially p. 107.

[2] *Cor.*, VI, 281; see also III, 153; IV, 314; VI, 286; VII, 284.

[3] See Ferrère: *L'Esthétique de Gustave Flaubert* (Paris, Conard, 1913), pp. 72–6, for a more detailed examination of this, and his conclusion, p. 76.

of God; he objects to atheists trying to prove His non-existence. He particularly objects, later in his life, to the Naturalists trying to prove their monopoly of literary truth and value. 'La rage de vouloir conclure est une des manies les plus funestes et les plus stériles qui appartiennent à l'humanité' (*Cor.*, V, 111), he says with characteristic assurance in 1863. This is probably the commonest theme of all in the *Correspondance*: it first appears in 1839, when Flaubert was eighteen, and is never forgotten. The conviction naturally had a profound influence on his approach to literature, and especially to his own works. Significantly, he believed that in refusing to 'conclude' he was following the example of the very greatest writers. Rabelais and Montaigne, two of his greatest literary heroes, have already been mentioned. Elsewhere, Flaubert says: 'Je vois ... que les plus grands génies et les plus grandes œuvres n'ont jamais conclu. Homère, Shakespeare, Goethe, tous les fils aînés de Dieu (comme dit Michelet) se sont bien gardés de faire autre chose que *représenter*' (*Cor.*, V, 111). Conversely, he criticizes Hugo, Zola, Feydeau, and Louise Colet, among others, for making rash judgements in their works.

Not 'concluding' means not having preconceived notions about life; the corollary to this is seeing life as it is, examining and accepting the facts—which brings us back to the original requirement of a scientific attitude. The many passages in the *Correspondance* containing phrases such as 'voir les choses comme elles sont', 'acceptons tout', and so on, are all slightly different aspects of the same critical idea.

All very well; but even a scientist is a human being, and regardless of intellectual concepts, human beings are apt to think of themselves and others in an emotional and subjective fashion. One cannot help one's own character, admits Flaubert,[1] and one cannot help interpreting human problems in the light of one's character and experience. Enough has been said by others of Flaubert's character; suffice it to recall here that he did 'conclude' very frequently, and that his conclusions were on the whole pessimistic, but almost fanatically idealistic as regards art. It is important to remember, however, that the pessimistic side was

---

[1] e.g. *Cor.*, V, 385, 397; VII, 280.

frequently tempered by a sense of the comic or of the obscene —the two often correspond. We can perhaps take the obscene aspect as read, in spite of the mutilations even to the 1954 Supplement of the *Correspondance*,[1] provided we do not pretend that it is not there. As for the comic aspect, it can in part be summarized in the grotesque stupidity of the celebrated *Garçon*, but this is not the whole story. There are many passages in the *Correspondance* showing Flaubert as a very ordinary person enjoying stupid little jokes and puns, and in general being just jovial. To ignore this is to draw a false and incomplete picture of him, to present him as a frantic romantic, completely and continuously miserable. Such exaggeration is unfortunate, the more so because it is so easily perpetuated as a tradition. Nicely put paradoxes—like Bourget's 'nihiliste affamé de l'absolu'—frequently seem more attractive than the simple truth.

Even allowing for these factors, and for the exaggerations inherent in the *Correspondance*, it remains true that Flaubert easily arrived at pessimistic judgements on life and his fellow men. But these judgements are not entirely incompatible with his desire for a scientific method. After all, a major tool in some sciences, especially the human sciences, is the method of comparison and contrast; and a major requirement of the scientist is that he should be capable of seeing both sides of a question. It is precisely by this method that Flaubert arrives at his conclusions: in observing a scene or an aspect of human behaviour, he frequently sees two contrasting elements of it, whereas many people would see only one. If he emphasizes the uglier or less worthy side at the expense of the other, this is usually because he is reacting against the failure of others to see it at all. The opposite of this sort of pessimism is not optimism, but complacency: Flaubert's 'pessimism' must be seen against the smugness of the majority of his contemporaries. Honesty, not cynicism, leads him to make a point of noticing both 'l'odeur des citronniers et celle des cadavres' (III, 137) while travelling in the Middle

---

[1] There exists a complete text of the *Supplément*, dated 1953, and apparently a limited edition. It did not achieve a place in the Bibliothèque Nationale's *Enfer*, but it is not in the general catalogue either.

East, to be aware always of 'autant de rubis dans le fumier que
de perles dans la rosée' (I, 297), to delight in ironic twists of fate.
Similarly he notes 'le grotesque de l'amour'—'l'idée du profil
étrange que je devais avoir dans ce moment-là me faisait tellement
rire . . .' (I, 236). This is also why he can see that 'mes compatriotes
ont des binettes gigantesques' (VI, 4), and why he stresses the
contrast between the 'gants blancs' of the Prussian officers and
the destruction for which they were responsible during the war
with France.[1]

His is a very personal pessimism, resulting partly from the
romanticism he so much admired when he was young, partly
from his bitter experiences in his later life (the most extreme
expressions of it are to be found in the early volumes of the
Correspondance, in the Œuvres de jeunesse, and in the letters written
during the Franco-Prussian War and the Commune), and partly
because he knew that he needed something to balance his latent
idealism in order to stop it from becoming ridiculous. But it is
also closely connected with his quite sincere intellectual desire
to observe life accurately and completely, to achieve a balanced
view of himself and others. He did not always succeed—the
other factors proved too strong for him—but he did try. Digeon's
conclusion is accurate: 'Le scepticisme de Flaubert est donc
plutôt une forme de discipline personnelle qu'une doctrine
assurée',[2] provided we keep in mind that there was a 'doctrine
assurée' first, and the 'discipline personnelle' is the product of
a slightly older, and considerably more thoughtful man.

The ideas discussed so far apply to Flaubert the man, and are
basic to his way of thinking. They are applicable not only to
literature but to everything that interested him—religion,
philosophy, ethics, and so on. When we turn to his specifically
literary theories, we are confronted with a paradox. While he
believes that man may never have enough facts at his disposal
to make any permanent decision about human problems, Flaubert
clearly credits art with a capacity for some sort of truth, here

[1] Cor., VI, 184, 203, 225; for other examples, see I, 30, 39, 79, 163, 319; II, 10,
32, 430; III, 129, 224, 407; VIII, 59.
[2] Digeon, op. cit., p. 111.

and now. What is the nature of this artistic truth, and how can it be attained? And, since Flaubert is normally dubbed a realist, what is the relationship between this literary truth and the reality of everyday life? His answers are orthodox: they place him in the mainstream of critical theory, while separating him decisively from most other nineteenth-century novelists.

Such a discussion can easily be diverted because of the inordinate importance Flaubert gave to 'documents', and because of the obvious similarity on this point between him and many of his contemporaries—Champfleury, Duranty, the Goncourt, and Zola, for example. The preoccupation with documents is a direct result of Flaubert's concern for scientific method, and of a characteristic attitude of his time. Since they constitute 'truth' of a certain kind, it is as well to dispose of them first.

Flaubert's passion for documents[1] has been the occasion of many jibes, of accusations that he wasted more time than he used, and even that he was a little mad. Perhaps that is true. But there is little point in arguing that such minute preparations are unnecessary, that other writers have produced masterpieces without such pedantry. The simple fact is that however unwieldy his methods may appear, they did produce great works, and that is what we have to be concerned with. Our job is to look at what he did, not to speculate on what he might have done if he had been someone else. It is especially pointless to prescribe what he ought to have done.

[1] Some examples: for *Madame Bovary* he read through several 'keepsakes' and children's books (*Cor.*, II, 370), went to the *Comices agricoles* (II, 466) and the funeral of a doctor's wife (III, 224-6), consulted a doctor on arsenic poisoning (IV, 99) and a lawyer on financial troubles (IV, 86), even copied out passages from *le Rituel de Paris* (IV, 139). For *Salammbô* he seeks out articles on Carthaginian gods (IV, 175) and photographs of Tunis and district (IV, 177), studies the *code civil* of Carthage (IV, 273), reads an enormous number of books on his subject (fifty-three by May 1857: IV, 189; one hundred by July: IV, 202), and finally goes to Africa. For *l'Education* he visits Sens (V, 156), Sèvres and Creil (V, 293), Fontainebleau (V, 387), and even Père-Lachaise cemetery (VI, 7). He also studies the methods of art dealers (V, 167), the making of porcelain (V, 201), the situation at the Stock Exchange (V, 261-2), and of course the whole history of the period, including legal and religious matters. All this in addition to his personal experience of the riots of 1848 (II, 338). The lists could be continued indefinitely.

Some interesting points emerge from an examination of Flaubert's mania for facts. We occasionally find that they were so important for him that he would re-write whole passages rather than tolerate a factual error. While writing *l'Education sentimentale* he discovered to his horror that he had made Frédéric and Rosanette take the train to Fontainebleau, but that in 1848 there was no railway line there. The result? 'Cela me fait deux passages à démolir et à recommencer.'[1] Such cases seem rare, however. Normally Flaubert has firmly in his mind the *type* of thing he wants to say, and then sets out to find facts which will fit his situation. The plan—and hence the action—of his novel controls the facts: the facts do not control the plan. Thus we find him asking the Goncourt for 'une théorie *quelconque* pour les portraits d'enfants' (XI, 172), and going to a great deal of trouble 'pour découvrir un certain paysage *que j'ai en tête*' (VII, 53), in which Bouvard and Pécuchet are to live: 'J'ai besoin d'un sot endroit au milieu d'une belle contrée, et que dans cette contrée on puisse faire des promenades géologiques et archéologiques' (VII, 152). He knew what he wanted before he started looking for it. Similarly, he asks a friend for 'une férocité d'enfant commise sur un chat' (XIII, 203) when he is about to write that lamentable episode; and the principle is implicit in his comments when he is uncertain about the authenticity of another detail: 'Et maintenant, ça me gênerait beaucoup pour mon plan qu'il en fût autrement' (XIII, 100). Almost all the fact-finding is carried out just before Flaubert begins to write the relevant section of his novel, when his plan is finalized, when he knows exactly what he wants to say, and is searching only for a means of giving it expression. He is not particularly concerned with what facts he uses, so long as they *are* facts, and will fit in with his plans. Other aspects of his work are much more important to him. To some extent the *Correspondance* can be blamed for misleading critics here: Flaubert's letters are so full of demands for this or that piece of information, that this appears to be his major preoccupation. But surely it is more likely that Flaubert,

---

[1] *Cor.*, V, 409; see also III, 422–3 for a similar statement about part of the *pied bot* episode of *Madame Bovary*.

pressed for time, will mention only the things he needs help with. The very fact that he feels able to enlist other people's help so freely in gathering details suggests how peripheral they really were. The vital human element of his books comes entirely from him, and from his observations of behaviour, which he had cultivated as a habit from an early age.[1] He requires no help from anyone here, nor does he ask for any:[2] the book is either in his head or in his plan before the 'research' begins. Consider, for example, *l'Education sentimentale*. The first plan of this work dates from early 1863,[3] while the first definite evidence we have of fact-finding for it is not until August 1864 (V, 156). Most of the intervening period was spent working on the plan. The same principle applies to *Madame Bovary* and to *Bouvard et Pécuchet*, although not quite so rigidly to *Salammbô*, where a great deal of initial reading seems to have preceded detailed work on the plan. Yet even so, Flaubert mentions very early (about July 1857) that his real difficulty with this book is not in the facts: 'Ce qui m'embête à trouver dans mon roman, c'est l'élément psycho-logique, à savoir la façon de sentir' (IV, 200); and the following month there is a suggestion that he is going on with his fact-finding only because the human element is proving too difficult: '. . . je recule comme un lâche devant *Carthage*. J'accumule notes sur notes, livres sur livres, *car* (italic mine) je ne me sens pas en train. Je ne vois pas nettement mon objectif. . . . ce qui me turlupine, c'est le côté psychologique de mon histoire.'[4]

The precedence of plans over supporting facts (of conception

[1] Frequently he observes behaviour patterns *in case* these may later be useful: *Cor.*, I, 97, 168, 417; II, 144; V, 127; XI, 116. Gothot-Mersch: *La Genèse de Madame Bovary* (Paris, Corti, 1966) confirms my argument: see pp. 90–110 (passim).

[2] Except perhaps from Bouilhet, in regard to fairly minor details—e.g. see the letter from Bouilhet to Flaubert about a scene from *Salammbô*, quoted in Albalat: *Gustave Flaubert et ses amis* (Paris, Plon, 1927), pp. 17–18. Note, however, that this is after the passage has been written, and is mere revision.

[3] Durry: *Flaubert et ses projets inédits* (Paris, Nizet, 1950), pp. 137, 141–2.

[4] *Cor.*, IV, 215, 216; cf. IV, 189. It is not implied here that his plan was finalized in all its details before he began writing. On the contrary, he began his novels with only an outline—the 'idée mère d'où toutes les autres découlent' (IV, 463)—and the final plan for each chapter was made separately just before he began to write that chapter. But this does not materially affect the argument.

or invention over reality) becomes an explicit principle when Flaubert comes into contact with other novelists. His criticisms of his friends at this time are especially valuable because they are not mere theories, but codifications of his own previous practice. One of his clearest statements on the question comes in a letter to Feydeau, criticizing that author's *Daniel*:

> *L'incroyable docteur!* Ah! celui-là est folichon! Où diable as-tu vu qu'il en existât de pareils? tu vas me répondre par un nom propre; je connais ton modèle physiquement, n'est-ce pas? mais là s'arrête la vérité. ... voilà de la fantaisie ou je ne m'y connais pas (IV, 294).

Clearly, truth for Flaubert does not lie primarily in facts, even when they concern people. And this was written in 1858, when he was going to so much trouble over facts for *Salammbô*.

The more he had to do with the Naturalists, the more definite he became. In 1875 he says:

> Ceux que je vois souvent ... recherchent tout ce que je méprise et s'inquiètent médiocrement de ce qui me tourmente. Je regarde comme très secondaire le détail technique, le renseignement local, enfin le côté historique et exact des choses. Je recherche par-dessus tout la *beauté*, dont mes compagnons sont médiocrement en quête (VII, 281).

The following year he pronounces *l'Assommoir* 'ignoble, absolument'; and explains: 'Faire vrai ne me paraît pas être la première condition de l'art. Viser au beau est le principal, et l'atteindre si l'on peut' (VII, 351). He had held this theory for at least twenty years—in 1857, speaking of his researches for *Salammbô*, he says: 'Cela importe fort peu, c'est le côté secondaire. Un livre peut être plein d'énormités et de bévues, et n'en être pas moins fort beau';[1] what he regarded as the exaggerations of the Naturalists simply prompted him to formulate it more decisively and more often.

Unfortunately, these quotations, clear as they are in intention, lead to a dead end. Passing from 'Truth' to 'Beauty' like this is merely passing from one unknown to another. We shall have to look elsewhere for a more positive idea of what Flaubert wanted. Yet it is worth remembering that invariably, when he

---

[1] *Cor.*, IV, 211; see also IV, 136; V, 35, 92; VII, 359; VIII, 374; XII, 130.

connects these two magic words, Beauty is the one which takes precedence.

Happily Flaubert sometimes develops his theories in terms which show more clearly what he really means. For example in speaking of Daudet's *Nabab*, having once again emphasized that facts are merely an accessory—a 'tremplin'—he adds, by way of explanation: 'il ne s'agit pas seulement de voir, il faut arranger et fondre ce que l'on a vu' (VII, 359; cf. VIII, 224); and writing to Taine on his 'Idéal dans l'Art': '... on ne peut faire vrai qu'en choisissant et en exagérant.—Toute la différence consiste à exagérer harmonieusement' (XI, 118). Here there is a new dimension. Flaubert obviously realized that reality cannot be reproduced in a work of literature (he has not always been credited with even this minimal perspicacity).[1] Further, even if that were possible it was not one of Flaubert's aims: this decisively separates him on a major issue from contemporaries such as Champfleury.[2]

The literary artist, then, chooses and combines his facts to achieve a level of truth which is beyond that of the reality with which he began. Somehow the transformation takes place in the process of writing, depends entirely on the author and not at all on his material. This, I believe, is all he was trying to say in the famous passage on the 'livre sur rien': if such a book were possible, it would simply prove that the subject is immaterial, that all the value comes from how the subject is handled.[3] It is certainly the force of the statement about the 'truth'of Tacitus. What would happen if we found authentic documents proving Tacitus had written nothing but lies? 'Qu'est-ce que ça ferait à la gloire et au style de Tacite? Rien du tout. Au lieu d'une vérité, nous en aurions deux: celle de l'histoire et celle de Tacite' (VIII, 374).

[1] The question is more fully treated in Cormeau: *Physiologie du roman* (Bruxelles, la Renaissance du Livre, 1947), e.g. pp. 20 et seq., 161 et seq.

[2] See Beuchat: *Histoire du naturalisme français* (Paris, Corrêa, 1949), vol. I, pp. 208 et seq.; Martino: *Le Roman réaliste sous le Second Empire* (Paris, Hachette, 1913), pp. 154 et seq.

[3] This is made much clearer in *Cor.*, IV, 225, about *Salammbô*: 'tout dépend de l'exécution', etc., q.v.

Truth of this sort can never be achieved by bare facts, but by the proper arrangement of *significant* facts. Significant facts, for Flaubert, are those which indicate to the reader eternal, or universal, aspects of human behaviour (another indication of Flaubert's orthodoxy). He is convinced of this above all by the example of the greatest writers of the past:

Ce qui distingue les grands génies, c'est la généralisation et la création. Ils résument en un type des personnalités éparses et apportent à la conscience du genre humain des personnages nouveaux. Est-ce qu'on ne croit pas à l'existence de Don Quixotte comme à celle de César? Shakespeare est quelque chose de formidable sous ce rapport (III, 31).

Conversely, he criticizes others who do not seem to him to meet this requirement: Dante's work, he says, 'est loin des poètes universels', 'faite pour un temps et non pour tous les temps' (II, 408); *Uncle Tom's Cabin* is 'actuel', a quality opposed to 'la vérité seule, l'éternel, le Beau pur'; it is 'une chose spéciale, fausse' (III, 60). In another place he declares that 'on n'est vrai qu'à force de généraliser' (V, 379). If any further proof is required that these are not just facile generalizations, of the type for which the *Correspondance* ought to be far more notorious than it is, but reflect a fundamental principle of his art, the idea recurs in Flaubert's *Préface* to the *Dernières Chansons* of Bouilhet. This preface is the only real piece of literary criticism Flaubert published. Unlike the *Correspondance*, it was written with the care he normally lavished on his published writing, and is therefore a more reliable source for his theories.[1] In it he praises Bouilhet in the following terms: '... il prenait la grande route, c'est-à-dire les sentiments généraux, les côtés immuables de l'âme humaine ...'.[2] There is, moreover, in the letter to Taine quoted above (XI, 118), as well as in the passage on *Uncle Tom's Cabin*, a suggestion that he believed this principle to be so basic that the Beauty, as well as the Truth, of a work of literature, would be ruined without it: 'En effet une œuvre n'a d'importance qu'en

[1] See *Cor.*, VI, 303, 306, 313, 317, 321.
[2] *Cor.*, VI, 484; for other statements of the same principle, see I, 46; III, 213; IV, 425, 429; V, 338; VI, 456; VII, 281.

vertu de son éternité, c'est-à-dire que plus elle représentera l'humanité de tous les temps, plus elle sera belle.'

In practice, too, the principle of truth through universality is an essential part of Flaubert's view of literature, for it appears even when he is thinking about a tiny section of a novel in progress, rather than the enunciation of grand theories. When he is searching for 'documents' for Emma's early life, he speaks, not of Emma, but of the sort of person she is to represent: 'Voilà deux jours que je tâche d'entrer dans les rêves de jeunes filles' (II, 370). He speaks of her in the same terms some months later: 'Tu me parles des misères de la femme; je suis dans ce milieu. . . . Si mon livre est bon, il chatouillera doucement mainte plaie féminine; plus d'une sourira en s'y reconnaissant' (III, 11). He sees Emma as a type, as well as an individual; her life is a collection of facts which are significant and representative. When he observes a funeral, it is a *type* of funeral which interests him: 'J'espère faire couler les larmes aux autres avec ces larmes d'un seul, . . . il faut que mon bonhomme (c'est un médecin aussi) vous émeuve pour tous les veufs' (III, 225). This explains his delight when he discovers on occasions that he has actually anticipated reality: his method is vindicated when his work is so utterly typical that it *becomes* fact. For example, in *le Pays* he finds a journalist writing about Switzerland in the style he had ascribed to Emma and Léon; in a newspaper report of a mayoral speech he finds a sentence which he claims is identical with one used by the *Conseiller municipal* at the *Comices* (III, 285). Nearly twenty years later he recalls that 'tous les pharmaciens de la Seine-Inférieure, se reconnaissant dans Homais, voulaient venir chez moi me flanquer des gifles' (VI, 107). This is Flaubert's truth, the sort which justifies his immodest assertion: 'O bêtise humaine, te connais-je donc?' (III, 243.)

Such general statements on truth and universality, while not being directly incompatible with Flaubert's practical aesthetic as seen in his works, do suggest a certain tension between what he thought and what he actually did. If he really did regard all these small facts as being of so little importance, why did he spend such a large proportion of his time searching them out?

His ideals are not normally associated with the fact-grubbing type of writer. He could have adopted Stendhal's more cavalier approach without changing his theories in the slightest.[1] After all, Stendhal's occasionally blatant disregard for factual con- sistency does not really diminish the value of his works—any more than Flaubert's are diminished by the few amazing errors (such as Rosanette's twenty-five month pregnancy) which escaped his notice.[2] The explanation probably lies in an uneasy relationship between Flaubert's ideals and his personal tendencies, and between his ideals and those of the period in which he lived. On the one hand, he knew that many great writers had not bothered with such trivialities, and their works were not much the worse for it; on the other hand, he needed to curb his natural tendency to wander from one generality to another, without ever getting down to facts—a tendency clearly to be seen in both the *Œuvres de jeunesse* and the *Correspondance*. The very greatest can ignore the minutiae of painstaking technique, as they have 'something' which compensates for their grossest errors in detail (*Cor.*, I, 385–6; III, 32). But Flaubert had tried this broad, bold path with signal lack of success: one can only approve his 1853 judgement of *Novembre*, and add that it is even more true of some of his other juvenilia: 'Ah! quel nez fin j'ai eu dans ma jeunesse de ne pas le publier! Comme j'en rougirais maintenant!' (III, 379.) Moreover, both personal pride and his high regard for literature led him to hunt down factual errors for another reason: he knew that reviewers, in their inability to handle the central issue of a book's literary worth, constantly criticize trivia. This happened to *Salammbô* in particular—the book for which facts were most difficult to establish. He must have foreseen the situation, for there is a strong element of rationalization in his many statements of this period about *probabilités* in literature: 'On ne pourra pas me prouver que j'ai dit des sottises d'arché- ologie' (IV, 202). 'Personne ne me prouvera que j'ai dit des

---

[1] For details, see Blin: *Stendhal et les problèmes du roman* (Paris, Corti, 1954), pp. 37–40.

[2] See Castex: *Flaubert: l'Education sentimentale* (Paris, Centre de documentation universitaire, 1959), pp. 58–9.

absurdités' (IV, 210). Flaubert's pride is quite as important as his theories, and he does not much like the prospect of being proved wrong by mere journalists or critics; nevertheless he is uncertain of some of his facts, and even before the book is written he is preparing his reply to the Froehners of this world. When the attack came, he was ready with such shockingly paradoxical phrases as, 'Je me moque de l'archéologie.' He nevertheless cannot refrain from showing that at the same time he knows all about it.

That a man like Froehner could even contemplate a criticism of the archaeology of a book published as a novel, shows the extreme reverence for the scientific idol in this period. Contemporary social pressure undoubtedly reinforced Flaubert's personal decision to impose this discipline upon himself. He explicitly acknowledges the fact in his somewhat hysterical criticism of *les Misérables* and its 'bonshommes en sucre': 'L'observation est une qualité secondaire en littérature, mais il n'est pas permis de peindre si faussement la société quand on est le contemporain de Balzac et de Dickens' (V, 34–6). He saw clearly the weaknesses of *les Misérables*; he also saw clearly the dangers inherent in his own method—'L'étude de l'habit nous fait oublier l'âme', etc. (IV, 211–12); 'si un roman est aussi embêtant qu'un bouquin scientifique, bonsoir, il n'y a plus d'Art' (IV, 441). He knew that he had to produce work which lay between two extremes, which would not be inconsistent with either, but would combine the best elements of both. The tension is thus a continuous attempt at compromise. He never defined theoretically the limits of this compromise—it is doubtful whether he could have—but he certainly defined them in practice, in each one of his mature works. We are back to the inevitable conclusion: important works of literature extend and enrich their author's aesthetic theories, and are not confined within them. We must not regard Flaubert's works as any sort of 'practical application' of the theories of the *Correspondance*.

We have already seen the close connection between the concepts of truth and universality, and Flaubert's final goal of Beauty.

We must now consider this last more closely, remembering to give it due emphasis. While Flaubert's intense desire for artistic beauty has not gone unnoticed by the critics, all too often it is conveniently forgotten after a passing reference to its importance. This is doubtless due in part to the difficulty of discussing in clear terms so vague and abstract a quality. Most people freely admit that Beauty (whatever it may be) ought to be found in great literature; that Flaubert wanted it in his works, and that indeed it is there; after which, they prefer to talk about something else. Fairly recently, certain critics[1] have come to insist rather more on the structural aspects of Flaubert's work, and to connect these with the concept of Beauty. But there have been few serious attempts to analyse what the *Correspondance* has to say on the subject.

It must first be emphasized that the *Correspondance* does in fact provide very few explicit guidelines. Flaubert had as much difficulty as anyone else in making clear what he means by *le Beau*, and it would be idle to expect a real definition in a collection of hastily-written and quickly forgotten letters. Certainly he frequently mentions Beauty in general terms, as an absolute quality which transcends all such accidents as literary 'schools' and historical periods: 'Il n'y a *qu'un Beau*. C'est le même partout, mais il a des aspects différents; ...' (III, 336); 'Un bon vers de Boileau est un bon vers d'Hugo.'[2] But really meaningful statements are non-existent. The best we can do is draw inferences from other attitudes more clearly stated; for if we accept Flaubert's oft-repeated assertions that his ultimate goal was always Beauty, it follows that the things he criticizes in his fellow writers are opposed to his concept of Beauty. For example, his stubborn refusal to regard literature as a saleable commodity stems largely from his belief that concern for money usually results in compromises and sacrifice of literary ideals.[3] Similarly, when he accuses Louise Colet in terms like these: 'Toi tu mêles au Beau

[1] e.g. Rousset: *Forme et signification* (Paris, Corti, 1964); Moreau: *Flaubert: Madame Bovary* (Paris, Centre de documentation universitaire, 1949).

[2] *Cor.*, III, 249; see also II, 37; VII, 294, 312; VIII, 118, 128, 144.

[3] See especially IV, 342, and his remarks about Gautier, II, 398–9. This seems to be the prime reason for his phobia about journalists.

un tas de choses étrangères, l'utile, l'agréable ...' (I, 307) '... le patriotisme, l'amour, ...' (II, 65); or when he berates her for envying Corneille's *glory* rather than his works (II, 64); or when he makes jibes at Balzac's ambitions (VII, 384, 386; VIII, 58), Du Camp and Feydeau's sermonizing (VIII, 144; IV, 391), Lamartine and Musset's sentimentality (II, 397–8; X, 252–3), Taine's pre-occupation with 'explaining' art (XI, 88, 118); it is obvious that for him all these things are incompatible with *le Beau*.

But surely this cannot be all there is to say about Flaubert's concern for Beauty. If his much-vaunted idealization of the whole business of literature is sincere, it must have had a profound and continuous influence on the way he wrote. It did: ultimately we shall be forced back to the novels to discover what he meant by Beauty, for it is they which constitute his definition of it. Mean-while, our search for it in the *Correspondance* is on the wrong track if we look for it in the grandiose generalizations where it is mentioned by name. Flaubert is talking about Beauty whenever he is talking about literature: it is not after all an abstract quality which one can hope to isolate and define, it is simply synonymous with good literature. It is in fact the combination of all the pre-cise details of technique of which he speaks. When we have examined these, we have examined what Flaubert thinks artistic beauty is.

The 'tour d'ivoire' idea—the author shutting himself off from contemporary life—occurs very frequently, and should be men-tioned here. Flaubert's reasons for adopting this attitude are twofold: it allows him to avoid direct contact with what disgusts him, and it provides the necessary conditions for working towards his ideal of Beauty. The second reason has perhaps not been stressed as much as it should be. By necessary conditions, Flaubert does not mean simply the obvious physical requirements of peace and quiet. He believes that by separating himself from the world he is able to look at it and write about it more objectively, by the mere fact that he is not 'involved', that life does not affect him personally. It is both a psychological and an aesthetic require-ment. He is thus avoiding the danger to which Du Camp, Fey-deau, George Sand, Gautier, and even, on one occasion, Bouilhet succumbed: he is not led, through personal involvement, into preaching about problems local and immediate. He can distinguish the eternally important human questions, and concentrate solely on them.[1] Hence the ivory tower is sometimes replaced by the pyramid, a structure more suited to Flaubert's requirements—'élevée et la base solide' (II, 428). When serious problems really do intrude upon him (the War, the death of his mother, the ruin of his niece), he is incapable of writing, not only because of his understandable sense of despair, but also because past experience had shown him that when he was emotionally involved he wrote badly. For some writers, severe emotional shocks eventually prove to be a source of inspiration, the catalyst resulting in, say, a polemical document (Bernanos, Hugo), or, by reaction, a highly idealized or escapist piece of work, or perhaps a lyric poem (Milton's *Lycidas*, the work of several of the Romantics, both English and French). For Flaubert, it is the reverse: when emotion begins, art stops.

Flaubert's belief in the value of hard, patient labour as a means of producing works of art has become legendary. Fortunately, there is an increasing awareness that the torture involved much more than perfecting his 'style' in the narrow sense to which several critics have limited their discussions. Some of his more outrageous statements about style—'de la forme naît l'idée', for example—are no longer taken seriously.[2] Indeed, they could never have been given much credence if the *Correspondance*, and gossipy reports from people like the Goncourt and Du Camp, had been treated more critically: it is inconceivable that a man who really believed such things could have written *l'Education sentimentale*. Yet it is true that the *Correspondance* does contain many passages where 'style' is given precedence. The only way of resolving an apparent contradiction between what Flaubert said he wanted to do, and what he actually did, is to conclude that

[1] e.g. *Cor.*, II, 268–9; V, 197; VI, 17. Brombert: *The Novels of Flaubert: a study of themes and techniques* (Princeton University Press, 1966) pp. 13–16, has some very interesting comments on the deep-seated reasons for Flaubert's 'monastic urge' and on some of its manifestations. These reasons are additional to, but not incompatible with the more rational ones discussed here.

[2] Durry, op. cit., pp. 40–1.

'style' was not limited to the polishing and re-polishing of individual phrases or sentences. Such an extended conception of style is after all not unusual, but for some reason it is seldom used in Flaubert studies. Consider, for example, the following passage about Bouilhet from the *Préface aux Dernières Chansons*:

Peu d'auteurs ont pris autant garde au choix de mots, à la variété des tournures, aux transitions—et il n'accordait pas le titre d'écrivain à celui qui ne possède que certaines parties du style. Combien des plus vantés seraient incapables de faire une narration, de joindre bout à bout une analyse, un portrait et un dialogue! (VI, 485; see also II, 202; IV, 165.)

Clearly the questions of structure and of composition referred to in the second sentence are being put forward as aspects of style. A similar broadening is implied in a letter to Louise Colet: 'Le style est tout et je me plains de ce que, dans *la Servante*, tu n'as pas exprimé tes idées par des faits ou des tableaux' (IV, 10). In some letters he goes even further, and uses the word 'style' as synecdoche, standing for 'literature', or 'art':

Depuis qu'on fait du style, je crois que personne ne s'est donné autant de mal que moi. Chaque jour j'y vois plus clair; mais la belle avance si la faculté imaginative ne va pas de pair avec la critique! (II, 358.)
... l'été prochain je verrai à tenter *Saint Antoine*. Si ça ne marche pas dès le début, je plante le style là, d'ici à de longues années. Je ferai du grec, de l'histoire, de l'archéologie, n'importe quoi, toutes choses plus faciles enfin (II, 53–4).

Ah! quels découragements quelquefois, quel rocher de Sisyphe à rouler que le style, et la prose surtout! *Ça n'est jamais fini*. Cette semaine pourtant ... j'ai fait un grand pas. J'ai arrêté le plan du milieu de mes comices ... (III, 362).

Style goes far beyond an obsession with the harmonious sound of individual sentences or paragraphs; it can also mean what others have called 'composition' or 'forme'—the combination and harmonious arrangement of all the elements of a work, the whole complex range of mechanical processes which together give complete expression to the Idea, the basic conception.

There are other elements which Flaubert clearly regarded as essential in achieving Beauty. By far the most important of these is the concept of Unity. The theme occurs constantly in the *Correspondance*, from the enthusiastic outburst of 1846 to considered criticisms of young writers like Huysmans thirty years later:

> Travaille, médite, médite surtout, condense ta pensée, tu sais que les beaux fragments ne sont rien. L'unité, tout est là! L'ensemble, voilà ce qui manque à tous ceux d'aujourd'hui, aux grands comme aux petits. Mille beaux endroits, pas une œuvre (I, 375).

Unity has not received nearly enough attention in Flaubert criticism, although it was briefly noted in Sainte-Beuve's article on *Madame Bovary*.[1] Until recently, the idea of unity has been taken in Flaubert studies to mean either of two things. First Dumesnil, reacting against the theory that Flaubert thought of nothing but stringing pretty words together, spoke of the intimate connection in his work between thought and language.[2] Secondly, Dumesnil speaks of Flaubert's 'unity' in the sense that he has certain themes and methods which constantly recur from his earliest works to his latest. This idea was put forward largely in reaction against Faguet's thesis that Flaubert could not decide whether to be a Romantic or a Realist, so reached an arrangement with himself whereby he would alternate from work to work.[3] While both these ideas are perfectly valid, they do not underline Flaubert's real preoccupation with unity: that every element of each novel—action, characters, dialogue, style and so on—should be so combined and integrated as to form a complete and harmonious whole, in such a way that nothing could be added to, and nothing taken away from the finished work, without in some way spoiling it. The idea is not new—again it places Flaubert

---

[1] Sainte-Beuve: *Madame Bovary*, lundi, 4 mai, 1857. Quotations from Sainte-Beuve's articles are taken from *Les grands écrivains français* (études des *Lundis* et des *Portraits* classées selon un ordre nouveau et annotées par Maurice Allem, XIXᵉ siècle, *Les Romanciers*, II, Paris, Garnier, 1927).

[2] Dumesnil: *Gustave Flaubert. L'homme et l'œuvre* (Paris, Desclée de Brouwer, 3ᵉ édition, 1947), pp. 318, 418; *Vocation*, pp. 211–12. Frejlich: *Flaubert d'après sa Correspondance* (Paris, Société française d'éditions littéraires et techniques, 1933), pp. 384 et seq., also speaks of this sort of unity, though in rather a confused manner. The idea occurs many times in the *Cor.*, e.g. I, 321; II, 339, 416; III, 141, 336; IV, 243; VII, 290.

[3] Dumesnil: *L'homme et l'œuvre*, pp. 303 et seq.; *Vocation* p. 206.

squarely in the orthodox camp—but originality of theory has never been a prerequisite of a great writer. Besides, if we must use the *Correspondance*, we must use it to give a complete picture, and not concentrate too much on the unusual, the bizarre, and the *fait divers*.

There are so many statements insisting on the necessity for unity that our only difficulty is the embarrassment of choice. Most of them are all the more significant in that they occur in what might be termed the 'practical' letters—those giving precise details of what Flaubert himself is trying to do at a given moment, and those criticizing works by other people which he has just finished reading. It is these letters, rather than those containing hastily developed, high-sounding generalizations, which most faithfully reflect Flaubert's real attitudes.

Lack of unity is the basic fault he sees in most of his early works when he turns to them later with a more critical eye. Significantly, these criticisms are made while he is writing *Madame Bovary*. The early version of *Saint Antoine*, he says, contains plenty of pearls, 'mais les perles ne font pas le collier; c'est le fil'.[1] Later, when he comes to rewrite *Saint Antoine*, he is constantly concerned with ways of avoiding the fault.[2] He is concerned with it, too, when he remarks on how difficult it would be to publish fragments of the work, and tries to find a passage 'qui ferait le mieux un ensemble' (II, 319). In the same way, he protests violently at the deletion of some parts of *Madame Bovary* in *la Revue de Paris*; although these cuts were very short compared with the length of the work, he inserted a note disclaiming all responsibility for the novel, and asking the reader to regard it as merely fragments.[3]

---

[1] *Cor.*, II, 362. This is also quoted by Fairlie: *Flaubert: Madame Bovary* (London, Edward Arnold, 1962), p. 24. This is one book which can certainly not be accused of ignoring the question under discussion: it has many interesting points to make. See also *Cor.*, II, 344; and for *Novembre*, III, 379; *Par les Champs*, II, 76, 384; first version of *l'Education*, II, 343–4.

[2] e.g. see *Cor.*, IV, 104, 105, 115, 124.

[3] Quoted by Dumesnil: *Madame Bovary de Gustave Flaubert* (Les grands événements littéraires, Paris, SFELT, 1946), p. 80; see also Flaubert's letter to Laurent-Pichat on the subject, *Cor.*, IV, 137–8. Maynial: *Flaubert* (Paris, Editions de la Nouvelle Revue Critique, 1943), pp. 102–3, also brings up this point, but only quite briefly, and does not appear to give it any real significance.

Again, he is quick to react when Sainte-Beuve, speaking of *Salammbô*, commits the supreme heresy by suggesting that many of the descriptions would be better appreciated if they were removed from the novel and published as anthology pieces. Flaubert's reply is categorical, and well worth meditating upon: 'Il n'y a point dans mon livre une description isolée, gratuite; toutes *servent* à mes personnages et ont une influence lointaine ou immédiate sur l'action' (V, 60–1).

It is clear from several of Flaubert's statements—and also from his method of writing—that he believed the unity of a novel to result primarily from the author's original conception, and his efforts to put this, and only this, across to his reader.[1] His own starting-point, as can be seen from his early plans, was normally a very simple set of circumstances which illustrated one or two basic human reactions. All subsequent details and ramifications served only to amplify and illustrate the original idea. Before he began to write he had the whole book before him in its general outline, and this was not subsequently changed without a good deal of careful thought.[2] Then, before he began to write the separate chapters, he did a more detailed plan of each—again amplifying, not changing the original outline without a very good reason. His method, up to the end of the first draft, was always one of expansion, never of linear development. The connection with his ideas on unity is obvious: having a detailed plan and sticking to it means that any extraneous matter is quickly spotted and eliminated. It is rather amusing to see this basic rule of any schoolboy composition being applied with such stunning effect. Indeed, Flaubert takes the importance of the plan so far that in at least one case he seems to identify 'plan' with 'conception': 'Médite bien le plan de ton drame; tout est là, dans la conception' (III, 140). Elsewhere his statements are less extreme, but never different. A writer must know what he wants to say before he can say it well.[3]

---

[1] e.g. see *Cor.*, II, 339; III, 20; IV, 315. See also a fuller treatment of this point in Durry, op. cit., pp. 41 et seq.

[2] It may be that this refusal to change his orginal plan was partly responsible for his well-known difficulties with *Madame Bovary*: see *Cor.*, II, 351.

[3] *Cor.*, II, 362; III, 127, 248, 401.

It is precisely because Flaubert knew what he wanted his book to say, that he was so merciless about scenes like the *Comices*. In such passages, there was a conflict between the over-all intention of the book and the requirements of the passage in itself. In the many rewritings of the *Comices*, Flaubert frequently sacrificed cherished phrases, no matter how perfect he thought them: if they did not contribute to the development or atmosphere of the whole book, out they went: 'Je fais des sacrifices de détail qui me font pleurer, mais enfin il le faut. Quand on aime trop le style, on risque à perdre de vue le but même de ce qu'on écrit. Et puis les transitions, le *suivi*, quel empêtrement!'[1]

This passage reflects a further stage in Flaubert's method of writing. Having gone to the trouble of devising a detailed plan, he goes far beyond it in the actual writing of a chapter, apparently losing himself in the sheer delight of torment. He works, for weeks if necessary, until he brings the style of the whole passage to near perfection, and only then returns to a consideration of his original intention, and realizes he must omit a good deal. He would give an efficiency expert ulcers, but he is convinced that this is the correct method for him. He even recommends it to his friends. Feydeau, whose work is indeed not remarkable for its unity, is offered this probably unwelcome advice:

Prends, au hasard, une des pages que j'indique comme lentes ou mal écrites; lis-la, indépendamment du reste, en elle-même, en ne considérant que le style. Puis, quand tu l'auras amenée à toute la perfection possible, vois si elle se lie avec les autres et si elle est utile. . . . Le sujet t'emporte et tu n'as pas l'œil assez ouvert sur l'ensemble; les paliers, dans ta maison, sont trop larges et trop nombreux (IV, 297).

In spite of the topsy-turvy method, however, it is plain that Flaubert will sacrifice anything for unity, and cannot understand a lack of similar high-mindedness in others. Incidentally, it should be remembered that this letter was written while Flaubert was writing *Salammbô*.

Since the achievement of unity involves the exclusion of all

[1] *Cor.*, III, 381–2; cf. in the second version of *Saint Antoine*: 'Je biffe les mouvements extralyriques, inversions qui vous déroutent de l'idée principale' (IV, 104).

3—T.N.F.

matter which does not contribute to the novel as a novel, any
tendency by the author to 'preach', to interrupt the development
in order to tell the reader his personal views, will not be permissible. Thus Flaubert has an artistic reason as well as a philosophical
one (*vérité, ne pas conclure*) for limiting himself entirely to *repré-
sentation*. This too is brought out in his criticism of *Daniel*, where
he draws a strong contrast between 'tout ce qui est essentielle-
ment du livre' and Feydeau's incurable tendency to '*faire le
monsieur*'.[1]

There is a close connection in Flaubert's mind between the
concept of unity and the concept of harmony. Harmony involves
structure, the disposing of the various parts so that there is an
over-all balance. For Flaubert, the problem was largely one of
giving due emphasis to the important parts of the novel, and
omitting or toning down the rest. It is thus a fairly mechanical
quality, but of great importance in that it reflects the author's
basic intention—his 'conception'. Hence, in criticizing a novel
by Maricourt, he cites a scene which is just a scene: it does not
result in anything significant, it does not contribute to the novel
as a whole, and therefore it is too long. It should not have
been presented as a scene at all, but merely as a transitional
passage.[2]

Once again, the significance of such criticism lies in the fact
that Flaubert is wishing on others what he wanted for himself.
He saw the failure of the first *Education* in terms of wrong emphasis or proportions, implying on one occasion that the book was
incomplete rather than bad: 'une qualité n'est jamais un défaut,
. . . Mais si cette qualité en mange une autre, est-elle toujours une
qualité?' (II, 344.) He struck the same problem with *Bovary*, for
novels intended primarily to show reactions to a situation, at the
expense of action or story, were rare at the time. Flaubert was
not quite sure that such a 'lack of proportion' was permissible.

---

[1] *Cor.*, IV, 289–90; cf. IV, 309: '. . . tu verras comme tes personnages parleront
bien du moment que tu ne parleras plus par leur bouche'.
[2] *Cor.*, V, 179; cf. V, 296–7, 302, 321; VI, 103; and IV, 292: 'Tu ignores l'art
de mettre dans une conversation les choses nécessaires en *relief*, en passant leste-
ment sur ce qui les amène. . . . Je ne dis pas de retrancher les idées, mais d'*adoucir
comme ton* celles qui sont secondaires.'

Yet this was how he had planned his work, and he did not feel he could tamper with his 'conception':

Le pire de la chose est que les préparatifs psychologiques, pittoresques, grotesques, etc. qui précèdent, étant fort longs, *exigent*, je crois, un développement d'action qui soit en rapport avec eux. .... j'aurai fort à faire pour établir une proportion à peu près égale entre les aventures et les pensées. ... Mais il aura donc 75.000 pages, ce bougre de roman-là! (III, 393; cf. IV, 70.)

(It is fortunate that in this case he overcame his scruples: he may well have removed one of those very qualities which place *Bovary* so far above most of the novels of his contemporaries.) His theory that the definitive *Education* lacked 'la fausseté de la perspective' (VIII, 223–4, 309) shows that even in 1879 he was still concerned with the same question.[1]

Statements concerning unity and related problems—harmony, composition—recur so consistently in the *Correspondance*, and over such a long period, that it is inconceivable that Flaubert did not really mean them. Sooner or later, he considers every part of the novel in terms of unity. He mentions, for example, description, dialogue, plot, characters, logical deduction of facts, linking, and transitions; and he speaks of them all as so many parts of a super-jigsaw, which have somehow to be fitted together.[2] However enthusiastic and idealistic the general theories, the writing of a novel is for Flaubert a slow, patient, intellectual task —not only as regards style, but in every aspect of planning and construction. It follows that the proper reading of such a novel is a task of some magnitude too. The more rapidly this view is fully accepted, the sooner we shall be able to consider Flaubert as an artist, in the full sense of that term:

... les livres ne se font pas comme les enfants, mais comme les pyramides, avec un dessin prémédité, et en apportant des grands blocs l'un par-dessus l'autre, à force de reins, de temps et de sueur, et ça ne sert

[1] See also *Cor.*, VII, 318 for the same idea regarding *Un Cœur simple*, and V, 100 regarding Feydeau's *Monsieur de Saint-Bertrand*.
[2] See, in addition to passages already cited, *Cor.*, II, 386; III, 388; IV, 434, 439; VI, 480. Of all writers, Moreau most clearly uses this attitude as his starting-point (op. cit., pp. 1–4, 29–30).

à rien! et ça reste dans le désert! mais en le dominant prodigieusement
(IV, 239–40).

Impersonality and point of view

Few aspects of Flaubert studies have occasioned so much discussion as his theory of impersonality. I have left it till last because
it is best examined in the light of what has already been said
about the other elements of Flaubert's art, and in particular about
unity.

The question is a complicated one, and has been further complicated by the large number of sometimes rather hasty critical
pronouncements it has stimulated. Many critics are content to
re-quote a few of the best-known and most striking passages
from the *Correspondance*, imposing upon them a meaning which
is not always consistent with other parts of Flaubert's theory.
Some merely state what they believe Flaubert ought to have
meant. The whole matter is important enough to warrant another
look.

In general, the debate about whether or not Flaubert was impersonal has centred round the question of whether he recorded
his own experiences in his work. Demorest and Ferrère, for example, argued that since he was so insistent in his *Correspondance*
that one ought to be impersonal, it is highly unlikely that he did
write about himself. Others, including Dumesnil, Gérard-Gailly
and the long line of discoverers of the original Madame Bovary,
applied themselves to proving that he did indeed record his own
experiences; and some of these critics argued that he was therefore
not impersonal at all.[1] Yet others, hypnotized by the man's
private life—and especially his love-life—use Flaubert's works
almost exclusively to reinforce the latter argument.

This controversy is a side issue. A man who spent as much time
as Flaubert thinking and writing about literature could not have
been so simple-minded as to equate impersonality with not
recording his own emotions and feelings, his own experiences
and personality in anything he published. It is not in the least
surprising that so many traces of him have been found in his

---

[1] Mme Durry inclines to this point of view: op. cit., pp. 126, 149 (note).

works, and the effort and ingenuity expended have hardly been repaid by the result. *Of course* Flaubert's works reflect—in part—all these things. It would be more shattering if someone could prove that a work—any work—did *not* do so.

Part of the trouble comes from the *Correspondance*, and from what Flaubert is claimed to have said. He is responsible for both 'Madame Bovary, c'est moi' and 'je n'y ai rien mis de mes sentiments ni de mon existence'. He also said '... aucun modèle n'a posé devant moi. Madame Bovary est une pure invention. Tous les personnages de ce livre sont complètement imaginés, ...' (IV, 191–2). Yet his plans contain actual names of real persons who obviously did serve as models, at least for some minor characters,[1] and at least some of the evidence adduced for the identification of the 'real' Madame Bovary is no doubt valid. The same applies to *l'Education*. After years of discussion and disagreement about whether or not Madame Schlésinger is Madame Arnoux and Flaubert Frédéric, Mme Durry published the now celebrated document which most have regarded as conclusive: 'Le mari, la femme, l'amant tous s'aimant, tous lâches. — traversée sur le bateau de Montereau, un collégien. — Me Sch. — Mr Sch. moi.' It is also well known that he used some of his own experiences, and those of many of his friends, in *Bouvard et Pécuchet*.

But is Flaubert really being inconsistent? The more reasonable critics have pointed out that several of the contenders for the title of the real Madame Bovary probably have a case, that the character of Emma is almost certainly composed of elements taken from various sources.[2] The same appears to be true of Homais, and doubtless of others. He produced them by the method we have outlined in the section on 'truth': collecting facts, and then selecting and combining those which were suitable to his preconceived purpose. He is merely treating parts of the lives of real people as 'documents'. The method is not radically different from that adopted for *Hérodias*, except that, as Ferrère points out,

---

[1] See Pommier and Leleu: *Madame Bovary: Nouvelle version précédée des scénarios inédits* (Paris, Corti, 1949), pp. 3, 54, 56; cf. Durry, op. cit., p. 28.

[2] V. Gothot-Mersch, op. cit., Pt. I, especially summary, pp. 81–6.

reading necessarily replaces direct observation. The source of his facts is not nearly as important as the use to which he intends to put them. To this extent he is correct in saying 'aucun modèle . . .'. At the same time, the selection and the combining of the relevant material reflect his own 'conception': all goes to illustrate a 'truth' about the world which is his alone and can only be his. He is also correct in saying, 'Madame Bovary, c'est moi.'

The same principles apply to Flaubert's other works. The subject-matter of a book can come from one of only two sources, or from a combination of them. These sources are (a) the author's personal experience, whether it be things that actually happened to him, or his imagination, and (b) the experience of other people, whether told to him, observed by him, or read about by him. Since it is manifestly impossible to reproduce all this experience in a book, a choice of the material available is inevitable. The choice must be the author's, and how and what he chooses reflects something of his personality. In this sense, no work of art will ever be completely impersonal.[1]

It is not entirely without value to reduce the argument to its basic terms in this manner. It demonstrates that in looking for signs of Flaubert's impersonality or otherwise in his subject-matter, or in the sources of his characters, we are doomed to arrive at the only possible conclusion: he took his subject-matter from reality, and changed it to suit himself. We are merely saying that Flaubert adopted the same procedure as any other writer who ever lived. We are not getting at the problem of what is specifically Flaubert, except to say that he altered his sources more than some writers, and less than others—an equally uninspiring conclusion. It may be mildly interesting to know whether or not Flaubert slept with Mme Schlésinger, or whether one's neighbour sleeps with his cook. But Flaubert wrote l'Education sentimentale, and the neighbour did not, and this is what we are really interested in. Sexual successes—or failures—do not suffice to produce works of art; and if Flaubert had never heard of Mme Schlésinger he would still have produced works of art. If it is true

---

[1] The point is not original: see, for example, Pouillon: *Temps et roman* (Paris, NRF Gallimard, 1946), p. 66; but it needed to be re-stated.

that Mme Schlésinger is behind both versions of *l'Education* as well as *Mémoires d'un fou* and *Novembre*, this shows, as critics have maintained, how important she is to Flaubert; but for literary criticism what it really shows is how unimportant was the nature of the subject-matter in the Flaubert novel. It does not prove that he remained forever faithful to the *Fantômes de Trouville*, but that he recognized the basis of a good novel when he saw it, and stubbornly worked at it until he made it a good novel. Moreover, we must not ignore the possibility that the famous 'Me Sch. Mr Sch. moi' may refer only to the scene with which it is linked in Flaubert's plan—the opening boat scene. Given Flaubert's view of art as the very opposite of a 'déversoir à passion', given the fact that many of Flaubert's other characters appear to be composites of his own invention, it is improbable that Madame Arnoux represents anything approaching a faithful portrait of Mme Schlésinger; and if she did it would tell us very little about *l'Education* as a work of art.

When they are not speaking about impersonality, most critics agree that for Flaubert the subject-matter of a novel is of minor importance. A novel must of course have subject-matter, but where it comes from makes no difference to its potential value as an element of the work of art to which it contributes. The Ganges is in itself no more poetic than the Bièvre, but the Bièvre is not more so than the Ganges.[1] Personal sentiments and experiences are theoretically neither more nor less suitable than those of others. All can be used, and all begin as 'documents', worthless in themselves except as a starting-point. Flaubert did not object to autobiographical elements as such, but rather was aware of the artistic danger inherent in using them. This would appear to be his meaning in the two passages in which he compares Byron and Shakespeare. Despite his admiration for Byron, he was in no doubt as to which of the two was the greater writer. He believes that Byron's unique personality was such that it covered a multitude of artistic sins, but that it was a dangerous path to try to follow: writers like him 'n'ont qu'à crier pour être harmonieux,

---

[1] *Cor.*, VIII, 225; cf. IV, 212 on the desert and a bed of cabbages, IV, 225 on Alexander and a louse.

qu'à pleurer pour attendrir, qu'à s'occuper d'eux-mêmes pour rester éternels'. Shakespeare, on the other hand, and people like him, 'résument l'humanité'. And they do this by *not* showing what they thought, what their personal likes and dislikes were.[1] Flaubert had tried Byron's method and failed. Musset, he believed, failed for the same reason.

There are one or two other suggestions that Flaubert accepted the possibility of using one's own experiences and sentiments as a starting-point for art. At the end of the *Préface aux Dernières Chansons* he states what sort of people he thinks ought to be writers. One of the conditions he regards as necessary is that 'les accidents du monde, dès qu'ils sont perçus, vous apparaissent transposés comme pour l'emploi d'une illusion à décrire, telle-ment que *toutes les choses, y compris votre existence*, ne vous semble-ront pas avoir d'autre utilité . . .'.[2] Again, in praising a novel by an unknown contemporary, he uses these words: 'L'autobio-graphie perce sous le roman, *mais sans déclamation ni étalage de personnalité.*'[3]

If this is so, how can we reconcile it with the many well-known passages from the *Correspondance* which seem to say precisely the opposite? It is, of course, possible to dismiss those quoted above as not representing Flaubert's true beliefs at all. Certainly a corres-pondence of this size is bound to contain contradictions; and there are admittedly very few passages explicitly accepting the possibility of using autobiography in a novel, but many apparently excluding it. Nevertheless, one of the above passages is from the *Préface aux Dernières Chansons*, which, I have argued, is more

[1] *Cor.*, I, 385–6; cf. II, 380, where Homer, Rabelais, and Michelangelo are placed with Shakespeare on the 'impersonal' side, and said to be greatly superior to Byron.

[2] *Cor.*, VI, 487; italic mine. This passage is also quoted by Bertrand: *Gustave Flaubert* (Paris, Ollendorff (Albin Michel), n.d.), p. 19, although I do not entirely agree with the conclusions he draws from it.

[3] *Cor.*, IV, 414; italic mine. It is true that Flaubert may simply be being polite here; but in the *Cor.* in general, when he wishes to be polite, he normally selects for praise those elements of a book which he regards as good, and conscientiously avoids those of which he does not approve. For further examples of this habit, see Sherrington: 'Des Dangers de la Correspondance de Flaubert', in *Les Amis de Flaubert*, mai, 1964, pp. 27–37.

likely to contain his considered opinion, carefully and precisely expressed. In any case, it is now firmly established that Flaubert did in fact sometimes employ autobiography in his own novels. If there is inconsistency, what he did must take precedence over what he said he did. But we should first reconsider the letters in which autobiography seems to be excluded, in order to see how deep the apparent inconsistency goes.

Like so many of Flaubert's literary doctrines, this one is first announced to Louise Colet: '. . . rien de plus faible que de mettre en art ses sentiments personnels', he states in 1852 (II, 378), and later in the same letter, 'tu prendras en pitié l'usage de se chanter soi-même'. This is followed by the comparison between Byron and Shakespeare already quoted. In the following year, he informs both Louise and Bouilhet that he had now decided not to write his memoirs or to put any more 'tristesses juvéniles' into his works (III, 315, 320, 383). In 1857, having denied that *Madame Bovary* contained anything at all of his personal sentiments or of his own life, he adds: 'C'est un de mes principes qu'il ne faut pas s'écrire.' Later he criticizes *Lui* by Louise Colet in similar terms (IV, 344) and is even scornful of his old hero Michelet for the same reason (VIII, 79).

In almost every one of these cases the bare statement (the part that is usually quoted) is developed in such a way that there is no doubt why Flaubert so often adopts this attitude. He never says that autobiographical elements are in themselves bad, even when giving this impression. What he does say is that they interfere with, or completely neutralize, the more important (artistic) qualities of the work. In the first letter quoted, he goes on to tell Louise that if she avoids personal sentiments, she will be more able to concentrate on style and human reactions; she will achieve the essential 'sérénité' and maturity, and characters which appear real. When he decides not to write his memoirs he equates 'personnel' with 'relatif'—he is thinking in terms of universality;[1] elsewhere he concedes that he might attempt his memoirs

---

[1] Cf. *Cor.*, II, 462: '*Moins on sent une chose, plus on est apte à l'exprimer comme elle est* (comme elle est *toujours* en elle-même, dans sa généralité et dégagée de tous ses contingents éphémères).'

when he is old, 'quand l'imagination est tarie' (III, 383). In criticizing *Lui* he remarks 'quelles tristes œuvres ça fait'. This is particularly brought out when he speaks of Musset: 'En voilà un qui a été peu critique! Il me paraît avoir eu sur l'humanité le coup d'œil d'un coiffeur sentimental!' (X, 252.) In all these passages Flaubert is saying the same thing: apart from the painful egotism of the writer who believes himself to be so interesting and worthwhile a person that everyone wants to know about him, there is the constant danger that a proper sense of proportion will be lost—and with it, any possibility of universal truth. Such writers, like Musset, too easily cease to be 'critical',[1] and tend to equate personal emotion with artistic worth ... 'Musset n'a jamais séparé la poésie des sentiments qu'elle complète' (II, 460).

Such ideas are intimately connected with Flaubert's conviction that writing a novel is essentially an intellectual procedure. It must be emphasized again that he was always extremely suspicious of anything resembling 'inspiration' in the Platonic sense.[2] 'On n'écrit pas avec son cœur, mais avec sa tête, ...'; 'tout doit se faire à froid, posément.'[3] If the writer lets himself get carried away, if he relinquishes the smallest part of his conscious control over what he is doing, then the chances of his failing *artistically* are greatly increased. And what more likely way of losing this control, than by writing about things which deeply affect one personally?[4] If, on the other hand, it is possible for a writer calmly to contemplate and analyse his own emotions, so that, in effect, he regards them simply as *facts*, separates them from his own specific personality, he is then at liberty to use them for an artistic purpose. Thus, in discussing the possibility of one day writing 'un roman métaphysique et à apparitions' (probably *la Spirale*, the plan of which has been discovered), based entirely

---

[1] Cf. T. S. Eliot's opinion that the greatest part of creative labour is critical labour: 'The Function of Criticism', in *Selected Essays* (London, Faber, 1949), p. 30.

[2] In this he is not unusual—it seems that most writers would agree with him. The inspiration idea seems to be more of an *idée reçue* than a fact.

[3] *Cor.*, III, 30; III, 104; cf. I, 420; III, 50; IV, 206.

[4] This general distrust of inspiration, as opposed to what Flaubert regarded as the artistic approach, has been pointed out by Ferrère, op. cit., pp. 7, 149, 232; Bertrand, op. cit., p. 11. But neither gives it due importance.

on some of his own hallucinations, he says, '. . . il faut attendre, et que je sois loin de ces impressions-là pour pouvoir me les donner facticement, idéalement, et dès lors sans danger pour moi ni pour l'œuvre' (III, 146). Flaubert's position here is strikingly similar to that of T. S. Eliot. Some of the points made in 'Tradition and the Individual Talent' fit his theory and practice exactly:

The poet has, not a 'personality' to express, but a particular medium, which is only a medium and not a personality, in which impressions and experiences combine in peculiar and unexpected ways. Impressions and experiences which are important for the man may take no place in the poetry, and those which become important in the poetry may play quite a negligible part in the man, the personality. . . . Poetry is not a turning loose of emotion, but an escape from personality. But, of course, only those who have personality and emotions know what it means to want to escape from these things.[1]

For Flaubert, as for Eliot, the question is an artistic, and not a sentimental one. Autobiographical elements are perfectly acceptable as subject-matter, but they then cease to have any autobiographical significance. They are raw material, like any other, and must submit to a 'refonte plastique et complète par l'Art'. Note also the order of the process described in another letter: 'J'ai imaginé, je me suis ressouvenu et j'ai combiné.'[2] Flaubert shows no inconsistency on this question, either from one letter to another or from his letters to his works. Condemning 'déclamation', puerile sentimentality, is just not the same thing as condemning autobiography.[3]

[1] Eliot: 'Tradition and the Individual Talent', in Selected Essays, pp. 13–22. The whole essay is relevant to the present discussion. See also Daiches: Critical Approaches to Literature (London, Longmans, 1959), pp. 143 et seq., where the theoretical implications of this position are discussed in more detail; and Cormeau, op. cit., p. 164.
[2] Cor., I, 254. 'Literature and Biography' in Wellek and Warren: Theory of Literature (London, Jonathan Cape, 1961), pp. 67 et seq., convincingly argues the dangers of using a writer's works for finding out about his life.
[3] This is also Bonwit's general conclusion (op. cit., p. 282). Similar points are made, but less clearly and without any attempt at justification, by Martino, op. cit., p. 167; Colling: Gustave Flaubert (Paris, Arthème Fayard, 1947), pp. 198–204; and by Dumesnil, Evénements, op. cit., p. 173, who, however, ignores the implications of his own statement by continuing to accept the old autobio-

It is as well to repeat here the warning of certain critics that Flaubert's highly intellectual approach does not necessarily imply a lack of feeling or sensitivity. For one thing, it is clear from the *Correspondance* that a good deal of his artistic effort was specifically aimed at controlling an excessive sensitivity. For another, it was certainly part of his literary theory that one's own emotions and sensitivity *contributed to* the writing of a novel: he was merely against their *dominating* it: 'C'est avec la tête qu'on écrit. Si le cœur la chauffe, tant mieux: mais il ne faut pas le dire. Ce doit être un four invisible. . . .'[1] Besides, it is just not in the nature of insensitive persons to undertake the writing of analytic novels of the type of *Madame Bovary* or *l'Education sentimentale*. One can only agree with Dumesnil, who, in dismissing the idea of Flaubert's 'coldness', simply says: 'En accuser Flaubert, c'est ne l'avoir point lu ou l'avoir mal lu.'[2] On the other hand, it is forcing the evidence to go to the other extreme, with the theory that Flaubert was so involved with his characters that he identified himself with them. At this point it is customary to quote the famous passage about his having the taste of arsenic in his mouth, and being physically sick, while describing Emma's death. Colourful though the idea is, one may doubt whether it gives a valid idea of Flaubert's approach to his work, even after due allowance has been made for the manifest exaggeration (Flaubert himself mentions the word 'indigestion') (V, 350). Whether it is true or not, it is an isolated example, completely at variance with the majority of Flaubert's statements on his methods of writing.[3]

---

graphical theories, particularly in regard to *l'Education*; see Dumesnil: *l'Education sentimentale de Gustave Flaubert* (Paris, Nizet, 1962), pp. 15–78, and *Vocation*, op. cit., p. 61, where he calls this book 'une autobiographie à peine romancée'. This statement is absurd.

[1] *Cor.*, III, 50; cf. III, 146, 383; IV, 243; Sand's letter to Flaubert on this subject in *Correspondance entre George Sand et Gustave Flaubert* (Préface de Henri Amic, Paris, Calmann-Lévy, 1904), p. 50 and Flaubert's reply, p. 53; also another letter p. 126.

[2] *Evénements*, op. cit., p. 175; cf. Frejlich, op. cit., pp. 352 et seq. and Brombert, op. cit., pp. 21–3.

[3] See Colling, op. cit., pp. 202, 223 for examples of this approach. This writer appears to accept quite literally every word of the *Correspondance*.

There is another important aspect of impersonality as Flaubert conceived it: a writer must never state his personal opinions. He must not inform his reader what his political, religious, social or literary views happen to be, he must never become a party to polemics of any sort. He must not make moral judgements on his characters and their actions, either approving or otherwise. In short, he must not 'preach' in any way. He was probably the only novelist of the period who believed completely in this restriction, although he was not the only one to say he believed it. Thus he criticizes prefaces by Zola (VI, 314), by Edmond de Goncourt (VIII, 263), and by Paul Alexis (VIII, 368);[1] and he was continually criticizing Feydeau, as we have already noted.[2] By contrast, he gives high praise to a completely unknown novelist, Amédée Pommier: '. . . vous n'appartenez à aucune boutique, à aucune église, . . . il n'est question, dans votre volume, ni du problème social, ni des bases, etc.' (IV, 397). This essential aspect of Flaubert's thought is very well known, and does not require further proof. It is, however, necessary briefly to consider the reasons for his position, and some of its implications.

As we would expect, almost every time Flaubert gives a reason for this theory, it is an artistic reason. It is impossible to over-emphasize this point, which, like others, is too frequently noted at the theoretical level and then forgotten in discussions of the works. 'L'homme n'est rien, l'œuvre tout' (VII, 280) is not merely a fine slogan. It is the reference point for everything Flaubert did, the complete summary of his whole being. The more fully we realize this, the more likely we are to view his works as they deserve.

We have already noted (p. 24) that he believed preaching interfered with unity. Another reason is that it endangers the universality of the work, its general validity:

Il me serait bien agréable de dire ce que je pense et de soulager le sieur Gustave Flaubert par des phrases; mais quelle est l'importance dudit sieur? (VII, 280.)

L'élément particulier, relatif, le petit fait, qui t'avait frappée, a nui à la conception du caractère. . . . Tu as écrit tout cela avec une passion

---

[1] See also *Cor.*, IV, 216, 309, 318.   [2] See also *Cor.*, IV, 216, 309, 318.

personnelle qui t'a troublé la vue sur les conditions fondamentales de toute œuvre imaginée. L'esthétique est absente.[1]

A third reason commonly given is that preaching precludes a proper scientific approach: the writer will not be impartial, so his chances of achieving 'truth' will be seriously impaired:

Il faut pourtant que les sciences morales [it is clear from the context that Flaubert is here including the novel in this category] prennent une autre route, et qu'elles procèdent comme les sciences physiques, par l'impartialité. Le poète est tenu maintenant d'avoir de la sympathie pour *tout* et pour *tous*, afin de les comprendre et de les décrire.[2]

Whichever way we turn, we are confronted with the same idea of the primacy of the work of art in itself, as something separate from everyday morals or polemics, something which relies for its value on perfection of form and permanent validity of content. 'Tu tiens trop à établir tes idées, et tu prêches souvent', says Flaubert, in a letter already quoted in part (IV, 297–8). 'Tu me diras que c'est *exprès*, tu as tort, voilà tout; tu gâtes l'harmonie du livre, tu rentres dans la manie de presque tous les écrivains français, Jean-Jacques, G. Sand; tu manques aux principes, tu n'as plus en vue le Beau et l'éternel Vrai.'

Impersonality as Flaubert conceived it does not mean the exclusion of personal opinions, of a message or a moral, any more than it prevents autobiographical elements or personal emotions. Flaubert was certainly aware that a writer's view of the world will always be seen, in general terms, in whatever he produces. He does compare the silence of the artist to the silence of God, who created the world, but told nobody what he was trying to prove by doing so;[3] but in one case, he amplifies the comparison,

---

[1] *Cor.*, X, 173. Cf. the reasons for his not wanting to write about an artist: 'l'art n'est pas fait pour peindre les exceptions', etc., V, 253 and II, 378.

[2] *Cor.*, IV, 243; cf. IV, 164; V, 257, 397; and Bonwit, op. cit., pp. 279 et seq., who attempts to define the differences between 'impartialité', 'impersonnalité', and 'impassibilité'. I believe it is preferable to underline the connection between closely related ideas, rather than separate them into categories in which they are sometimes uncomfortable. Such an approach might be justifiable if the *Correspondance* formed a closely reasoned complete system of aesthetics. But Bonwit does put forward some interesting points here.

[3] e.g. *Cor.*, IV, 318; V, 227, 253; VII, 280.

and in doing so qualifies it: 'qu'on le sente partout [i.e. the artist] mais qu'on ne le voie pas' (IV, 164). Elsewhere he declares that although personal opinions are not explicitly stated, an intelligent reader will always see in a book 'la moralité qui doit s'y trouver' —provided the book is a good one.[1] Baudelaire had made precisely this point in his article on *Bovary* some twenty years before, as well as stating it in more general terms: 'En effet, il faut peindre les vices tels qu'ils sont, ou ne pas les voir. Et si le lecteur ne porte pas en lui un guide philosophique et religieux qui l'accompagne dans la lecture du livre, tant pis pour lui.'[2] In a letter to George Sand, Flaubert is even more explicit: having said that he refuses the novelist the right to 'accuse' any person or party, he adds: 'Je ne crois même pas que le romancier doive exprimer *son* opinion sur les choses de ce monde. *Il peut la communiquer, mais je n'aime pas à ce qu'il la dise*'.[3] Moreover, he was convinced that he *had* communicated his opinion in his own works. Speaking of *l'Education*, he says: 'Mais je vous réponds que les conservateurs ne sont pas ménagés. J'écris maintenant trois pages sur les abominations de la garde nationale en 1848, qui me feront très bien voir des bourgeois! Je leur écrase le nez dans leur turpitude, tant que je peux.'[4] And of le *Candidat*: 'J'y roule dans la fange tous les partis' (XII, 96). But when he is asked to include allusions, tirades, direct explicit criticism of contemporary events, in *le Candidat*, he refuses utterly: 'Je trouve cela facile, canaille et anti-esthétique' (VII, 108). The fact that the moral of a book is not spelt out in so many words does not mean that it is not there: it merely means that Flaubert credited his reader with more intelligence than did most of his contemporaries.

As regards the over-all criticism of life and humanity, then, Flaubert's ideas are not very different from those of most other

[1] *Cor.*, VII, 285; also quoted by Fairlie, op. cit., p. 14.

[2] Baudelaire: 'Les Drames et les romans honnêtes', in *l'Art romantique* (Genève, Editions d'art Albert Skira, 1945), p. 284; cf. *Madame Bovary*, ibid., p. 390. It will be recalled that this latter article was one of the very few on *Bovary* which Flaubert liked.

[3] *Cor.*, V, 396; italic mine; cf. XIII, 274 to Du Camp: 'Laisse donc le lecteur penser pour lui-même'.

[4] *Cor.*, V, 407–8; cf. V, 385, 397.

novelists, though they are more subtle than some in their practical application. But generalizations are easy; when it comes to the means of *applying* his ideas, he reduces the whole problem to impossibly simple terms. An author, he said, should simply 'peindre', describe things as they are—or rather, as he believes them to be: we have seen that Flaubert never pretended to have a monopoly of philosophical or moral truth. '. . . je me plains de ce que, dans *la Servante*, tu n'as pas exprimé tes idées par des *faits* ou des *tableaux*', he writes to Louise Colet (IV, 10); and twenty-five years later, to Du Camp: '. . . tu qualifies ces messieurs d'assassins, de monstres, etc. A quoi bon? puisque tu *montres* qu'ils l'ont été. L'effet eût été plus écrasant sans réflexion aucune, . . .' (XIII, 168). Such statements on method, despite their apparent clarity, obscure a multitude of practical difficulties. It may be easy enough for Du Camp to show us monsters, simply by describing monstrous actions; but what of a novel about a Frédéric Moreau, who is neither monster nor angel? Frédéric is a very ordinary human being—that is, he has many sides to his character, some good and others bad; and he comes into frequent contact with many other ordinary mortals, all of whom have this same mixture of good and bad. He is also involved with historical events of great significance, once more showing both good and bad characteristics. And all this has to be *shown*, rather than told, to the reader, in such a way that it forms a single harmonious unit. The problems of presentation and organization of material which Flaubert set himself are immense; methods of resolving them in practice are not even hinted at in the *Correspondance* theories, which do not venture beyond stating what the problems are. Again we see how inadequately this body of letters projects Flaubert's ideas on what constitutes a novel; again we see that only his works will tell us what his works are.

The problem goes even deeper. We must also take some account of the many violently expressed opinions in the *Correspondance*. Since Flaubert almost invariably disagreed with the majority of his compatriots, his decision not to tell them so undoubtedly put a strain on him. He refused to succumb to the temptation, but he often almost wished that he would. He needed some means of incorporating his opinions in his works, but in such a way that they would not interfere with his clearly-stated artistic principles. The problem is brought up explicitly only once in the *Correspondance* (in a letter to G. Sand), but his works provide strong evidence of his line of thought. In 1867 he writes: 'Quelle forme faut-il prendre pour exprimer son opinion sur les choses de ce monde, sans risquer de passer, plus tard, pour un imbécile? Cela est un rude problème, ...' (V, 347); and although here, too, he goes on to state that 'le mieux est de les peindre, tout bonnement, ces choses qui vous exaspèrent. Disséquer est une vengeance', his tone indicates that even at this late stage he was not entirely sure that this was the complete answer. There is a particularly interesting short passage in *l'Education* which, if taken in conjunction with some of the letters, illustrates one secret method by which he reconciled the artistic demands of impersonality with the purely personal desire to 'vuider son fiel'. It is also a good practical demonstration of the fact that impersonality was for Flaubert *a means of presenting* his subject-matter, and independent of the subject-matter itself. The passage concerns Thiers, who on no fewer than forty-one occasions appears in the *Correspondance* as the perfect bourgeois, and therefore the subject of Flaubert's vehemence at its most entertaining. As an example, consider the following:

... rugissons contre M. Thiers! Peut-on voir un plus triomphant imbécile, un croûtard plus abject, un plus étroniforme bourgeois! Non, rien ne peut donner l'idée du vomissement que m'inspire ce vieux melon diplomatique, arrondissant sa bêtise sur le fumier de la bourgeoisie! Est-il possible de traiter avec un sans-façon plus naïf et plus inepte la philosophie, la religion, les peuples, la liberté, le passé et l'avenir, l'histoire et l'histoire naturelle, tout, et le reste! Il me semble éternel comme la médiocrité! Il m'écrase (V, 346-7).

Then returning to *l'Education*, he adds: 'Je tâcherai du reste, dans la troisième partie de mon roman, ... d'insinuer un panégyrique dudit ...'. And, in fact, we find, in *l'Education*: 'On exaltait avant tout M. Thiers pour son volume contre le Socialisme, où il s'était montré aussi penseur qu'écrivain.' From this apparently harmless statement, two points emerge. The first is that it is completely in character, for it is made in the home of the reactionary M. Dambreuse, at a period when it was considered safe to be once again opposed to Socialism. When read in conjunction with other statements by the Dambreuse group on other politicians and writers scattered through the book, this short passage helps to build up a picture of fear, pretentiousness, self-interest, inconstancy and ignorance in the conservative camp. By contributing to our picture of a group which played an influential part in both the revolution and Frédéric's 'sentimental education', it helps to communicate (but without specifically drawing attention to the fact) Flaubert's opinion of the Dambreuse group. In context, its apparent innocence vanishes. The second point about the sentence is that when it is read in conjunction with certain *Correspondance* passages, Flaubert can be seen to be quite literally and seriously *stating* his opinion of Thiers too, but covertly, for himself and a few initiates alone: '*aussi* penseur qu'écrivain'—that is, nil on both counts! He is using the same sentence both to imply and to state. But whether or not a reader knows Flaubert's opinion of Thiers, his understanding of the *novel* is not in the least affected. Like the women Flaubert slept with, the point is artistically irrelevant. Its inclusion gave him some slight personal amusement and satisfaction, but of an extra-literary kind, something which he had no intention of sharing with the public—again like the women he slept with. It would not have made *l'Education sentimentale* a better novel if he were to have announced it out loud.

The same principles operate in *Bouvard et Pécuchet*. For example, the discussions on art and literature constitute an almost unbelievable hotch-potch of theories of diverse origins. Some are contemporary and some are very old, some appear reasonable while others are obviously the product of profound ignorance. The only thing they have in common is that not one is thoroughly examined, there is only the most perfunctory attempt to follow out the implications, and when two theories are found to be in opposition, one or both of them is assumed to be totally wrong. Now the *Correspondance* shows that some of the theories discarded by the two *bonshommes* were held quite seriously by Flaubert. But of course the book was never intended to be read with the *Correspondance*: the non-specialist reader, depending only on the novel, would find it impossible to isolate Flaubert's views. This ordinary reader would, however, be able to see that the way Bouvard and Pécuchet handled aesthetics is consistent with the way they handle other fields of knowledge: their *Bovarysme* has infected them so thoroughly that they cannot be aware of their inability to distinguish the sublime from the ridiculous. The passage tells the reader something about Bouvard and Pécuchet, but nothing about Flaubert, even though some of Flaubert's personal opinions are there.

This is the central point about the way Flaubert put into practice his theory of impersonality. Whether it concerns autobiographical details or firmly-held personal opinions, the impersonality is to be seen not in the subject-matter but in the way it is expressed. Impersonality is a method of presentation, a technique as a result of which it is impossible to tell, without recourse to external documents, whether or not a given statement or situation reflects the author's personal views or experience.[1] While personal elements are frequently present in Flaubert's works, their presentation is such that this fact makes no contribution whatever to an assessment of the artistic merit of the works.

Having decided what impersonality is, and having seen that it was only one of many requirements of the work of art as Flaubert conceived it, we must now consider what methods of achieving it were open to him. The direct 'preaching' approach, or the one incorporating an obviously laboured thesis, would never be employed. There should be no overt communication between author and reader: the author must not intervene as a separate personality. Therefore the method adopted by Stendhal and some earlier English novelists (in particular Fielding and

---

[1] The point is made by Frejlich, op. cit., pp. 357–64; Dumesnil, *Evénements*, op. cit., p. 176; Lubbock: *The Craft of Fiction* (London, Jonathan Cape, 1957), p. 67; but in all of these it is stated as a bare fact, with very little attempt at justification.

Sterne) is excluded—even though the 'personal opinions' expressed by these authors are not always what they really believed.[1] Of course, a sort of impersonality is achieved by this method, simply because one cannot assume that authors like Stendhal think what they say they think. But as a literary technique, it has disadvantages. It very easily leads to charges that the author is either a fool or a *mystificateur*, which, although non-literary judgements, are sometimes sufficient to bring a work into disrepute and blind people to its real qualities. This was Sterne's fate for a very long time, and also appears to be one of the reasons why Flaubert had no taste for the works of 'cet idiot de Stendhal'. It brings with it the danger that the author often becomes so preoccupied with the effect he will produce—whether humorous, cynical or merely bizarre—that the purely formal and aesthetic qualities of the work assume a secondary role. The concern with putting over a literary personality, even if it is not the author's real personality, involves the same hazards as those of which Musset was victim.

One of the novelist's main functions is (at least it was in the middle of the nineteenth century) to present a set of human characters involved in a situation, and to analyse, in terms of their personality and their background, their reactions to that situation. The author who will not allow himself direct comment on his characters is obliged to *show* their personality through what they think, what they believe, and what they say or do. The author who wishes at the same time to include his personal opinions can do this only by ascribing these opinions to one or more of his characters. The usual result was that the author ascribed his opinions to a single character, who was normally the hero, so that it was clear who was thus honoured (or burdened) with his creator's message. In the simplest cases, all characters opposing this one are obviously villains, and all those supporting him can be regarded as subsidiary message-carriers. The situation results not so much from the author's sympathy with the main character, as is usually assumed, as from the author's admiration for his own opinions and standards. But if an author is

[1] See Blin, op. cit., pp. 217–98, for a detailed study of this in Stendhal.

humble (or realistic) enough to see that his opinions are unlikely to be eternally valid, this solution is as unsatisfactory as direct preaching. Besides, just as no novelist has a monopoly of truth, so no hero does either: such a system is not valid philosophically. The only way out is for the author to distribute his opinions among several of the characters, whether 'heroes' or not, and also to ascribe to each a mixture of opinions from other sources, thereby simultaneously presenting less 'novelistic' characters and disguising his personal views. The distribution comes from the work itself: each character has opinions which are consistent with his personality, or which tell us something new about his personality. The author thus disclaims all personal responsibility for any views expressed. He has safeguarded himself (in theory, but not in fact) against all accusations of foolishness, irresponsibility, shortsightedness, and so on: he has merely 'reported' the views of his characters. One or more of the characters may well be foolish, etc., but the author cannot be blamed for that.

How can such an author convey a moral criticism if he will not commit himself in the usual way? And how can he do it while maintaining those standards of style, unity, harmony and so on which he has set himself? How, in other words, can he be both absent from and present in his work? One of his major technical problems will clearly be the point of view from which the work is presented. It is the purpose of this study to examine the ways in which Flaubert solved the problem.

Twentieth-century writers have experimented widely with methods of achieving extra realism by limiting the novelist's hitherto widely-accepted omniscience. In its extreme form, such a limitation results in presenting the entire novel as the experience of a single character. The author works from inside the character's mind, as it were, viewing everything as the character would. He restricts his field of vision, and therefore his knowledge of other characters: he never knows what others are really thinking, so that anything they say or do can be regarded merely as isolated phenomena having no infallibly discernible motivation. Within this convention, the author either lets his selected character describe, or he himself describes in the third person, only what that character sees and hears and thinks. Without going into the many ways in which the results differ from one another, we can say that *Ulysses*, *les Faux-Monnayeurs*, *l'Etranger*, *la Nausée*, Golding's *Pincher Martin* and Robbe-Grillet's novels are examples of limited point of view techniques. In all of these novels, the author, at some time or another, pretends to renounce his position as intermediary between characters and reader, and lets the reader 'discover' the outcome by following the consciousness and experiences of one or more of the characters.[1]

Of course, the basic principle is considerably older than the twentieth century: it is the very foundation-stone of the first-person novel, where it has frequently been used to create a sense of immediacy and suspense. In the times when the story of the novel was considered more important than it is today, it was a useful means of keeping the reader wondering what was going to happen next, with the author pretending he did not know either. This can be seen in, say, Apuleius' *The Golden Ass*, and Defoe's *Moll Flanders*. It is also basic to the epistolary novel, in which the character writing the letter normally relates only what happened to him on a particular occasion, and to find what happened next or to discover whether this character's version is complete, the reader has either to wait for a subsequent letter, or gradually to piece together the full story by comparing several letters from different characters. *Les Liaisons dangereuses* is a good example.

Some sporadic dabbling in limitations of omniscience is also common in what might be called 'traditional' third-person novels, as a glance at almost every work of this sort will show. Professor Blin has made a serious study of its implications in the works of Stendhal, where it is used to some purpose; but on the whole it seems fair to say that most of Flaubert's predecessors, and some of his important successors, including Zola,

[1] Naturally some of these books apply the method more completely than others: Gide is continually placing himself, as author or narrator, between his characters and the reader; Robbe-Grillet almost never does. For a brief historical survey of twentieth-century interest in this technique and a summary of problems and types involved, see Friedman: 'Point of View in Fiction: the Development of a Critical Concept' in *PMLA*, vol. 70, 1955, pp. 1160–84.

tended to restrict its use to the demands of a particular isolated situation from time to time. Some of the less able, such as Champfleury, seem to use it indiscriminately, according to whim. In general, it is more common in scenes, much rarer in transitional, or 'panoramic' passages.

That such writers do not bother to limit their apparent omniscience with rigorous consistency is not surprising. Most chose the third-person form in the first place precisely because it allows them to make clear that they as authors *are* quite separate from their characters, that they, not the characters, are writing the book and are in direct contact with the reader. They *want* the freedom to break in on the story whenever they wish, to explain to the reader anything they may regard as necessary to his comprehension of the book: character traits, motives, causes, what was going on simultaneously elsewhere, and so on. Even quite recently, such writers as E. M. Forster and F. Mauriac have unashamedly taken advantage of the omniscience which they know all novelists have in fact.

Thus although one of the characteristics of twentieth-century novel-writing is its experimentation with point of view techniques, the experimentation is in fact often concerned with new ways of applying old principles. Contemporary novelists have invented some new techniques; but in much of their work they are exploring the implications of those which have always been an integral part of novel-writing. They are searching for conscious and consistent application of these techniques, in the light of new feelings about what a novel is or should be.

It is precisely because Flaubert was one of the most self-conscious of nineteenth-century novelists, and also because he is so often connected with the main stream of novel development, that his case would seem to be a profitable one to study. His use of point of view has not, indeed, gone unnoticed. The best studies of it are an article by Jean Rousset and two studies by Pierre Moreau, all dealing with *Bovary*. Percy Lubbock devotes the main chapter of his *Craft of Fiction* to this aspect of *Bovary*, which is also mentioned in this light in Auerbach's *Mimesis*, Ullmann's *Style in the French Novel*, and an article by Nathalie

Sarraute.[1] Even Faguet had some awareness of the matter, although his main argument develops along other lines. One or two other critics have mentioned it in specific isolated applications —e.g. Ferrère for *Salammbô*—without appearing to attach much importance to it. More recently, H. F. Mosher has given the question much more attention in a comparative study of Flaubert and Ford Madox Ford.[2] This is the most systematic approach to the problem which I have seen. It happens that on more than one occasion Mosher makes similar points to those I shall be developing, sometimes using the same material. On the other hand, our conclusions are at times quite different, and there seemed to be enough divergence to justify a closer study. By starting within a framework of definitions which forces him to assume that Flaubert's basic method was a traditional omniscient one, Mosher is, I believe, unable to bring out the subtleties and innovations which make restricted point of view techniques so important in Flaubert's work. This statement is intended to make clear, in so far as that is possible in a brief generalization, the main area in which we differ. It is not intended to detract from what remains a valuable study, as more detailed references to it later should show.

Flaubert's use of point of view must naturally be seen in relation to what he wanted his novels to do. A totally subjective presentation, where the point of view is entirely that of a single character and where there is no hint of authorial omniscience, may at first seem to answer Flaubert's requirement of impersonality, as discussed above: the author as a separate active identity is banished, and any views expressed can be imputed to the character alone. But he would quickly have seen that this technique was only

[1] Rousset, op. cit., pp. 109 et seq.; Moreau, op. cit., and 'L'Art de la composition dans *Madame Bovary*' in *Orbis Litterarum*, 12, 1957, pp. 171–8; Auerbach: *Mimesis: The representation of reality in western literature* (translated from German by Willard Trask, New York, Doubleday Anchor, 1957), pp. 425 et seq.; Ullmann: *Style in the French Novel* (Cambridge, University Press, 1957), pp. 94 et seq., also briefly on *l'Education sentimentale*, pp. 161–7; Sarraute: 'Flaubert le précurseur' in *Preuves*, février, 1965, pp. 3–11.

[2] Mosher: *Point of View in the Fiction of Gustave Flaubert and Ford Madox Ford* (University of Texas Ph.D. dissertation: Ann Arbor, University Microfilms, 1967).

partly suited to his purpose. To convey a moral criticism by such a method, he would have to choose a character who was either a simple *porte-parole*—obviously undesirable and in any case equally possible with a traditional omniscient method—or a sufficiently unusual personality for the criticism to be implicit in his reactions. He may, for example, be a person with considerable education or acuity of judgement, capable of looking critically at his own and other people's actions, as Stephen Dedalus or Leopold Bloom are (sometimes) in *Ulysses*; he may suffer from an exceptional level of self-awareness, a veritable mania for analysing life and his position in it, like the central figure of *la Nausée*; or he may be an utterly passive person to whom strange things happen, like those of *l'Etranger* or *le Voyeur*. In any of these cases he would not be a typical character, and could not satisfy Flaubert's requirement of universality.

Again, if the author were to be logical in recording the experiences of a single character, it would all have to be done in the language and style of that character. If the character is a typical human being, the language of the entire novel would have to be very ordinary. Although this is recognized, and accepted with equanimity, by many modern novelists, it is incompatible with Flaubert's respect for fine language. Flaubert's selected character would therefore have to be a great writer, so that the book could be well written, but then he ceases to be typical . . .

A totally consistent restriction of authorial omniscience is thus impossible for Flaubert, because it would conflict with some of his major artistic theories. But it is true that a measure of restriction is capable of solving some of the problems of presentation associated with his views on impersonality. It remained for him to find a means of adapting the technique so that it did not interfere with other criteria. We shall see that in his earliest and least literary works, he was already using the elements of a limited omniscience technique. When he came to think seriously about methods of presentation, he was therefore in a position to develop techniques which had long been common property, but in which he found an unsuspected richness. Whether he did this consciously is not certain; it can only be said that the technique is there, that it is not incompatible with the explicit theories of the *Correspondance*, and that given his highly intellectual approach to novel-writing, it is unlikely to have been an accident.

II

THE EARLY WORKS

In search of a witness

WHENEVER a writer abdicates all or part of his omniscience, a character must assume one of his responsibilities by taking over the role of observer. It seems significant for Flaubert's use of point of view that he nearly always introduces an observer into his writing, even where this is totally unnecessary: it amounts almost to a quirk of style with him. He even uses an 'observer' to present many of the descriptions of the *Notes de Voyage*, which one would expect to be far removed from the domain of novel technique. For the very reason that these *Notes* have only the barest literary pretensions—they are mostly impressions jotted down while Flaubert was travelling, with minor revisions after his return to Croisset[1]—they provide an excellent opportunity for studying the simplest form of Flaubert's use of the observer technique.

The only possible observer in such a work is Flaubert himself, for there are no characters; and time and again he transforms himself into a sort of rudimentary character, solely, it would seem, so that he can have an observer within his work. In other words, he continually creates an implicit separation between himself as observer and himself as author. He seldom describes a scene directly from memory. Instead, he uses his imagination and memory first of all to put himself back on the vantage point from which he had viewed the scene (the top of a hill, for example), and then describes, in an orderly fashion, what he can see. Facts are almost invariably accompanied by impressions—the size and

---

[1] See Naaman: *Les Débuts de Gustave Flaubert et sa technique de la description* (Paris, Nizet, 1962), pp. 117–24 for details of how and when the various *Voyages* were written.

appearance of distant objects, the effect of light and colour at the precise moment in question, and so on. The result is a sense of immediacy and authenticity, a feeling that none of this can possibly be invented, for it is being described as it is being viewed—a simultaneous translation of sights into words. Flaubert remembers not the scene, but himself looking at the scene. Sensations and motives are those of the moment of seeing, not of the moment of writing. This intimate connection between observer and observed recurs continually in his published novels, as we shall see. For the moment, some of the dozens of cases of it in the *Notes* will demonstrate the method. Consider, for example, the following:

Du haut du Liban, sur la crête aiguë de la montagne, on a à la fois (il ne s'agit que de se retourner) la vue de l'Anti-Liban, de la plaine de la Bequaa, le versant oriental du Liban, d'un côté et de l'autre, celle de la vallée des Cèdres et de la mer, bleue et couverte de brume, au bout de cette gorge teinte d'ardoise avec des traînées rouges et des tons noirs. La vallée part d'en face de vous, par une courbe incline sur la gauche, puis redevient droite et s'abaisse vers la mer. De là-haut, elle a l'air d'une grande tranchée taillée entre les deux montagnes, fossé naturel entre les deux murs géants. Sur son ton, généralement bleu très foncé, places noires; ce sont des arbres, dans lesquels on distingue des petits dés gris, qui sont des maisons. Aux premiers plans, à droite, mamelons qui descendent vers la vallée, comme des épines dorsales régulières de couleur rose, pâle d'ensemble; la crête de chacun est presque rouge et graduellement, en descendant vers le fond, va s'apâlissant en gris, pour se marier aux terrains blancs inférieurs. Quelques traînées blanches au milieu des mamelons, entre chacun d'eux; ce sont les sentiers des ravins à sec. . . . A gauche, grand mouvement de terrain, creusé comme une vague, lisse à l'œil et tout gris, sans verdure aucune; c'est un peu plus bas que commencent les couleurs vertes. . . . Le village de Bercharra, au milieu de ses arbres longs et verts, comme seraient des sapins (ce sont des peupliers trembles), a l'air tout penché sur l'abîme, et la vallée (dont, à cause de la hauteur où l'on est, on ne peut voir les pentes qui y mènent) a l'air creusée à pic.

Quand on se tourne vers l'Anti-Liban, on a d'abord le Liban; au premier plan, la partie dégarnie de la montagne, puis le plateau qui monte vers la partie boisée. Son fond est grisâtre, çà et là parsemé de bouquets verts, le terrain fait gros dos et va joindre la forêt de caroubiers dont on ne peut voir le versant oriental. Vient, en y faisant suite, la plaine de Bequaa, qui a l'air de monter et va s'asseoir aux pieds de l'Anti-Liban qui accumule les unes derrière les autres ses chaînes successives.[1]

Throughout this rather long passage, a number of expressions serve to emphasize the actual presence of an observer on the mountain-top: 'On a la vue'; 'il ne s'agit que de se retourner'; 'la vallée part d'en face de vous'; 'à cause de la hauteur où l'on est, on ne peut voir . . .'. The sense of immediacy is reinforced by statements of how various items *appear*: the valley 'a l'air d'une grande tranchée taillée entre les deux montagnes'; the trees are simply 'places noires', houses 'des petits dés gris'; the village 'a l'air tout penché sur l'abîme', and so on. Colours are carefully noted, especially their gradations and the way they merge one into the other. Finally, at least one observation—the fact that the sea is shrouded in mist—and very probably some of the colours noted, show that this is not a description valid for all times, but for a particular moment when the observer happens to be there.

None of this, it is true, is in itself very surprising or very original. Similar remarks could be made about passages in Chateaubriand and many other writers, including Fromentin, whose *Voyage en Orient* (1869) employs an almost identical method. The significance of the passage quoted lies, first in the fact that it is so typical of the *Notes de Voyage*,[2] so that the method appears to be almost second nature to Flaubert, and secondly in the fact that it is the simplest manifestation of a method which is to be found throughout Flaubert's mature work. We are tracing the *development* of a technique, and if its starting-point happens to be unexciting and unoriginal, it is certain that its later forms are not.

Since impressionism is a vital aspect of Flaubert's mature technique, it is important to emphasize its beginnings here. Basically, an impressionistic technique is one in which temporary and fleeting aspects of a scene are stressed. These are presented not

---

[1] *Voyages*, I, 363–4.
[2] Minor examples can be found almost by opening the book at random; some of the more noteworthy ones are: vol. I, pp. 111–13, 164, 167–8, 171, 173–4, 176, 185–6, 207, 210, 225, 302–3, 314, 347–8, 394; vol. II, pp. 70–1, 72, 76, 78–9, 84–5, 100–1, 134, 135–6, 145, 155–6, 160–2.

as we know them to be, but as they appear in the circumstances of the moment: our intellectual knowledge of the nature of objects, as gained from past experience, is temporarily subordinated to our sensory impressions of them. In the passage I have quoted, the part played by the subjective impression is small: although the houses are first described as 'des petits dés gris', it is explained almost immediately that they are in fact houses: the intellectually known objective fact is explicit. Frequently, however, the fact becomes less important than the impression. This is a method of involving the reader more closely, by forcing him to follow the workings of the observer's mind, to receive the impressions as the observer receives them, and gradually to piece together the facts as the observer does. Consider, in the light of this, the following description of the approach of two desert caravans, one of which passes in the middle of a sandstorm; and note how carefully the changes in the appearance of both the caravan and the landscape are recorded:

Il fait chaud, à notre droite un tourbillon de khamsin s'avance, venant du côté du Nil, dont on aperçoit encore à peine quelques palmiers qui en font la bordure; le tourbillon grandit et s'avance sur nous, c'est comme un immense nuage vertical qui, bien avant qu'il ne nous enveloppe, surplombe sur nos têtes, tandis que sa base, à droite, est encore loin de nous. Il est brun rouge et rouge pâle, nous sommes en plein dedans; une caravane nous croise, les hommes entourés de coufiehs (les femmes très voilées) se penchent sur le cou des dromadaires; ils passent tout près de nous, on ne se dit rien, c'est comme des fantômes dans des nuages. . . . Il m'a semblé, pendant que la caravane a passé, que les chameaux ne touchaient pas à terre, qu'ils s'avançaient du poitrail avec un mouvement de bateau, qu'ils étaient là-dedans et très élevés au-dessus du sol, comme s'ils eussent marché dans des nuages où ils enfonçaient jusqu'au ventre.

De temps à autre nous rencontrons d'autres caravanes. A l'horizon, c'est d'abord une longue ligne en large et qui se distingue à peine de la ligne de l'horizon; puis cette ligne noire se lève de dessus l'autre, et sur elle bientôt on voit des petits points; les petits points s'élèvent, ce sont les têtes des chameaux qui marchent de front, balancement régulier de toute la ligne. Vues en raccourci, ces têtes ressemblent à des têtes d'autruches.

Le vent chaud vient du midi; le soleil a l'air d'un plat d'argent bruni, une seconde trombe nous gagne. Ça s'avance comme une fumée d'incendie, couleur de suie avec des tons complètement noirs à sa base, ça marche . . . ça marche . . . le rideau nous gagne, bombé en volutes par le bas, avec ses larges franges noires (I, 241–2).

In the following passage, the same elements are present, but this time greater attention is paid to the fleeting effects of colour and lighting. The subjectivity of the description is obvious, and is doubly interesting here because it involves a description of people—another important element of Flaubert's mature descriptive technique:

Le soleil perce les nuages, ils se retirent des deux côtés et le laissent couvert d'un transparent blanc qui l'estompe; le ciel, noir sur la gauche, devient bleu outremer très tendre, avec des épaisseurs plus foncées dans certains endroits; le bleu a un ton gris perle fondu sur lui. Les masses se dissipent, le bleu reste bordé de petits nuages blancs déroulés; derrière l'acropole d'Argos, à notre droite, près de nous et sur elle, un petit nuage blanc, cendré. La lumière, tombant de ma droite et presque d'aplomb, éclaire étrangement François et Max à ma gauche, qui se détachent sur un fond noir, je vois chaque petit détail de leur figure très nettement; elle tombe sur l'herbe verte et a l'air d'épancher sur elle un fluide doux et reposé, de couleur bleue distillée.[1]

Flaubert's habit of using an observer to record partly fact, partly subjective impression, seems to have come so naturally to him in the hastily-revised *Voyages* that one can never be sure

[1] *Voyages*, II, 143. In some cases Flaubert actually notes the time of day, since this affects what he sees (II, 315, 558, 562, 568). See also Naaman, op. cit., pp. 226–7, 263–6, 347; and p. 377 for an interesting example of how Flaubert records a given colour in different ways, depending on the light and the position of the viewer. Bruneau: *Les Débuts littéraires de Gustave Flaubert, 1831–1845* (Paris, Armand Colin, 1962), pp. 300–1, also draws attention to 'le goût et le sens de la lumière' in *Corse*.

Bart: *Flaubert's Landscape Descriptions* (Ann Arbor, University of Michigan Press, 1956), pp. 2–14 (passim), 27–30, quotes many passages from the *Notes de Voyage* in his study of Flaubert's notations of exact nuances of colour and the effects of light, and mentions various attempts to involve the reader in the descriptions and associate him with what is being observed (pp. 12–14, 20). But as his book is concerned specifically with landscape descriptions, it has a different emphasis and orientation from the present study. It therefore seemed useful to repeat some of what he has already said.

whether he was conscious of it or not. But the same method occurs quite as frequently in the two sets of notes which he did make some attempt to rewrite, apparently at first with a view to publication: the *Voyage en Corse* and *Par les champs et par les grèves*. These still do not show Flaubert's mature literary technique—he was only nineteen when he wrote the earlier one.[1] Nevertheless, the fact that the usual liberal sprinkling of 'seeing' words, the strictly progressive, observed descriptions, and the same elements of subjectivity—both temporary aspects of the scene and emotions inspired by the scene—should all have survived this literary reworking in such large numbers,[2] suggests that Flaubert really did know what he was doing. But this is not a question which can finally be settled in the *Voyages*, and it is time to examine the early creative works.

The *Œuvres de jeunesse* consist of over forty separate pieces, of varying length and merit, written between 1835 and 1849. They include the first versions of *la Tentation de Saint Antoine* and of *l'Education sentimentale*. None has much permanent literary value compared with his published works, although some are quite amusing. But the majority of them, and especially the first *Education sentimentale*, can be considered literary works in the sense that when Flaubert began to write them he presumably had some ideas about publishing them, and they are nearly all attempts at true creative works, whereas the *Voyages* are merely records. They range from plans and unfinished sketches to pieces which have obviously involved much thought and hard work, and therefore demonstrate Flaubert's literary technique as it stood before *Madame Bovary*. A complete study of them would be a long and tedious task, and probably not worth the effort, but it is not difficult to summarize those aspects of interest to the present study.

---

[1] See Bruneau, op. cit., pp. 293 and 304, and Naaman, op. cit., p. 117 for details of the position of these *Notes* in Flaubert's work.

[2] e.g. *Par les champs et par les grèves*, pp. 20, 45–9, 63–5, 75–6, 106–7, 114–17, 161, 162–4, 199–201, 219–20, 225–7, 375, 382–3, 385–9, 407–8, 422–5, 431–2, 437–8, 444, 448–9, 468.

First, however, a general comment on attitudes to these works. My examination of their techniques does not imply literary value, or even that they necessarily foreshadow the great writer Flaubert was to become. It is important to see these juvenile ramblings, which have survived only because Flaubert happened to be a hoarder, in their proper perspective: there has been an unfortunate tendency to ascribe consciously mature literary techniques, and even a whole philosophy, to a child. In fact, if all these pieces had been lost, French literature would have been not one iota worse off, and Flaubert studies very little worse. There is nothing spectacular, or even unusual, about most of them: civilization has produced few child prodigies, and Flaubert was not one of them. Thousands of children make pronouncements like 'Le jour de l'an est bête', and thousands attempt to produce literary masterpieces. Probably the majority like to write and produce plays with their friends, and pester their families into being the audience. The fact that Flaubert is known to have done all these things proves nothing about his later career. We should expect to find few, if any, signs of incipient genius; much more likely will be evidence of a vociferous and unruly schoolboy, highly impressed with his own value, who is writing down his thoughts largely because that is what 'thoughtful' schoolboys do, especially at the height of the romantic period. Literary technique, apart from style (in the narrow sense) and the few rules learnt at school, is a subject which barely occurs to such writers. It is normally limited to the awareness of a need for variety and originality in presentation, often with a surprise reserved for the end. The variety and 'originality' both come, in general, from the imitation of methods which appealed to the writer in works by others. Both are used mainly to demonstrate what a clever fellow the writer is, this last being the most pressing necessity of all. It is only at the post-adolescent stage, when most people grow out of their play-acting and their writing, as their energies are diverted into the practical channels about which Flaubert complained so bitterly, that a continuing interest in literary experimentation becomes really significant. But as we cannot know exactly at what point in his youth Flaubert began to be aware of the real problems of technique, and seriously began to search for ways of solving them, we can never be sure when a given technique ceases to be fortuitous. We must not pretend that literary technique is something consciously evolved from the age of fourteen.

Like most of the second-rate authors of the nineteenth century, and several of the major ones, the younger Flaubert saw creative writing as an expression of controversial opinions and a literary personality. The most constant aspect of his early technique is direct exposition of his theories in a pseudo-conversation with the reader. This usually takes the form of brash cynicism, and occurs in almost every one of the works in question.[1] Apart from this, the *Œuvres de jeunesse* display a wide variety of modes of presentation. For example, Flaubert experimented briefly with the method of having a character read a letter, which by being printed in full helps to advance the narrative.[2] He attempted the 'anti-preface', as an unusual means of introducing his story (*Quidquid volueris*, I, 204). He had characters recount their life story within the story (*Novembre*, II, 214 et seq.); he had his hero recall in writing a previous oral account to friends of part of his own life story (*Mémoires d'un fou*, I, 517 et seq.). He pretended to adopt a sort of journal form, by having his hero intimate that everything would be written down in the order it occurred to him, without any attempt to impose an artificial order (*Mémoires d'un fou*, I, 484).[3] He tried the convention of an editor publishing an old manuscript and attempting some kind of external explana-

---

[1] See Bruneau, op. cit., pp. 97–8, 137–8, 181–3, 215–16, 338–9 for examples and a statement of the frequency of such interventions in the various types of works. Their occurrence is so obvious that it is superfluous to cite further examples here.

[2] *Un Secret de Philippe le Prudent*, I, 60–2. The technique is employed in its most basic form, with no regard for verisimilitude in style or content. Since Flaubert is really concerned only with continuing his story and putting across his 'message', the letter is an artificial complication, apparently introduced solely for variety.

[3] This looks very much like a convenient excuse for avoiding the hard work involved in structure and composition: it is a method still in favour at a certain level of novel-writing for the same reason. I should point out, however, that Bruneau (op. cit., p. 253) gives Flaubert credit for more sincerity here, and takes his statements as the announcement of a seriously-worked-out literary principle.

tion and judgement (*Novembre*, II, 243 et seq.). He also made two gestures in the direction of the first person novel. Every one of these experiments has the air of resulting from a passing whim, of being an artificial appendage to a story which could quite as easily have done without it.[1]

When we turn to those aspects of technique directly connected with point of view—the problems of the relationship between author and character, and between author and reader—a similarly confused picture is to be found. Those elements which we have already noted in the *Voyages* do occur fairly frequently, and more frequently in the later *Œuvres de jeunesse* than in the earlier ones; but their occurrence is somewhat haphazard. For example, there is still a proliferation of words containing the ideas of seeing, hearing, etc. (that is, implying that a witness is present at the scene being described), and besides, the witness is now quite often one of the characters, instead of the author.[2] This is a very definite, although not in itself very conclusive, step in the direction of a restricted point of view technique. The author is beginning to suppress his own personality, and temporarily allows the character to advance the narrative. We are told the character's thoughts and feelings, instead of the author's (although of course the two frequently coincide), and we see only those events which the character sees. This does not, of course, apply only to descriptions, but to all aspects of the work; the technique of the *Voyages* has been extended. But it seldom occurs in its pure form—that is to say, without commentary and explanation from the author in his own name—and seldom occurs for long. It was just one method among many: there is a good example of it in *le Moine*

[1] See Mosher, op. cit., pp. 85–145 for a much more detailed consideration of various point of view techniques in Flaubert's earlier works. Mosher has some interesting points to make, but in my opinion takes Flaubert's youthful experiments too seriously.

[2] e.g. *Œuvres de jeunesse*, vol. I, pp. 9, 11–21, 29, 46, 55–6, 62, 64–5, 78–86, 148, 149–50, 208–9, 211 et seq., 215–20, 465, 467–8, 473–5. See also Naaman, op. cit., pp. 348 et seq., for examples of the continuation, in the 'creative' works, of visual elements and the effects of light. Although Naaman does not say so, many of the examples he gives of 'tremblements et vibrations' (p. 353) and of auditive elements which the *characters* notice (pp. 354–6) underline the temporary and subjective orientation of the passages.

des Chartreux (I, 29–30), one of Flaubert's very earliest works,[1] and it is not consistently used again for several years.

After several sporadic appearances—in particular in *Rêve d'Enfer*, where Bruneau sees a very definite attempt to integrate description with action by means of the characters' emotional attitudes[2]— the technique assumes new importance in *Quidquid volueris*, where several quite long passages are entirely from the point of view of Djalioh. It is in this work, too, that we see a further advance: a connection, more definite than in *Rêve d'Enfer*, between descriptions and the feelings of the witnessing character. Consider, for example, this passage describing Adèle dancing:

> Djalioh était debout, appuyé sur un battant de la porte, la valse passait devant lui, tournoyante, bruyante, avec des rires et de la joie; chaque fois il voyait Adèle tournoyer devant lui et puis disparaître, revenir et disparaître encore; chaque fois il la voyait s'appuyer sur un bras qui soutenait sa taille, fatiguée qu'elle était de la danse et des plaisirs, et chaque fois il sentait en lui un démon qui frémissait et un instinct sauvage qui rugissait dans son âme, comme un lion dans sa cage; chaque fois, à la même mesure répétée, au même coup d'archet, à la même note, au bout d'un même temps, il voyait passer devant lui le bas d'une robe blanche, à fleurs roses, et deux souliers de satin qui s'entre-bâillaient, et cela dura longtemps, vingt minutes environ. La danse s'arrêta. Oppressée, elle essuya son front, et puis elle repartit plus légère, plus sauteuse, plus jolie et plus rose que jamais (I, 225).

The effect of this scene on Djalioh's mind is very important to the development, so it seems significant that the description is presented from his point of view. That it *is* from his point of view is made plain by the frequent 'seeing' words, and by impressionistic details such as 'un bras qui soutenait sa taille' (the owner of the arm is not described, as only the arm being where it is is important), and 'le bas d'une robe blanche . . .' (not a full description of Adèle, but only the part Djalioh could see as he looked down). Then follows an exposition of Djalioh's thoughts (omitted from the quotation) occasioned by what he had just seen of Adèle. For all the romantic bombast, it is these thoughts which are the essential part of the passage: the description is

---

[1] 1835–6, according to Bruneau, op. cit., p. 13.   [2] Ibid., p. 180, q.v.

included only to show what caused them. So, too, with the later description of the swans (I, 229), which occurs when it does because a picture of a handsome and contented pair is required at the moment when Djalioh is bitterly resenting his ugliness, and the fact that Adèle will never love him because of it.[1]

The gradual development of a descriptive technique calculated to underline the connection between a character's feelings and reality as observed by that character, is followed in more detail by Bruneau. He, too, mentions *Quidquid volueris* as important in this development, but regards *Passion et Vertu*, written a few months later, as being much more so. It is here, he says, that 'Flaubert établit une relation entre la psychologie du personnage et le paysage qu'il regarde, et lui fait prendre conscience du rapport profond qui existe entre la nature et lui-même . . .';[2] and while conceding that the example he quotes is not outstandingly successful, and probably copies a procedure taken from romantic writers, he classes it as 'le premier exemple, dans l'œuvre de Flaubert, de ces merveilleuses descriptions qui rempliront les grands romans'. This last comment is probably exaggerating the importance of the passage: Flaubert's method here results in something uncomfortably like ordinary pathetic fallacy. Descriptions like these are merely a step towards Flaubert's mature technique, and the difference between them and later ones is not, as Bruneau suggests (as does Demorest, whom Bruneau quotes), simply a difference in mastery of language and style. What such descriptions lack above all—and will continue to lack throughout the *Œuvres de jeunesse*—is the critical dimension which allows Flaubert to show his *characters* indulging in pathetic fallacy, while at the same time showing that he himself is not taken in.[3] For the moment, Flaubert is at the stage in which he

---

[1] The rape scene, I, 235–9, is also entirely from the point of view of Djalioh.

[2] Bruneau, op. cit., pp. 140–1. See also Mosher, op. cit., pp. 117 et seq.

[3] Naaman, op. cit., pp. 226–7, notes that Flaubert frequently allows his descriptions to be influenced by his personal health and state of mind, that they are often partial and subjective. He also notes (p. 201, n. 58) several early examples of pathetic fallacy, and Flaubert's increasing tendency to include precise details in his descriptions. But when he states that later 'la nature cesse de se marier aux sentiments des personnages et de se conformer à leur état d'âme, comme dans ses

will later portray his characters, after he himself has passed it.[1]

The *Mémoires d'un fou* is an extraordinarily verbose piece of work, of which little can be said except that it has already had much more than its fair share of critical attention. But when the tiny incident about which this mass of words is built occurs—the adolescent saving the lady's scarf from the sea[2]—the technique employed is precisely that which we have already noted in *Quidquid volueris*. The only difference is that the first person is used, but this is not a significant difference in the present case. The narration of the incident constitutes the only real scene in the whole of the work, and it is possible that a definite novel technique is beginning to emerge here. It must be added, however, that the story of the two English girls, which also occurs in the *Mémoires*, is not presented in this manner, but is simply a '*récit*'.

In *Novembre*, the last of Flaubert's works before his first attempts at *Saint Antoine* and *l'Education sentimentale*, signs of a similar development are to be found. This is by far the longest of his early works, and the action is more developed than in *Mémoires*, with proportionately less 'philosophical' commentary by the author (although this is still considerable). It seems, too, that it was much more carefully written: Bruneau argues (p. 312) that it took up to two years to complete, and calls it 'la première véritable création littéraire de Gustave Flaubert'. There is thus more chance for Flaubert to develop a technique which would be suitable for a novel. Besides, he was by now twenty-one, and there is little doubt that he was consciously searching for the method of presentation which would best suit his purposes. It therefore seems significant that once again the central incident is entirely from the point of view of the hero. When he decides to go to the brothel, the reader goes with him, up the stairs and into

---

écrits d'écolier, sauf de rares exceptions; . . .' (p. 201), his conclusions diverge from those of Bruneau, and from the evolution we have been tracing here.

[1] See also Bruneau, op. cit., pp. 257–9, for similar comments on *Mémoires d'un fou*.

[2] *Œuvres de jeunesse*, I, 505–6.

the room, following not only his actions in strict chronological order, but also his thoughts and feelings, and seeing things only as he saw them.[1] When he enters the room, it appears large because of the darkness; this makes him notice the reason for the darkness, and the colour of the light. Then he notices 'une femme' —no amplification for the moment, as the hero knows nothing about her, and besides it is rather dark. Even simple variations in word order emphasize the point of view: 'Il fallait qu'elle ne m'eût pas entendu, car elle ne se détourna pas quand j'entrai; . . .' This could have been stated as a simple fact, but it is stated as a deduction. And because the woman did not hear him come in, he has time to stand and look at her. Quite naturally, it is here that her description begins, and it is introduced by a 'seeing' phrase: 'je restai debout sans avancer, occupé à la regarder'; this is reinforced by several similar expressions scattered through the passage. It is to be noted, too, that this first description is not complete, but records only what the hero can see as she sits at the end of the room in semi-darkness—mainly her hair, which is catching the light. Only when the woman realizes he is there and looks up is he able to describe her face, and again the effect of the light is noted. The whole of the scene progresses in this way, with every action, every sight, every word and feeling being revealed to the reader as it was revealed to the hero. This is the most complete and strictly ordered scene in Flaubert's work to date. The effort was apparently too much for him, for a few pages later he lapses back into his philosophic generalities. Nevertheless the advance seems quite definite, and scattered through *Novembre* there are several more short passages showing the same technique: they certainly occur more frequently in this work than in the previous ones.[2]

It should be pointed out that Bruneau, who also mentions this description of Marie,[3] contends that it is merely 'esquissé' in comparison with descriptions of people in Flaubert's novels. His

---

[1] *Œuvres de jeunesse*, II, 197 et seq.

[2] Bruneau, op. cit., pp. 332–5, quotes other examples, concerning pure descriptions. Like Bart, he mentions Flaubert's debt to Chateaubriand.

[3] Ibid., p. 335.

general comments fit with the argument I have developed here, but his conclusions are precisely the opposite:

> Flaubert cherche plutôt à rendre dans les lignes qu'il lui [à Marie] consacre l'impression de beauté et de volupté qu'elle crée dans l'esprit de son héros: [here Bruneau quotes the description]. Description assez imprécise où les adjectifs 'adorable', 'palpitantes', 'chaude' préparent le lecteur aux voluptés qui vont suivre. Flaubert est loin encore des portraits des grands romans.

I hope to show that in fact Flaubert is coming very close to the portraits of his great novels.

Novembre is interesting for another reason: the extra factor of judgement and criticism of the hero which is introduced. Previously Flaubert had normally made his hero someone shunned by bourgeois society (a pirate, an actor, a person who commits rape and murder) and clearly announced his sympathy for the outcast. Most of his voluminous explicit criticism is reserved for the reader or for society—an attitude typical of many romantic works. This habit continues in *Novembre*, with the apology for the prostitute, but in addition there are suggestions that the *hero* may have made a mistake in some of his judgements, and this is a new note.[1] Such suggestions are introduced in two ways. First, the 'editor' of the manuscript explains that the hero was the sort of person who sometimes overrated his capabilities. We are told, for example, that he was deluding himself in believing that he was capable of significant works of art (II, 244). The second method is more important: the hero himself, on looking back over the events he has been recounting, realizes he may have unconsciously exaggerated his feelings. This is illustrated in his informing the reader, after sixty pages convincing us that he has been talking about the most beautiful and most intelligent creature alive, that 'elle n'était peut-être ni plus belle ni plus ardente qu'une autre; j'ai peur de n'aimer qu'une conception de mon esprit et de ne

---

[1] Although there is already a hint that this will happen in *Mémoires d'un fou* (I, 530): '. . . il y a des peintres qui voient tout en bleu, d'autres tout en jaune ou tout en noir. Chacun de nous a un prisme à travers lequel il aperçoit le monde.' This statement, which will have important echoes in an early version of *Madame Bovary*, is not yet specifically applied to the hero.

chérir en elle que l'amour qu'elle m'avait fait rêver' (II, 238). Another example—not a very subtle one, and therefore all the more useful as an example—is the description of the women the hero passes in the street—'toutes merveilleusement belles; . . . les duchesses . . . semblaient me sourire, m'inviter à des amours sur la soie; . . . les dames en écharpe 's'avançaient pour me voir. . . . Toutes m'aimaient dans leur pose, dans leurs yeux, dans leur immobilité même, je le voyais bien' (II, 197).¹ And so on. As a picture of a street scene it is obviously distorted by the hero's feelings—and yet it is presented as if it were factual. The critical dimension is also effectively illustrated in the long descriptive passage on pp. 188–92. The hero is happy, and rejoicing in nature: nature is described only in its beautiful and joyous aspects. But the same evening, when the buoyant mood has subsided, the hero retraces his steps, looks at the same scenes, and sees nothing: 'il me sembla que j'avais rêvé'. Now it is extremely important to notice this denial of what had gone before—Bruneau, for example, notes only the description, which leads him to talk about Flaubert's mystical and pantheistic experiences.¹ Flaubert is not in fact saying that there is a 'harmonie entre les paysages et les états d'âme': he is saying that the hero has discovered that there is no such harmony. The hero sees nature in a particular way as a result of his feelings, and the emphasis is on the feelings more than on the description. The description occurs for the light it throws on the feelings; when the feelings go, so does the scene: description depends upon point of view. This is the logical conclusion of the tendency towards impressionism which occurs so frequently in Flaubert's early works. And the passage can serve as a warning: here the hero realizes, and tells us, that his impressions cannot be accepted as solid fact. The warning seldom occurs so explicitly again.

Of course, the first of these examples must inevitably call to mind Frédéric Moreau, and the others summarize the character of the future Emma Bovary; but their real significance here is that they show that Flaubert has become aware of an important psychological fact—the basis of *Bovarysme*—which would be

¹ Bruneau, op. cit., p. 334.

excellent material for a novel if a suitable method of presenting it could be found. It must have been obvious to him that the methods tried here were inadequate: if the hero is capable of seeing his mistakes, he would have been less likely to make them in the first place; and the convention of an external editor to present and judge the work is outmoded and unconvincing. What is required is a 'hero' who is the victim of his illusions—if possible one who is also introspective, so that he can be shown to be a victim of his illusions even while examining his actions and motives—and a method of presentation which makes this clear without the intervention of anyone external to the story, whether author or 'editor'.

It must be emphasized that although the restricted point of view method is employed with increasing frequency up to *Novembre*, it is never as common as the technique of the omniscient author, where the reader is continually reminded that he is being given a full account of a completed event, with explanations and commentary added as the author sees fit. Between these two extremes, there are numerous passages where Flaubert, wishing to present a more graduated description or exposition without totally sacrificing his omniscience, pretends to restrict temporarily his knowledge of what is to come. Several works begin with such a description, but then continue with an explanation from the author of its significance. In such a situation, he often begins with a hypothetical witness, a person who is not part of the story, but who would be able to see this or that event if he chanced to be present at the right time. This is a technique frequently employed by Balzac, and we shall have occasion to return to it.[1]

All these methods of presentation are widely used in books Flaubert had read. All served his primary purpose of getting his ideas down on paper, and by using them more or less indiscriminately he also achieved the requirement of variety in presentation. He is still apparently fairly indiscriminate in *Mémoires d'un fou* and *Novembre*, but the ever-increasing tendency towards restriction of point of view is by now probably significant. In addition, the

[1] e.g. *Œuvres de jeunesse*, vol. I, pp. 55–6, 78, 148, 208 et seq., 465–7, 473–5. For general similarities with Balzac, see Naaman, op. cit., pp. 342–7.

fact that both these works are in the first person suggests that he has at least become aware of the problem. The use of the first person to retell a story is a convenient way of combining the advantages of the omniscient narrator (since it happened to the narrator, he knows what is going to happen in the future), and the restricted point of view technique (since it happened to him, he can remember how he thought and felt at the time, and to what extent his knowledge of the situation was limited). But we are still a long way from the Flaubert of *Madame Bovary*, and it is now time to see what advances were made in the first version of *l'Education sentimentale*.

A technical impasse

From the technical point of view, the most obvious characteristic of the 1845 *Education* remains the continual presence of the author. From the first sentence ('Le héros de ce livre, un matin d'octobre, arriva à Paris avec un cœur de dix-huit ans et un diplôme de bachelier ès-lettres') to the last ('Ici, l'auteur passe son habit noir et salue la compagnie'), a facetious, mocking strain is never far from the surface. Flaubert is still preoccupied with presenting a literary personality—although this personality is very different from that of earlier works, and is itself a measure of the progress he has made in at least one direction. In addition, there are a large number of digressions and authorial interventions, and the greater part of the book is presented through an omniscient narrator. These interventions include direct commentaries, and explanations and criticisms of the actions and motives of all the characters.[1]

Nevertheless the experimentation continues. It may even be that this partly explains why the 1845 *Education* is an unsatisfactory novel, for one feels that some of the techniques used are

[1] See Bruneau, op. cit., pp. 435–6 for a more detailed examination, and examples of the more important types. Little can now be said on the first *Education* without reference to the comprehensive study by Bruneau. Some of the arguments presented here, although differently orientated, use basically similar material. See also Mosher, op. cit., pp. 92, 140 et seq. for other considerations arising out of Flaubert's use of point of view in this work.

experiments alone, that they do not grow from any inner logical necessity, that form is superimposed upon content without being intimately connected with it.[1] For example, most of what concerns Jules in the early part of the book is allowed to 'tell itself', through Jules's letters to Henry. Now although these letters are full of useless verbiage (e.g. III, 7–10, 33–7) and largely lacking in the most elementary form of verisimilitude, they do at least correspond with what Flaubert later regarded as a necessity, in that they *show* a character, without explanations and analyses by the author. It might be argued, too, that by presenting Jules in his letters to Henry, Flaubert is able continually to emphasize the links between his two heroes, and thus contribute towards the unity of his novel.[2] But quite suddenly, and without any apparent reason (it occurs before the exchange of letters between the two friends diminishes in frequency), this method ceases, and we begin to follow Jules's experiences more directly, more in the order and at the time in which they occur. No longer content to allow the character to present himself, Flaubert reverts to the omniscient author technique in order to give himself freedom to provide a running commentary. This sudden change (from III, 96) is the more noticeable for occurring only a few pages before Henry returns home for holidays (III, 102) and, we are told, takes part in long conversations with Jules. Had Flaubert really been interested in *showing* his characters, and the contrasts and similarities between them, and indeed in the formal unity of his novel, he could have used this opportunity to introduce significant conversations (as he does, for example, near the beginning of the 1869 *Education*, to present Deslauriers). He obviously still prefers explicit authorial analyses.

One effect of Flaubert's desire to make it plain that he, as author, is inventing and regulating the development of his novel is a technique strongly reminiscent of Balzac's. In particular, the presentation of the Renaud establishment and its inhabitants

---

[1] This is also Mosher's view, op. cit., pp. 139–42.

[2] In which, we must add, it is nevertheless sadly lacking. The two stories and the two developments remain quite separate, a fact which Flaubert later recognized (*Cor.*, II, 343–4).

cannot but recall Balzac's introduction to the *pension Vauquer* in *le Père Goriot*. True, there are important differences: the description is not as long as Balzac's, nor as specific about locality (III, 11); and there is less of the idea that the house and furnishings intimately reflect the character of the owners. But Flaubert temporarily introduces the same convention of a disinterested passer-by used to 'witness' the exterior of the house, then to enter and speak to M. Renaud, who is thus presented to the reader. This witness is quickly dispensed with to give way to the omniscient author, relayed from time to time (without apparent reason) by some of M. Renaud's pupils, and thus M. and Mme Renaud are presented in some detail to the reader[1] before the action of the novel really begins.

Another experiment occurs in the important interview between Henry's parents and M. Renaud after the lovers' flight to New York. There is a sudden lapse into theatre-type dialogue, with the little remaining prose description presented almost in the form of stage directions (III, 199–212). One can imagine reasons for this: it allows the characters to present themselves, and it helps to involve the reader by the sense of immediacy and the mental picture it presents. Nevertheless its sudden occurrence in the middle of a novel is bizarre to say the least (but is this necessarily a fault? Joyce does the same thing in *Ulysses*), and it is not used consistently: when direct speech becomes inadequate, the author breaks in to explain. Nor is it really necessary to show the characters here—this has already been done by other means. In fact, it shows nothing except a burlesque picture of the bourgeois in a crisis. It does, however, indicate—as do several other passages (e.g. III, 55–6, 58–9, 85 et seq., 130–6, 167–73)—that Flaubert has not yet learned to use dialogue in a novel, at least in the way he later believed appropriate. Like Champfleury, he spends a great deal of time indicating, in a relatively realistic manner, what a group of people would probably say in a given situation. This means including much material which is not 'significant', which does not, for example, advance the action, add to our knowledge of the speakers' characters, show a contrast between what the

---

[1] But not completely, as Bruneau points out, op. cit., p. 433.

characters say and what they believe, and so on. It is useless dialogue, which Flaubert later rejected. It is life and not art.

Again, when Flaubert wishes to indicate that his characters think in *idées reçues*, he does not scatter their favourite theories through their conversation or their thoughts as in the later novels, but produces a long Rabelaisian list, at the same time clearly indicating his contempt. So we have the sarcastic authorial summary of the conversation at the Renaud dinner (III, 30, 31–2), the long introduction to the character of Henry's father (III, 190 et seq.), and the artistic and intellectual beliefs which Jules had come to reject (III, 255 et seq.).

Flaubert also experimented briefly in this novel with recounting important scenes indirectly, after they had happened, no doubt as a means of increasing the impact on the reader. (An example of this technique brought to perfection is the coach scene of *Madame Bovary*.) After following in some detail the ups and downs of Henry's progress with Mme Renaud, and after a period which has been largely down, without warning we are given a letter from Henry informing Jules that his efforts have been successful (III, 112 et seq.). But the impact is partly neutralized by the fact that the letter goes on to recount in detail what led up to the happy event, and exactly how it occurred. Thus after the initial announcement the reader is taken back in time and made to follow the scene as if it were just happening, which could quite as easily have been done by the omniscient narrator technique which is normally used for Henry's experiences. The letter convention is a superfluous embellishment. So, too, is the method used in the scene where Henry recounts to Morel his misfortunes on the day he went riding (III, 89 et seq.). If this scene is important (which itself is doubtful), it could have been presented by the narrator technique too—as indeed it is in part: Flaubert seems to forget his original convention, especially towards the end of the scene, where he coolly informs us that in spite of all appearances, he is not recording Henry's version of the scene at all: 'Le lecteur imagine sans peine qu'il raconta ses chagrins en d'autres termes que nous ne l'avons fait, . . .'(III, 93).

Finally, although the author is frequently aggressive in his omniscience, he also sometimes goes to the other extreme, and coyly advises the reader that he does *not* know what is going on in the mind of one of his characters. This is particularly noticeable when it comes at the end of an exposition of a character's thoughts, as it does, for example, in III, 46.

In the midst of all this uncertainty and variation, some attempts at a restricted point of view presentation are to be expected as well, but we shall be obliged not to take them too seriously unless they are very numerous. In fact, they are not numerous, they do not occur consistently, and when they do occur they represent little advance on the examples already examined. For instance, when Mme Renaud comes into Henry's room for the first time, she has already been described to the reader in general terms by the omniscient author technique, and no mention is made of her appearance for some time. The scene begins with a dialogue, which surprisingly quickly takes a significant turn—Mme Renaud is less distant than Mme Arnoux will be. At this stage her gesture of squeezing the key in her hand draws Henry's attention to that hand, which is then described: '... les yeux d'Henry y étaient singulièrement attirés' (III, 19). The paragraph is insignificant in itself, but we shall later see Charles looking at Emma's hand and Frédéric looking at Arnoux's. In these descriptions there will be a similar mixture of objective and emotive terms, but a different use of the emotive terms.

The description of Mme Renaud's eyes later in the same scene (III, 23–4), which might also seem at first to be subjective and impressionistic, requires some comment. First, it is not so carefully arranged as the description of the prostitute in *Novembre*, for although the eyes ostensibly come within Henry's experience of the moment and are obviously described only because of their effect on him, it is four o'clock on a winter afternoon (December according to III, 24, January according to III, 18); it is almost dark, what light there is is shining on Henry (III, 20) and therefore not on Mme Renaud; so that in fact Henry would be unable to see her eyes well enough to register the details given. Secondly, Henry's 'subjective' approval is explicitly supported by the author—'J'aime beaucoup ces grands yeux des femmes de trente ans ...' etc.—and is therefore endowed with a certain objective validity. Thirdly, the emotive terms used here are very similar to those of the original description of Mme Renaud (III, 13–15), which was given by the omniscient narrator, so for this reason too they can be regarded as 'true'. Flaubert has not yet seen the logical consequences of a subjective description, and the possibilities of using it to separate himself from his characters and thereby achieve impersonality of presentation. As with the other methods, the subjective technique here seems to be just another variation, with no real reason for its presence.[1]

The most complete and consistent point of view scenes concern Jules and his heroine. Although we first hear of the theatrical troupe and of Lucinde in Jules's letters, and therefore in the first person, we are taken back to the beginning and introduced to developments progressively, as if following Jules's experiences as they occurred. The technique is similar to that of the prostitute scene of *Novembre*, especially when the physical appearance of Lucinde and her mother is gradually revealed to Jules and the reader as sufficient light becomes available (III, 68; see also III, 67, where the effects of a ray of sunlight in the darkened theatre are noted). Not surprisingly, Lucinde, too, is presented as being unusually beautiful. But while the reader, like Henry, is for the moment willing to accept Jules's judgement on this matter, it is not long before he is forced to change his mind. When Henry sees the girl for himself, his opinion—'Elle n'est pas mal'—reinforced by Jules's belated attempts at rationalization and explanation (III, 105–7), reveals Jules's delusion. This is then verified by the author:

Lucinde avait pour Jules les mêmes qualités [i.e. as those which

---

[1] Other passages using Henry's point of view, but which add little to what has already been said, include III, 52 (where Henry waits in vain for Mme Renaud to keep a rendez-vous, just as Frédéric will do); III, 80–4 (Henry, torn between desire and jealousy, watches Mme Renaud dancing with others); III, 110–12 (Henry's return to Paris by coach, which cannot but remind us of Frédéric's return from Nogent, except that Henry's joyful self-confidence proves to be justified); III, 179–80 (the view of the port, and Henry and Mme Renaud's last evening in France).

Henry has just stated to be Mme Renaud's] et, de plus, comme elle était jeune fille, et partant, vierge, il la dégageait de toute la matérialité de la vie, sans lui supposer ni boyaux dans le ventre, ni cors aux pieds, et la posait au septième ciel, sur des nuages à franges d'or. Henry, plus dans le vrai et moins soumis au *subjectif*, comme diraient les philosophes, aimait Mme Emilie telle qu'elle était. . . .[1]

Jules, too, is eventually forced to admit his error of judgement (III, 117–20). More than this, he revises his entire moral and artistic attitude—he is forced to admit that even in the most vital areas his judgement had been falsified by the way his mind worked. It seems significant that the scene marking the end of his first moral attitude is also one of the most striking point of view passages in Flaubert's work so far: the well-known episode of the stray dog, ending in a hallucinatory vision. The hallucination is in fact the last of Jules's early delusions: it was quite an ordinary dog really, as Flaubert indicates at the beginning of the next chapter: 'Ce fut son dernier jour de pathétique: depuis, il se corrigea de ses peurs superstitieuses et ne s'effraya pas de rencontrer des chiens galeux dans la campagne.'[2] Point of view is beginning to be used to show delusions actually at work—although not yet without a supporting statement from an external commentator.

It is unnecessary to consider in detail what has become of descriptions of nature in this novel. The question has been thoroughly treated by Bruneau,[3] who notes the continuing preoccupation with colour and light, and with connections between nature and the psychological development of the characters. But

---

[1] III, 106. Deslauriers passes the same judgement on Mme Arnoux, much to Frédéric's anger; but Deslauriers does not have the overt support of the author, and in addition has reasons for not encouraging Frédéric too much. Mme Arnoux's beauty remains an unknown quantity, but repetition of the same scene as here might lead us to suspect that it is Deslauriers, not Frédéric, who is right.

[2] III, 255. Needless to say, the statement has wider application than to this episode alone: it begins the chapter which shows just how radically Jules has changed. Naaman, op. cit., pp. 147–8, and Bruneau, op. cit., 425–9, both review the various explanations which have been advanced for the dog scene, and add their own. Most consider the philosophical or symbolic possibilities, which do not immediately concern us here.

[3] Bruneau, op. cit., p. 434.

I cannot subscribe to Bruneau's conclusion, which is similar to the ones he reached for *Passion et vertu* and *Mémoires d'un fou*: 'Flaubert a tiré les conséquences de sa découverte de la nature, de l'harmonie universelle. Son récit est situé dans la nature, ses personnages sont en harmonie avec elle, le roman établit la même unité que la vie elle-même'.

While it is true that for much of the book this correspondence occurs, Bruneau's assumption that this is the orientation of Flaubert's mature technique is not a necessary consequence. On the contrary, such an assumption is unequivocally negated by this passage from the novel:

> La nature extérieure a une ironie sans pareille: les cieux ne se couvrent pas de nuages, quand notre cœur est gros; les fleurs parfument l'air, quand nous le remplissons de nos cris; les oiseaux gazouillent et font l'amour dans les cyprès sous lesquels nous enterrons nos plus tendrement aimés (III, 143, quoted by Bruneau, p. 440).

This is the same critical dimension as was found in *Novembre*: it is a retraction by Jules (and by the author) of what he had believed about harmonies and correspondences. Even though he does hold that his earlier beliefs were responsible for his most poetic period (as Bruneau points out), he nevertheless considers that he now has a truer view of life. In future books, Flaubert will not need such an explicit renunciation: he will contrive to show his character being aware of superficial correspondences, while simultaneously implying that they are merely part of the over-all delusion.

Restricted point of view techniques in the first *Education* are of relatively little importance in terms of the proportion of the novel thus presented. They cannot yet be regarded as a major weapon in Flaubert's literary arsenal. But there are other important indications in this work that Flaubert may soon be able to make full use of such techniques. First, he has begun to show an interest in a new sort of hero. Henry in particular is very different, for he is a much more ordinary person; and although Jules has affinities with the heroes of *Mémoires d'un fou* and of *Novembre*, Bruneau reminds us that he survives his tragic adolescent period, and instead of wasting away (the hero of *Novembre* had died 'par la seule force de la pensée'), he too manages to readjust to life. Secondly, and more importantly, Flaubert is now more conscious of the way people's personal attitudes contribute to a falsification of their lives. Unsubtle and childishly cynical though it still is, this cornerstone of Flaubertian psychology is given real prominence, if not mature expression, in the 1845 *Education*. These two new elements prefigure the total disappearance of heroes and author's mouthpieces, and their replacement by ordinary (medi-ocre) central characters. They also prefigure therefore a radical separation between characters and author, who of course did not regard himself as mediocre.

The simplest manifestation of Flaubert's new attitude is his oft-repeated announcement that the judgement of ordinary people is unstable and unreliable, that it is influenced by the most trivial external circumstances. For instance, when Henry, already doubtful about the duration of his love for Mme Renaud, already foreseeing the sheer monotony of what he had so recently believed was his purpose in life, begins to feel the 'vide' which Flaubert always portrays after the initial passion (III, 188–90), at least part of his disillusionment is brutally put down to seasickness: 'on voit volontiers les choses en noir quand on vomit de la bile'. Henry was always much more optimistic when his boredom was alleviated by Mme Renaud's practical demonstrations of her love.[1]

Notwithstanding the previously-quoted statement (p. 71) that Henry is less given to subjective deformation of reality than Jules, both heroes suffer from this typically Flaubertian malady: Henry's attack is in fact more serious, for it turns out to be incurable. Indeed, the very passage in question prepared us for this, for it continues:

Henry . . . aimait Mme Emilie telle qu'elle était, avec son entourage de chaque jour, le milieu où elle vivait, avec tout son corps et toute son âme, avec tous ses caprices et ses dédains; c'était tout cela qui la

---

[1] Other obvious examples occur on pp. 37–8 (Henry's attitudes to Jules's letters influenced by the weather and Mme Renaud), and pp. 41–3 (Henry's attitudes to Morel influenced by what the latter happens to say).

constituait, qui la faisait telle qu'elle était, qui la distinguait des autres femmes, c'était pour tout cela qu'il l'aimait (III, 106).

Yet it was precisely because he hated her milieu and her entourage that he took her to America, and he was not always particularly pleased with the other elements mentioned either. This is another early example of a method which Flaubert came to use more and more: stating as indisputable facts things which a character thinks he believes, and which the author does not believe at all. Again, just before Henry's attempts to seduce Mme Renaud succeed, and at a time when it appears that they never will, we find Henry exaggerating his heroine's charms, manipulating the facts and indulging in the sour grapes rationalization which Léon will apply to Emma and Frédéric to Mme Arnoux when they are in similar situations:

> Henry lui disait [i.e. à Jules] qu'il ne voulait pas d'un amour charnel, qu'il lui fallait autre chose, et il lui faisait de Mme Renaud des descriptions charmantes, sans ajouter qu'elle avait peut-être un peu trop d'embonpoint, ni que, dans l'hiver, le froid lui rendait le bout du nez rouge et les joues toutes plaquées; . . . Il lui avoua cependant une partie de ses ennuis, mais vaguement, sans préciser les faits, grandissant les petites choses et poétisant les vulgaires, embellissant un peu l'histoire pour faire plus d'effet (III, 103-4).

When Henry and Mme Renaud decide to return to France, Flaubert attempts to explain their excitement and the apparent resurgence of their love in similar terms. They are incapable of objectively comparing the present moment with similar occasions in the past, of learning by experience:

> . . . liés de plus près par cet espoir commun, leur amour assoupi se réveilla tout à coup devant le bonheur qui réapparaissait pour eux dans un avenir infaillible, illusion à ajouter aux autres et dont Henry fut encore la dupe. Content de s'en retourner à des pénates connus et de reprendre une vie plus sûre, il crut qu'Emilie était pour quelque chose dans sa joie, que sans elle il ne se sentirait pas si heureux, et il l'en aimait davantage, contre-coup du plaisir nouveau dont il la croyait être la cause.
> Tout ce qui leur avait manqué en Amérique, tout ce qui avait

menti à leurs vœux, ils le replacèrent en Europe, pour l'avenir, dans les mêmes conditions que par le passé. Espérant toujours un bien-être indéfini qui n'arrivait jamais, rien n'aurait dû le leur faire présager; ils le croyaient cependant, et leur cœur en battait d'avance, comme à chaque année qui vient, malgré l'expérience des aînées, toujours l'on s'attend vaguement à quelque chose d'inéprouvé et de meilleur (III, 231; cf. III, 227).

It is not only because of their immediate relevance to the present argument that I have quoted such extracts from the first *Education*. Flaubert was already an adult (aged twenty-four) when he wrote this book. His own passage from adolescence to maturity in ideas, which is reflected in it, was completed; his views of human behaviour and motives are less likely to change radically from now on. Now in spite of superficial differences, the 1845 *Education* shows some unmistakable similarities, in orientation and in the psychology of its characters, to the 1869 version. It sometimes makes explicit certain aspects of behaviour which will be much more subtly presented in the mature work, and which as a result easily go unnoticed. Some of the passages quoted above will be useful for comparisons later. For the same reason, a few further authorial comments, although of a rather miscellaneous nature, could be mentioned here: they, too, show Flaubert at his most unambiguous on some important points.

Although Flaubert frequently portrays Henry as being deluded and extremely changeable, he specifically states that this is not the result of hypocrisy (except, of course, on a subconscious level). Henry's inconstancy, whether political (III, 286) or amorous (III, 283–4), is explained entirely in terms of mistaken but sincere rationalization, an inability to stand off from life and analyse it objectively. We should remember this in considering not only Frédéric, but almost all the other characters of the great *Education* —and in particular M. Dambreuse.

The author's comments on the attitudes of Henry and Mme Renaud towards each other are also important. Although Mme Renaud is indisputably more forward then Mme Arnoux— Flaubert uncompromisingly portrays Henry as 'béant et affamé devant ce mets qui fumait pour lui seul' (III, 60)—there are analogies between the central situations of the two books. When Henry presses his suit, Mme Renaud, like Mme Arnoux, speaks at first of chastity and virtue and duty. For a time, Henry is convinced by these arguments, and does not pursue the matter. Later, his reaction is identical with that of Frédéric, except that the younger Flaubert is more explicit about motives on both sides: 'Henry comprit bien qu'il venait de faire une faute [i.e. in taking Mme Renaud's protestations at face value], il s'en voulut et s'en gronda vertement, puis il s'en loua et s'en estima davantage, tournant sa timidité en vertu et sa sottise en délicatesse, comme cela arrive toujours' (III, 60). When Frédéric is put off in this way, he is even less clear than Henry about the real state of affairs; and we shall not then have the author to explain what we cannot see for ourselves. A few pages later, a reaction which is psychologically similar, even though it develops in the opposite direction, is ascribed even more brutally to Henry; and once more we should remember Frédéric's inability to scrutinize his deeper motives:

Et elle s'en allait ensuite, ayant longtemps attendu une réponse [i.e. to her moral arguments against her sleeping with Henry] qui n'était pas venue, et qui sait? peut-être même une réfutation triomphante.

Henry se disait alors: 'Pourquoi irais-je troubler cette eau pure? faner cette fleur? pourquoi afin de satisfaire l'appétit d'un moment, la plonger dans la honte et les regrets? ce serait pour moi-même la descendre de ce piédestal où mon amour l'a posée; elle m'aime de l'amour des anges, le ciel n'est-il pas assez vaste? cet amour n'est-il pas assez doux?'

Et puis, par une réaction ordinaire, il en venait à jurer horriblement et à frapper du pied de façon à défoncer le parquet. Ce juron voulait dire que l'eau pure est faite pour désaltérer, et les fleurs pour être senties; que l'amour des anges n'est pas celui des hommes, et qu'il était homme, et qu'en conséquence, etc. (III, 65).

There is no confusion possible about Flaubert's intentions here: in the 1869 version there is room for doubt, but an identical interpretation cannot be ruled out.

Jules, as we have seen, is for a time subject to the same type of error, and for the same reasons, as Henry. At this stage he represents what will become the 'romantic' side of Frédéric's character. He is portrayed as 'un enfant crédule et sans défiance', who 's'exaltait en écrivant, devenait éloquent à force de parler, s'attendrissait lui-même, et s'aimait parce qu'il se sentait bon.' Flaubert continues: 'Ce qui le rendait à plaindre, c'est qu'il ne savait pas bien distinguer ce qui est de ce qui devrait être; il souffrait toujours de quelque chose qui lui manquait; il attendait sans cesse je ne sais quoi qui n'arrivait jamais' (III, 101).

Jules, too, is incapable not only of seeing reality as it is, but also of accepting even what he sees. But unlike Henry and Frédéric, he then develops a habit of searching self-criticism, a habit which somewhat improbably results from the flight of Lucinde, and the concomitant (magic?) realization that his play, on which all his hopes for the future had rested, was worthless (III, 120). Unfortunately, when he does come to dominate his 'grandes dispositions pour chercher le parfum de l'oranger sous des pommiers' (III, 165), he turns into a mouthpiece for the new Flaubert (see especially III, 255 et seq.). After a struggle to free himself from his characters, Flaubert has retired beaten to the safety of his earlier technique. More than ever before, a Flaubert character has come to self-realization; but Jules represents a dead end after all, and his like will never occur again in Flaubert's works. His self-knowledge was an artistic mistake.

Thus the first *Education* represents an advance in Flaubert's awareness of the problems and the people he has to present, but the problem of how to present them has scarcely begun to be resolved. He has achieved the critical dimension which can turn a novel into a great novel, but has only attached it to the surface of the work, like a patch on an old pair of trousers: he has not yet discovered the more modern art of invisible mending. For Henry, who never achieves self-knowledge,[1] the criticism is unashamedly superimposed by the author's direct comments—the patch is not even the same colour as the trousers. For Jules, it is contrived by allowing the character to change so that he becomes perspicacious enough to be his own critic. Both solutions were unsatisfactory: neither is impersonal, and both depend upon the premise that the

[1] Although he is sometimes on the verge of it—e.g. III, 217, 287, 302–3.

author is always right, even if the characters are not. He subsequently decided that this premise is untenable. In addition, the solution adopted for Jules, even if it were properly motivated, automatically raises the character above the ordinary run of humans, makes him special and atypical. And Flaubert obviously found it impossible to provide a reasonable-sounding explanation for the profound change which takes place in Jules. What single event, no matter how momentous, can be credited with causing this sort of personality readjustment? Flaubert knew very well that it could happen—it happened to him—but the problem was to present it as part of a novel structure, not merely to affirm its possibility in real life. Besides, if Jules can change so radically once, renouncing all his earlier beliefs, he can clearly do the same thing again. How can we be sure that he is more right the second or third time than the first? Although the second Jules obviously enjoys the sympathy of the second Flaubert, he has nevertheless 'concluded', and this the third Flaubert will refuse to do. In the final analysis, Jules *cannot* be right. Flaubert cannot approve any character and remain true to his own philosophy. The only real solution is for Flaubert to separate himself completely from his characters; to make them typical humans and thus subject to the same weaknesses as Henry and the early Jules; to *show* them concluding, according to their lights at any given moment; and to show them to be wrong in concluding, no matter what their conclusions are, while no longer giving any authorial indication of which conclusions are considered right and which wrong. Although in this novel Flaubert has become more Flaubertian, in that he refuses to associate himself with most of his characters, he is still too involved with Jules. On the one hand, his reaction against his earlier methods is too extreme, and his sarcastic commentaries on people like Henry and Mme Renaud are often exaggerated and misplaced; on the other, his method has not really changed at all. After the first *Education sentimentale*, his itinerary for the future is traced out, but the actual journey is not much farther advanced than at the end of *Novembre*; he has still to find a 'hero' who *remains* the victim of his illusions, and a method of portraying him.

III

MADAME BOVARY

Description as subjectivity

HAVING found some attempts at a restricted point of view
technique in Flaubert's early works, we shall not be
surprised at its use in *Madame Bovary*. What is more
important is that now, quite suddenly, it assumes striking proportions. Not only is it applied with remarkable frequency and
consistency, but also it has become an integral part of the novel's
structure, to the extent that the meaning of the book is expressed
through it. We know that in the years between the first *Education
sentimentale* and his first great work, Flaubert had carefully
re-examined his views on the purposes and techniques of the
novel. Whatever methods he employs in *Bovary*, we can be
quite sure that he had good reasons for choosing them in preference to others. It is in this book that point of view becomes
significant.

I have already pointed out that Flaubert's use of point of view
in *Bovary* has not gone unnoticed in the past. Even some of his
earliest critics were to some extent aware of the basic elements of
the techniques in question. For instance, Sainte-Beuve remarks[1]
that in a description an author should not include details which a
person present at the scene would not be able to see for himself
(although he claims that Flaubert does not follow this precept in
Salammbô, and in any case his remarks do not preclude a hypothetical witness, as employed by Balzac and Stendhal, and by Flaubert
in his early works).[2] Faguet praises Flaubert for integrating his

---

[1] Sainte-Beuve, lundi, 22 décembre, 1862; op. cit., pp. 235–6.
[2] e.g. at the beginning of *le Père Goriot*, the witness is sometimes 'vous',
sometimes 'un Parisien égaré', sometimes 'les passants'; at the beginning of
Eugénie Grandet, it is 'vous' or 'les amis du moyen âge'; in *le Rouge et le Noir*

descriptions with the action of the novel more completely than did Balzac, by transferring the role of witness from author to characters, thereby making their experiences our experiences, and simulating the processes by which we all gain our knowledge of people and things in real life.[1] Beuchat, apparently developing Faguet's statements, argues that this allows the reader to forget that there is an author, a 'translator' between himself and the characters; thus the author's impersonality is guaranteed.[2] Ferrère, and, more recently, Bart and Moreau, have pointed out how not only descriptions, but also images, in Flaubert's work, are usually based upon things directly experienced by the characters ('choses vues', says Moreau, and particularly shapes, nuances of colour, effects of light), and are intimately connected, either in content or in tone, with the character's personality or state of mind.[3] Henry James, with his own preoccupation with the 'angle of vision' from which an author presents his novel, is clearly aware of some of the implications of the choice of an Emma or a Frédéric as 'reflectors and registers'.[4]

The points raised by these and other critics are frequently illuminating; but on the whole, their main arguments are only incidentally relevant to problems connected with point of view, or their relevance is not established in any systematic way. There is clearly much more that could have been said about Flaubert's

---

it is 'le voyageur'. Although the reader sees at least part of the scene in question through the eyes of these various hypothetical observers, they are not used consistently, nor do they really have anything to do with the book itself: they are introduced for the occasion and then dropped.

[1] Faguet: *Flaubert* (Paris, Hachette, 3ᵉ édition, 1913), pp. 70–3, quotes as an example the reader's progressive 'discovery' of Rouen with Emma and Léon; cf. p. 162, where he examines the 'witnessed' aspects of the *conseiller's* arrival at the *Comices*. At this level, Flaubert's technique is not original: it is frequently used in Hugo's *Notre-Dame de Paris*, a novel which Flaubert admired.

[2] Beuchat, op. cit., vol. I, pp. 268–70.

[3] Ferrère, op. cit., pp. 165–8, 196. Bart, op. cit., pp. 33 et seq. Bart cites some very interesting examples—e.g. Charles's reaction to the Norman countryside on his first journey to Les Bertaux—to support his statement that 'landscapes exist only to give the characters a setting which brings them out more fully'. See also Moreau: *Bovary*, op. cit., pp. 43–8.

[4] James: 'Gustave Flaubert' in *The House of Fiction* (London, Mercury Books, 1962), pp. 199 et seq.

presentation techniques. Even the two very rewarding articles which deal most fully with the subject[1] must be regarded as only a beginning, for they have opened up a whole new field of study for this already much-studied book. Moreover, the *development* of Flaubert's use of point of view in subsequent novels has had almost no attention, yet there is evidence that in them it is sometimes even more interesting and more subtle. To appreciate this fully, an adequate view of how it is used in *Bovary* is necessary.

It is a simple matter to show that Flaubert has integrated descriptions with action more fully in *Madame Bovary* than in any previous work: more than ever before, a progressive presentation of the subjective way in which the witnessing character looks at a scene establishes an intimate connection between witness and witnessed. In addition, at least three new elements—all the logical outcome of this situation—have been introduced, to achieve a completely functional use of a mature point of view technique. First, it is no longer just occasional descriptions, but nearly all scenes and actions, which are now seen through the eyes of the characters; secondly, *only* scenes and actions which can be seen through the eyes of the characters, and which are of importance to them, are now presented; and thirdly, since the main characters are no longer of the type which enjoy the author's unmitigated sympathy or respect, it follows that the very presentation of their subjectivity by these means—once we realize that this is what is being done—can be used to provide the critical dimension which had created so many problems in the first *Education*. The first two of these elements can be discussed together, before we pass to the third, which is the most important.

The first descriptions of Emma (already examined in similar, but briefer terms by Rousset)[2] provide a good starting point, for they also reveal an interesting parallel with those of the prostitute in *Novembre*. At this point the reader is still viewing the action through Charles, the only important character so far introduced. We follow him into Les Bertaux, noticing, as he does, the external

---

[1] Lubbock, op. cit., pp. 60 et seq.; Rousset, op. cit., pp. 109 et seq.
[2] Rousset, op. cit., pp. 114–15.

(misleading, but we do not know that yet) signs of a well-to-do establishment. Then 'une jeune femme, en robe de mérinos bleu garnie de trois volants'—this is all that Charles notices about his future wife—takes him into the kitchen, then upstairs to attend the patient. Only when he is forced to interrupt his work to wait for her does he notice anything more, and then in the most natural way: she is sewing, pricks her finger, and as she brings it to her mouth, Charles sees her hands and her eyes, which are then described. As usual, it is made clear that it is in Charles's mind that the description first occurs, that the author is merely recording: 'Charles fut surpris de la blancheur de ses ongles.' Some time later. he has the opportunity of noticing one or two more details: her lips, her hair, her cheeks. Again it is noted that the details are given because of Charles's interest: '. . . avec un mouve- ment ondé vers les tempes, *que le médecin de campagne remarqua là* pour la première fois de sa vie'. Moreover, the point of view is emphasized throughout the passage by Emma's being referred to as 'Mlle Emma' or 'Mlle Rouault,' while Charles is simply 'Charles'.[1] The reader already knows Charles well, whereas he is still on somewhat formal terms—as Charles is—with Emma.

The impressionism which we have come to expect is not very obvious in this presentation of Emma's appearance, except in the sense that only details which force themselves upon Charles's awareness are mentioned. But several other details about this first visit to Les Bertaux do emphasize the unique, temporary nature of the whole situation. Prominent among these are the objects mentioned when Charles first enters the kitchen: the fire, with its reflections on metallic objects—effects of light again—the meal in preparation, the clothes drying. In the same way, the next view we have of Emma shows her, too, in a particular setting, which Charles notices and remembers *because* it is particular, momentary, outstanding: sunlight, coloured as it passes through her sunshade, playing on her face. It is not a description, but an impression.

Charles does not risk any further interest in Emma until the death of his wife. In the intervening period, although he has been

[1] There is one exception—an example of *style indirect libre*, which will be re- ferred to later.

back to Les Bertaux, she is not even mentioned. But after a transitional paragraph briefly tracing the acquisition of his new independent spirit, the stage is set for Emma to return to his thoughts. When she returns to his thoughts, she returns to the book: another scene has been prepared, and it is presented in precisely the same manner (pp. 29–30). As Charles enters the kitchen, he sees almost nothing, for, as in *Novembre*, 'les auvents étaient fermés'. Naturally, this fact draws attention to the patterns of light filtering through the shutters and coming down the chimney to strike the ashes in the fireplace. Then he sees Emma, and notices only one thing about her: 'sur ses épaules nues de petites gouttes de sueur'. Rousset has an interesting comment on this last notation.[1] He points out that an earlier version of this sentence read 'ses épaules blanches étaient roses'. It is likely that one of Flaubert's reasons for changing this is that such an observation, at least in these terms, would be beyond Charles's limited sensibility.

Thus Emma is not described so much for herself, as she is, but as she appears to Charles—perhaps even as he would like her to be. Further, she is described only because she causes a deep impression on him: the description is where it is because of her importance to Charles. Flaubert's revisions corroborate this. The *Nouvelle version* contains several references to scenes and actions which Charles could observe any time he visited Les Bertaux: 'Emma d'ordinaire se trouvait dans la cuisine, . . .'; 'Les jours qu'il arrivait de bonne heure dans l'après-midi. . . .'[2] Such passages, showing the habitual situation, are reduced in the final version, so that *particular* scenes, those which stand out in Charles's mind because of their unique quality, are to the fore. This is emphasized further by the addition, in the final version, of a sentence which does not occur in the earliest ones: Charles returns home, thinking about Emma, going over in his mind what she has said, trying to imagine her past: 'Mais jamais il ne put la voir, en pensée, différemment qu'il ne l'avait vue la première fois, ou telle qu'il venait de la quitter tout à l'heure' (p. 31). These revisions tend to the same end as the subjective and impressionistic

---

[1] Rousset, op. cit., p. 115.   [2] Pommier et Leleu, op. cit., pp. 165–6.

elements: the reader sees only the circumstances which have impressed the character.

The description of Charles and Emma at the theatre in Rouen (pp. 307 et seq.) affords another good example. As usual it is strictly progressive, and words emphasizing direct experience and participation by those present occur several times. More important, words emphasizing *Emma*'s participation are even more frequent: 'Elle sourit ... en voyant la foule ...'; 'et Madame Bovary les admirait d'en haut ...'; 'Emma se penchait pour le voir ....'. It is her experience in which we are interested, and the way in which she seizes upon parts of the opera as a basis for her lamentations. The opera itself is not, of course, described in detail. It would be impossible for anyone who did not already know *Lucia di Lammermoor* to gain much idea of it from Flaubert.[1] The point is that Emma is not following it as an opera, in spite of her fascination: 'Elle se retrouvait dans les lectures de sa jeunesse, en plein Walter Scott. Il lui semblait entendre, à travers le brouillard, le son des cornemuses écossaises se répéter sur les bruyères.' She continually forgets the opera to think of herself, and the development of the description faithfully reflects the workings of her mind. Thus one of her reveries about Rodolphe, based on Lagardy's singing, is suddenly interrupted by applause, and Emma realizes there is to be an encore. Only during the encore are the contents of the aria mentioned, and even then only vaguely. During the first performance, Emma had been so preoccupied that she had not even been aware of what the performers were singing about. By the end of the second act she has become so carried away by her romantic dreamings that she is not even using the opera as a starting-point, but Lagardy himself: 'Il devait avoir, pensait-elle, un intarissable amour, pour en déverser sur la foule à si larges effluves' (p. 313). These thoughts become so intense that they end in semi-hallucination: '... de la scène, tout en jouant, il l'aurait regardée. Mais une folie la saisit; il la regardait, c'est sûr!' (Note the force of this sole present tense.)

By the beginning of the third act Léon has arrived, and the

[1] Bopp: *Commentaire sur 'Madame Bovary'* (Neuchâtel-Paris, la Baconnière, 1951), pp. 346–7.

description of the opera is modified accordingly: 'Mais, à partir de ce moment, elle n'écouta plus; et le chœur des conviés, la scène d'Ashton et de son valet, le grand duo en *ré* majeur, tout passa pour elle dans l'éloignement, comme si les instruments fussent devenus moins sonores et les personnages plus reculés' (p. 315). She now has no need of the opera as a basis for her romantic ramblings, for she has a much closer, more *possible* one. She is thinking of her past with Léon, who at this moment is literally breathing down her neck: the opera fades out of the book. Its magic and its fascination have disappeared, so that when Léon asks Emma if she is interested, she can quite truthfully reply: 'Oh! mon Dieu, non, pas beaucoup' (p. 316) and even discover that 'le jeu de la chanteuse lui parut exagéré'.

Once more, then, the description is presented from the point of view of a character, and the same general remarks are applicable to this scene as to Charles's view of Emma. The subjectivity of the witnessing character is of prime importance: the description constitutes a significant part of what Flaubert is telling us about his characters. We should be interested less in the thing described than in the way it is seen. Description is a means of conveying a state of mind or a trait of character.[1]

Flaubert's plans show that in other major scenes he intended to convey this same impression of presenting only what a given character particularly noticed. The La Vaubyessard episode is an outstanding example. Emma, who is so impressed by the luxury and the aura of mysterious and illicit love, is again the major witness. Everything, even the exterior of the chateau, is therefore described in detail, from the moment she arrives. The plans make the position clear: 'le bal — c'est un tourbillon *qui passe devant le nez d'Emma*'; 'bal — jeunes gens — caractère général des lions...' —to which he added, significantly: 'Lions [mêlez à la danse *à cause de l'effet qu'ils doivent produire sur elle*].'[2] Not that the explicit

---

[1] It is naturally no accident that the opera Emma sees is *Lucia di Lammermoor*. Flaubert picked this one *because* it was capable of having so much personal significance for Emma. Léon Bopp (op. cit., pp. 347–53) lists the large number of ways in which this passage either recalls or foreshadows details about Emma scattered through the novel. Some of the implications of this will be discussed later.

[2] Pommier et Leleu, op. cit., pp. 24, 49, 50. Italic mine.

statement is necessary in this case for us to see the effect on Emma
—this has long been recognized.[1] But it does show that Flaubert
was *consciously* applying a principle which frequently operates
more subtly than here.

Further evidence is to be found in the omission of some passages
from this scene: the *Nouvelle Version*[2] contains conversations
similar to those of the soirée scenes of *l'Education sentimentale*,
where 'bourgeois' of different types and social classes discuss in
pompous and pretentious terms subjects of no importance. The
reasons for the final rejection of these pages seem clear enough:
the ball scene is intended to be specifically significant for Emma.
She could not have been present at such a conversation among
men—she is not mentioned at all in the passage in question; and
if she had been present, what they were saying would not have
fired her imagination in the same way as the meal, the ball, the
surreptitiously passed note, or the snippets of 'romantic' conversation: it is the sort of conversation she would not notice. It
would represent the breaking-in of the author, in a scene which
was otherwise from Emma's point of view. Difficult as it must
have been for Flaubert to forego this opportunity of displaying
the bourgeois in action, he suppressed the passage in the interests
of significant descriptions and of unity.

The conversations which remain are, on the other hand, perfectly consistent with Emma's point of view, while still allowing
opportunity for irony. Again the text indicates in the usual way
that these snippets *are* heard by Emma (p. 71): 'A trois pas
d'Emma, un cavalier en habit bleu causait Italie ...'; 'Emma
écoutait de son autre oreille une conversation pleine de mots
qu'elle ne comprenait pas'. Again it is clear that what she hears
is recorded because of its importance to her: Italy, with its obvious
romantic associations, and the mysterious world of luxury and
high living associated with horse-racing. But there is an additional
level of meaning which is beyond Emma, an ironic judgement
on both her and those she admires. These people may be aristo-

[1] e.g. see Ferrère, op. cit., p. 176 for similar remarks on part of this scene (the
detailed description of the table); Lubbock, op. cit., p. 69; Sarraute, loc. cit., p. 9.
[2] Pommier et Leleu, op. cit., pp. 209–12.

crats, but they still talk in *idées reçues*, like everyone else in the book: 'la grosseur des piliers de Saint-Pierre'; 'le Colisée au clair de lune'—these are the things which the authentic tourist *must* talk about, like the 'poésie des lacs' in Switzerland, with which Léon later bewitches Emma, like the Riviera or St Mark's, Venice, for the modern tourist. The conversation of these people is worthless, and it is a judgement on Emma that she is impressed.

Even in very small details we can sometimes see from the plans how Flaubert kept firmly in mind the connection between the thoughts of his characters and the way things were described. Of Emma's thoughts about the cigar-holder which Charles found, he writes: 'porte-cigarres [*sic*] qui lui a fait? — maîtresse [glisser dessus *ce ne doit pas être net dans sa tête*]'.[1] When Léon and Emma take an evening boat-ride near Rouen, and Emma sings—significantly—Lamartine, her voice is described in the definitive version (p. 354) as 'harmonieuse et faible'. In the plans it is 'chevrotante et maigre'. As the editors of the *Nouvelle version* point out, Flaubert has substituted Léon's subjective, admiring impression, for his own more objective one.[2]

The witness technique is occasionally reinforced by Flaubert's making the observer 'deduce' facts, rather than stating them outright. In the first scene, Charles's coat '*devait* le gêner aux entournures'—the witness does not really know, for he cannot tell what Charles's feelings are. On page 2, the witness expresses some doubt as to why Charles did not rid himself of his cap as the others did: '. . . soit qu'il n'eût pas remarqué cette manœuvre ou qu'il n'eût osé s'y soumettre . . .'; and later (p. 6): 'Grâce, *sans doute*, à cette volonté dont il fit preuve, . . .'[3] This is an extremely common literary procedure, and is also very frequent in Flaubert's early works, especially the first *Education*. Nevertheless, its use in *Bovary* is usually more significant than in, say, the works of Balzac or Zola. Both these novelists normally use the 'omniscient narrator' method of presentation. In such cases it appears illogical for the author to pretend, for only a sentence or two at a time, *not* to be omniscient, and to use the method of statement by

---

[1] Pommier et Leleu, op. cit., p. 52. Italic mine.   [2] Ibid., p. 107.
[3] Other examples occur on pp. 128, 188, 233, 267, 394, 395, 396, 402, 422–3.

deduction. It seems to be merely a means of varying the form of the sentence, or of the author reminding the reader he is still there. But if, as in *Bovary*, almost the whole novel is presented by someone who is *normally* not omniscient, statements of this type are to be expected, and emphasize, rather than contradict, the normal technique.[1]

The use of characters' names also seems to be significant in emphasizing that people, as well as scenes, are normally viewed through the eyes of a character-witness. It has already been noted that Emma is normally referred to as 'Mlle Rouault' or 'Mlle Emma' in the scenes where Charles does not know her very well, and this represents a general (although not completely consistent) attitude throughout the book. Charles begins by being simply 'le nouveau', then becomes 'un nom inintelligible', 'Charbovari', 'Charles Bovary', and finally, when we begin to follow his point of view, just 'Charles'. Emma's father is 'M. Rouault' for some time before he becomes 'le père Rouault'. When Léon is looking at or thinking about Emma, he is normally called 'Léon' and she 'Mme Bovary'; when the point of view is Emma's Léon becomes 'M. Léon'.[2] This distinction ceases when they become more intimate.

The necessity for a witness in this book appears so strong that when it is not possible, or not desirable for one of the main characters to serve in this capacity, Flaubert has no hesitation in using some of his many minor ones. Mme Tuvache and Mme Caron take over the point of view for a single page, in order to watch Emma's visit to Binet (pp. 422–3); sometimes we see Emma through the eyes of Justin (e.g. p. 299, where he watches her comb her hair; pp. 433–4, where she demands the key of the poisons room); when she gives in to Léon in the carriage, it is merely the driver and the passers-by who 'witness' the fact (pp. 336–8).

---

[1] Even Flaubert is not entirely consistent. In one passage presented largely from Emma's point of view, in which her motives are in general quite clear, the point of view is suddenly and inexplicably restricted by the use of 'peut-être' (p. 372). Other examples are on pp. 57, 150, 269, 327, 354. See also Mosher, op. cit., pp. 228–9.

[2] pp. 116, 128, 132, 320, 334; 126, 130, 316.

At the wedding feast, it is not sufficient simply to *state* how Charles behaved when he was alone with Emma: it is added that '*on l'apercevait* de loin, entre les arbres, qui lui passait le bras sous la taille', and so on (p. 41). Towards the end of the book, during the period of Charles's despair, the villagers in general act as witnesses: 'On le vit pendant une semaine entrer le soir à l'église' (p. 476), and even 'un curieux se haussait par-dessus la haie du jardin, et apercevait avec ébahissement cet homme à barbe longue, .' (p. 479).

Such cases are relatively rare, however, and the point of view of minor characters never continues for more than a few paragraphs at a time. By far the greater part of *Bovary* is presented through Emma, Charles, Léon, or Rodolphe. But the main point is that Flaubert has now firmly come out in favour of the witness technique: almost without exception,[1] the point of view is that of somebody within the work itself, a character rather than the author. Apart from the presentation of Charles's mother and father, all the major descriptions contain at least some of the elements we have noted, and all therefore suggest the subjective and non-permanent nature of what is being described. True, the author still frequently breaks in, and he very seldom allows the reader entirely to forget that he is in charge. True, the point of view changes very frequently, so that sometimes he successively adopts the perspective of several different characters within a few pages, and sometimes that of several characters at once. All these aspects of the question will have to be examined. But it is already obvious that a method of presentation which had occurred spasmodically in many of Flaubert's early works has now emerged as a major literary tool, in constant use.

The large number of reveries occurring in *Bovary* are a development of this intimate relationship between external appearances and the workings of a mind. Almost all are triggered off by the sight or sound of real objects, which are sometimes briefly described, and sometimes merely mentioned, at the beginning.[2] It

---

[1] The most important exceptions will be dealt with later, pp. 128 et seq.

[2] See Mein: 'Flaubert, a Precursor of Proust' in *French Studies*, vol. xvii, July 1963, pp. 218–37, for a fuller development.

is the Vicomte's cigar-holder which makes Emma dream of Paris, and then buy a map of Paris and read fashion magazines and novels (pp. 79 et seq.); and then all these combine to create a romantically-oriented mental picture of the city. At the Ball, the noise of the windows being broken makes her turn her head, and see the local peasants looking in at the dancers; this takes her thoughts back to her father and Les Bertaux (p. 72). Later it is her father's letter which, in another period of crisis, makes her dream of those 'happy' days on the farm (pp. 238–9). At the *Comices*, the perfume of Rodolphe's hair reminds her of the Vicomte and at the same moment the sight of *l'Hirondelle* in the distance reminds her of Léon (pp. 203–4); this causes a confused picture of all three men in Emma's mind, allowing the only one who happens to be present to reap the benefit. It is the ringing of the Angelus which in a period of boredom (pp. 152–3) recalls her convent days and the joys of religion there, and leads her to try to talk to Bournisien; in Rouen, when she is beginning to tire of Léon, the sight of the walls of her convent causes her to reflect on her whole life (p. 392).

Being by their very nature subjective, such reveries merge very well with the subjective technique of description which we have been examining; and the way they are introduced serves to emphasize once more that what is important in this book is not so much reality, but reality viewed by a character.

One of the interesting aspects of the Flaubertian reverie is the frequent use of the *style indirect libre*. This has been studied in detail elsewhere, but it is worth noting here how convenient the device is, within the context of the subjective presentation which concerns us. One of the basic elements of *style indirect libre* is the changing of the verb tense from the present, as it would be if the author were directly quoting the character's thoughts or words, to the imperfect of normal indirect speech. Now Flaubert habitually uses the imperfect tense in narrative as well, so that if the character's reverie and the author's narration are not specifically separated from each other, it is not always obvious to the reader whose word he is being asked to accept: if it is the author stating a fact, then it can be taken as a fact; but if it is the author *reporting*, in *style indirect libre*, what a character believes to be a fact, the situation is very different.

Normally there is no particular difficulty about distinguishing between the two types of imperfect tense, because passages of *style indirect libre* also contain a sufficient number of emotive words to make it clear that we are not dealing with a simple narration. For example, towards the end of the *pied-bot* episode, when Emma is cursing herself for her stupidity, the following passage occurs:

> Emma, en face de lui, le regardait; elle ne partageait pas son humiliation, elle en éprouvait une autre: c'était de s'être imaginé qu'un pareil homme pût valoir quelque chose, comme si vingt fois déjà elle n'avait pas suffisamment aperçu sa médiocrité. . . .
>
> Comment donc avait-elle fait (elle qui était si intelligente!) pour se méprendre encore une fois? Du reste, par quelle déplorable manie avoir ainsi abîmé son existence en sacrifices continuels? Elle se rappela tous ses instincts de luxe, toutes les privations de son âme, les bassesses du mariage, du ménage, ses rêves tombant dans la boue comme des hirondelles blessées, tout ce qu'elle avait désiré, tout ce qu'elle s'était refusé, tout ce qu'elle aurait pu avoir! Et pourquoi? et pourquoi? (p. 255.)

It is clear enough that after the first three verbs these are Emma's thoughts about Charles, and that being a direct result of her humiliation, they are not necessarily consistent with the facts. For instance, while it is true that 'vingt fois déjà elle avait suffisamment aperçu sa médiocrité', Emma has forgotten her recent more ambitious and optimistic mood: 'En effet, Bovary pouvait réussir; rien n'affirmait à Emma qu'il ne fût pas habile...' (p. 241). Similarly, references to her intelligence and her 'sacrifices continuels' are more likely to be her estimate than Flaubert's, as his plans for an earlier scene show: 'Elle en veut beaucoup à Charles de ne pas s'apercevoir du sacrifice (qu'elle ne fait pas)!'[1]

After the interruption caused by Hippolyte's scream, Emma's thoughts become more and more unjust towards Charles, and yet are still stated as if they were facts: 'pour cet être, pour cet

---

[1] Pommier et Leleu, op. cit., pp. 59, 64; see also Ullmann, op. cit., pp. 106 et seq.; Thibaudet: *Gustave Flaubert* (Paris, NRF Gallimard, 1935), pp. 246–7; Fairlie, op. cit., p. 20.

homme qui ne comprenait rien, qui ne sentait rien! Car il était là, tout tranquillement, . . .' etc. For the reader, who on both the preceding page and the following one is also shown what Charles is thinking, it is not difficult to see how wrong Emma is.

The passage describing Emma's thoughts just before she is to run away with Rodolphe (p. 271) is also clearly of this type, with mere hopes and dreams stated as if they were facts. So too are Emma's speculations about the owner and the maker of the cigar-holder (p. 78)—Emma merely *assumes* (because it suits her) that it belonged to the Vicomte and that it was lovingly hand-woven by his mistress. And so, as it turns out, are Charles's assumptions about le père Rouault's fortune (p. 31).

Is the distinction between fact and appearances—between the author's statements and the characters' statements—always so clear? We cannot be sure. In doubtful cases, it would seem advisable to charge the character, rather than the author, with the responsibility, for this would be consistent with both the over-all tendency of the book, and Flaubert's repeatedly expressed desire for the author not to intervene. Take, for example, the contrasting descriptions of Charles and Léon, at the time Emma is just beginning to realize that the latter loves her (p. 141):

> Mais elle tourna la tête: Charles était là. Il avait sa casquette enfoncée sur ses sourcils, et ses deux grosses lèvres tremblotaient, ce qui ajoutait à son visage quelque chose de stupide; son dos même, son dos tranquille était irritant à voir, et elle y trouvait étalée sur la redingote toute la platitude du personnage.
>
> Pendant qu'elle le considérait, goûtant ainsi dans son irritation une sorte de volupté dépravée, Léon s'avança d'un pas. Le froid qui le pâlissait semblait déposer sur sa figure une langueur plus douce; entre sa cravate et son cou, le col de la chemise, un peu lâche, laissait voir la peau; un bout d'oreille dépassait sous une mèche de cheveux, et son grand œil bleu, levé vers les nuages, parut à Emma plus limpide et plus beau que ces lacs de montagne où le ciel se mire.

Although short, the descriptions follow the normal pattern. As Emma is already inclined to find Léon attractive and Charles repulsive, it is not surprising that both descriptions should be (a) incomplete, (b) composed of the elements which Emma is pre-disposed to notice and (c) highly emotive. Like so many other passages, this one tells us more about Emma than about the two men; but the reader must notice that some of the 'facts' given are only Emma's impressions: 'son dos même, son dos tranquille était irritant à voir'—for Emma only: no one else is likely to be irritated by it! Only she could find 'toute la platitude du personnage' on the back of his coat, or make his lips indicate semi-imbecility. As an earlier version shows, poor Charles is merely suffering from the cold—that same cold which makes Léon pale and interesting. Nor is there anything intrinsically handsome or attractive in any of the parts of Léon described: the contrast with Charles, such as it is, is also imposed by Emma's mind. Who else would liken Léon's eyes to 'ces lacs de montagne où le ciel se mire?'

Earlier versions of this passage show a more extreme contrast between the two men, and also make it clearer that the 'descriptions' are really a reverie, a minor emotional crisis expressed with the help of *style indirect libre*:

> Emma tout à coup se sentit monter en elle-même un flot de colère, comme une nausée. Il lui parut hideux et détestable tout à fait. Quel pantalon, d'ailleurs, que ce pantalon noir, râpé, trop court et qui marquait aux jambes la tige large des bottes! . . . Son dos même, son dos tranquille était irritant à voir, il semblait à Emma être sot de lui-même et elle trouvait étalée ainsi sur la redingote toute la platitude du personnage. . . . Si Charles l'eût touchée, elle eût poussé un cri.[1]

Then, to emphasize the abnormality of these thoughts, which could not be occasioned by the facts, a further paragraph suggests that they may be caused by the effect of the cold on Emma's nerves, just as Henry's emotional crisis had been the result of seasickness.

And what of the description of Emma after her adultery with Rodolphe, which also occurs during a reverie? If we take it as authorial statement, we are accepting that Flaubert wants us to believe that an afternoon's fornication has changed her appearance: 'Mais, en s'apercevant dans la glace, elle s'étonna de son

---

[1] Pommier et Leleu, op. cit., pp. 285–6.

visage. Jamais elle n'avait eu les yeux si grands, si noirs, ni d'une telle profondeur. Quelque chose de subtil épandu sur sa personne la transfigurait' (p. 225). Again the corresponding passage in the *Nouvelle version* decides the issue:

Cependant elle s'aperçut dans la glace, et elle eut presque de la stupéfaction en reconnaissant son visage. *Comment n'exprimait-il rien de ce qui emplissait son âme? Comment se faisait-il qu'elle pût paraître la même?* Alors elle avança de plus près pour se considérer, et elle se trouva tout à coup extraordinairement belle. Elle n'avait jamais eu les yeux si grands, si noirs, ni d'une telle profondeur. Son front poli luisait, ses dents étaient plus blanches. Elle s'en chérissait davantage et tout en désagrafant sa robe, elle clignait ses paupières et se cambrait la taille, avec une pose naïve de courtisane et d'impératrice.[1]

Emma first realizes that her activities have not changed her appearance, and then, because she thinks they should, talks herself into believing that they have. In the final version, Flaubert removes even this modest amount of perspicacity, so that from the beginning she accepts wishful thinking as fact.

Flaubert's modifications to these two passages reflect the general pattern of change from the first *Education* to *Bovary*. The early version shows him handling Emma very much as he handled Henry: telling us her thoughts, and making it clear that they resulted from an inaccurate summing-up of the real situation. The definitive version restricts itself more nearly to presenting the thoughts, leaving the reader to see the rest for himself. The author is both drawing nearer to Emma, following her point of view more closely, becoming more 'involved', and also, by this very fact, becoming more impersonal, leaving her thoughts to be judged on their own merits. The total meaning is not changed, but rendered more subtle.

How far can one go in presenting impressions as facts? Surely it is safe to assume that if a character believes it is raining, for example, then it must be raining: Flaubert could not have gone to such extremes as to hint that it was not. Perhaps not, but he certainly went further than most novelists, for even physical

---

[1] Pommier et Leleu, op. cit., p. 381. Italic mine.

characteristics of people may not always be what they seem. One definite example can be cited: the colour of Emma's eyes. Critics have noticed that Emma's eyes are sometimes black, sometimes blue, and, on one occasion, brown! Now if Balzac said that his heroine's eyes were blue, one would accept this as a fact; and if he later said they were black, this tiny detail would eventually be reported in a long list of similar slips in an article called 'Le Réalisme de Balzac' or something of the sort, and all would be forgiven. In Emma's case, however, the three colours are not a mistake at all, but part of the technique under discussion: the *apparent* colour does in fact change, according to the play of light. Flaubert knew exactly what he was doing: 'Noirs à l'ombre, bruns au jour et même bleu sombre au grand jour, ils avaient des épaisseurs de couleurs les unes sur les autres, ...'[1] The corresponding sentence in the definitive novel (p. 45) leaves out the mention of brown, but still makes it clear that the colour changes according to the light. So does the first mention of Emma's eyes (p. 19): 'quoiqu'ils fussent bruns, ils semblaient noirs à cause des cils'. In subsequent passages, only one colour is mentioned each time, but the changes are consistent: Charles sees them as black in the mirror at La Vaubyessard at night, (p. 69); Léon sees them as black in the *Lion d'or* the first night, (p. 114) but as blue when he meets Emma during the day (p. 324). Rodolphe sees them as black the first time he meets Emma (p. 180) as does Emma herself when she looks in her mirror, also at night (p. 225). There is one doubtful case: Rodolphe sees them as blue when Emma comes to ask him for money, although the same passage (pp. 428–9) mentions 'la clarté du crépuscule' and 'un dernier rayon du soleil' (but presumably if she were so positioned that the light shone directly on her eyes it would still be possible to see them as blue). In any case, a single possible exception is insufficient to negate the general validity of the principle. Even those details which are at

---

[1] Leleu, op. cit., vol. I, p. 136. The sentence is also quoted by Bopp, op. cit., p. 28, who appears sceptical, and is in any case more interested in pointing out that the 'real' Madame Bovary (he does not say which one) also had eyes which could change colour. See also Bollème: *La Leçon de Flaubert* (Paris, Les Lettres nouvelles, Julliard, 1964), pp. 156–7.

first sight most definite can hold unexpected significance in this book. Not that it is uncommon, in real life, for people to have eyes which seem to change colour: there is nothing magic about it. But *in novels* we are not accustomed to such nuances, so that they can easily go unnoticed, or, if noticed, misinterpreted.

We cannot of course infer that all physical traits recorded in *Bovary* are figments of somebody's imagination. Nevertheless, this invasion of the subjective into a field of description in which writers are normally accepted at their word, should lead us to examine more fully the general question of Flaubert's descriptions of people.

As is well known, Flaubert seldom gives a complete, once-for-all physical description of his main characters; such portraits as exist are built up gradually from elements scattered throughout the book. Now in view of the consistently subjective presentation of *Bovary*, this fact is obviously important. The normal explanation is that such gradual and progressive descriptions reflect more nearly the psychological processes of everyday life, and are therefore more realistic than the total portraits of a writer like Balzac. This is true, but there are other reasons. One is that if people are described as they are seen by other people, different witnesses will notice different attributes according to their own character, mood and preoccupations. Descriptions of people, like descriptions of things, can be used to reveal the observer as well as the person described. Thus Charles notices nothing about Emma until he has nothing better to do, and is capable of noticing such unpicturesque details as beads of sweat on her shoulders. Rodolphe, on the other hand, notices the shape of Emma's body as she bends over (p. 179) and 'le pied coquet' (p. 180). Léon, like Charles, is not immediately struck by sexual possibilities (pp. 109, 116): her dress is very much a barrier at first, a fact which symbolizes the pedestal on which he has already placed her: 'Son vêtement, ensuite, retombait des deux côtés sur le siège, en bouffant, plein de plis et s'étalait jusqu'à terre. Quand Léon, parfois, sentait la semelle de sa botte poser dessus, il s'écartait, comme s'il eût marché sur quelqu'un' (p. 136). The contrast between this attitude and

Rodolphe's (p. 181: 'il revoyait Emma dans la salle, habillée comme il l'avait vue, et il la déshabillait') is an adequate commentary on the differences between the two men.

Similarly, Léon is introduced to the reader simply as 'un jeune homme à chevelure blonde' (p. 110). It is hardly necessary to emphasize the prestige of blond hair in nineteenth-century France: Emma is noticing something which distinguishes Léon, and which she associates with love and luxury. Later, she also notices the black velvet collar of his coat (not quite a fulfilment of her earlier dream of 'un mari vêtu d'un habit de velours noir à longues basques' (p. 56), but a step in the right direction!), his carefully combed hair, even his well cared-for fingernails (p. 130).[1] Later still, she notes that he is pale and has blue eyes (p. 141)—two more characteristics of some prestige for a romantic woman, apart from the contrast with Charles which this passage emphasizes.

Rodolphe, too, is described—or, more exactly, not described—in a similar manner. It is important to our knowledge of both Rodolphe and Emma that what she first notices is his clothes: although it is a working day, as the gaiters show, he wears a velvet coat and gloves (p. 177)—he is seen as something which Charles is not. He is also something Léon is not—here, as at the beginning of the riding scene (pp. 218-9) Emma recognizes the velvet coat of her dreams.[2] At the *Comices*, the clothes again make the man (pp. 191-2): of Rodolphe himself, she notices only the eyes (p. 203), and even they serve only as a starting-point for a reverie involving the Vicomte and Léon. There is, in fact, no real portrait of Rodolphe, as Faguet pointed out.[3] The nearest approach to one occurs after the *pied-bot* episode, when Emma compares him *in her mind* with Charles (p. 260), but even here there is not a single mention of him as an individual (pp. 271-2).

[1] There is considerable irony in the fact that Charles noticed that Emma's fingernails were not those of a working peasant, just as Emma notices that Léon's are not those of a working bourgeois.

[2] See Gothot-Mersch, op. cit., pp. 112-13 for an interesting comment on the way this coat was from the beginning associated with Flaubert's picture of Rodolphe.

[3] Faguet, op. cit., p. 163.

The passage begins with 'Au galop de quatre chevaux *elle* était emportée . . .'; the pronoun subsequently becomes *ils*, but never more precise. The *ils* are Emma and her dream ideal: Rodolphe is an accidental incarnation, a mere antidote to Charles. As his features are irrelevant, we never see them.

What are the implications of this subjective presentation? First, unless the characters whose point of view is utilized demonstrate a quite unusual perspicacity, their view of the facts will be deformed. The characters in *Bovary*, unlike Jules, are all fairly ordinary people (this, indeed, is part of the point): none has the balance, the broadness of mind, and in particular the detachment, necessary for an adequate view of reality. In short, none has what Flaubert called the scientific attitude, none was objective enough to 'accepter les choses comme elles sont'. Hence we shall expect the characters to 'conclude'—to accept appearances as facts, without close examination. Flaubert can use the subjective presentation to portray his characters deluding themselves, without continually breaking in to tell the reader about it. By continually making it clear that he is showing us characters' *impressions*, he is continually inviting us to suspect the validity of these impressions. Since the story is mostly about Emma, and it is usually Emma's impressions that we have, we ought to suspect her most of all.

The technique has two main dangers, one inherent and the other accidental. The first is that Emma, who naturally assumes she is correct in her summing-up of a given situation—we all suffer from this evil—is not much given to self-examination, to continual probing and questioning of ideas and impressions.[1] The more strongly she feels, the less she questions. Now should the author faithfully record, without external comment, such a character's experience, the reader will inevitably be influenced by the character's judgement. We have already seen how impressions and opinions are recorded as if they were facts. After a time, this has a cumulative effect on the reader, and even though he realizes intellectually the danger of accepting the character's

---

[1] Fairlie, op. cit., p. 44, defines the situation very well in speaking of Emma's 'self-consciousness without self-knowledge'.

impressions as valid, he nevertheless tends to do so. It is the psychological effect of propaganda and advertising. Eventually he is
likely to assume that what the character thinks is also what the
author thinks, and therefore what *he* is supposed to think.[1] In
the case of *Bovary*, the tendency has been given impetus by the
'Madame Bovary, c'est moi' myth, which is nearly always
lurking in the back of the reader's mind: even if he is reading
Flaubert for the first time, editors seldom fail to relay this piece
of information in their introductions.

The second danger involved—the accidental one—is that most
novelists do in fact approve of their heroes, even if they do not,
like Stendhal, continually say so. While not condoning every
action and every thought, they usually convey a general air of
sympathy, or at least of pity, for the main character. With this
experience of novels, it is easy for the reader to assume a similar
attitude in Flaubert, especially as Flaubert is on the surface such
a conventional novelist. It is obvious, too, that Flaubert's attitude
towards Homais and the other bourgeois is traditional enough;
since Emma is not like these people who are obviously being
satirized, she must have the author's sympathy. Flaubert is not
quite so simple. It is essential to remember those of his statements
which reveal a healthy disrespect for his heroine, a disrespect not
very different from his attitude towards Homais:

Je suis à faire une conversation d'un jeune homme et d'une jeune
dame sur la littérature, la mer, les montagnes, la musique, tous les
sujets poétiques enfin. On pourrait la prendre au sérieux et elle est
d'une grande intention de grotesque. Ce sera, je crois, la première fois
que l'on verra un livre qui se moque de sa jeune première et de son
jeune premier.[2]

---

[1] Some such process seems to be the basis of the judgement of Mason: *Les
Ecrits de jeunesse de Flaubert* (Paris, Nizet, 1961), p. 26, that Emma represents
'l'être d'élite, l'âme poétique'. Cf. p. 30.

[2] *Cor.*, III, 42, Cf. IV, 168; also Pommier et Leleu, op. cit., where we find the
plans speaking of Emma 'pleurnichant sur elle-même' (p. 48), appearing in a
'toilette putain' at the *Comices* (p. 77; cf. p. 52: she is already 'un peu putain' at
Tostes), and the fact that her name was originally Lestiboudois (p. 7). Cf. Gothot-
Mersch, op. cit., p. 195; Thibaudet, op. cit., p. 16; Tillet: *On Reading Flaubert*
(London, Oxford University Press, 1961), pp. 14 et seq.; etc.

With these dangers in mind, let us return to the theme of suspicion of Emma, and see how easily one can be persuaded by her deformed idea of herself and her surroundings as a result of following her point of view. The reader's view of Charles, for instance, is largely conditioned by what Emma thinks of him, for once she is introduced Charles's point of view occurs infrequently. Emma's view of Charles—when she thinks about him at all—is conditioned by her mood. Before they are married, when she is dissatisfied with life on the farm, it is *Charles* who is a romantic possibility, a kindred soul: she treats him as she later treats Léon, showing him sentimental souvenirs, talking about the boredom of living in the country, and so on (pp. 22, 30–1, 47, 55). Only when she realizes that he cannot be a romantic ideal does she begin to find fault with him: her attitude is clearly an attempt at rationalization. She had relied on Charles to save her from reality, had thought that through him 'elle possédait enfin cette passion merveilleuse qui jusqu'alors s'était tenue comme un grand oiseau au plumage rose planant dans la splendeur des ciels poétiques' (p. 55).[1] Then came the calm of married life, the first escapist dreams, and therefore 'un insaisissable malaise', which is soon rendered less abstract by being centred on Charles. Emma begins to blame him for not being what she had pretended he was. It is at this point that the first unfavourable picture of him occurs; and, characteristically, her thoughts are expressed as though they were facts: 'La conversation de Charles était plate comme un trottoir de rue, et les idées de tout le monde y défilaient dans leur costume ordinaire, sans exciter d'émotion, de rire, ou de rêverie' (p. 57). Now although this is not an exaggerated criticism of Charles, and doubtless expresses Flaubert's idea of him (the plans speak of his 'inanité'), the statement contains another level of meaning within the context of Emma's thoughts. That *she* should make this judgement is ironic: she has the right idea for the wrong reasons. For her, Charles has 'les idées de tout

---

[1] A similar point is made by Cook: 'Flaubert: The Riches of Detachment' in *The French Review*, vol. xxxii, December 1958, p. 125, although he tends to go to the other extreme by exaggerating Charles's sensitivity. He does, however, point out that Emma is 'his true wife, as the title hints, and her tragic flaw is in not recognizing it'.

le monde' because he never felt the need to go to see Parisian actors when he was in Rouen;[1] because he could not swim, shoot, or fight with a sword; and because he could not explain an expression concerning horse-riding which she had found—naturally —in a novel. Because he is not, in short, a character in one of her novels. Two pages later, Emma is disappointed that her attempts to excite passion in him by approved methods did not work: 'Au clair de lune, dans le jardin, elle récitait tout ce qu'elle savait par cœur de rimes passionnées et lui chantait en soupirant des adagios mélancoliques'. Emma herself has 'les idées de tout le monde', but of a different type; her judgement of Charles is deformed because it is based on false premises. She is as bourgeois as he is, within Flaubert's meaning of the term.[2] Indeed, this is made explicit: Emma is 'incapable, du reste, de comprendre ce qu'elle n'éprouvait pas, comme de croire à tout ce qui ne se manifestait point par des formes convenues'. Flaubert is not yet relying completely on his point of view technique—which makes it all the more remarkable that such comments have so often gone unnoticed. But the passage does show the direction of his development: the author's comment is superfluous for the discerning reader. In later books, Flaubert will allow the facts to speak for themselves.

From this time on, it is a *parti pris* with Emma to find fault with her husband. Faults are not, of course, lacking; but what is more interesting is that as a direct result of the point of view, they are invariably presented in a twisted way which finally accuses Emma rather than Charles. Only after Emma's boredom makes her turn on him, the only victim available (apart from herself, which is unthinkable), does he become the ugly, vulgar, unfeeling incompetent. Many of the 'faults' she finds, even when

[1] This has at least three important echoes later: when Emma meets Léon, one element of their 'sympathie commune' is 'spectacles de Paris' (p. 116); when her love for Léon is developing, he mentions his intention of going to the theatre in Rouen (p. 131); and their liaison begins again when Charles finally does take his wife to the theatre. Such continual echoes contribute greatly to the novel's unity: see Moreau, op. cit., pp. 7–12, for others having structural importance.
[2] Cf. Fairlie, op. cit., p. 42, who makes a similar point, and Thibaudet's discussion of Emma's *idées reçues*, op. cit., p. 112.

based on facts, are utterly unreasonable (even her final desperate realization that Charles was capable of forgiving her everything increases her loathing); most are selfish; all depend on Emma's mood. And because her point of view predominates, better sides of Charles's character go unnoticed, except when Emma is in one of her rare moods of kindliness. There is no better illustration than the *pied-bot* episode, so often regarded as showing Charles's incompetence. It will be recalled that it was Emma who, at the instigation of Homais and for entirely selfish reasons, persuaded Charles to attempt the operation. Knowing his own capabilities, he would never have dared to take such a risk otherwise. He is an *officier de santé*, not a surgeon; the operation was new and unusual; his failure was highly probable. Only Emma and Homais (it is significant that they work in concert, and that their reactions to the failure are substantially the same) could have been ambitious enough to encourage Charles, and only they, who need to disguise their part in the affair, could see it as a proof of his stupidity.[1] Within his limits, Charles was in fact reasonably efficient: there is a paragraph to this effect on pp. 84–5, and, in fact, if he had been a less successful doctor a good proportion of his troubles would never have occurred. After all, he cured Emma's father, the gamekeeper who gave Emma the dog which helped crystallize her dreams of 'disillusionment' (p. 61), the marquis d'Andervilliers, who invited them to the ball (p. 64), and of course Rodolphe's servant.

Emma turns to Charles, then, when she is being pushed aside by Rodolphe: and when Hippolyte's operation appears to have been successful, Charles is suddenly a different man:

Elle lui sauta au cou; . . . La soirée fut charmante, pleine de causeries, de rêves en commun. . . . et elle se trouvait heureuse de se rafraîchir dans un sentiment nouveau, plus sain, meilleur, enfin d'éprouver quelque tendresse pour ce pauvre garçon qui la chérissait. . . . mais ses yeux se reportèrent sur Charles: elle remarqua même avec surprise qu'il n'avait point les dents vilaines (p. 245).

[1] Thibaudet, op. cit., pp. 107–9, certainly exaggerates Charles's stupidity; see, on the other hand, Gothot-Mersch, op. cit., p. 136, and Moreau, 'Composition', loc. cit., pp. 172–3.

This is the *only* time Emma and Charles have 'rêves en commun'; it is also the only time she notices a favourable physical characteristic in him. When the operation fails, she returns to her more normal attitude, that of 'sacrifices continuels'. The 'rêves en commun' go their own ways: 'Elle ne partageait pas son humiliation, elle en éprouvait une autre'; and instead of his good teeth, 'Tout en lui l'irritait maintenant, sa figure, son costume, ce qu'il ne disait pas, sa personne entière, son existence enfin' (p. 256).

Physical descriptions of Charles consistently reflect and reinforce the pattern of attitudes changing with moods: the facts are invariably presented in such a way that they cannot provide a true picture. For one thing, there are no descriptions of Charles when Emma is first attracted to him, when we could expect a favourable view. This is partly because at this stage the point of view is Charles's; partly because Emma at first sees him more as a means of escape from her environment than as a man, so that his appearance is unimportant to her; and partly because he has no striking distinguishing features anyway—the earlier statement that his face had become 'presque intéressante' (p. 11), and père Rouault's opinion that he was 'un peu *gringalet*' (p. 32), have sufficiently characterized him. Thus Charles is never really described until after Emma's disillusionment begins, so that he is automatically the victim of an emotional chain reaction. A picture of domestic monotony is followed by an unflattering portrait of Charles in bed and a description of his rough country boots.[1] The more Emma reflects on her boredom, the more flaws she sees in Charles's character, the uglier and more vulgar he becomes. This is sometimes quite as clear as if it had been stated outright: on page 86, for example, having decided Charles is a 'pauvre homme', the text continues:

Elle se sentait, d'ailleurs, plus irritée de lui. Il prenait, avec l'âge

[1] p. 59. Ferrère, op. cit., pp. 162-3, speaks of this passage while showing how Flaubert builds up a scene from his notes. He rightly remarks that the details included are to illustrate 'l'incurable et béate insignifiance du personnage'; but he fails to take account of the fact that the reader is already aware of this insignificance, and that if the scene did no more than this it would be unnecessary repetition. It is *Emma*'s discovery, and not the reader's, which gives the passage its meaning.

[within a year of his marriage!] des allures épaisses; il coupait, au dessert, le bouchon des bouteilles vides; il se passait, après manger, la langue sur les dents; il faisait en avalant sa soupe, un gloussement à chaque gorgée, et, comme il commençait d'engraisser, ses yeux, déjà petits, semblaient remonter vers les tempes par la bouffissure de ses pommettes.

Even little tics, like his habit of cutting the corks, annoy her. Emma, of course, has similar tics—'elle ... s'amusait, avec la pointe de son couteau, à faire des raies sur la toile cirée' (p. 91), but *these* are to be interpreted as a sign of her noble *ennui*, not annoying vulgarity: everything depends on the point of view.[1]

The pattern continues in subsequent descriptions, which require no further comment: Charles is unfavourably contrasted with Léon (p. 141); Emma, pleased with his apparent success in the operation, notices his good teeth (p. 245); Charles is contrasted with Rodolphe: 'jamais Charles ne lui paraissait aussi désagréable, avoir les doigts aussi carrés, l'esprit aussi lourd, les façons si communes qu'après ces rendez-vous avec Rodolphe, quand ils se trouvaient ensemble' (p. 260); finally, when Charles's father dies, the depressing contrast between her home and her carriage-ride with Léon, and even Charles's sorrow (with Hippolyte's opportune appearance to remind her of Charles's 'incurable ineptie') make her turn against him once more (p. 347).

Emma's view of her child fits the same pattern: when she thinks she is fighting to keep Léon at bay, Berthe, like Charles and the Church, receives an embarrassing amount of attention (p. 147); when she returns from her abortive visit to the *curé*, 'C'est une chose étrange, pensait Emma, comme cette enfant est laide!' (p. 161); when she is having doubts about Rodolphe (p. 240), and later when Rodolphe has broken off the relationship (p. 298), the child is again in favour.

L'abbé Bournisien, too, has been slandered by many readers'

---

[1] Cf. Emma's disgust for Charles because he is too tired to concentrate on his medical journals (p. 85), as opposed to her self-pity because she is too upset to concentrate on her novels (p. 84); also her disdain for Charles's carrying a pocketknife 'comme un paysan' (p. 142), as opposed to the absence of any derogatory comment when, just after she has given in to Rodolphe, he produces a knife to fix the bridle of one of the horses (p. 224).

equating Emma's view of him with the author's. The same principle of description according to mood applies. Emma invariably turns to the Church for non-religious reasons, as was carefully explained in the chapter on her school-days.[1] Her only motives for visiting Bournisien are sentimental: these are set out on pp. 153-4, and summarized in the words: '. . . et ce fut sans en avoir conscience qu'elle s'achemina vers l'église, disposée à n'importe quelle dévotion, pourvu qu'elle y absorbât son âme et que l'existence entière y disparût' (p. 154). Sleepwalkers normally have rude awakenings. Emma is predisposed to expect from Bournisien something which she had no right to expect: her hopes are as rash and meaningless as trying to find in Rodolphe or in Charles a romantic hero. Even on her way to the church, 'l'existence entière', far from disappearing, keeps on pushing in on her, in the form of Lestiboudois, the noisy children, the bleak cemetery, and the dark little church. It is in these conditions that we must see the unflattering physical description of the priest:

La lueur du soleil couchant qui frappait en plein son visage pâlissait le lasting de sa soutane, luisante sous les coudes, effiloquée par le bas. Des taches de graisse et de tabac suivaient sur sa poitrine large la ligne de petits boutons, et elles devenaient plus nombreuses en s'écartant de son rabat, où reposaient les plis abondants de sa peau rouge; elle était semée de macules jaunes qui disparaissaient dans les poils rudes de sa barbe grisonnante. Il venait de dîner et respirait bruyamment (pp. 155-6).

This view of Bournisien sets the tone of the ensuing conversation, and makes it impossible for Emma to get any comfort from him. Now although Bournisien doubtless possessed all these undesirable characteristics, it is important that they should be mentioned only now. They have never been noticed before—not even by Homais—nor will they be noticed again. When Emma is ill and repentant, the priest takes on quite a different appearance (p. 295): 'Il s'enquérait de sa santé, lui apportait des nouvelles et l'exhortait à la religion dans un petit bavardage câlin qui ne

[1] Cf. Pommier et Leleu, op. cit., p. 42: 'catholicisme amoureux mais en lire plus de propension à l'amour qu'à la religion, car n'est pas mystique mais poétique (et sensuelle plus tard) — peu de véritable sentiment et de jugement'.

manquait pas d'agrément. La vue seule de sa soutane la récon-
fortait'—very likely the same revolting cassock which had been
described in the earlier passage.

Besides, there is a specific statement by Flaubert that he did not
intend to present Bournisien as the ugly, nasty being which
Emma sees in this chapter. This is one side of his character, but
he has some saving graces:

> Je veux exprimer la situation suivante: ma petite femme, dans un
> accès de religion, va à l'église; elle trouve à la porte le curé qui, dans
> un dialogue (sans sujet déterminé) se montre tellement bête, plat, inepte,
> crasseux, qu'elle s'en retourne dégoûtée et indévote. Et mon curé est
> très brave homme, excellent même, mais il ne songe qu'au physique
> (aux souffrances des pauvres, manque de pain ou de bois), et ne devine
> pas les défaillances morales, les vagues aspirations mystiques; il est très
> chaste et pratique tous ses devoirs.[1]

Flaubert does present the more favourable side of Bournisien in
the book, partly in the conversation with Emma, and partly in the
early stages of the inn scene, before the Bovary arrive (pp. 105–6).
The evidence necessary to counter-balance Emma's extreme
view is not lacking, but it is not so obviously present as Emma's
opinion—again, because the reader follows Emma's point of
view more than anyone else's.

Silent criticism

It was certainly part of Flaubert's intention to portray both
sides of Emma's environment (and in particular Charles, as the
symbol of this environment) in this manner, giving only apparent
weight to her views. Once again, his plans support our contention:
of Yonville itself, he notes: ' — le présenter d'abord comme un
endroit assez agréable, Emma s'y plaît au commencement puis
comme atroce d'ennui aux époques où elle l'exècre'; 'chaque
malheur qui arrive réagit en rage contre sa vie, contre son mari'.[2]
The tragedy lies not so much in what Charles was, as in what

---

[1] *Cor.*, III, 166–7. The point is also made by Fairlie, op. cit., pp. 18–19, but
without attaching it to the techniques under discussion here.

[2] Pommier et Leleu, op. cit., pp. 26, 19.

Emma thought he was, compared with what she thought he ought to be. What he was is bad enough, and one can sympathize with Emma. What she thought he was is much worse, and what she thought he ought to be is, in the circumstances, fantastic. It is part of Flaubert's irony that while she had some justification for reacting against Charles, her actual reaction is caused by a mistaken assessment, and by pursuit of a mistaken ideal. Moreover, she believes she sees in both Léon and Rodolphe different aspects of what she wanted to see in Charles, so that she is also attracted to them for wrong reasons; and she eventually discovers that the qualities she saw in them are not there anyway. And all the time some of the qualities she might reasonably have sought—such as the undying love she believes she wants—are possessed by no one but Charles! The total situation is thus much more complex than that of a romantically-minded heroine imprisoned in a dull everyday life, which is the normal assessment of this book.[1] Such a situation is both real and universal: it is seldom possible to separate right from wrong, as most people, and most situations, contain a mixture of both; and most people act from a mixture of right motives and wrong ones, while firmly believing that they are acting only from right ones.

There is an interesting parallel here with a passage from one of Flaubert's letters, written while he was busy with *Bovary*. He is astounded that his brother, whom he regarded as the type of the bourgeois, should be enthusiastic about poets he himself admired:

Sais-tu que mon cher frère lit avec rage Régnier, qu'il en a trois éditions, qu'il m'en a récité des tartines par cœur? il a dit devant moi à Bourlet à propos de *Melaenis* [by Bouilhet]: 'Si tu n'as pas lu ça, tu n'as rien lu.'

Que je sois pendu si je porte jamais un jugement sur qui que ce soit!

La bêtise n'est pas d'un côté et l'esprit de l'autre. C'est comme le vice et la vertu: malin qui les distingue.

Axiome: Le synthétisme est la grande loi de l'ontologie.[2]

---

[1] Moreau, *Bovary*, op. cit., p. 15 mentions 'l'incompréhension mutuelle' but in the examples he gives he hardly draws attention to the fact that it really is mutual; but cf. Fairlie, op. cit., pp. 12, 61–2.

[2] *Cor.*, IV, 83.

This passage is not entirely facetious. It reflects a general attitude frequently found in the *Correspondance*, and which is closely
connected with the concept of 'ne pas conclure'. In addition, the
concluding 'axiome' is found again at the end of a plan for the
final part of *Bovary* (Emma's death, etc.).[1] The editors of the
Nouvelle version believe it has nothing to do with the plan, but a
more probable explanation is that it occurs there because Flaubert
regarded it as a summary of his intention in the novel. It fits
perfectly if interpreted from the context of the letter quoted
above. There is not one character in the whole novel who does
not have this mixture of good and bad, of sensible and inane, of
right ideas and wrong ones. Justin, a symbol of inarticulate,
idealistic love, is directly responsible for his idol's death, and
eventually becomes a 'garçon épicier'; Charles's mother, nasty
as she is, acts only from love for her son—'la faire bonne un
peu. aime Charles',[2] and even at her most bourgeois has some
insight, for when Emma is ill she is largely correct in her diagnosis
about Emma's boredom and preoccupation with bad novels.
True, she regards all novels as bad, thinks that they invariably
have an undesirable effect. But in Emma's case she is close to the
truth, even so close as to call the book-lending trade a 'métier
d'empoisonneur!' (p. 175). In the same way, Canivet's harangue
against Charles's stupidity over Hippolyte is justified, but for
the wrong reasons: he is one of those doctors whose mind is
closed to any new developments, and is content to regard anything he cannot do himself as impossible: ' — Ce sont là des
inventions de Paris! Voilà les idées de ces messieurs de la Capitale!
c'est comme le strabisme, le chloroforme et la lithotritie, un tas
de monstruosités que le gouvernement devrait défendre!' etc.
(pp. 251–2). Even Charles's ridiculous posthumous love for Emma
has a certain pathetic idealism which somehow helps to justify
it, as Flaubert noted in his plans: 'redécouvertes. — [reamour.
aime ses amants pour parler d'elle] ['venez nous causerons d'elle']
[étonnement de Rodolphe] [L'amour comme un soleil dore les
immondices]'.[3]

---

[1] Pommier et Leleu, op. cit., p. 122.   [2] Ibid., p. 99.
[3] Ibid., p. 124.

The subjective point of view technique seems eminently suitable for the presentation of a situation of such complexity, which would be difficult to explain adequately, even if there were no requirement of impersonality. Flaubert has to present simultaneously two completely separate levels of facts—the facts of a character's experience (and the character's assessment of it), and the fact that the character's assessment is partly mistaken. It is a fact, for example, that Emma thought Charles was a monster; it is also a fact that Charles was not a monster. By presenting the book subjectively, largely through the eyes of Emma, Flaubert effectively puts the first level of facts before us; and by continually making it plain, through 'seeing' words, impressionistic and temporary elements, changes in the appearance of things and people according to the observer's mood, that the book is presented subjectively, he is at least hinting at the second level of facts.

It has already been noted, however, that the method has its dangers, in that the reader, unprepared for such a subtle and unusual presentation, will tend to identify Emma's point of view with Flaubert's. If he does so, the second level of facts (the continual implicit criticism of Emma) will be lost. Such a reader may criticize Emma for her stupidity, but still believe that Flaubert approved of her romantic escapism. This is, indeed, still a common interpretation of the book, especially by those who like to portray Flaubert as a romantic fighting to escape from romanticism into realism. On its own, the method ensures impersonality, but it is not certain to make the author's intentions clear; and we have seen that for Flaubert the two were not incompatible. Flaubert recognized this danger—'On pourrait la prendre au sérieux et elle est d'une grande intention de grotesque'—and besides, such a method offers limited scope for other elements which he regarded as highly desirable, if not essential. These would include in particular the comic and the ironic, neither of which is possible by following exclusively the point of view of a person who takes herself as seriously as Emma does.

Flaubert's solution to the problem has been implicit in much of what has already been said: clearly the point of view is not always Emma's. She is not introduced until the book is well under way, and dies before the end of it, a fact which Rousset says first made him think about the point of view technique. Somewhat earlier than Rousset, Lubbock argued that such changes in point of view could not be the result of caprice or of chance in a writer as careful as Flaubert. The reason, he suggests, lies in the subject of the book: it is not only the story of Emma, but 'the history of a woman like her in just such a world as hers, a foolish woman in narrow circumstances; so that the provincial scene, acting upon her, making her what she becomes, is as essential as she is herself'.[1] If this is so, Emma's environment must be as clearly presented as Emma; but it is part of the point that neither Emma nor any of the other characters has the humour and irony necessary to do this objectively, so the task falls to the author. Therefore, the author must not follow Emma's point of view too closely, as he must be free to adopt his own every so often, without this transition being too brusque or obvious. He is always slightly aloof from her, so that he can sometimes be entirely so. Finally, some of the book is presented from Charles's point of view, which forces a comparison between Emma's view of herself, and Charles's view of her: this shows us the inanity of Charles and therefore of Emma's environment. For the same reason, the end of the book is not Emma's death, but Charles's silly reaction to it and all that it revealed. Thus, 'the whole book, mainly the affair of Emma herself, is effectively [one might add: symbolically] framed in this other affair, that of Charles, in which it opens and closes.'[2]

Lubbock sometimes oversimplifies the case, and one is naturally not obliged to accept all his conclusions. Yet it is difficult to overstate the importance of his chapter on *Bovary*, which insists that the form of a novel—in this case, through a point of view technique—can reflect the subject and therefore be an integral part of it, rather than a mere adjunct. Developing Lubbock's conclusions a step further, it can be said that this intimate connection between form and subject, to the extent that the subject is ex-

---

[1] Lubbock, op. cit., p. 80.   [2] Ibid., p. 91.

pressed *in* the form, as well as by it, is one aspect of that over-all unity which we know Flaubert desired. The whole concept is the equivalent, on a much grander, more complex and more subtle scale, of Flaubert's oft-repeated theory of the *mot juste*— the idea that, within a sentence, sounds, rhythms, and even syntax are as important as the meanings of the words themselves in expressing the exact nuance in the writer's mind. Some of the principles stated by Lubbock are therefore of great value; but his implication that the presentation of the book largely alternates between Emma's point of view and the author's, and that those parts from Charles's point of view serve only to show Charles's inanity, does not do full justice to the subtlety of Flaubert's technique. It is necessary to discuss these questions in more detail.

In the first place, it is not only at the beginning and the end of the book that Charles's point of view occurs. Although it is overshadowed by Emma's (as Emma's personality overshadows Charles's) it is briefly presented at several important points. When it does occur, it nearly always serves the same, rather complex purpose: it shows Charles's inanity, as Lubbock says; it places Charles in strong contrast with Emma, thereby under-lining the inevitability of subsequent developments; but it con-tinually shows the reader that Emma's ideas are not quite accurate, thereby emphasizing what was implicit in the subjective presenta-tion of Emma's thoughts and feelings; and finally it hints at some interesting *parallels* between Charles and Emma, thereby increas-ing the irony of the apparently unbridgeable contrasts.

Thus the early part of the book, as well as portraying Charles's obviously unattractive characteristics, suggests that he is, in his own, slow, inarticulate way, something of a dreamer, an idealist whose ideals escape him—an immediate parallel with Emma. But the parallel serves in the long run only to aggravate the incompatibility, for when Charles is in the city *he* dreams of living in the country. He looks forward to his first marriage as a means of escaping from his mother, just as Emma wanted to escape from her father and *his* environment. Like Emma, 'Charles avait entrevu par le mariage l'avènement d'une condition meil-leure, . . .' (p. 13), and, like Emma, he was sadly disappointed.

Again, he quickly decides his marriage to Emma is ideal (pp. 45–7) at the very moment Emma is deciding that it is not; Charles proves to be woefully wrong, while Emma, as we have noted, is right, but for largely the wrong reasons.

Other occurrences of Charles's point of view, or of the author following Charles's actions rather than Emma's, show that these observations are substantially valid in almost every case.

pp. 83–5: The picture of Emma, utterly bored, and blaming Charles for this state of affairs, is interrupted by the strongly contrasting picture of Charles's difficult and distasteful life as a country doctor. Because of this life, he returns home exhausted in the evening (when Emma expects him to be the fiery romantic hero), and is charmed by Emma's 'délicatesses', the small elegant touches of dress, of habit, of food, and the little luxuries of exotic materials, such as 'un nécessaire d'ivoire, avec un dé de vermeil' (p. 84). He is, in short, delighted with those very aspects of Emma to which she believes him to be completely insensitive, and which will later be a major cause of their mutual ruin. Ironically, these elegant touches are not in any case intended by Emma to be for his benefit, but for her own—they are a result of her boredom and the longing for luxury which began with La Vaubyessard. This ironic intention is made explicit in both the plans and the novel. When she tries to make Charles conform a little more to her ideal of elegant manhood, 'ce n'était pas, comme il croyait, pour lui; c'était pour elle-même, par expansion d'égoïsme, agacement nerveux' (p. 86). 'Charles en est attendri (à propos qu'elle l'habille) et au contraire à ce moment même elle est agacée contre lui.'[1]

pp. 92–4: As Emma's nervous state worsens, it gradually dawns on Charles that something ought to be done, and, after consultation with another doctor, he concludes that the environment does not suit her. Again the various levels of irony are obvious. Charles is correct in his conclusion but wrong in his reasons: 'Charles imagina que la cause de sa maladie était sans doute dans

---

[1] Pommier et Leleu, op. cit., p. 51; cf. p. 52: 'essaie de l'éléganciser par pur égoïsme'. This is one of the relatively few cases where the author's intentions are specifically stated in the book.

quelque influence locale ...' (p. 93). And having reached the correct conclusion, his solution is to move a few miles away to precisely the same sort of town. But this should not obscure the fact that Charles is *willing* to do anything for Emma's good, at the risk of his practice and therefore his (and her) personal situation. Emma, blinded to Charles's good points—and especially to his love for her—by her own feelings and troubles, is barely aware of this fact. A specific problem of presentation arises here, for Emma's point of view has to look reasonably plausible, at least superficially. Charles's good points have to be pushed into the background, and yet not so much that they are not noticed, for this would destroy the irony. The problem would appear to have occurred to Flaubert in these terms, for in the earliest plans published in the *Nouvelle version* it is stated simply that the idea of moving is Emma's: 'elle finit par prendre le pays en exécration et force son mari à le quitter'. Flaubert then saw the chance for an ironic development, for in the next plan he added: 'a des vapeurs, des besoins de pleurer où elle s'enferme. — Charles croit que l'air du pays lui est mauvais et quitte sa clientèle.' Later still, there is a further addition: 'Chagrin de Charles qui fait tout ce qu'il peut pour la rendre heureuse' (the underlining is Flaubert's). But then he must have decided that if he insisted too much on Charles's feelings, this would draw the reader's attention away from Emma, and make her feelings appear too unreasonable, for in two subsequent plans he reduces Charles's role again, mentioning merely 'inquiétudes de Charles'.[1] In the early versions of the passage in question, Charles's worries are still quite explicit: Charles 'se tourmentait à réfléchir sur sa maladie', 'elle ne dit rien et certes, si elle eût témoigné son désir cependant, Charles eût obéi bien vite'.

Pour elle, il eût cassé du caillou sur les grandes routes et battu à la grange! Le soir, lorsqu'il rentrait chez lui, il ne l'abordait qu'avec angoisse et quand elle lui avait répondu comme de coutume, par son éternel: 'Laisse-moi, je souffre', son cœur se navrait, il s'écartait sans rien dire.[2]

[1] Pommier et Leleu, op. cit., pp. 4, 8, 25, 51 and 53.
[2] Ibid., p. 236; Leleu, op. cit., vol. 1, pp. 282–3.

The definitive version (p. 93) has dropped all such explicit statements of Charles's feelings, but has retained enough to make it
clear that Charles, in his own bumbling way, still has them, even
though Emma does not think so.[1]

p. 175: Throughout the development of the 'adultère moral'
with Léon, Charles is kept well in the background, except for
unfavourable comparisons. When Léon leaves and Emma relapses
into her state of boredom and frustration, her husband's point of
view returns very briefly to show once again how worried he is
about her condition—so worried that he takes the most extreme
step he can think of: he sends for his mother! This is precisely
what he ought not to have done, yet the stupidity of his action
should not obscure the fact that, like Emma, he is merely trying
to realize his ideal.

pp. 242–4: Charles begins to study the question of Hippolyte's
foot in preparation for the great operation. The accumulation
and confusion of medical terms in these passages, together with
the all-pervading sense of doubt, and the impossibility for the
lay reader to gain anything more than a vague idea of what it is
all about, all these demonstrate that the point of view here is
Charles's, and that he himself knows very little more than the
reader. Again the irony: it is Emma who has pushed him into
this strange world of *stréphocatopodie, stréphendopodie, stréphexo-
podie, stréphypopodie,* and *stréphanopodie,* on the grounds that 'rien
n'affirmait à Emma qu'il ne fût pas habile'—something which
she does not really believe anyway. When the operation fails
(pp. 254–7), Charles, worried sick (although Emma thinks he is
not) and encouraged by Emma's recent renewed show of love
for him, turns to her in his trouble and is astounded by her violent

---

[1] Moreau, *Bovary,* op. cit., pp. 4–5, draws attention to Flaubert's omission of
many pages concerning Charles during his revisions; and argues that he has thus
changed the 'éclairage' of his novel, removing the sympathy he formerly held
for Charles, who was originally, much more than Emma, the 'méconnu'. This
argument would be valid only if Charles had *changed* in character and situation
during these revisions. In fact, he remains a 'méconnu'—not more than, but as
much as Emma, but in a different way. The only difference is that the fact is less
obvious in the final version, because the point of view is predominantly Emma's.
It is only the apparent emphasis which has changed.

outburst of ill-humour. Charles's point of view occurs more frequently in this chapter than it had for some time previously, because here more than elsewhere Emma's alone would have been insufficient to achieve the terrible irony which Flaubert required. It was necessary to keep on showing the reader that Charles was only partly what Emma believed, in order to give greater weight to Charles's pathetic discovery that she was not what he believed.

p. 270: The decision has been made to run off with Rodolphe. Emma and Charles, side by side in bed, are simultaneously making entirely different plans for the future. It has usually been assumed that this passage emphasizes the total incompatibility of Charles and Emma, and Charles's bourgeois approach to life as opposed to Emma's romantic, idealistic one.[1] This is true enough, but once again it should not be permitted to hide the parallels, which are equally important, and which certainly increase the ironic effect. Although the content of their reveries is very different, both are equally naive in their dreams of the future. Both make plans which depend on the love and support of someone else— Charles depending on Emma, while Emma depends on Rodolphe. Both are destined to return to reality with a jarring shock, because both have been too blind to look for possible disappointments in their own personality. And here, too, it is emphasized that just as Emma's tragedy is that neither Charles nor Rodolphe is what she believes them to be, so Charles's is that Emma is not what he believes her to be.

pp. 290–1: Another crisis in Emma's life (Rodolphe has left without her). Again Charles's love for Emma is mentioned, but not emphasized: the fact that he totally neglected his patients— at the very time when, through Emma's follies, he was most in need of the money—to look after her unceasingly for forty-three days, is mentioned only in passing. Charles's feelings are kept in the background, so as not to divert the reader's attention from Emma's plight.

It is not until after Emma's death that Charles's personality begins to occupy the reader's attention again, and the final irony

[1] e.g. see Faguet, op. cit., p. 166.

begins: all those ideas and habits which Emma had spent her life
searching for—in her own mind, then in Léon and Rodolphe—
suddenly blossom forth in a weird, fatuous way in Charles himself. His letter of instruction about Emma's burial (p. 452), his
sudden thought that by some influence of magnetism (a subject
last mentioned by Rodolphe as part of his campaign against
Emma's virtue during the *Comices*, p. 205) she might return to
life (p. 455), his memories of the 'happy' days gone by (p. 459),
his sudden interest in dress and appearance and related disregard
for money (p. 472), all these things are the result of Emma's influence, and form a comment on the emptiness of Emma just as
much as that of Charles. In addition, they show that Emma
would, after all, have had more chance of forming Charles to
her wishes than either Léon or Rodolphe, neither of whom
possessed the one necessary characteristic—unfailing, unquestion-
ing, entirely disinterested love for her, resulting in a total sub-
mission to her whims, no matter how silly. In this connection,
another note in Flaubert's plans comes to mind: of Charles, he
says: 'Adore sa femme et des trois hommes qui couchent avec
elle, est certainement celui qui l'aime le plus — [c'est ce qu'il faut
bien faire voir].'[1]

It is principally because of the unreliability of Emma as chief
witness that Flaubert is also obliged to show us from time to
time the workings of both Léon and Rodolphe's mind. Both
these men became entangled with Emma (willingly enough, it
is true) largely because she was reacting against Charles.[2] In
these circumstances, she is obviously not disposed to judge them
impartially: she will certainly not see them as Flaubert did. She
would hardly realize, for example, that Léon is a 'nature pareille
à celle de Charles, mais supérieur, physiquement et moralement
(plus d'intelligence mais moins de bon cœur)', that all that is
stopping this apparently ethereal young man from seducing her

---

[1] Pommier et Leleu, op. cit., p. 21.

[2] Ibid., p. 69: 'plus occupée à haïr Charles qu'à aimer Léon'; p. 93: 'elle revient
à Rodolphe, haine de Charles . . . — amour furieux, (et compromettant) plutôt
par haine.'

is his 'couillonisme profond', his 'intérieur mollasse'; nor that Rodolphe 'empoigne Emma par la blague', that 'il voulait tout bonnement s'amuser'.[1] By introducing the point of view of Léon and of Rodolphe from time to time, Flaubert is able to show these things to the reader, without being forced to the expedient of explaining them from his privileged position of omniscient narrator. Again his changes in point of view form the basis of his irony, by making it known that these two are not what Emma believes them to be, any more than Charles is. But here, too, the irony is more complex than would appear at first sight; again it works both ways, for Emma is not what they believe her to be either. For example, while Léon is busy being the timid romantic (pp. 136–9) (which his first conversation with Emma would have led him to believe was the right approach), Emma is in a mood to respond to the other sort of romantic approach: 'L'amour, croyait-elle, devait arriver tout à coup, avec de grands éclats et des fulgurations, ...' (p. 139). By the time he summons up the courage to make his declaration (p. 146), she has realized he loves her, decided he is a danger, and has adopted the virtuous loving wife role (pp. 146–8). Much to her chagrin, Léon accepts this at face value (pp. 148–9), and proceeds to idealize her instead! '... ne semblait-elle pas traverser l'existence en y touchant à peine, et porter au front la vague empreinte de quelque prédestination sublime?'[2] Like Charles, Léon is unfortunate in that he has the right sentiments at the wrong time. This is a favourite theme of Flaubert's which he develops more fully in *l'Education sentimentale*.

At a different level, the same applies to Rodolphe. He is primarily interested in sex, as is made clear on the first occasion we follow his point of view (pp. 180–2; this was made even clearer in an earlier version, with Rodolphe making statements like: 'Elle doit bien baiser pourtant!'). Rodolphe's campaign is mounted on the assumption that Emma will feel the same way, and when she succumbs to him so easily, he is no doubt confirmed

---

[1] Pommier et Leleu, op. cit., pp. 9, 59, 69; 28, 29.
[2] Cf. our comments on this attitude in the first *Education sentimentale*, supra, pp. 74–6.

in his view. But the reader knows that Emma succumbs because of a special set of circumstances about which Rodolphe knows nothing, and that he is merely very lucky to have happened along at the critical moment.[1] Rodolphe is therefore surprised and embarrassed when he comes to realize that his physical charm is a relatively minor part of her attraction to him. Thus when she suggests that he ought to have his pistols ready to defend himself against Charles (p. 235), Rodolphe begins to notice that 'elle devenait bien sentimentale' (!) The 'devenait', which shows that this paragraph represents Rodolphe's point of view (it could not be that of the author, who has spent the last two hundred pages showing that Emma was always so), also shows that if Rodolphe was a disappointment for Emma, she was equally so for him. This is not surprising: Emma is not, of course, alone in viewing people subjectively, in seeing in them the things she wants to see, and ignoring the rest. Rodolphe, for all his experience of women (or perhaps because of it, as he had hitherto known only one sort—see p. 265), is not immune to this disease.

Meanwhile, the ironic developments continue. Rodolphe, perceiving that Emma is not what he at first believed, but is nevertheless completely under his spell, proceeds to take advantage of her and *make* her what he thought she was: 'Il jugea toute pudeur incommode. Il la traita sans façon. Il en fit quelque chose de souple et de corrompu', and so on (pp. 265–6).[2] As a result, when Léon re-enters the picture, *his* view of Emma, as the sentimental, romantic woman, which was correct (although he did not fully realize it at the time) when he was in Yonville, is now much less correct. She has not, it is true, lost her sentimentality, but thanks to Rodolphe's attentions, it is now a more violent, more aggressive and more experienced kind, so that instead of proving 'l'amoureuse de tous les romans, l'héroïne de tous les drames, le vague *elle* de tous les volumes de vers, … par-dessus tout Ange!' which he bargained for (p. 367), she begins to frighten him with her experience, and becomes in his eyes

---

[1] Pommier et Leleu, op. cit., p. 89: 'il l'a toujours plus fascinée qu'elle ne l'a aimé'.

[2] The plans are even clearer (p. 93).

almost a Satanic being, dangerous and sinister.[1] Emma is of course concurrently discovering what the reader knew all along to be Léon's character: a timid, effeminate bourgeois who is dabbling in 'romantic' adventures simply because that is what young bourgeois do before they think seriously about establishing themselves as pillars of society (even Charles had succumbed a little to this temptation when he was studying in Rouen).

Thus there is another curve of non-correspondence in character and sentiments between Emma and her men, running from Léon to Rodolphe and back to Léon. This is superimposed on the non-correspondence between Emma and Charles, and on the similarities between them all, which keep on being discovered by the wrong persons at the wrong times, and going unnoticed when they would be important. There are literally dozens of these cross-currents, which together build up an incredibly complex network: in fact, the more one studies this amazing book, the stronger one's impression that its ramifications are unlimited. A large number of them result from the basic fact which we have been examining: reality is frequently *almost* what it appears to be, but seldom quite—not, at least, at the opportune moment. This is also true of most of the minor characters: there is the same lack of comprehension, and the same ignorance of the true state of affairs, between Emma and Bournisien, or between Emma and Justin, or between Homais and Justin. Such complex interrelationships could not possibly have been shown if Flaubert had limited himself to Emma's point of view, or to any other single point of view. Only through continual changing of the point of view could he achieve a total picture, as well as an ironic one.

A frequently changing point of view is therefore capable of solving the dilemma inherent in *Novembre* and the first *Education*: how to show both the hero's experience at first hand, and also the fact that the hero's assessment of his experience was mistaken. *Bovary* does it through the continual juxtaposition of a number of equally subjective views of reality, and continually makes it plain, by the devices we have examined, that they *are* all

[1] p. 391. Léon is, of course, just as much mistaken in this judgement as in his earlier one.

9—T.N.F.

subjective; and the criticism comes automatically because the different subjective views are mutually destructive. As Sarraute says, one of the interesting aspects of *Bovary* is that 'le trompe-l'œil est présenté comme tel';[1] and this is one of the ways Flaubert achieves it.

Point of view, and changes in point of view, can be used for other reasons, although these are frequently complementary to the ones given above. Point of view can, for example, be used to convey a symbolic meaning. Rousset has an extremely interesting section on the use of windows and other devices which introduce the idea of perspectives and views in a literal sense, but whose use corresponds most markedly with Emma's state of mind.[2] It is no accident that at certain periods in Emma's life, when she is exalted and apparently about to realize some of her dreams, she is able to look down from a height on her normal environment as something small and futile. This is true of her first real conversation with Rodolphe, when they are in the upper floor of the *Mairie* looking down on the *Comices*; it is true of their horse ride in the woods, where she looks down on Yonville, and it is specifically stated that 'jamais ce pauvre village où elle vivait ne lui avait semblé si petit' (p. 220); it is true, too, in a certain sense, of her visits to Rouen to see Léon: as she enters the city, it gradually ceases to be a mere impression in the mist, and becomes a part of her reality. At least one of these cases—the *Comices*—was certainly regarded by Flaubert in this light, and Rousset could well have quoted the plans to support his argument. Much of the significance of the *Comices* episode is lost if it is not seen as forming Emma and Rodolphe's field of vision. They are not in the least oblivious to what is going on round them, as is commonly supposed: their continual awareness of it all is part of the point. The *Comices* is divided into two symbolic parts: the first, when they are actually taking part in it, walking about and viewing it with some interest, shows that this after all is their environment; and the second, when they go up into the *Mairie*, signifies their—or at least Emma's—attempt to escape from this environ-

---

[1] Sarraute, loc. cit., p. 8.   [2] Rousset, op. cit., pp. 124-7.

ment. But they cannot escape from it, because it keeps on intruding upon them. All this is clear from the plans. They are used as 'witnesses' to the *Comices* from the beginning, because it is part of them: 'La description générale des comices dans un dialogue entre Emma et Rodolphe. — Rodolphe a Emma à son bras — ils se promènent.' 'Rodolphe se moquant des Comices qu'au fond il respecte un peu'[1] (in the novel Rodolphe stops occasionally to admire 'quelque beau *sujet*', he has a ticket which he proudly shows to the authorities, and he is obviously on friendly terms with M. Derozerays de la Panville). When Rodolphe and Emma go up into the *Mairie*, the plans continually refer to their looking at and experiencing directly what is going on, together with the symbolism of the windows as a possible means of escape: 'Emma regarde à la vitre'; 'vue sur les têtes et chapeaux des dames'; 'toutes fenêtres ouvertes — coup de vent frais faisant [word omitted by Flaubert] les bonnets et le tapis de la table de la mairie — blés coupés dans la campagne — Hivert dans le lointain. . . . — (bien marquer la double vue)'; 'vue des champs par la fenêtre ouverte — odeur des foins secs par cette fenêtre-là, la rêverie par l'autre'.[2]

In the same way, descriptions of nature, such as there are in this book, are also frequently used symbolically: the brighter seasons are introduced whenever there seems a chance of Emma's achieving happiness, and vice versa. It is summer when she is attracted to Charles, and when it is decided that they will marry (p. 29), and spring when they are married (p. 34); when Emma begins to be overcome by the boredom of married life, the description of the country-side contains such elements as cold winds and the setting sun (pp. 62–3);[3] and most of the period of her boredom is covered by the following winter: 'Les carreaux, chaque matin, était chargés de givre, et la lumière, blanchâtre à travers eux, comme par des verres dépolis, quelquefois ne variait

---

[1] Pommier et Leleu, op. cit., pp. 77, 79, 80, 81.

[2] Ibid., pp. 81, 82, 83. For a fuller treatment of the symbols of this book see Demorest: *L'Expression figurée et symbolique dans l'œuvre de Gustave Flaubert* (Paris, Conard, 1931), pp. 453–71.

[3] See Ferrère, op. cit., pp. 165 et seq. for an expanded explanation of the significance of this passage.

pas de la journée'.[1] The symbolic and the real winter end together: it is March (p. 94) when the Bovary leave Tostes. When
Emma goes with Léon to visit her child in the country—when
their love begins to develop—it is summer, and the accompanying description of nature contains suggestions of hope and beauty
(pp. 130–1). By the time Emma begins to fight against her love
for Léon, it is winter again (p. 148). When it occurs to her that
she might turn to the church and Bournisien, the chapter begins
on a hopeful note with a description of spring (p. 153), but the
symbolic mood is quickly changed during the description of
Bournisien, for his face is lit by the setting sun, as Emma's hopes
begin to set (p. 155). As Léon leaves Yonville for Paris, and again
Emma's future looks dark, there is a heavy rainstorm (p. 167).
When she meets Rodolphe for the first time, and the *Comices*
take place, it is summer; although she gives in to him in the glow
of an October sunset (p. 219). After the temporary lapse in
Rodolphe and Emma's affair, their love develops again in spring
(p. 239). It is autumn when Rodolphe decides he cannot run
away with Emma (p. 273), so that her illness and convalescence
occupy the following winter: 'L'hiver fut rude. La convalescence
de Madame fut longue' (p. 294). She recovers, and it is spring
again when she meets Léon at the theatre (p. 300). In the same
way, it is probably no accident that it is spring when Charles's
first wife dies (p. 25), or that the description of Emma's father
returning from her funeral includes a picture of the setting sun:[2]
it is not only for Emma that the seasons and the time of day have
symbolic significance.

Symbolic details are always introduced unobtrusively, and in
the most natural manner. They invariably have a normal, everyday, realistic level of meaning as well as their symbolic one, so
that the latter can easily go unnoticed. Emma never obviously
looks out of a window in order that symbolism can be introduced
at a given point. In the same way, it is perfectly natural that her

---

[1] pp. 88–9; cf. p. 91, the reference to the fire burning at night, and the plans
(Pommier et Leleu, op. cit., p. 53), where this particular case is made explicit:
'Le temps pleure comme elle.'

[2] p. 469; see Ferrère, op. cit., p. 167.

wedding should take place in the spring, or that the *Comices* should be held in the summer: it would be ludicrous to stage either event in mid-winter. But it has been shown many times that Flaubert introduces even the tiniest details only with good reason; the consistency of such correspondences rules out any likelihood of mere chance.

Another piece of symbolism which Flaubert had intended to present by means of the restricted point of view technique was the 'coloured glass' episode. The day after the ball, Emma, walking in the grounds of La Vaubyessard, comes upon a small pavilion, one window of which is composed of small pieces of glass of different colours. She looks in turn through the blue, the yellow, the green, and the red panes, and notes the changes in the countryside; she then looks through the other window, which is of clear glass, and sees things as they are.[1] The implications of the passage are obvious: metaphorically, this is what Emma spends her whole life doing, and this is what the point of view technique continually emphasizes. The episode was finally omitted, partly, no doubt, because it does not really fit Emma's experience—not once does it occur to her to look through the clear glass. It is likely, too, that the passage finally seemed too forced, as if Flaubert were openly negating his heroine's way of looking at things, as he had done in the first *Education*. But the attitudes involved, and the importance to Flaubert of the phenomenon of a deforming subjectivity set in motion by *choses vues*, are again underlined.[2]

---

[1] Pommier et Leleu, op. cit., pp. 215-17; cf. plans, ibid., pp. 41, 47.

[2] The metaphor was dear to Flaubert. An early form of it appears in *Mémoires d'un fou* (v. supra, p. 62, note 1); and it occurs again in 1844: 'Vous connaissez ces verres de couleur qui ornent les kiosques des bonnetiers retirés. On voit la campagne en rouge, en bleu, en jaune. L'ennui est de même. Les plus belles choses, vues à travers lui, prennent sa teinte et reflètent sa tristesse' (*Cor.*, I, 151-2). When he was writing the *Bovary* passage, he says: 'Je ne suis pas de ceux qui regardent la vie à travers des carreaux de couleur' (quoted by Pommier et Leleu, op. cit., p. xix; cf. *Cor.*, II, 412; III, 130; IV, 243-4). In this letter, he seems to be consciously separating himself in spirit from Emma, even though his point of view presentation brings him so close to her at this point of the novel. There could be no firmer indication that, for Flaubert at least, 'identification' with his characters is a technical matter, entirely distinct from the so-called identification, in the psychological or sentimental sense, often used by critics.

The existence, in *Madame Bovary*, of various levels of meaning beyond the literal one has long been recognized, and several writers have contributed to the now very long list of details which are significant in this way.[1] In the present context, these non-realistic levels raise an important question: how does their communication to the reader fit in with a subjective point of view? If we are following only the character's experiences, how can there be a pattern of meaning which, in some cases at least, is beyond the perception of that character? It is improbable, for example, that Charles would attach a symbolic or prophetic significance to the shying of his horse as he enters Les Bertaux for the first time.[2] The existence of such additional meanings is sometimes taken as a sign that this novel does not in fact depend on restricted point of view, but on authorial omniscience, for its meaning. This is too easy. Flaubert *is* omniscient, of course— but then all novelists are, no matter what convention of presentation they adopt. Symbolic meanings are not necessarily a consequence of the point of view adopted, and can occur as easily in a first-person novel as in an omniscient one. The extra level of meaning usually comes when a novel is re-read, when the *reader*, having seen the over-all pattern, is omniscient as compared with the character. This is a basic fact which is frequently ignored. No matter how many times the book is lived through, the characters are condemned to the same ignorance and errors, while the reader increases in knowledge. The result is that the reader can often see much more than the characters in a given set of facts, and can interpret them differently, even if these facts are entirely from the character's point of view. Thus the shying of Charles's horse is less important to him than to the reader, even though it is noted because it forced itself on Charles's attention. The value of the point of view technique is not nullified by the existence of an extra level of meaning. On the contrary,

---

[1] e.g. Cook, loc. cit., pp. 122–4, who states that 'every last detail of his narrative is made to do double duty, as observed detail and as correlative of the action'; Faguet, op. cit., pp. 155–6; Bart, op. cit., pp. 33 et seq.; Fairlie, op. cit., pp. 35, 43, 70–1; Thorlby, op. cit., p. 45; Bollème, op. cit., pp. 156–7; Gothot-Mersch, op. cit., pp. 134–5, 226–7.

[2] See also Fairlie, op. cit., pp. 70–1.

it is increased, for the use of the technique results in an ironical *décalage* between the character's and the reader's interpretation of a single fact.

It should be added that this *décalage* varies in degree, in Flaubert's work, from character to character and from novel to novel. The minds of several characters are naturally attuned to a certain kind of symbolism in surrounding everyday objects. For example, the romantic leanings of Frédéric and Emma tend to make them more sensitive than Charles to 'moods' of nature, and the social background of Mâtho and Salammbô encourages them to look constantly for symbolic significance. But Flaubert often turns the tables on these characters too, and includes levels of meaning of which they cannot be aware. Thus it is likely that Emma sees most of the parallels between her situation and the time of day or the season, and between her situation and the moral size of Rouen and Yonville; but it is equally likely that she does not see the prophetic significance of the autumn sunset as she yields to Rodolphe, even though that sunset, like the long, cold winters, is presented as part of her experience. The question will be raised again in relation to subsequent works. Meanwhile, it seems clear already that the point of view presentation, when used in conjunction with the over-all structure of the work—for it is this last which finally permits the reader to perceive the extent of the *décalage*—makes a real contribution towards an extra level of meaning.

The normal point of view technique, as used by Flaubert for most of his novel, can also be varied with a particular effect in mind. As Moreau has pointed out, Flaubert takes delight in changing the angle of vision in order to give a fresh view of scenes which might otherwise be hackneyed, but which are a necessary part of his development.[1] The best examples of this are the scene where Emma gives in to Léon in the carriage, and that in which she tries to persuade Binet to help her, before the distant but scandalized eyes of Mesdames Caron and Tuvache. Apart from the immediate impact of the unusual point of view, such scenes are normally full of irony. The reader has been

[1] Moreau, *Bovary*, op. cit., pp. 29–30.

sufficiently acquainted with the point of view of one of the characters (in both these cases, Emma) for him to know what is going on; it is unnecessary for him actually to see or hear, and at the same time he can enjoy the ignorance of the spectators, and their speculations.

Author and narrator

In spite of the foregoing, *Madame Bovary* remains very much a third-person novel in several ways, and one's immediate impression is that although the author seldom intervenes in an obvious manner, he is present in every single line. Taken as a whole, *Bovary* is undeniably quite different from many modern novels, whose use of point of view is far more rigorous. Reasons for this are not very difficult to find: in general they are a consequence of Flaubert's aesthetic preoccupations, which were examined earlier. While the point of view technique is an excellent means of achieving impersonality, impersonality alone does not make a work of art. For instance, Flaubert considered a good literary style essential. If the point of view technique is applied with absolute consistency, the style will change with the point of view, and will always be strictly limited to the capabilities of the character concerned. The resultant novel will be in a very poor style indeed—imagine how Emma would write! For a writer like Flaubert, there can only be one answer: even though he closely follows the point of view of the various characters, he must do so in his own language and style. But such a solution gives rise to a further dilemma, for Flaubert apparently believed[1] that because of the intimate connection between thought and expression, anything which was clearly thought out and worth saying, could easily be well expressed. Conversely, difficulty in expression, or bad expression, was the direct result of worthless or fuzzy thinking. But for a good proportion of *Bovary* he was trying to reverse this axiom (it is fortunate for him that its validity is doubtful, as his own practice does in fact show), and express bad thoughts well. It is to this that he ascribes much of

[1] e.g. *Cor.*, II, 361; III, 48.

his difficulty in the *Comices* passage: 'Bien écrire *le médiocre* et faire qu'il garde en même temps son aspect, sa coupe, ses mots même, cela est vraiment diabolique. ...' 'Quand j'aborde une situation, elle me dégoûte d'avance par sa vulgarité; je ne fais autre chose que de doser de la merde.' He probably had the same problem in mind when he claimed that if successful in *Bovary*, he would have achieved 'du réel écrit'—that is, vulgarity well expressed.[1]

In spite of these partly self-imposed difficulties, this is the method Flaubert usually adopted: there are a large number of passages which record simultaneously the perception of a character, and the language of Flaubert. Examples are not difficult to find—several are given by Ullmann and Auerbach[2]—and need not delay us here. The point is that Flaubert's determination to present his novel in a literary style inevitably resulted in a compromise, a dilution of the point of view technique in the interests of a broader view of the work of art. The impersonality achieved by the juxtaposition of conflicting subjective views is tempered by the style. Here is one element of the novel where the personality of the author is continually and massively present— which is exactly as Flaubert wanted it.

Another very obvious aspect of the third-person novel, which is often found in *Bovary* and which apparently interferes with the point of view technique, is that there is a narrator regulating the appearance of the characters, arranging scenes and dialogues, deciding whose point of view the reader will follow next, and generally directing the whole development of the book. The variety of narrators in *Bovary* suggests that Flaubert had quite a problem here; and his subsequent books give the impression that he was not satisfied with the solutions he adopted. The basic difficulty can be stated in these terms: the more obvious the narrator, the less the reader is in direct contact with the characters —the less he can see the characters' subjectivity actually at work, and therefore the less impersonal the book will be. Every time

---

[1] *Cor.*, III, 338, 345; II, 405; III, 20, 24, 268, 423.

[2] Ullmann, op. cit., pp. 112–14; Auerbach, op. cit., pp. 427–8; see also La Varende: *Flaubert par lui-même* (Paris, éditions du Seuil, 1958), pp. 98–9.

the narrator is interposed between the action and the reader, no matter how unobtrusively, the reader has a right to question the authenticity of the action. If the reader sees Emma thinking Charles is a monster, he is more willing to accept this as a fact than if he merely has the narrator *telling* him that she thought so. (It is understood, of course, that both methods of presentation are conventions: in either case the reader is really accepting the author's word for the authenticity of what is portrayed. The direct method increases the pretence of authenticity, not the authenticity itself.) Therefore, for a writer like Flaubert, who wanted to put only the 'facts' of the case before the reader, and leave the interpretation to him, the continual presence of a narrator is something of a nuisance. On the other hand, Flaubert also wanted to *guide* the reader to an interpretation, which he does by showing the reader several different sets of 'facts'. In other words, he is sometimes limiting our knowledge to that of the heroine, and sometimes extending it to areas of the heroine's ignorance; he is asking us to accept two separate literary conventions at once, and to change from one to the other when it suits him. In these circumstances, a narrator, while a nuisance on the one hand, becomes a necessity on the other, for it is he who must arrange the transitions at the relevant points. He must remain as unobtrusive as possible, of course, for when we are following the point of view of one character only, the illusion of limited knowledge must not be destroyed; and those passages where he directly takes over the advance of the story must not be too startlingly different in tone from the others, or the novel will have a disjointed, stop-and-go appearance. Besides, even in those passages where the narrator is in control, it is desirable to continue the illusion that he is presenting only facts, and not interpretations.

Whether Flaubert actually thought the problem out in these terms can never be known. One can only say that the handling of the narrator passages in *Bovary* is consistent with some such reasoning. In the first place, the narrator himself is frequently a 'witness', just as if he were a character. In the opening scene, he is part of the class, and consistently refers to himself as such;

and as we have already noted, this scene contains all the elements of the witness technique which are so liberally used by Flaubert throughout the book. It is probable that this particular solution was adopted primarily to increase the sense of immediacy and authenticity of the scene described.[1] But in spite of the use of the witness technique, this scene has a totally different quality from, say, the description of the opera, which is from Emma's point of view. It would never occur to the reader to question the objective validity of what he is told in the classroom scene, and this vague *nous* speaks with more authority, and his statements are more worthy of being accepted at face value than Emma's. The *nous* is a device for presenting facts, as opposed to the subjective impressions we shall so frequently be given.

Having served his purpose, this particular type of narrator seems to have become a distinct embarrassment: he is unobtrusively dropped within a few pages, never to reappear. But even though the *nous* drops out, the reasons which made it necessary to introduce him remain, so that other devices have to be found to replace him. The most straightforward of these, and the one which had for long been in favour among novelists, is to be found only once in its pure form in *Bovary*: in the formal description of Yonville at the beginning of Part II. There is still a witness in this passage, and the town and its environs are described strictly in order, as the witness leaves the main road, looks down on the whole area from a hill-top, crosses the bridge and surveys the town, and even goes inside the church. His presence is continually emphasized, as usual, by a sprinkling of 'seeing' words. But this description is in no way incorporated with the action, and there are no characters present. The 'witness' knows the area and its history well, and is not above making explicit value comments. The whole description is in the present tense (one of only three or four cases where this happens in Flaubert's mature work), and the 'witness' eventually reveals that he is also the omniscient narrator: 'Depuis les événements que l'on va raconter...' (p. 100).

[1] Gothot-Mersch's suggestion (op. cit., pp. 114, 244) that the *nous* of this scene indicates that Flaubert was recording personal memories does not provide a satisfactory explanation for its survival into the definitive version.

In short, this description is very much in the manner of Balzac, as both Faguet and Thibaudet have pointed out; it is most unusual in the works published by Flaubert. The similarity with Balzac is further emphasized by the implication that Homais's pharmacy and Bournisien's church are reflections of the characters of their respective incumbents (although Flaubert does not actually state this, as Balzac would). Nowhere in Flaubert does the narrator so clearly draw attention to his omniscient position for such a long passage, and nowhere else are there so many value judgements which must clearly be ascribed to the author. The plans give no indication of why Flaubert should have chosen to adopt this straightforward expository method here, in contrast with his more normal manner. Thibaudet's explanation, that there was no need to describe Tostes because the problem was merely posed there, whereas Yonville is the setting for the events which are to resolve it, and therefore has to be described in detail (pp. 98–99), is inadequate for at least two reasons. First, other places in other novels—Carthage, Paris, Nogent, Chavignolles—are equally the décor for the working out of problems, and the background of essential events, but none is described in this manner. Secondly, the description which comes nearest to this one in manner—that of Fontainebleau forest in *l'Education*—cannot be regarded as an essential part of the background for the resolving of the problems posed in that book, or at least not as essential as Paris or Nogent.

Simple exposition of this type seems to represent a less mature stage in the development of Flaubert's technique. The plans show that in several places he originally intended to use this method, but subsequently abandoned it in favour of a more scenic presentation, with exposition more integrated with the action. The earliest notes for the beginning of the book indicate that both Charles and Emma were to be introduced by the simple narrator technique, with the disposal of their antecedents and present situation before any action began. The first plan begins: 'Charles Bovary officier de santé 33 ans quand commence le livre veuf déjà d'une femme plus vieille que lui ...', etc.; and later Flaubert added: 'commencer par son entrée au collège'. Similarly, having sketched

Emma's background, he added this note: 'poser ces antécédens [*sic*] dans le cours des développemens postérieurs . . .'. Flaubert also intended at first to describe Charles's house at Tostes before he married Emma, but later decided to defer this description, presumably because the house was significant mainly as an element of the environment to which Emma objected: by placing it after the marriage he could present it from Emma's point of view. The same applies to their house at Yonville, which was to have been described with the rest of the village at the beginning of Part II. Finally, it was not for some time that Flaubert hit upon the idea to 'commencer par une réunion au Lion d'or' in order to present so many of the inhabitants of Yonville and the mutual attraction between Léon and Emma: all this, too, would have been presented in a simpler, narrative rather than scenic, manner.[1]

If Flaubert's normal development was away from the orthodox narrative method of the Yonville description, this single case is an even greater puzzle. It is true that he uses it to give us an objective picture of the town, and also places himself, as author, on a higher level than what he is describing, thereby setting the tone for the subsequent satire of its inhabitants; but this complicates the question rather than solves it, for he normally uses other methods when he wants to present an objective picture, and the satire would still be perfectly plain without this initial description.

Another important scene which is presented through a witness who is not directly involved is Charles and Emma's wedding. This is a single event, not something which remains true for all time, so that it is described in the imperfect rather than the present; but this change of tense, natural as it is, gives the wedding scene a completely different tone from that of the Yonville description. The narrator frequently gives the impression that he is present as a reporter, or even as one of the guests, for he temporarily forsakes his omniscience: 'Les gamins, vêtus pareillement à leurs papas, *semblaient* incommodés par leurs habits neufs . . . et l'on

---

[1] Pommier et Leleu, op. cit., pp. 3, 7, 9, 40, 56, 61.

voyait à côté d'eux ... quelque grande fillette de quatorze ou seize ans, leur cousine ou leur sœur aînée *sans doute* ...' (p. 36). This effect is heightened by references to 'Mme Bovary mère' and 'M. Bovary père', and by the fact that there is not one value judgement that is not a quotation from one of the guests—not even on the monstrous taste of the wedding cake decoration.

At the same time, this description is clearly the work of someone who is also capable of penetrating the minds and thoughts of anyone he chooses, of knowing that some of the boys were wearing boots for the first time in their lives (this in the very sentence where he also pretends not to know all about them, quoted above), that there were various spectacular mishaps on several different roads as the guests returned home, and so on. The author's attitude in this passage is strangely ambivalent, neither as detached as in the Yonville description, nor as involved as in the class-room scene. Yet the over-all effect of the scene is the same as the others: without forsaking the advantage of immediacy inherent in the witness method, the narrator gives us an objective picture of what is going on. Once again, it would not occur to the reader to doubt the validity of what he is told here.

The beginning of the *Comices* chapter, before Emma and Rodolphe appear, is very similar in tone, except that the narrator never draws attention to his omniscience, and places himself in the position of any villager who was present.[1] The impression that it is just any local, not necessarily Rodolphe and Emma specifically, who is viewing the scene, continues even when, as we noted earlier, the point of view is taken over by the future lovers: throughout the passage the pronouns used are *on* and *vous*, rather than *ils*. This fact has two important consequences. First, it emphasizes that even though the scene is partly from the point of view of these two important characters, it is not to be regarded in the same light as, say, the ball or the opera. What they see here is not greatly influenced by character or mood, since it is not particular to them. As Lubbock puts it,[2] we are

---

[1] See also Faguet's comments on the arrival of M. Lieuvain, op. cit., p. 162.
[2] Lubbock, op. cit., p. 70.

looking as much at the external reality of the scene as at the characters, whereas in the ball scene the effect on the character was much more important. Secondly, because Emma and Rodolphe *do* see the same as what *on* sees, this means that they are part of *on*—the presentation emphasizes that this *is* their environment, that they are no more aloof from it than Homais or Tuvache, in spite of what they may think.

In this passage, then, the narrator, by identifying his point of view with that of everyone present, manages to give the impression that he is describing objectively, even though he is using a witness technique: we have here not one witness, whose views may be open to question, but many witnesses, with the evidence of one corroborating that of the others, as it were. This is a technique which we might call the 'combined point of view', and which seems less subject to the vagaries and errors of a single observer—a principle which becomes extremely important in *Salammbô*.

The tendency of the narrator to identify himself with the point of view of the villagers in scenes such as this has even led one critic to postulate a 'bourgeois narrator', a narrator who is almost a character, who reflects the base, collective mind of the community almost as much as he reflects the superior mind of the author.[1] This is an attractive theory, especially as such a method would increase the possibility of two characteristics dear to Flaubert: irony and impersonality. Irony is possible because, as both Bersani and Ullmann[2] point out, Flaubert can use a mixture of *style indirect libre* and his own style in such a way that he simultaneously presents the mode of thought of the villagers and an implied criticism of this mode of thought. Impersonality is possible because the reader cannot always be sure whether he is being given the author's view or the view of *on*: it is a variation, on a different register, of the constant changing between reveries and reality. And because of this, another sort of irony is possible, at the expense of the reader: for if he accepts as Flaubert's view

[1] Bersani: 'The Narrator and the Bourgeois Community in *Madame Bovary*' in *The French Review*, vol. xxxii, no. 6, May 1959, pp. 527–33.
[2] Ullmann, op. cit., pp. 107–9.

what is merely that of the Homais of this world, then he himself
is 'caught', is partly a Homais himself. Although this is an extra-
literary consideration, Flaubert almost certainly took a perverse
delight in its possibility. It is merely the other side of the idea,
frequently expressed, that his books were intended for an *élite*,
that the bourgeois could take them as he would. It is the basis
of the *Dictionnaire des idées reçues*—and who can honestly deny
that some of the items in that terrifying book seem sensible
enough? It is also the idea expressed in the letter about the possibility of the reader taking seriously the 'poetic' conversation
between Emma and Léon at the inn, and in this letter about
another section of the novel: 'J'ai une tirade de Homais sur
l'éducation des enfants (que j'écris maintenant) et qui, je crois,
pourra faire rire. Mais moi qui la trouve très grotesque, je serai
sans doute fort attrapé, car pour le bourgeois c'est profondément
raisonnable.'[1]

There are several ways in which Flaubert encourages such
confusion, and guarantees the impersonality of most of his narrative passages. The most obvious, his habit of italicizing certain
expressions, or explaining outright that the expression is not his,
as in the sentence, 'Malgré ses airs évaporés (c'était le mot des
bourgeoises d'Yonville) ...' (p. 174), can be misleading, for
Flaubert does not always dissociate himself so clearly from the
opinion of the community. As Ullmann points out,[2] he does this
only in the more extreme cases, where what he records comes
closest to the actual words used by the character concerned. It
does not follow that everything in narrative passages which is
not in italics is the opinion of the author.

In addition, there are at least two different sorts of *on* employed
in the narrative passages, and distinguishing between them is not
always easy. The *on* of descriptive passages like the *Comices*, we
have seen, is a device for increasing the immediacy of the description, while remaining objective. There is also the *on* used in
reporting the content of M. Derozerays's speech at the *Comices*:

M. Derozerays se leva, commençant un autre discours. Le sien, peut-

---

[1] *Cor.*, III, p. 184.   [2] Ullmann, op. cit., pp. 98, 108–9.

être, ne fut point aussi fleuri que celui du Conseiller; mais il se recommandait par un caractère de style plus positif, c'est-à-dire par des connaissances plus spéciales et des considérations plus relevées. Ainsi, l'éloge du gouvernement y tenait moins de place; la religion et l'agriculture en occupaient davantage. On y voyait le rapport de l'une et de l'autre, et comment elles avaient concouru toujours à la civilisation (p. 205).

Or the *on* of the passage describing Canivet's arrival:

On discutait chez l'épicier sur la maladie d'Hippolyte; les boutiques ne vendaient rien, et Mme Tuvache, la femme du maire, ne bougeait pas de sa fenêtre, par l'impatience où elle était de voir venir l'opérateur. ... et l'on apercevait sur l'autre coussin près de lui une vaste boîte, recouverte de basane rouge, dont les trois fermoirs de cuivre brillaient magistralement. .... On disait même à ce propos: 'Ah! M. Canivet, c'est un original!' Et on l'estimait davantage pour cet inébranlable aplomb' (pp. 252–3).

It is very much the sentiments of the village which are given in such passages: the very stupidity of their content prevents them from being associated with Flaubert's opinion, and they could not possibly be regarded as objectively valid. Other passages in similar vein would include the description of Léon's habits and talents on pp. 119–20, which is swarming with *idées reçues*; the scandal about Emma and Léon begun by Mme Tuvache (pp. 127, 138); the periods when Emma temporarily appears virtuous, and is therefore frequented and approved of by *on* (pp. 147, 149, 298–9); the scandal about Emma and Rodolphe (p. 266) (in an earlier version of this passage *on* is actually identified as Mme Tuvache);[1] and, to a certain point, the explanation of the changes which had taken place in Léon since he had left Yonville (p. 319). These are all fairly definite examples of the use of the bourgeois narrator, who, while advancing the action, is simultaneously reflecting the collective sentiment of the village; but in how many other places does Flaubert make statements which he considers bourgeois and stupid, but which do not appear so to the reader? The untrustworthy narrator, who, like the characters, is capable of serving us *idées reçues* in the guise of

[1] Pommier et Leleu, op. cit., p. 424.

solid facts, seems to be the Flaubertian equivalent of the literary smoke-screen which earlier writers—Stendhal, Sterne, Fielding, Defoe—delighted in raising around their personal opinions. The apparent guilelessness with which these authors announce opinions frequently masks, rather than clarifies, their real sentiments. In Flaubert's case, it pays not to forget his dictum: '*On* est un immense sot collectif.'[1]

Such caution will not, however, explain away all the apparent authorial intrusions in *Bovary*. Some sections of the novel are certainly presented by the orthodox omniscient narrator method, and are accompanied by comments which unambiguously orientate the reader's attitude. For instance, although Flaubert partly dramatizes his presentation of Charles's early life, by beginning with a scene, he then reverts to an ordinary expository technique to summarize Charles's boyhood and his parents' background. These passages are tempered very little by the use of the *style indirect libre*.[2] During the 'flash-back' on Emma's life at the convent, too, there are many criticisms of her attitude, both implied and explicit, which could only be the author's. It is a clear case of Flaubert's ignoring his own statements about not intervening. This is probably partly because the book is still at the stage of posing the problems: it would be uneconomical, and would delay the development too much, to present other points of view. The chapter is also a good example of Lubbock's contention that the author always remains a little aloof from his characters, so that he can sometimes be entirely so.[3] These authorial judgements (which in spite of their directness are largely ignored by critics who regard Emma as a dramatic embodiment of Flaubert's personal aspirations) clearly show that Flaubert

---

[1] *Cor.*, XII, p. 146. Mosher, op. cit., pp. 211–13 seems to regard this ambiguity of attitude as a fault, an abdication of the author's responsibility to his reader. I believe I have shown that Flaubert had ample literary and philosophical justification for his method.

[2] Cf. the explanatory passage about the Marquis d'Andervilliers, p. 64, and his reasons for inviting the Bovary to the ball.

[3] For similar comments on this scene, but a very different explanation of Flaubert's motives and subsequent developments, see Bart: 'Aesthetic Distance in *Madame Bovary*' in *PMLA*, vol. 69, 1954, pp. 1112–26.

lavished no more respect or sympathy on his heroine than she deserved, and no more than on other characters:

Ce n'étaient qu'amours, amants, amantes, ... *messieurs* braves commes des lions, doux comme des agneaux, vertueux comme on ne l'est pas, toujours bien mis, et qui pleurent comme des urnes. Pendant six mois, à quinze ans, Emma se graissa donc les mains à cette poussière des vieux cabinets de lecture (p. 51; cf. pp. 52, 53).

It is not sufficient to say that in such passages Flaubert is satirizing the excesses of bad romanticism, and their authors. This is true, but he is being equally critical of the gullibility of Emma, who is incapable of distinguishing between the good and the bad. As Flaubert's notes say, she is 'sans goût artistique, elle est peu artiste mais poétique'.[1]

Author's interventions, to comment or explain, or to generalize from a particular case, occur particularly when the point of view is Emma's and she lets her dreams take over. We see it again after her return from the ball, when she dreams of Paris (p. 81); when her difficulties are compared with the 'vocation arrêtée' of the hairdresser (!) in Tostes (p. 89); when Emma and Léon are returning from the visit to her child, and their developing love makes them tongue-tied (p. 132); when there is a warning, in general metaphorical terms, that this love may cause trouble by being repressed: 'Elle ne savait pas que, sur la terrasse des maisons, la pluie fait des lacs quand les gouttières sont bouchées, et elle fût ainsi demeurée en sa sécurité, lorsqu'elle découvrit subitement une lézarde dans le mur.'[2]

In view of the number of these explicit comments, it may

---

[1] Pommier et Leleu, op. cit., p. 6; 'poétique' here has the special pejorative sense which Flaubert reserved for those of the Romantics—Lamartine and Musset —whom he detested. Cf. the use of the word in the judgement of her religious sentimentality, p. 105, note 1.

[2] p. 139; other examples pp. 17, 19, 22, 92, 116, etc. The last-mentioned, criticizing the spire of Rouen cathedral, is one of the more interesting doubtful cases referred to earlier. This spire, in cast iron, but in pseudo-Gothic style, was added in the nineteenth century. It was the subject of considerable controversy in Rouen, and is also criticized by Maupassant in *Bel-Ami*. It is possible either that Flaubert could not resist adding his own comment, or that the spire represents one of those *scies* which so annoyed him. The fact that the reference occurs in a

seem surprising that until recently critics have seldom stressed that Flaubert's famous 'nul lyrisme, pas de réflexion, personnalité de l'auteur absente'[1] represents a desire rather than a fact. There is always a danger of taking the will for the deed, of looking for the novel in the *Correspondance*. The maxim quoted above was formulated when Flaubert had been working on *Bovary* for less than five months. Early versions, written after this statement, contain a very large number indeed of such interventions. Flaubert did make an immense effort to eliminate them[2]—the very thoroughness of his suppressions shows his determination to find a new technique—but we should not be surprised that some signs of the struggle should remain.

It must be said, too, that listing the authorial interventions of *Bovary* as we have done gives them an emphasis which they do not enjoy within the context of the novel. They are not nearly as frequent as in the works of most third-person novelists, and they are usually very short—often no more than a few words, at most five or six lines. Besides, they are always apposite: not one could be regarded as a digression, nor a case of the author's being wise and ponderous at the expense of a captive reader. It is this which one frequently finds in third-person novels, both before and after Flaubert, and it is doubtless to this habit that he was referring in many of his letters about impersonality. On the whole, the intrusions in *Bovary* do contribute to the over-all technique of presentation.[3] In particular, they help to counterbalance those long passages where the author adopts the point of view of various characters, and emphasize that he does this

---

passage from Léon's point of view, and in a metaphor about Léon's love, would support the latter hypothesis. The comment could then be regarded as Léon's, and a sign of his bourgeois preoccupations.

[1] *Cor.*, II, p. 361. Fairlie, op. cit., pp. 15, 19, is one of the few critics to emphasize these interventions, and in her analysis of characters and motives (passim) indirectly demonstrates how useful they are for an understanding of the novel. Cf. Mosher, op. cit., pp. 173 et seq.

[2] See Gothot-Mersch, op. cit., pp. 261 et seq.

[3] There are some cases of superfluous interventions, which merely reinforce what was already discernible through the point of view presentation. One was mentioned *supra*, p. 101; another is the comment on Emma's 'prostitution' to Rodolphe, p. 425. Cf. Mosher, op. cit., pp. 206–7.

for reasons other than the desire to identify himself with his characters. It is a means of disclaiming personal responsibility for what the characters think and say and do.

Changing the viewpoint

All these different facets of the narrator's position in the novel, combined with the frequently changing points of view, presented a considerable problem of organization, for one of Flaubert's essential aims was unity, and this would naturally include unity of tone. The *Correspondance* shows that transitions, from one idea to another, from one section to another, from psychological analysis to action, caused Flaubert a great deal of difficulty; this is also reflected in the plans, where the order of events and explanations is frequently changed. There is no doubt that he overcame these difficulties, for the reader is seldom aware of the constantly shifting viewpoints, and there is no impression of discordance or discontinuity. It is necessary to look into how he did this, for the methods of merging one point of view into another constitute one of the essential elements of this extremely complicated technique.

Some of the more obvious factors contributing to unity of tone have already been mentioned. First, the ubiquity of the basic witness method tends to disguise the fact that it is put to many different uses. Secondly, Flaubert's personal literary style, while partly adapted to suit the thoughts and speech of individual characters, is basically constant. Thirdly, his habit of diluting his style with quotations from his characters—whether direct or indirect—is also constant: it occurs almost as much in narrative passages as in reveries or 'point of view' descriptions.

These consistent elements help to disguise the fact that frequently the change from one point of view to another is quite sudden. Sometimes such brusque changes are desirable, for they underline sharp contrasts in mood or thought, as when we see Charles and Emma's conflicting dreams of the future (pp. 270–2), or their conflicting thoughts about the *pied-bot* operation.[1]

[1] p. 255; this and other passages quoted by Rousset, op. cit., p. 120.

Similarly, the sudden changes from Charles's point of view to that of Emma's father when Charles is steeling himself to ask for Emma's hand (pp. 31–3) give ironic point to Charles's confusion, because (a) Les Bertaux was not nearly as profitable as he supposed, so that Emma could not have hoped for a better suitor; (b) Emma was not the asset he imagined, so that her father was glad enough to get rid of her; and (c) he had unwittingly made his designs so obvious already that père Rouault was only waiting for the question in order to bestow his consent.

The hand of the narrator is sometimes even more obviously present in the regulation of changes in point of view. Sometimes there occurs a whole series of sudden changes, each point of view being indicated by only a few words, so that the presentation is that of an omniscient narrator, who briefly penetrates the thoughts of several people, but gives prominence to none. It is unnecessary to dwell on the mechanism of these passages, which is obvious enough; but it is noteworthy that they occur most frequently in chapters where the action is to be advanced, where events rather than thoughts and impressions are recorded. They are a means of moving more or less imperceptibly from a static to a dynamic situation, or from one static situation to another. For example, at the end of Part I (pp. 91–4), the rapidly changing points of view lead within three pages from Emma's apparently interminable boredom and frustration in Tostes to hope of a bright new life in Yonville. A similar series, after Emma's visit to Bournisien (pp. 160–3) introduces another decisive change in her situation by very suddenly, and yet naturally and smoothly, removing Léon from the scene at a critical moment. Others occur in chapters relating Emma's decision to run off with Rodolphe and events resulting from this; Charles's financial difficulties and Lheureux's manipulations; Emma's affair with Léon, her successive encounters with Lheureux and her narrow escapes from being discovered; and Emma's actions after her final appeal to Rodolphe.

It is not uncommon for Flaubert to smooth over his changes in point of view by means of an intervening passage of either direct speech or *style indirect libre*. Consider, for example, the section of the ball scene between the dinner and the dancing, when Charles and Emma are dressing (p. 69). Flaubert requires an opportunity to give a physical description of Emma, for which he needs to change from Emma's point of view to Charles's. The transition is achieved by means of a brief conversation. Similarly, when the description is completed:

> Charles vint l'embrasser sur l'épaule.
> — Laisse-moi! dit-elle, tu me chiffonnes.
> On entendit une ritournelle de violon et les sons d'un cor.
> Elle descendit l'escalier, se retenant de courir.

It is the few words pronounced by Emma which brought the point of view back to her, so that we can see the dancing through her eyes.[1]

Frequently, too, this smoothing over is achieved by a simple association of ideas. This is the method studied by Rousset in 'l'Art des modulations'.[2] It is probably the most subtle of the methods employed by Flaubert; but it is very doubtful whether, as Rousset implies, it is the most common one. Nevertheless, examples of it are not difficult to find. When Emma and Charles are first married, we see the house at Tostes through Emma's eyes, and continue to follow her point of view as she meditates changes. One of these changes is to have a carriage (p. 45); it is stated that Charles bought her one, and this simple mention of Charles, as if in passing, brings about a change in the point of view, for the following paragraphs show *his* view of Emma and his new life.

Later, Charles's further reflections on his happiness lead to the statement that he is in good health and that his reputation is well established; and imperceptibly the point of view has changed from Charles's to that of *on* (mixed with a comment from the omniscient narrator) to show that he was highly thought of as a

---

[1] Such brief passages of direct speech are usually significant in several other ways as well, but these do not concern us here. For other examples of this type of transition, see pp. 138 (villagers—Binet—Léon), 230 (Emma—Binet), 175 (Emma—Charles), 325 (Léon—Emma), 336 (Léon—coach driver).

[2] Rousset, op. cit., pp. 117–22.

doctor (pp. 84–5). Continuing this theme, we are told how he subscribed to a medical journal 'pour se tenir au courant', but that he usually fell asleep while reading it; and we suddenly realize that the sight of Charles asleep over his reading has brought us back to Emma's point of view (p. 85). At the beginning of the *Comices* scene the change from the general description to the point of view of Emma and Rodolphe is equally careful. The general description ends with a view of Mme Lefrançois cursing the organizers for setting up a refreshment marquee. Homais, during a conversation with her, sees Emma with Rodolphe, and rushes off to greet them. Rodolphe sees him coming, and his point of view begins (pp. 185–8). Later, the reader follows Rodolphe's point of view as he writes his farewell letter to Emma; having finished it, he places it in the basket of apricots, and orders his servant to take it to Emma. The servant carries the reader with him, from La Huchette to Yonville, for from the moment he arrives at Emma's house her point of view takes over.[1]

In spite of the very large number of these changes, there remains a readily discernible over-all pattern, as both Lubbock and Rousset have pointed out. The book begins with the narrator, who introduces us to Charles, seen externally, as we would see anyone in real life; we then penetrate gradually, through a summary of his background, into Charles's character and consciousness. From there we see Emma—again, at first, as an object; and, largely by means of a summary of *her* background, we penetrate her consciousness. From now on her point of view predominates, until she takes the poison, when the point of view becomes a skilful but extremely complicated mixture of Charles, Homais, the omniscient narrator, and *on*, with the last two gradually taking over. Thus, at the end of Emma's life she is viewed from the outside, as when she was first introduced; and at the end of the book Charles tends to be viewed from the outside, as when he was first introduced: 'On le vit pendant une semaine entrer le soir à l'église' (p. 476); 'On s'étonna de son découragement. ... Alors on prétendit qu'il *s'enfermait pour boire*' (p. 479), and even his death is discovered by Berthe, who, like

[1] p. 283; cf. pp. 47, 119 et seq. (example quoted by Rousset), 134–7, 176–7, 332.

nous at the beginning, plays the part of the uncomprehending witness. But of course Charles is no longer an object for the reader, who, having frequently followed his point of view, can see the discrepancy between what *on* thinks and what the facts are. The result is the same type of dramatic irony as in the scene where Emma goes to Binet.

Interspersed with this irony is that of Homais's triumph. Unlike the other major characters, Homais has always been an 'object', in the sense that he has been presented almost entirely from the outside, with no more than a few sentences from his point of view. Apart from some brief explanations, by the omniscient narrator, of his sometimes questionable motives, his character has been portrayed by simply recording what he said, either directly or in *style indirect libre*. Rousset is probably correct in assuming (p. 113) that Flaubert purposely kept him in this unprivileged position so that he could be used to such effect in the epilogue, in order that the pattern external–internal–external should be complete. It might be added that Homais's unprivileged position is also symbolic, in that for Flaubert people like him *are* objects; it was unnecessary to show his thoughts, because he seldom has any which he does not express. Homais is the only character in the novel for whom Flaubert has apparently no sympathy whatsoever, because he is not a human being, but a symbol. All the others, including Emma, have some bourgeois traits and, in varying degrees, bourgeois leanings; Homais is the pure bourgeois, the embodiment of all the worst aspects of all the other characters. He is not, moreover, a bourgeois only in the social sense. He does not represent a particular class, so much as the total unthinking mass of humanity. He is not a type, as critics have—perhaps uneasily—maintained, but *the* type: he is humanity. This, at least, is what Flaubert intended, as the following note testifies: 'Homais vient de Homo=l'homme'.[1]

If this is the pattern of the changing point of view, then clearly the most important transition in the novel is that from Charles to Emma. Rousset describes the mechanics of this transition,[2]

[1] Pommier et Leleu, op. cit., p. 118.   [2] Rousset, op. cit., pp. 118–19.

but not entirely satisfactorily, and the question is important enough to merit reconsideration. It is true, as Rousset asserts, that up to the first description of the garden at Tostes (p. 44), the reader has never penetrated Emma's thoughts, while by the second, very subjective description (p. 89) he probably knows more about her than he does about Charles. Rousset is also correct in implying that the transition is very gradual, differing in this from most of the less important ones. But in fact, it begins just before the first description of the Tostes garden, which is already from Emma's point of view, even though it is not, like the second one, charged with emotion. It is extremely important to realize that we are first seeing Charles's home through Emma's eyes. If the preceding remarks on Flaubert's descriptions are valid, this one is certainly far more than a 'simple état des lieux, constat objectif des surfaces et des matériaux, tel qu'il peut émaner d'un tiers observateur . . .'.[1]

Rousset's reason for this statement seems to be an assumption that the reader knows nothing about a character until he penetrates that character's consciousness. But, original as he was, Flaubert was not as revolutionary as that. We already know a good deal about Emma, both from her early conversations with Charles, and from passing descriptive statements. We know, for example, that Emma 'ne s'amusait guère à la campagne' (p. 20); that she over-estimates her value and sees only her own side of a situation: compare her statement 'qu'elle était chargée presque à elle seule des soins de la ferme' (p. 20) with Charles's observation of her carefully looked-after fingernails (p. 19), and her father's thoughts on the matter: 'Le père Rouault n'eût pas été fâché qu'on le débarrassât de sa fille, qui ne lui servait guère dans sa maison' (p. 32). We know that she already suffers from the 'étourdissements' which prefigure her nervous illnesses, and that she is sentimental and pretentious (pp. 20, 30–1, 34). By the

[1] Ibid., p. 118. Rousset adds the following note, in support of his argument: '"Un tiers, qui les eût observés, vis-à-vis l'un de l'autre . . ." lit-on dans le brouillon, à ce moment-là.' 'A ce moment-là' has to be interpreted liberally if it is to contain any truth; the sentence does not refer to the *brouillon* description of the garden, as Rousset's note would lead one to believe, but to a later passage dealing with Emma's attitude to sex, entirely suppressed in the definitive version.

time Emma reaches Tostes, she may still be an 'object', but she is quite a familiar one.

In addition to giving a fairly objective—or, at least, non-emotive—picture, the first Tostes description develops and emphasizes some of these traits, and presents some basic differences between Emma and Charles. This is Charles's house, and, in the tradition of Balzac, it is part of Charles and expresses Charles. But it is also Emma looking at Charles, and therefore expresses Emma too. Emma's point of view is implied in the usual ways as she progressively 'discovers' the various parts of the house,[1] and emphasized by the passage about the wedding bouquet:

C'était un bouquet de mariée, le bouquet de l'autre! Elle le regarda. Charles s'en aperçut, il le prit et l'alla porter au grenier, tandis qu'assise dans un fauteuil (on disposait ses affaires autour d'elle) Emma songeait à son bouquet de mariage, qui était emballé dans un carton, et se demandait, en rêvant, ce qu'on en ferait, si par hasard elle venait à mourir (pp. 44–5).

This, coupled with the fact (noted earlier) that Flaubert changed the position of this description, obviously thinking it was more useful here, shows that the passage is certainly not a 'simple état des lieux'. It is important for our knowledge of Charles that he was careless about tidiness and about interior decoration and furnishings, that his taste was doubtful ('un papier jaune serin relevé dans le haut par une guirlande de fleurs pâles'), that almost the only book in the house was a *Dictionnaire des sciences médicales* with the pages uncut, that tact was not his most obvious quality; it is equally important that it is Emma who notices all these things, and not one good one to make up for them. From the moment she steps into Charles's house their troubles have begun: Emma immediately begins to change the house (p. 45), thereby emphasizing their differences, asserting a dominant position, and spending a considerable amount of money.

---

[1] With one small exception: Emma could not know at this stage that she would be able to hear the voices of the patients through the thin walls of Charles's surgery.

If this passage is already from Emma's point of view, we must look further back for the transition. It is achieved, in fact, by means of the whole preceding chapter, which describes the wedding. This, we have seen, is a 'narrator' chapter, and the withdrawal of the point of view from Charles prepares the way for Emma to take over. After the wedding and the couple's departure for Tostes, it is the reminiscences of Emma's father which occupy our attention at first; père Rouault's point of view is also a device for achieving a smooth transition between two important parts of the book, as it will be between Emma's death and funeral.[1] Then quite suddenly (p. 42) we leave père Rouault and transfer to Tostes, where Charles and Emma are just arriving. It is here that the first description of the house occurs.

This is not, however, the end of the matter; for after the description of the house (p. 45) Charles's point of view returns for a few pages, before the 'flash-back' on Emma's early life. This 'reverie' chapter (VI) is definitely from Emma's point of view, as is made clear at both the beginning and the end; it is Emma examining her own past. Yet, as Rousset says, the chapter is also liberally sprinkled with comments making it plain that the *author* has arranged the reverie, and that he is very condescending about it. We have still not reached the stage where Emma's point of view is presented in its pure form for any length of time.

This reverie, however, does lead to another (p. 56), which in turn leads to Emma's growing dissatisfaction with Charles (pp. 57-9); but again her point of view is interrupted by the narrator (pp. 60, 61). Then comes Emma's walk in the country with her dog, and the reverie culminating in her exclamation: 'Pourquoi, mon Dieu, me suis-je mariée?' (p. 62). At this point her dissatisfaction has reached a peak, and discovered a definite object for complaint. The problem has now been posed in the clearest terms, and if the reader has been following closely, he will have seen that there is right and wrong on both sides. It is now safe for

---

[1] For the second occasion, it is explicit in the plans that the change in point of view is introduced specifically to achieve the transition: 'le père Rouault (transition entre la fin des veillées et l'enterrement)' (Pommier et Leleu, op. cit., p. 126). The parallels between the two scenes are thereby reinforced.

Flaubert to concentrate on presenting Emma's side of the picture; the reader has enough information to maintain a correct perspective by using his intelligence. He is now in a position superior to that of any of the characters; having ensured this, Flaubert lets Emma's point of view predominate.

The other means of presentation open to Flaubert is, of course, direct speech. The subject could constitute a separate study; it is mentioned here to emphasize that whatever the advantages of the point of view method and its variations, Flaubert is not a slave to any single technique, but utilizes all the resources available to him. It will be sufficient, then, briefly to summarize a few general principles.

Dialogue is normally restricted to important scenes, when the action of the book, having reached a crucial stage, slows down: the inn scene, Emma's first interview with Lheureux, her first meeting with Rodolphe, the *Comices*, the ride in the woods, and so on.[1] It is also used for satirical purposes when Homais is present, as in the scene with Bournisien by Emma's deathbed. In either case, it introduces or emphasizes character traits: the inn scene provides a perfect example. The procedure is so obvious that it requires little comment,[2] except perhaps to underline how thoroughgoing it is. Among Flaubert's notes for the scene we find: 'Homais se fout un peu de l'exactitude',[3] which in the novel becomes a simple, bland statement (which is irrelevant as well as inaccurate) that the Fahrenheit equivalent of 30°C is 54°. Homais also shows that, like Emma, he has certain literary pretensions, but absolutely no judgement: his 'meilleurs auteurs' are Voltaire, Rousseau, Delille, Walter Scott, and *l'Echo des feuilletons* (pp. 115–16)—the same hotch-potch, in a different field, as Emma's Bernardin de Saint-Pierre, Chateaubriand, keepsakes, *la Corbeille, le Sylphe des salons*, Eugène Sue, Balzac, and George

---

[1] This was a conscious principle of Flaubert's, and in his *Correspondance* he sometimes criticizes other writers for using dialogue apparently on impulse, instead of limiting it to important scenes. See *Cor.*, IV, 291; V, 321; VI, 103; cf. remarks on the first *Education*, supra, p. 67.

[2] See Fairlie, op. cit., pp. 16–17.

[3] Pommier et Leleu, op. cit, p. 60.

Sand.[1] In the same way, Léon and Emma's conversation at the inn is composed of 'petites choses significatives'.[2] Even incidental statements emphasize character, as when Emma is looking for a name for her daughter, and Homais says: 'M. Léon ... s'étonne que vous ne choisissiez Madeleine, *qui est excessivement à la mode maintenant*' (p. 124). The last phrase sums up both Homais and Léon, and puts them on the same side of the fence.

Taken in conjunction with other parts of the book, direct speech contributes a great deal to the unity and the irony. For example it is significant that Emma, Léon, Charles, and Homais all have substantially the same idea of Paris, and that all express it in the form of *idées reçues*: Emma and Léon in reveries, when we are following their respective points of view (pp. 80–2 and 163–4), and Charles and Homais in a conversation (pp. 168–9). In his description of the Bovarys' new house, Homais mentions in passing (p. 114) the door which permits one to leave the house without being seen, remarking how convenient this is for a doctor—not to mention his wife. Mme Lefrançois, in her jealousy of the *Café Français*, darkly predicts that its owner will come to a sticky end (p. 102); Tellier is next mentioned in a seemingly innocent conversation between Emma and Lheureux, during which the merchant speaks of him as if they were great friends (p. 145); then, at the beginning of the *Comices*, in the conversation between Homais and Mme Lefrançois, these two threads are brought together, with the news that Lheureux has brought about Tellier's ruin (pp. 187–8) by the same methods as he will use to ruin Emma; and to emphasize the point, at that very moment they notice Emma and Rodolphe with Lheureux (p. 188). Irony often occurs in statements which are on the surface completely insignificant,

---

[1] pp. 48–52, 80–1. It is important to note that in both cases it *is* a hotch-potch, that neither reads entirely bad literature. Consistently with his dictum on 'synthétisme' which we considered above, Flaubert places the fault not in what they read but in their lack of judgement. If this is not understood, it is easy to misinterpret the novel. Faguet, for example, reads into certain passages a criticism of romantic literature, and Bersani (loc. cit., p. 527) appears to make the same sort of mistake. Digeon, by reaction, seems to go to the other extreme (op. cit., p. 159). For a more balanced view, see Fairlie, op. cit., pp. 29, 63.

[2] Pommier et Leleu, op. cit., p. 61.

as when Charles writes to Rodolphe 'que sa femme était à sa disposition' (p. 218), or to Léon, about his marriage: 'comme ma pauvre femme aurait été heureuse' (p. 471); when Homais, watching Rodolphe and Emma go off riding, says: 'Un malheur arrive si vite! Prenez garde!' and 'Bonne promenade! ... De la prudence, surtout! de la prudence!' (p. 219); or when Lheureux, after Emma's death, says: 'Une si bonne personne! Dire pourtant que je l'ai encore vue samedi dernier dans ma boutique!' (pp. 467–8).

Dialogue in *Bovary* is not realistic, in the sense that it does not attempt to reproduce the speech of real people. Emma's father, for example, does not speak like a Norman peasant of the time—one has only to turn to Maupassant to be assured of that; Léon does not speak like a timid country clerk; and of course Homais speaks like no one who ever lived. Nearly all the characters use certain expressions which are typical of their situation, so that the speech of, say, Bournisien is differentiated from that of Rodolphe; but these identifying elements are incorporated into a good, semi-literary French style, which is that of Flaubert, in a manner very similar to that of the passages of *style indirect libre*. In short, dialogue in *Bovary* represents yet another compromise, best expressed in a letter by Flaubert about 'du dialogue trivial qui soit bien écrit'.[1] This last requirement also fits well with Flaubert's concept of universality: if the dialogue merely reproduced the speech of real people—as does that of Champfleury, for example—it would be (a) partly incomprehensible to a modern reader (a difficulty frequently met in Zola) and (b) dated and particular, without the wider human significance which makes the speech of people like Homais so enjoyable today. This is the difference between Homais and the bourgeois characters of such books as *les Bourgeois de Molinchart* or of *M. Prud'homme*. The latter are simply nineteenth-century French

---

[1] *Cor.*, III, 20; cf. III, 24; IV, 79, 292; and III, 359: 'Quelle difficulté que ce dialogue, quand on veut surtout que le dialogue ait du *caractère*! Peindre par le dialogue et qu'il n'en soit pas moins vif, précis et toujours distingué en restant même banal, cela est monstrueux. ...' See also Thibaudet, op. cit., pp. 274–7; Durry, op. cit., p. 35; Fairlie, op. cit., p. 23; Gothot-Mersch, op. cit., p. 266.

bourgeois, whereas Homais is everywhere about us, albeit in diluted form.[1]

Unity in diversity

Clearly Flaubert's presentation techniques in his first great novel are both numerous and complex. He has by no means abandoned the techniques of the third-person novel, which he inherited from Stendhal and Balzac. He has, however, modified them, especially by drastically reducing the role of the author as a personality or a preacher. Even when he appears to address the reader directly, he is frequently doing no more than expressing the sentiments of *on*, hiding behind his book even when he seems to be coming out in the open.

More important than this, Flaubert was obliged, as a result of his ideas about impersonality, to find a means of presentation which would both minimize the necessity for him to comment openly and also allow him to make his point. He found the basis of this new technique in a method he had been using all his life. This witness method was capable of being extended and modified in such a way that the author could shelter behind his characters and deny all personal responsibility for anything he wrote. He could, in effect, make implicit in his book what many earlier writers made explicit in their Preface: if anything herein offends or angers the reader, it has nothing to do with me, for I am merely reporting actual happenings. He could thus attribute to his characters thoughts, actions, and feelings with complete indifference as to their source, whether personal or otherwise, secure in the knowledge (or so he no doubt believed) that if all were presented as the *characters'* experience, it would be both impossible and irrelevant for readers to distinguish between what he personally admired and what he scorned. This impersonality, this separation between author and characters, is thus achieved simultaneously with the immediacy which one expects from the author who

---

[1] Moreau: *Bovary*, op. cit., pp. 35–6, tends to dismiss Homais as a manifestation of a contemporary literary fashion. He is this; but if he were only this, he would long since have sunk into the oblivion of M. Creton du Coche.

'identifies' himself with his characters. Further, by not limiting this presentation to one character, he can do the same thing many times over, so that several characters will be shown to have this confusing mixture of good and bad, and the author's own opinions will be even more effectively disguised. The changing of points of view will also help to make it clear that all the characters see things as it suits them, according to background or to mood, and not necessarily as they are. Changing the point of view scores a philosophical point without the necessity of a philosophical treatise, reveals the background and the mood of the character concerned, gives at least some objective information about the thing or person being described, and leaves the way open for irony and humour, by the juxtaposition of conflicting points of view—and all without endangering the impersonality of the author.

There are occasions, however, when objective pictures are desirable. In such cases Flaubert rejects his characters as a worthy means of presentation, and takes over himself, as narrator. But even so, he usually smooths over this change by identifying to some extent with an actual witness who was present. The extent of identification varies with the particular case.

Finally, none of the above methods is taken to its logical extreme, and where any of them might interfere with other desirable elements of a work of art, such as style, it is curbed accordingly. Flaubert's art is continually one of compromise, notwithstanding the impression one gains from his correspondence. He uses all the methods, both traditional and personal, which are available to him, and selects the one best suited to his purpose of the moment; but he never allows any one to predominate to the detriment of another. His methods lack the thoroughgoing logic of certain modern works, but, unlike those of, say, Murger, they are never so unspeakably illogical and casual that they alienate the reader. All the pieces are skilfully filed so that they fit perfectly, and welded to present a smooth, polished surface, with no joins visible at normal viewing distance. Perhaps compromise is a desirable step towards a successful work of art. The history of literature suggests that the unbridled theorists, those who have

a 'revolutionary' idea and stick to it, occupy an important
historical place, but that after a time their works are read largely
in anthologies, if at all. What student of French does not bow
before the importance of the *Bataille d'Hernani*, yet how many
have read *Hernani*? Is *Hernani* in fact worth reading?

Madame Bovary has for so long held a leading place in world
literature that one easily forgets it is only a first effort. While
critics were content to fondle it or walk on it, Flaubert saw it as
just a promising beginning. He was anxious to move on to better
things, to develop the techniques he had learnt, and to apply them
to greater ends. After 1857, he quickly outstripped many of his
readers.

IV

SALAMMBÔ

The crowd and objectivity

Quant à la description en elle-même, au point de vue littéraire, je la trouve, moi, très compréhensible, et le drame n'en est pas embarrassé, car Spendius et Mâtho restent au premier plan, on ne les perd pas de vue. Il n'y a point dans mon livre une description isolée, gratuite; toutes *servent* à mes personnages et ont une influence lointaine ou immédiate sur l'action. . . .

J'arrive aux richesses d'Hamilcar. Cette description, quoi que vous disiez, est au second plan. Hamilcar la domine, et je la crois très motivée. La colère du Suffète va en augmentant à mesure qu'il aperçoit les déprédations commises dans sa maison. . . . *Qu'il ne gagne pas à cette visite*, cela m'est bien égal, n'étant point chargé de faire son panégyrique; mais je ne pense pas l'avoir *taillé en charge aux dépens du reste du caractère*. L'homme qui tue plus loin les Mercenaires de la façon que j'ai montrée . . ., est bien le même qui fait falsifier ses marchandises et fouetter à outrance ses esclaves.[1]

THESE important extracts from Flaubert's letter to Sainte-Beuve clearly state his principle of using only integrated or significant descriptions. Whether he was actually successful or not, Flaubert certainly *intended* to present his descriptions in terms of the personality of his characters and the over-all development of the novels, not solely because he enjoyed writing them. It is particularly important that he should make this point in terms of *Salammbô*, the very novel which seems to contain the greatest proportion of descriptions for their own sake. Again, this letter to Sainte-Beuve, like the *Préface aux Dernières Chansons*, is worthy of more credence than the general run of the *Correspondance*, for Flaubert was aware that Sainte-Beuve intended to publish it.[2]

[1] *Cor.*, V, 60–1, 63. [2] See Sainte-Beuve, op. cit., pp. 243, 250.

Intentions, however, are not as important as results. This letter puts us on the track of a continuing point of view technique: it does not establish its existence, which can be determined only in the novel itself.

Salammbô appears to differ from *Bovary* in the original motivation, the basic starting-point. As far as one can judge, the original idea of *Bovary* was the story of Emma's life,[1] whereas Flaubert seems to have viewed *Salammbô* first of all as an exposition of another world, a society before an individual. The first mention of it in the *Correspondance* speaks of 'un travail archéologique':[2] Flaubert is obliged, by the very nature of his new subject, and in particular by the lack of documentation about individual figures, to think first in terms of the milieu. To create an Emma Bovary, he had only to think like a nineteenth-century Frenchman, and to look about him; he had already done most of the 'archaeological' work by living. For *Salammbô*, he was obliged to deduce his characters and their attitudes and therefore thoroughly to learn all the possible influencing factors first.

Deducing credible characters—credible, that is, in terms of both their specific milieu and of humanity as a whole—with only archaeological data to guide him, gave Flaubert considerable trouble in the early stages.[3] But his main problem was one of presentation: the characters also had to *look* satisfactory to a reader ignorant of Carthaginian archaeology. This means including within the novel sufficient archaeological detail to justify his contention that Salammbô or Hamilcar or Mâtho were indeed what he claims they were. Now the presentation technique most frequently used in *Bovary* is eminently suitable for showing an external reality which is not necessarily authentic, but often a reflection of the characters' deformed view; the emphasis is on the character, rather than the thing described. It was unnecessary to describe Charles's house in detail, because readers could easily form their own mental picture. By contrast, a detailed presentation of Salammbô's palace is vital, because in addition to mould-

---

[1] See in particular Gothot-Mersch, op. cit., pp. 89–90.
[2] *Cor.*, IV, 164.
[3] *Cor.*, IV, 240–1; cf. IV, 175, 200, 212, 216, 243, 244, 245.

ing and reflecting her character, it is completely new to the reader, who could not understand her character, and that of her race, without this help. Detailed objective descriptions are essential in *Salammbô*.

In addition, *Salammbô* is clearly a less complicated novel than *Bovary*, as regards attitudes and motives of the characters. It is more schematic, dealing with large-scale conflicts on a number of relatively clear-cut issues: Carthage against Barbarians, Moloch against Tanit, Africa against man, and so on.[1] Human life and human struggles seemed to Flaubert to have the vastness and the fierceness of the country itself, and individualism among ordinary people appeared almost non-existent. Such an impression was strengthened by the Bible, and also by Latin and Greek writers on Africa: apart from a few leaders, one sees unfriendly hordes rather than people. Whether this generalization is valid or not, it did constitute an important part of the atmosphere of the country, which Flaubert wanted to depict. Besides, exotic countries and peoples have always seemed like this to the European, no doubt because he does not really know them: witness the 'epic' film of more recent times. Large crowds acting in concert, continually in turmoil, continually meeting head-on, are an inevitable part of the work.

But there is no evidence that Flaubert had altered his basic attitude to the novel or to humanity; nor is there anything to suggest that Salammbô and her contemporaries were any less likely than Emma to be mistaken about their role in life simply because they lived in more exotic surroundings. To some extent, then, the method of subjective presentation, with its suggestion of providing something less than the truth, will remain suitable. We might therefore expect, *a priori*, to find in *Salammbô* a method which is basically similar to that of *Bovary*, but with such modifications and changes of emphasis as are dictated by the nature of the subject.

It is not difficult to show that many descriptions in *Salammbô*

---

[1] Some of these are developed by Bertrand, op. cit., pp. 58–62, and mentioned by Flaubert in his letter to Sainte-Beuve, *Cor.*, V, 58 (about Salammbô herself), 64.

contain the elements found in earlier works, and which have already been sufficiently emphasized. An outstanding example is the description of Hannon as he comes to pay off the Mercenaries (or so they believe):

Un soir, à l'heure du souper, on entendit des sons lourds et fêlés qui se rapprochaient, et au loin, quelque chose de rouge apparut dans les ondulations du terrain.

C'était une grande litière de pourpre, ornée aux angles par des bouquets de plumes d'autruche. Des chaînes de cristal, avec des guirlandes de perles, battaient sur sa tenture fermée. Des chameaux la suivaient en faisant sonner la grosse cloche suspendue à leur poitrail, et l'on apercevait autour d'eux des cavaliers ayant une armure en écailles d'or depuis les talons jusqu'aux épaules.

Ils s'arrêtèrent à trois cents pas du camp, pour retirer des étuis, qu'ils portaient en croupe, leur bouclier rond, leur large glaive et leur casque à la béotienne. Quelques-uns restèrent avec les chameaux, les autres se remirent en marche. Enfin les enseignes de la République parurent, c'est-à-dire des bâtons de bois bleu, terminés par des têtes de cheval ou des pommes de pin. Les Barbares se levèrent tous, en applaudissant; les femmes se précipitaient vers les gardes de la Légion et leur baisaient les pieds (p. 43).

And so on for two more pages. The sequence is exactly that observed by the Barbarians: 'quelque chose de rouge' becomes a richly ornamented litter, escorted by soldiers; the emblems of Carthage appear; they see 'une main grasse, chargée de bagues' and hear 'une voix rauque'. At length the curtains open and the assembled soldiers see 'une tête humaine', which they recognize as Hannon's. When he gets out of the litter he is described.

The parallel between this appearance of Hannon and that of the *Conseiller de Préfecture* at the *Comices* is very striking, even though it is in a different key. In both cases the assembled multitude turns its collective attention to the visiting dignitary from the time his conveyance is first visible until he himself can be seen and described. In both cases the point of view is a collective one; and in both cases Flaubert utilizes this fact to present a description which is more complete and objective than would be the case if a single person, who might have emotional reasons for distorting the description, were viewing the scene. This does not, of course, preclude the possibility of emotive notations, for Flaubert, in common with other writers celebrated for their crowd scenes—Shakespeare, Zola, Conrad—regarded the human crowd as given to collective emotions, especially of the baser sort. M. Lieuvain represents an authority to which all Yonvillais gladly submit, so that the collective sentiment is that he showed 'l'apparence des plus bénignes'; Hannon represents an authority heartily detested by all the Mercenaries, and is also hated and distrusted as a person, so it is his ugly disease which is emphasized. In addition, while both descriptions are from a collective point of view, both include that of certain important characters, thereby linking them symbolically with the crowd: Spendius and Mâtho are as much Mercenaries—barbarians—as Rodolphe and Emma are Yonvillais—bourgeois—because they share the collective emotions.

Significant differences between the two scenes result from the differences in subject-matter discussed above. In *Bovary*, it was sufficient to mention 'un grand landau de louage, traîné par deux chevaux maigres, que fouettait à tour de bras un cocher en chapeau blanc' (p. 194). Since this was normal, no one would notice further details; and it was ample to give the contemporary French reader the desired picture of the typically tarnished glory of the provincial authority. But the trappings of an official representative of Carthage, unknown to this same reader, had to be set out in full. The excuse for this is that for the Mercenaries such riches are not normal. They would all be avidly taking in the smallest manifestation of this immense wealth: they are looking at it as envious strangers, so that their point of view is eminently suitable for recording the details which a European reader would need to know. But within the context of the novel such detail is significant in another way. As the Mercenaries believe that Hannon is coming to pay them, the trappings increase their hopes: it is obvious that Carthage can well afford to pay. They also emphasize the hollowness of Hannon's hypocritical speech, and (aided by Spendius' wilful mistranslation) convince the soldiers that they have been duped, and exacerbate their desire

for revenge. Hence although the emotive significance of the
Hannon passage is not explicitly emphasized much more than
that of the Lieuvain description, it is more important to the
development of the novel; and this is doubtless because the Yonville crowd is merely part of the background of Emma's personal
struggle, whereas the barbarian crowd is one of the chief 'characters' of the struggle of *Salammbô*. In this scene Flaubert has adapted
his 'combined point of view': while still using it for objective
description, he manages in addition to give it real emotive significance, even though it is largely devoid of emotive expressions.
This new technique is of great importance in *Salammbô*.

Since the riches of Carthage have been mentioned, let us examine the opening pages of the novel. Again the witness technique
is obvious, and again the witnesses are the Barbarians. The usual
'signpost' expressions are common throughout the first twelve
pages, until the appearance of Salammbô. Again the fact that the
Barbarians are foreigners, unaccustomed to such festivities,
motivates the detailed description of the opulence of the surroundings and of the fare: one is reminded of Emma, a stranger
to the wealth of La Vaubyessard, and therefore deeply impressed
by it, dwelling upon the delights of the table there. And just as
La Vaubyessard influences Emma's behaviour, so do the riches
of Carthage cause the Barbarians to act according to their character: envy, cruelty, rapacity, fear, and mistrust are all brought
out. Almost everything said about Carthage contains one of two
concepts which are relevant to the Barbarians' situation: plenty
or danger. Even Hamilcar's palace shows an 'opulence farouche'
(p. 2).

It is interesting that Flaubert changed his method of presentation
in this first chapter of *Salammbô*, as he had in several passages of
Bovary. His original version—the one written before he went
to Africa—is more academic in tone, and begins 'at the beginning'
by describing the site of Carthage, and how the town occupied
that site:

Carthage, bâtie sur une haute péninsule, était bordée à l'est, du côté
de la Cyrénaïque, par un golfe entouré de montagnes. Au nord, du
côté de la Sicile, la pleine mer battait sa falaise blanche, et au sud et à

l'ouest, le lac de Tunis et le golfe d'Utique échancraient l'isthme étroit qui la reliait à la terre ferme. Ainsi posée au milieu des ondes, elle tournait le dos à la mer avec l'insolente sécurité d'un maître, tandis qu'elle regardait l'Afrique tout en face et, allongeant vers elle son bras de terre, semblait la tenir attachée.[1]

The last sentence is a definite attempt to influence the reader: as with Balzac, the emotional situation is being established before any action begins, before the setting comes to life. The second paragraph of this version begins with a comparison with Athens and Alexandria, and continues by introducing the classic hypothetical traveller, whose eyes are then used to advance the description. Just as with *Bovary*, Flaubert later decided that the beginning was not after all the best place to start, and that the sense of immediacy (and hence the reader's interest), as well as an appearance of impersonality, could be increased by opening with a scene, by using the eyes of interested, instead of hypothetical witnesses, and by setting the emotional scene and introducing characters against a background of action rather than of description. Predictably, his refurbished description of Carthage in the definitive version (pp. 67-9) is presented from the point of view of the angry Mercenary army who have come to attack. The description now has an emotional and psychological significance, as well as a factual one: 'Ce spectacle de Carthage irritait les Barbares. Ils l'admiraient, ils l'exécraient, ils auraient voulu tout à la fois l'anéantir et l'habiter'. Its site and its defences are now recorded because they present military problems to the attacking armies. The description is now an integral part of the novel.

Similar principles operate when a group of Mercenaries decides to explore the grounds of Hamilcar's palace (pp. 11-12). The garden is described progressively and fairly objectively, until they come upon vessels containing strange moving objects, which are presented in an impressionistic and mysterious manner: 'et des lueurs rougeâtres emplissaient confusément ces globes creux comme d'énormes prunelles qui palpiteraient encore'. Again the stranger's eye is being used: those things he recognizes, like the garden, are straightforward; those things he does not recognize

[1] *Salammbô*, Conard edition, Notes, pp. 470-1.

are left vague, and emphasize the menacing strangeness that is inherent in the Barbarians' idea of Carthage. These awesome 'lueurs rougeâtres' may be nothing more than the reflections of the soldiers' torches, mentioned in the following line, but since this does not occur to the soldiers it is not explained to the reader. Similarly, when they eat the sacred fish, we know that we are still following their point of view, because of the statement about the origin of these fish: 'Tous descendaient de ces lottes primordiales qui avaient fait éclore l'œuf mystique où se cachait la Déesse' (p. 12). The Mercenaries, having fought with the Carthaginians, having seen the power of Carthage and therefore of the Carthaginian gods, would never question this belief, even though it is part of a foreign religion. They eat the fish not to show contempt for an alien religion, but through mere drunken bravado. Since they believe they are committing sacrilege,[1] their act will have a real influence on them. This is a principle of great importance in the development of the novel, and we shall return to it later. Suffice it to point out here that swift retribution followed, for the group who originally discovered the fish were the first to be massacred, and this did not go unnoticed by the Barbarian army (see p. 51). Again the point of view technique establishes the emotional and psychological situation.

The appearance of Salammbô provides another example. The Barbarians' attention is fixed upon her, but she is too far away for them to see what she looks like (and, besides, the light is behind her): they can only see that she is 'couverte de vêtements noirs' (p. 13). With the Mercenaries, the reader watches her slowly descend the steps. It is not until she is actually among the soldiers that she is described; and the description is introduced by the appropriate 'signpost' words:

> ... et elle marchait lentement entre les tables des capitaines, qui se reculaient un peu en la regardant passer.
> Sa chevelure, poudrée d'un sable violet, et réunie en forme de tour selon la mode des vierges chananéennes, la faisait paraître plus grande. Des tresses de perles attachées à ses tempes descendaient jusqu'aux

---

[1] p. 12; cf. p. 390.

coins de sa bouche, rose comme une grenade entr'ouverte. Il y avait sur sa poitrine un assemblage de pierres lumineuses, imitant par leur bigarrure les écailles d'une murène. Ses bras, garnis de diamants, sortaient nus de sa tunique sans manches, étoilée de fleurs rouges sur un fond tout noir. Elle portait entre les chevilles une chaînette d'or pour régler sa marche, et son grand manteau de pourpre sombre, taillé dans une étoffe inconnue, traînait derrière elle, faisant à chacun de ses pas comme une large vague qui la suivait. . . .

Personne encore ne la connaissait. On savait seulement qu'elle vivait retirée dans les pratiques pieuses. Des soldats l'avaient aperçue la nuit, sur le haut de son palais, à genoux devant les étoiles, entre les tourbillons des cassolettes allumées. C'était la lune qui l'avait rendue si pâle, et quelque chose des dieux l'enveloppait comme une vapeur subtile. Ses prunelles semblaient regarder tout au loin, au delà des espaces terrestres (p. 14).

Several relevant points can be made. Now that Salammbô is close to them the soldiers realize that her clothes are not completely black, as they had thought. Because they are foreigners, her cloak is said to be made of 'une étoffe inconnue'. Since there is a large number of them, we have a combined point of view, so that the description, as far as it goes, can be assumed to be objective, and therefore also informs the reader of the sort of clothes a rich Carthaginian princess would wear. But since this is a particular group of foreigners, with one or two dominating collective passions, the description is not complete. Her personal attributes are barely mentioned, because, as we are told a little later (p. 15), the soldiers 's'ébahissaient de sa parure': they are interested in the wealth of Carthage, and Salammbô is covered in it. Apart from the brief mention of her mouth, they notice only her pallor, which they ascribe to her association with the gods. As with the fish, this explanation is stated as a fact, so that Salammbô finds herself honoured, solely by the point of view technique, with a mysterious power which will not be broken until she succumbs to the very human realities of Mâtho's tent. This first description of the heroine is entirely conditioned by the situation and the psychological state of those who are looking at her. For the Barbarians, she is a living symbol of Carthage, of its wealth which inspires envy and avarice, of its gods which inspire mysterious fear; and thus she appears to the reader.

The importance of the collective point of view in this first chapter of *Salammbô* indicates the extent of Flaubert's modifications to his technique. Although statistical methods rarely seem to 'prove' much about literary works, it is inescapable that this combined technique is used to a significantly greater extent than any other point of view. It occupies more than 200 of the total of 414 pages, while the point of view of Hamilcar (the next most important, largely because of the long chapter describing his return to Carthage), is found for just over forty pages, and Salammbô herself, Mâtho, Spendius, and the ordinary third-person narrator account for only about 35–40 pages each. Dividing the book into such clear-cut categories is of course quite artificial, and can serve only as a starting-point. In practice, when the collective point of view of the Barbarians is used, this often includes the point of view of Mâtho as an individual; similarly, the point of view of Carthage sometimes includes that of Salammbô. Nevertheless the distribution of the various techniques of presentation makes this novel noticeably different in tone from *Bovary*. It almost certainly accounts for much of the 'epic' effect of the novel. This last has often been ascribed to Flaubert's style and vocabulary, doubtless following statements by Sainte-Beuve and Gautier. But the style of *Salammbô* is not really an epic style, in the sense that, say, Virgil's or Milton's style is epic. It is actually very simple and restrained, a factual style.[1] There are relatively few long sentences, and those that are long are made so by lists of peoples, of machines, of actions, of weapons: their basic structure remains very straightforward. Although the cumulative effect of lists of, for example, the warriors and peoples taking part in a battle, is itself one of the stylistic devices of the great epics, this alone is insufficient. There are no complex, high-sounding metaphors or similes—nothing, for example, to equal

---

[1] See Thibaudet's comments on the 'style historique' (op. cit., pp. 143–4). While Thibaudet grants the characters of *Salammbô* 'une réalité épique', he never describes the style in these terms.

the 'steppes of Russia' metaphor of *Madame Bovary*. The descriptions of such epic accessories as the machines of war contain no reference to any possible fellow-feeling between them and their operators, no suggestion of personification, no trace of any special powers or other virtues—on the contrary, the painful inefficiency of these monstrous inventions is continually being underlined. The descriptions of these machines are sometimes difficult to understand, but they remain technical and factual, and there is an obvious attempt to simplify, for the modern reader, the confusing array of heavy weapons: 'Sous la variété infinie de leurs appellations (qui changèrent plusieurs fois dans le cours des siècles), elles pouvaient se réduire à deux systèmes: les unes agissant comme des frondes, les autres comme des arcs' (p. 304). The vocabulary is certainly exotic, but this is not necessarily an epic quality: in this case, it is merely giving the everyday names to objects and actions which, if strange to us, were perfectly ordinary to the people concerned. There is little attempt to make dress, habits, or speech larger than life: they are merely indicative of what life was. This is shown by the fact that in general it is only nouns which have an exotic flavour; verbs, adjectives, and adverbs are seldom very startling, nor are they used in ways which depart from the normal habits and structure of nineteenth-century literary French. Besides, epics glorify great heroes, tend to make them superhuman, so that they can either fight with reasonable success against supernatural forces, or actively be aided by these forces. *Salammbô* performs the reverse function: it reduces both superhuman and supernatural forces to strictly human terms—and terms of base, degraded humanity into the bargain.

Yet *Salammbô* does develop on a massive scale, in spite of the oppressive smallness of most of the individuals portrayed. In this very restricted sense, the novel can be said to be epic, and the effect is achieved by using such a large proportion of the book to show great numbers of people acting and thinking and feeling in unison, as if they shared but one small mind. The combined point of view technique serves both to express and to symbolize Flaubert's conception of the struggles of Africa.

The principles of the combined point of view, and in particular that of using a group of interested (as opposed to impartial) strangers to combine detailed but relatively objective descriptions with psychological involvement, are applied in most of the passages which stress archaeological or historical information. In other words, background information on Carthage is provided through the Barbarian point of view, and on the Barbarians through the Carthaginian point of view. As an extension of the same principle, since each Barbarian tribe or nation is relatively strange to the others, the Barbarian point of view is also used to point out the distinguishing characteristics of one group, as seen by the others. For example, the Carthaginian point of view is used to show us the Barbarian army leaving Carthage (pp. 26–9), the *Mangeurs de choses immondes* (pp. 71–2), the Barbarian camp (pp. 72 et seq.),[1] the Barbarians' battering-rams (pp. 307–8) the main part of the siege of Carthage (pp. 320–6), and the awesome *hélépole* (pp. 329–31). The Barbarian point of view shows us Hamilcar's palace in the first chapter, the countryside surrounding Carthage (which is an aspect of Carthaginian wealth and dominion, pp. 30 et seq.), the priestesses of Sicca (pp. 35–6), the arrival of Hannon (pp. 43–5) and the forced opening of his baggage (pp. 52–53), Carthage itself when they return to attack it (pp. 67–9), the arrival of Hannon's army and the ensuing battle (pp. 127–30), Hamilcar's army and the beginning of that battle (pp. 198–203),[2]

---

[1] Maynial, op. cit., p. 119, says: 'Au lieu de s'échapper aussitôt, s'étant donnée à Mâtho, Salammbô demeurait quelques jours sous la tente, et l'auteur profitait de l'occasion, — il le dit, — pour décrire le camp et les mœurs des mercenaires.' Apart from showing that Flaubert did indeed intend to use the point of view of his characters, and not the omniscient method, to describe the milieu of this book, this fact supports our present argument. The camp is not described through Salammbô's eyes in the definitive version, except in an impressionistic, symbolic manner (see *infra*, p. 222). Flaubert must have realized that he could not use Salammbô to give an objective, 'archaeological' picture, that for this he would have to use another method.

[2] The Barbarians' point of view is here reinforced by that of the people of Utique, who, being on the ramparts, have a better view. As the battle degenerates into confusion, the point of view, no doubt purposely reflecting this, ceases to be restricted to the Barbarians and oscillates rapidly from one side of the battle-field to the other.

and some at least of the Carthaginian defensive tactics during the last great battle (pp. 308–10).

The sacrifice to Moloch (pp. 341–51) may at first appear to be an exception: although it is partly intended to give background information about Carthage, the point of view is obviously that of the Carthaginians themselves. However, there is no real contradiction here, for this extraordinary manifestation of Carthaginian religion is not like, say, the palace of Hamilcar, which is before the people of the city every day, and which they may be expected to take for granted. Such sacrifices occur only in cases of extremity, for normally Moloch stays locked in his temple: 'on ne pouvait contempler impunément le Baal que dans l'exercice de sa colère' (p. 341). A ceremony centred round a normally hidden god is as unusual and as fearful for the Carthaginian populace as it is for us. Like Emma at La Vaubyessard or the Opera, they can realistically be astonished at some aspects of their own culture, and are therefore suitable witnesses, likely to notice enough to provide a detailed account for the European reader. Besides, for purely practical reasons, Flaubert was forced in this case either to use the point of view of the Carthaginians, or to fall back on the convention of the third-person narrator. The Barbarians are outside the city, and kept there by its defenders. They cannot know what is going on in Carthage, until, attracted by the noise and the flames, and realizing that for the moment they are not being watched, they climb up to a vantage point in time for the last stages of the holocaust (p. 351). Similarly, when the Mercenaries have been defeated and Carthage is celebrating the final victory, the Carthaginian point of view must again be utilized to present the festivities (pp. 404–8).

One may well ask whether the consistent use of such a technique is really worthwhile, in that, like other techniques, it simultaneously solves some difficulties and raises others of perhaps equal importance. The greatest advantages of the way point of view was used in *Bovary* were the opportunities for impressionistic description, for conciseness and subtlety, by suggesting, without having to state, a non-correspondence between the character's views and reality; for impersonality, by allowing the author to

shelter behind his characters' thoughts without being forced to
reveal his own; and for a measure of psychological verisimilitude,
by penetrating the thoughts of only one character at a time,
thereby imitating, within limits, the processes by which in real
life each individual gains knowledge of other people and of the
external world. The last of these advantages is automatically
cancelled by the combined point of view technique: if, as some
contemporary writers contend, it is 'unrealistic' for an author
to enter the mind of more than one character in any one book,
how much more so is it to penetrate those of a large number of
people simultaneously! The other advantages, too, are reduced,
in that it is primarily objectivity, and not implied subjectivity
which Flaubert is seeking in these passages—he is using his witness
technique for an effect opposed to that for which it is most suited.
Would it not have been simpler, and just as valid, to drop all
pretence of a witness and revert to the time-honoured convention of the omniscient narrator? After all, Flaubert is not entirely
opposed to this traditional convention. Besides, with several of
the normal effects of the point of view technique stripped away,
many of the passages referred to above are already similar in tone
to that of ordinary narration.

Against all this must be placed the fact that the witness technique
was by now so much a part of Flaubert's manner, with its roots
in his earliest attempts at creative writing, that he would be unlikely to abandon it unless it had no use whatsoever. This is not
quite the case in the passages under discussion, for the technique
still serves to create some illusion of authenticity. Flaubert prefers
not to say to his readers: 'You may believe me if you will, but
this, according to the books I have consulted, is what Carthage
looked like.' He would rather say: 'Those who were present saw
these details, so obviously they are authentic.' Logically, the two
statements are of equal validity, but for the reader interested in
the characters and the action (both of which he is predisposed to
accept for the moment as 'true'), as well as in the décor, the
second has a better chance of success. In addition, the combined
point of view is also frequently used, as we shall see, to present a
collective subjectivity, not very different in kind from the in-

dividual subjectivity of an Emma Bovary. The question of unity of tone therefore enters the argument: the technique *must* be used in certain parts of the book, so that it becomes desirable to use it also in those parts where it may not otherwise be essential.

Collective subjectivity

Some examples of the collective subjectivity achieved through the combined point of view technique have already been given, but this is such an important aspect of *Salammbô* that more are called for. In the first place, even in those passages in which Flaubert's main requirement was historical information, the emotive element is seldom entirely absent. This has been sufficiently demonstrated for Hannon's meeting with the Mercenaries, and for the opening scene of the feast. These scenes are typical: in every one of the examples cited above as giving objective information, one can also see psychological motivation for presenting the description at the precise moment it occurs.

In addition to such passages, there are many which are intended *primarily* to tell us about the emotions or the psychology of the character groups. In these, there is still a fairly large proportion of description, and archaeological information is still included; but the description tends to be of actions rather than of objects, while the archaeological information bears on habits and modes of thought, and is mentioned in passing rather than being given prominence. These changes are reflected in a change of the point of view: it is no longer that of the enemy. In passages intended primarily to show the psychology of Carthage, the point of view is usually that of the Carthaginians themselves, and similarly for the Barbarians. This is natural enough: people do not notice what they take for granted, but pay great attention to things which affect them closely. For the physical surroundings of Carthage, the Barbarian point of view is best suited; for the emotions and reactions of Carthage, it is their own which is called for.

Consider first some Carthaginian passages of this type. After the battle of the Macar, Hamilcar sends his prisoners back to

Carthage as a sort of deposit, with the promise that more will come. The scene at Carthage is a 'délire de joie', and Flaubert goes on to demonstrate this (pp. 214–16). There is some use of *style indirect libre* to show that we are closely following the sentiments of the populace: 'les autres ne tiendraient pas, la guerre était finie' (p. 214); 'La sanction des dieux n'y manqua pas; car de tous les côtés du ciel des corbeaux s'abattirent' (p. 216). Passing references to Carthaginian customs serve a similar purpose: 'l'on frotta de beurre et de cinnamome la figure des Dieux Patæques pour les remercier. ... ils semblaient vivre sous leur peinture plus fraîche et participer à l'allégresse du peuple'. 'Les servantes de la Déesse ... se prostituaient.' 'On vota ... des holocaustes pour Melharth, trois cents couronnes d'or pour le Suffète.' In fact, it is precisely by notations of this sort that Flaubert paints the joy, and, later in the passage, the extreme cruelty, of the Carthaginians. The emotions are suggested indirectly, by external manifestations, and are not actually described at all. Indeed, it is difficult to see how else it could be done. Given that Flaubert is trying to present a collective emotion, he cannot penetrate the minds of a series of people one after the other, as he did in several parts of *Bovary*. If he did so, he would obviously find a great diversity of ways of looking at this national joy, different emphases and different motives and different sentiments. To present all this would make the people of Carthage a series of individuals, while the point is that they have divested themselves of their individuality and are acting as a mob. The combined point of view, then, remains relatively externalized even in those areas where it comes closest to showing emotions directly. To this extent it is less intimate than the method employed in *Bovary*, and tends to preclude the possibility of the reader 'identifying' himself with the characters.[1] But this externalizing does not alter the fact that we are dealing with emotions, so that however they are presented, their validity is open to question on the same

[1] This is not necessarily a bad thing, although when people make this statement about a book, they usually imply a shortcoming. In fact, the more a reader 'identifies' himself the less critically he reads, and the less likely he is to do justice to his own intelligence and that of the author.

grounds as those of Emma. They represent a temporary and unstable state of mind, involving a suspension of clear thought and a deformation of the real nature of things. When the immediate cause of the emotion disappears, the emotion itself vanishes, and with them the false interpretation of the facts. Unfortunately, for the Carthaginian populace as for Emma Bovary, when one emotion disappears it is usually replaced by another, so that a different, but equally false, interpretation of reality takes over. Thus, some twenty pages after the passage just cited, when Hamilcar has suffered a temporary reverse in fortunes, the 'délire de joie' is replaced by a 'délire funèbre'. This passage (pp. 229–32) relies even more heavily than the previous one on *style indirect libre*. Phrases like 'on s'était cependant imposé d'assez lourds sacrifices!' are strongly reminiscent of the tone of some of Emma's musings, such as 'par quelle déplorable manie avoir ainsi abîmé son existence en sacrifices continuels?' The only difference is the externalization already referred to: while Emma's rhetorical question is in her mind, that of the Carthaginians is being bandied about from person to person, part of the general discussion of the problem facing them all. It represents the same basic unwillingness to look at facts, and also contains the same latent irony: in both cases past 'sacrifices' have been relatively unimportant and largely imagined, while real hardships for both are still to come.

Flaubert, we must repeat, regarded this unwillingness coolly to examine reality—to 'voir les choses comme elles sont'—as a social disease, resulting in a variety of other social diseases, and almost all his characters show symptoms of it. In the present case, it is responsible for the gradual degeneration of morale into something approaching panic and hysteria. The initial reaction of anger and hate is itself determined not so much by Hamilcar's defeat (although this is the only reason the populace will admit and therefore the only one explicitly given to the reader) as by the fact that right from the beginning Hamilcar, like other rich and powerful people, was feared and disliked (cf. p. 6), and he was recalled only when the Republic was already in dire difficulty (p. 136). Besides, it was sheer bad luck that Hamilcar's army had

been surrounded: the Mercenaries themselves had been
surprised (p. 222). The defeat could not rationally be regarded
as Hamilcar's fault—or even, as events subsequently proved, as
a defeat at all. Moreover, he would never have been forced into
this awkward position had the city sent the help he needed when
he had asked for it (p. 220). And in terms of sacrifice, if anyone
was suffering, it was Hamilcar and his troops rather than those
in relative comfort at Carthage (cf. the horrible descriptions
which emphasize this point, pp. 225-9). One could go on in this
manner, finding reasons to justify Hamilcar's position. Once
again, it is part of the depth of Flaubert's works that apparently
clear-cut issues—clear-cut because they are presented from one
limited point of view—are in fact very complex. The point is
that in the emotion of the moment, those who believe themselves
wronged become progressively less willing to consider such
matters. This does not relieve the reader of the responsibility of
considering them, if he will not be as limited as the people of
Carthage or Emma Bovary, but would prefer to try to keep up
with their creator. To this end, it is important to notice how the
passage in question opens: 'Carthage avait comme bondi de
colère et de haine'. This is a warning that what follows is true,
in that it is an accurate report of what people felt and said, but
that it is also false, in that these feelings and sayings are justified
only in the 'mind' of Carthage. Thence we follow the progressive deformation of reality, from a relatively cool appraisal of
the necessity of finding and arming reinforcements, through
recriminations about Hamilcar, regret for the 'sacrifice', and
turning against innocent groups, to the inevitable rationalization
that it was all a punishment from the gods for Hamilcar's 'sacrilege' (which here, as so often in the history of Christianity, is a
sanctimonious term for a less complete orthodoxy than the
avaricious priests would have liked). Only at this point is a real
difficulty introduced: the increasing heat and the developing
water shortage. This naturally serves to heighten the emotions
already present—they do not know that this water shortage is
as nothing beside the one they will eventually have to face—and
the whole city gives itself up to superstition, to groundless panic

alternating with lifeless dejection. Then, since their prayers are
not answered, comes the rising up against the unco-operative
goddess concerned. Finally, a scapegoat is necessary and as neither
Tanit nor Hamilcar is readily available for kicking, the collective
hate turns to the one person who is intimately connected with
both malefactors, and who has the additional qualification of
inability to fight back: Salammbô. Considered in isolation, this
whole passage is an admirable exposition of mob psychology,
of the unreasoned mobility of a group of people in difficulty;
but when it is compared with those showing the much greater
difficulties of the Carthaginian soldiers, and the equally unreasoned delight of these same people at the beginning of the
chapter, it takes on an extra significance of grim irony. As in
Bovary, Flaubert achieves this significance with no explanations
and no commentary. He simply presents the relevant point of
view, and leaves it to the reader to draw the conclusions and
make the comparisons.

These two passages give us the essential of the Carthaginian
character and of Flaubert's method of showing it. Subsequent
treatment of this gruesome people amplifies and diversifies, but
does not change the information to be gleaned here. The same
method of presentation is used on pp. 314–15 and pp. 320–3, to
show the now very real difficulties of the city blockaded by the
Barbarians, with the shortage of food, the heat which deformed
and putrefied the corpses, the agitation and the resulting violence,
and again the jeering at the gods (a reaction fairly common
among Flaubert's characters—e.g. Charles, Emma, Mme Aubain
—as is its reverse, equally ridiculous in Flaubert's eyes, of returning to one's gods when they do something to please their adherents
—Emma and Mme Arnoux, as well as the Carthaginian mob).
We also see their 'nourritures immondes' (they are not thinking
for the moment about their condemnation of the Garamantes,
but Flaubert certainly wanted his reader to do so), the eating of
the sacred beasts (by the people who had tried to have Hamilcar
condemned for sacrilege), the jealousies and selfishness, the
mutilations caused by the Barbarians' catapults, fired indiscriminately over the city, the plague, also caused by the Barbarians,

and even the obsessive commercial spirit of the Carthaginians, which prevents them from using the hair of slaves they hoped to sell later, even to save their own lives. Again, on pp. 341–51 we watch the progressive hysteria engendered by the sacrifice to Moloch, and on pp. 352–3 the 'resultant' rainfall. The irony inherent in the changing attitudes to the gods in these passages will not of course escape us. Finally, in the last chapter, the cruel, hysterical joy returns, with the gods again in favour. But here, too, is yet more mocking irony, additional to that gained by comparing this passage with the previous ones: as Levin points out,[1] the reader is aware that the Carthaginian victory is after all only temporary, for Rome is to be the real winner. The setting sun of Moloch has more than an immediate application to the story of Mâtho and Salammbô.

Against the unflattering portraits of Carthage, we must place those of the Barbarians. The best example is the 'Défilé de la Hache' episode: nowhere in the book is the collective technique under discussion more in evidence (pp. 357–69). The tone of collective subjectivity is set some time before the Barbarians are trapped, by the description (which recalls that of the approaching camels in the *Notes de voyage*[2]) of the harrying techniques employed by Narr'Havas:

Souvent, aux heures les plus lourdes, quand on avançait par les plaines en sommeillant sous le poids des armes, tout à coup une grosse ligne de poussière montait à l'horizon: des galops accouraient, et du sein d'un nuage plein de prunelles flamboyantes, une pluie de dards se précipitait (p. 357).

The description of the trap itself continues the Barbarian point of view: 'ils surprirent un corps de vélites; l'armée entière était certainement devant ceux-là, car on entendait un bruit de pas avec des clairons. ... [Needless to say, the deduction recorded here by means of *style indirect libre* is quite wrong, for the Carthaginian army is behind them.] On aperçut un homme en manteau

[1] Levin: *The Gates of Horn. A Study of Five French Realists* (New York, Oxford University Press, 1963), p. 282.
[2] See *supra*, p. 52.

rouge, c'était le Suffète.' (Even brief, simple statements like this reflect the point of view technique—they first see a man, then they recognize him.) Our realization that it *is* a trap comes only with that of the Mercenaries. After their first inspection of their prison, and the initial despairing reaction of the weaker and less rational, there occur two sentences which, we are now in a position to realize, have a wider application than to their immediate context: 'Quand le découragement se fut un peu calmé, on examina ce qu'il y avait de vivres . . . les estomacs étant remplis, les pensées furent moins lugubres'. The first returns us to the favourite theme of emotions taking precedence over intelligence. Like the Carthaginians, these barbarians sit down and think only after lives have been wasted. The second is a direct statement of what had been implicit in the presentation of the Carthaginian character: the 'facts' change with incidental circumstances.[1] By itself, this sentence does not demonstrate any world-shattering insight on Flaubert's part; it gains importance by being read in the wider context of the whole work, and indeed of all Flaubert's work. It is a signpost sentence, pointing to one of the possible interpretations of *Salammbô*: in spite of surface differences between Barbarians and Carthaginians, they share basic weaknesses which both unite them, and bring them uncomfortably near to ourselves.

Parallels between the Barbarians and the Carthaginians are in any case obvious, even though Flaubert, true to his desire for impersonality, does not draw attention to them. It is not long before the trapped army is cursing Mâtho and other leaders (p. 362), just as Hamilcar was cursed by his own people; and with the mobility we have already seen in the Carthaginians, this fact does not prevent, a few pages later, a complete change of attitude: 'D'ailleurs, Mâtho, qui était un brave, ne les abandonnerait pas. "Ce sera pour demain!" se disaient-ils.'[2] Those who have food

---

[1] Cf. the remarks on Henry's attitude to Mme Renaud, in the first *Education*, *supra*, pp. 73–6. The concept is a psychological platitude, but none the less true for that.

[2] p. 365; the *style indirect libre* here permits Flaubert to dissociate himself from this fickleness.

carefully avoid sharing it, as do the Carthaginian priests with
their secret supply of sacred horse-meat (compare pp. 320 and
362). Soon, on the example of the Garamantes, they are eating
those who have died; and although the Carthaginians do not go
quite as far as cannibalism, the eating of the sacred horses of
Eschmoûn must be at least as heinous a crime: again the two
sides are distressingly alike. Similarly, although the Carthaginians
do not actually eat their prisoners (compare pp. 215–16 and 364),
they did slowly torture them to death just for fun, and on a
previous occasion they had come very close to vengeful cannibalism (see p. 51). Finally, the Barbarians, too, come to hate and
despise their gods (pp. 365–6).

It is unnecessary to pursue the point in greater detail. Whether
the Barbarians are in distress (other passages of this kind are on
pp. 278–83, 313), or whether they are celebrating, they are controlled by a few basic emotions, unfettered by intelligent thought,
and always accompanied by brutality: Flaubert believed that
unreasoning humans—most humans—are something less than
human. We can now see a good reason for what first strikes one
as a monotonous repetition of situations and scenes, a repetition
which, incidentally, worried Flaubert long before it worried any
critics.[1] He wanted to give a complete picture, by showing that
whatever the imagined differences between these two groups,
both were at bottom equal. Because of his chosen doctrine of
not intervening, such a project involved so arranging his book
that each side would meet a series of situations analogous to
those experienced by the other. Since each has to face several
different situations, Flaubert can show the inconsistency and
irrationality with which each reacts; and since both have to face
a similar series, he can show the consistency with which people
react inconsistently and irrationally. The result is more complex
than what is suggested by a first reading: an exotic story, following a strictly chronological development, with bloodthirsty embellishments. Moreover, Flaubert, with his taste for irony, is not
content to stop here. He also shows each side self-righteously
disapproving of the behaviour of the other! We have already

[1] *Cor.*, IV, 287, 392, 406, etc.

noted the Carthaginian revulsion about the 'choses immondes'
which the Garamantes ate, and seen that both they and the
Mercenaries can be at least as revolting in their diet (compare pp.
71–2, 228, 320, 363). Already on p. 51—before they spoke so
slightingly of the Garamantes, and before there was any food
shortage—the Carthaginians had taken bites out of Mercenary
corpses hung up in the city's butcher shops. Similarly, the Mercenaries are indignant at the 'injustice' (p. 53) shown by the
Carthaginians in torturing and mutilating those who had been
left behind, and are horrified at the sight of the sacrifice to
Moloch (p. 351), Zarxas' treatment of a Carthaginian corpse
(p. 227), and the Carthaginian habit of crucifying lions (pp. 34–5).
On the other hand, the Carthaginians are exasperated at the
Barbarians' 'injustice' (p. 76), aghast at their treatment of Giscon
(pp. 226, 288), and fearful of their ferocity when Hamilcar forces
them to fight among themselves (p. 377). Such apparently minor
points are of the order of Emma's criticism of Charles for carrying a knife or for not taking an interest in reading, and, like these,
help build up the over-all irony and the author's implicit criticism. Their success depends on the reader's ability constantly to
establish cross-references. Of course, admitting that this was
Flaubert's intention will not remove the monotony if it is really
there; but in practice the novel seems less monotonous if the
'repetitions' are seen as echoes, intended to guide the reader
and to achieve that balanced structural unity to which Flaubert
gave such importance.

A most important point about the passages we have been discussing is that they are the ones which most easily escape from
the chains of milieu and moment, and which can make some
claim to having universal significance. They show us people not
only as products of a particular environment, but also as Flaubert
could still find them today—at a Hitler meeting, a football match,
an anti-nuclear demonstration, a coronation, a mass pilgrimage
or an underground railway station. The base crowd instincts
appear in any emergency, or what appears to be one. The particular manifestations of the instincts will vary with environment
—a frightened group of underground passengers is unlikely to

crucify a ticket-collector, or a football crowd to barbecue even the most unpopular umpire—but morally all are alike. When one considers that the Barbarians, who so closely resemble their enemies, are not a homogeneous group, but represent countries as far apart as France and central Africa, it is clear that this is one of the novel's most important moral comments. Levin's claim (p. 282) that 'Flaubert's sympathies are plainly with the Barbarians', does not adequately translate the significance of these parallels. It is true that they 'hold out with incredible bravery until they are betrayed by the bad faith of the Carthaginians'; but it is equally true that the Carthaginians are betrayed by the bad faith of the Barbarians, and that the Carthaginians are equally capable of bravery and stoicism under adversity and cruelty (cf. their sacrificing of almost all their remaining water during the Barbarian siege, and Giscon's attitude in captivity). As always, a closer reading will reveal that Flaubert's sympathies are plainly with no one. Levin comes closer to the truth when he speaks of the Carthaginian civilization as an 'institutionalized barbarism': this is the message of *Salammbô*, as indeed it is in large measure the message of *l'Education*: we are all Barbarians, and we need only the opportunity to demonstrate it.

Salammbô is not, then, merely an oriental orgy, a series of flamboyant incidents allowing Flaubert to wallow in sadism. It may well be, as Sainte-Beuve hinted and Mario Praz emphasizes,[1] that a writer must necessarily have sadistic tendencies in order to commit such a story to paper. This, however, is not really important. Flaubert was at least content to dream and write about such atrocities, while so many of his contemporaries, not to mention our own, practised them.

The narrator

We must now examine the position of the third-person narrator in *Salammbô*, since the combined point of view technique, especially when it is used to provide archaeological information,

[1] Praz: *The Romantic Agony* (London, Oxford University Press, 1933), pp. 161–162.

is sometimes not much different in tone from ordinary narration. Indeed, a decision about which of the two methods is being used may on occasions appear a little arbitrary, so carefully have the transitions been achieved.

The combined point of view technique can be said to be present when two conditions are fulfilled: the witnesses must be an important group of characters who are present at the scene, and the things reported or described must be limited to what these witnesses are capable of observing or knowing. With the narrator technique (for example, in the wedding scene of *Bovary*) these two conditions will not apply consistently. In the passages of *Salammbô* referred to so far, they apply for page after page— but not, it must be admitted, with absolute consistency. However, since inconsistencies are relatively infrequent and usually brief, I have left them out of consideration when calculating the importance of the combined point of view technique, and have ascribed to the narrator only passages of some length and importance, which, because of their content, could not possibly be assumed to be the observations or thoughts of witnesses. This is as accurate a division as can be expected: obviously we cannot pretend to establish any sort of scale, ranging from totally consistent application of the conditions mentioned above, through to 'total inconsistency', and decide on an exact point (50 per cent consistency?) at which the omniscient narrator ceases and combined point of view begins. That Flaubert should occasionally mix the two techniques is not surprising: already in *Bovary* his guiding principle was to use whatever method was most suitable to his purpose. 'Point of view' passages do contain extra information to help the reader, but only when it is *necessary*, rather than merely desirable. Such interpolations are far less frequent than in most other third-person novels. In the first chapter of *Salammbô*, for example, the only statements which are necessarily those of the narrator are the opening sentence; a few lines during the exposition of the reasons for the banquet, in which the words of the ruling council of Carthage are indirectly reported (p. 6); half a paragraph explaining the significance of the 'coupes de la Légion sacrée' (p. 8); and five lines explaining how Narr'Havas happened to be present at the banquet (p. 17). In addition, the passage in which Salammbô sings shows that although the reader is closely following the point of view of the soldiers, his knowledge of the situation is more extensive than theirs. Her lament is introduced as being part of their experience (p. 14: 'ils l'entendirent murmurer:'); yet we are twice told that they cannot understand what she is saying, even though the reader can. On the other hand, it is interesting to note that Flaubert has provided *some* witnesses who can understand Salammbô's words: the priests who accompany her. He has thus made it possible, by twisting the technique somewhat, for the reader to be simultaneously equal to and superior to the important witnesses. But to do this, he must, of course, introduce one or two short explanations, and therefore the narrator also briefly enters the picture.[1]

Very brief narrator interpolations of this sort are to be found scattered throughout the book,[2] but they have little importance for the over-all technique: in all, they would total only about five pages. Certain chapters do, however, rely on the narrator to a much greater extent, and these need closer attention.

Chapter VI (pp. 111–37) provides some excellent examples of the interweaving of different modes of presentation, including that of the narrator. When Narr'Havas comes to offer himself as an ally of the Barbarians, the point of view begins with Mâtho and Spendius (p. 112), but quickly changes to a more general, combined one for the swearing of the alliance (p. 113). We are then told of Mâtho's reception when he returned with the veil, in a paragraph which, while bringing the reader up to date, also introduces the narrator, so that he can proceed, immediately after the Mercenary chiefs' council of war results in the despatch of messengers to the peoples under Carthaginian domination, to an explanation of the relationship between Carthage and her tributary nations (pp. 114–15). The reader is then miraculously

---

[1] Cf. Hannon's speech to the Mercenaries, pp. 45–8.

[2] There are at least twenty of them, ranging in length from a line to a paragraph or two. Some of the longer ones are to be found on pp. 140–1, 233, 273–4, 385.

transferred to the messengers' various destinations (p. 115), so the point of view is again disturbed, this time by the sudden disruption in both time and place. With the end of this paragraph we return to the preparations of Spendius and Mâtho, then briefly to Carthage, back to the Barbarians, and again to political commentary (p. 116). This time, however, the political commentary is much more closely linked with a Barbarian discussion of strategy, and is certainly presented from their point of view.

An interesting fact about this apparently confused section is that the point of view eventually returns to its original starting-point—a conference between Mâtho, Spendius, and Narr'Havas. It is obviously not the same council, for too much has taken place in the interim; yet this return, combined with the fact that in the intervening pages, too, traces of their point of view are to be found, helps to smooth over the complex detours and commentaries. The process is similar to that which is sometimes found in transitional passages in *Bovary*. When he has to present details which do not form an important part of the action, but which lead up to an important development, Flaubert adopts the convention of the omniscient narrator in order to summarize; but he usually finds some means of making this summary relatively unobtrusive.

A second problem of transitions presents itself in this novel, for Flaubert has undertaken to show two sides of a struggle. Whether through a desire to be just or a desire for balance, he must continually transfer from the point of view of the Barbarians to that of the Carthaginians. In the chapter under discussion, he does it by another expedient already found in *Bovary*.[1] The Barbarian army has decided to move from the plains before Carthage, and the Carthaginians are naturally watching with great interest. The reader suddenly finds himself on the ramparts watching them watching, and instead of seeing the Barbarian army from within, now begins to see it from afar: 'La stupéfaction fut grande quand on vit l'armée se mouvoir tout à coup . . .' (p. 117). By the time their departure has been described for a paragraph, the transfer of point of view has been painlessly

---

[1] See *supra*, p. 141.

effected, and the reader is left behind in Carthage. But he does not retain the Carthaginian point of view for long, for the purpose of his being left behind is to provide him with an explanation of the city's political economy. By the middle of the following paragraph the narrator has dropped his disguise and ventured one of his rare statements of open criticism: 'Le génie politique manquait à Carthage', which he elaborates in no less forthright terms. This criticism is tempered somewhat by the inclusion of a sentence or two of *style indirect libre* (pp. 117–18), as if to suggest the continuing Carthaginian point of view; but the lucidity and conciseness of the exposition leave no doubt that this can only be the work of one with a view much broader and much less involved than that of any Carthaginian. This is the longest and most important passage so far in which the third-person narrator method occurs, and deserves closer scrutiny. One's first reaction is to ask why these facts about the internal organization of Carthage were not incorporated into a collective point of view passage, as are most other historical details. It could not, surely, be solely because Flaubert wanted to voice his criticism: this would be too far removed from his normal attitude. The subject matter of the passage suggests a reason. Collective point of view passages normally develop from things directly perceived by the senses, whereas this one deals in concepts and modes of thought. The theoretical organization of government is not something directly experienced by ordinary people, who normally see no further than simple day-to-day manifestations of it. Only the Carthaginian ruling classes would be able to formulate such generalized statements, and even they—like the corresponding classes in our own society—are too concerned with everyday questions to be much worried by first principles. (An illustration of this is to be seen in the meeting of the ruling council in the following chapter: both Hamilcar and his opponents take their position so much for granted that it would not occur to them to explain it or to trace its historical development.) Plainly, then, this sort of information cannot easily be forced into the point of view mould.

Once the narrator has performed his necessary function, he

again retires into the background as quickly and as unobtrusively as possible. Having explained the Syssites and described their meeting-place, Flaubert turns to their habits, and the general Carthaginian point of view begins to return: the first hint is a reference to the Carthaginian measurement of time: 'trois fois par lune', and soon we are told that 'd'en bas on les apercevait...' (p. 119). By the beginning of the next paragraph the technique by which the explanatory digression was begun has been re-established: 'Mais à présent ils ne pouvaient dissimuler leurs inquiétudes, ils étaient trop pâles;...', etc.

A similar situation—the need for an explanation from someone more competent and perspicacious than any of the characters— forces the narrator to intervene again later in the same chapter, to explain the Barbarians' attitudes towards religious beliefs (pp. 125–6). This brief interruption, again managed quite naturally and smoothly, is introduced by conversation between Mâtho and Spendius about the gods. It is tempered by *style indirect libre*, quickly returns to Spendius' personal beliefs and superstitions, and is finally passed over in favour of a description of Spendius' preparations for the siege of Utique. In addition, this short passage itself serves to disguise yet another transition: before the conversation the reader was with Mâtho before Hippo-Zaryte; at the end of it he has been unwittingly transferred to Utique with Spendius.[1]

Chapter III ('Salammbô'), which is a special case, must be considered separately. It opens with a description of Carthage by moonlight, containing most of the normal Flaubertian elements, including indications of a witness. In addition, whoever is contemplating the scene is clearly familiar with the topography of Carthage and its environs. But in fact there are no characters present at this moment, and there is no indication of where the

---

[1] The narrator intrudes (usually with similar precautions), on at least half a dozen other occasions. The most important are on pp. 354–7 (another transitional passage, between the sacrifice to Moloch and the Barbarians' being trapped in the *Défilé*) and p. 400 (half a page to tell the reader what had been happening in the *Défilé*, in preparation for the Carthaginian messenger to 'witness' the grisly scene). Others are on pp. 207–8, 295–6, 332, 376.

vantage-point is, except that subsequently Salammbô comes up on to the terrace of her palace. It would have been a simple matter to postpone this decription for a page or two, in order to utilize her point of view: the mood of the description is quite in keeping with her emotional state.[1] As it is, the description is only a setting of the stage, a preliminary creating of atmosphere. In this it resembles the first presentation of Yonville, except that there Flaubert usually limits himself to details which anyone could see at any time, whereas the Carthage description is very much a 'mood' piece, emphasizing effects of light and shade at the precise moment of the rising of the moon over the water; and this temporary aspect is reinforced by the use of the imperfect, rather than the present tense of the Yonville description. This is the only important description of *Salammbô* which is not clearly attached to any witnessing character. Possibly Flaubert decided that this was a better way to introduce the chapter than by beginning with the appearance of Salammbô, or perhaps he felt that if he had inserted it later it would have interrupted the flow of religious fervour to which the chapter is largely devoted. Neither of these explanations is very satisfactory, for it is not difficult to find passages where he does the reverse with no ill effects.

When Salammbô begins her devotions, the point of view seems at first to be that of her slave Taanach, conveniently introduced to serve as a 'reflector' for recording Salammbô's actions (as she does later, when Salammbô dances with the serpent). But there is also a physical description of Taanach (p. 57), and a brief explanation of one of her actions, which she herself would hardly think of formulating; and later in the chapter there are comments on Salammbô's upbringing (pp. 61–2), on Hamilcar's ambitions for her, and on the relationship of her personal religion to the national one. All of this suggests that the point of view is neither Salammbô's nor Taanach's, that most of the chapter, including the introductory description, is the work of an omniscient nar-

---

[1] Cf. p. 58: 'Ses yeux, un instant, parcoururent l'horizon, puis ils s'abaissèrent sur la ville endormie. . . .' Salammbô does actually look down over Carthage, but the city is not described at all at this point.

rator. Yet in spite of his apparent superiority over the characters, this narrator does not entirely separate himself from local superstitions. The following passage illustrates the purely Carthaginian nature of his 'facts':

Une influence était descendue de la lune sur la vierge; quand l'astre allait en diminuant, Salammbô s'affaiblissait. Languissante toute la journée, elle se ranimait le soir. Pendant une éclipse, elle avait manqué mourir.

Mais la Rabbet jalouse se vengeait de cette virginité soustraite à ses sacrifices, et elle tourmentait Salammbô d'obsessions d'autant plus fortes qu'elles étaient vagues, épandues dans cette croyance et avivées par elle (p. 61).

In fact, this passage, combined with the narrator's obvious familiarity with Carthage in the opening description, tempts one to postulate a Carthaginian narrator, parallel to the bourgeois narrator of *Bovary*: a storehouse of *idées reçues* which are ancient and exotic, but none the less *idées reçues* for that. Such a concept would not be beyond Flaubert, and there is some further evidence of it in his treatment of religion, as we shall see later. It is also apparent in the explanation about the Garamantes (pp. 71–2), who were hated by the Carthaginians 'à cause de leurs nourritures immondes'. Such a statement is not far removed, in spirit, from bourgeois statements from the *Dictionnaire des idées reçues* such as 'Cuisine de restaurant: toujours échauffante. — bourgeoise: toujours saine. — du Midi, trop épicée ou toute à l'huile.' This is particularly so because their moral indignation does not prevent the Carthaginians from tasting even more exotic dishes themselves, just as Homais's disapproval of restaurant cooking does not prevent him from enjoying it on occasions.

Whether the narrator is Carthaginian or not, the important point for the moment is that much of this chapter is presented by the narrator rather than the witness technique. For once the reason seems fairly obvious. This is largely an 'archaeological' chapter, in that it serves to give the reader details of Carthaginian religious rites. We would therefore expect the collective point of view, which, however, is manifestly impossible in this case: no witness, other than Salammbô's private slave, could reasonably

be present at her devotions, and Taanach is barred from knowledge of religious doctrine because of her race (p. 63). Taanach
is suitable as a reflector for Salammbô's dress, appearance, and
actions (and her point of view is used for these details, both here
and in the snake scene), but she could not know how Salammbô's
version of moon-worship differed from that of other Carthaginians, nor the psychological reasons for such differences.

But again Flaubert takes care that the narrator is not too much
to the fore. For much of the time he simply reports Salammbô's
words, and later those of Schahabarim. The reader can see for
himself that although both are speaking of the same religion,
Salammbô concentrates on the special relationship between Tanit
and humanity, notably herself, while the priest, more theological,
ranges from the principle of creation to a diversity of gods, of
which Tanit is one. A parallel with an over-all view of Christianity
from Genesis to the Resurrection, as opposed to the restrictive
adoration of the Virgin Mary, or some other isolated aspect,
was no doubt intended. Salammbô shows an affinity with other
important Flaubertian characters, and reflects her creator's
interest in personal versions of religion tending to degrade and
invalidate the original concept.[1] Direct speech in this chapter
allows Flaubert to tell us a great deal about Carthaginian religion
and Salammbô's character without the help of his usual witness,
while still keeping the narrator's intervention to a strict minimum.

The only other important cases where Flaubert drops the point
of view in favour of the omniscient narrator are in scenes of
battles and troop movements. This is particularly true of the
great Battle of the Macar (pp. 199–206), to which brief reference
has already been made. At first the reader is with the Barbarians,
whose view of the advancing Carthaginians permits a description
of the latter's equipment and tactics. This point of view continues for as long as the Mercenary army forms a single integrated

---

[1] e.g. in St. Antony's asceticism and Félicité's concept of the Holy Ghost, as
well as Mme Arnoux's belief that the illness of her child was a warning from God
not to sleep with Frédéric. It is often found in *Madame Bovary*—see, for example,
pp. 49, 154, 298.

mass; with the progress of the fighting, there ceases to be *a* Barbarian point of view. By this time the reader has been skilfully transferred to a better vantage-point[1] so that he continues to see the battle as a whole, to distinguish also what is going on in isolated sections of the battlefield, and to follow Hamilcar's strategy and motives as well as those of the Barbarians (pp. 204–6). The reader's knowledge is much greater than that of either side.

A similar situation is to be found in the last great battle (pp. 394–9); and in certain other passages, in particular pp. 222–5 (where Hamilcar's army is surrounded by the Barbarians) and pp. 290–3 (where the two armies are competing for a favourable military position, and both trying to seduce Utique and Hippo-Zaryte), the point of view oscillates so rapidly from one side to the other that the over-all result is not very different from the battle scenes.

There is probably some significance in this handling of the point of view in such passages. For most of the book, the two sides are firmly kept apart, at least on the surface. Even when they get within 'seeing' distance of each other, they remain two separate cultural entities, with no apparent points of contact. The continual changing back and forth of the point of view reflects this separateness. But we have already noted that this same changing of point of view also serves to suggest real similarities of basic attitudes which underlie the surface distinctions; and the two sides are most alike in their less savoury characteristics. Their sharing of a common point of view only in battle completes the picture: it is in cruelty and murder that they are really identical. Once again, the choice of point of view reflects the moral significance of the novel.

To summarize, then, we can say that the narrator method is used in *Salammbô* to present objective facts, to provide explanations, or to introduce explicit criticism of characters or society, just as it was in *Bovary*. However, explicit criticism plays an even

---

[1] Gautier had already made reference to a 'témoin oculaire' in speaking of Flaubert's handling of battle scenes. See Pléiade edition of Flaubert's works, vol. I, p. 735.

smaller part in Flaubert's second novel, and, although he had to provide many more objective facts, he had developed another, better method for this—the combined point of view. The result is that the narrator method is less important here than in *Bovary*, in spite of appearances, and in spite of *Salammbô*'s being the sort of novel where one would expect the reverse: it is now used only when other methods are completely impracticable.

The double point of view

The combined point of view is sometimes used for objective description when only two characters, instead of the more usual crowds, are present. This represents an intermediate stage between the collective technique, and the individual point of view to which we shall turn later. The method has its own advantages, the foremost of which is flexibility. Two witnesses are as suitable as a larger number for preventing misrepresentation of the facts, providing the two used are sufficiently different in character and preoccupations; on the other hand the author can, without obviously disrupting the flow of the narrative, also penetrate the thoughts of one or both before a given situation, thus individualizing them in a way which was impossible with large crowds. The method is not used very frequently in *Salammbô*, but when it is, its advantages are fully brought out. Each time the first requirement, that the two witnesses should be basically different, is met, and on most occasions there is a mixture of objective description and internal reflections which emphasizes these differences.

The first occurrence of this technique (pp. 20–5) is of particular importance, for it provides our first extended view of Spendius and Mâtho as individuals, as well as showing the beginnings of their alliance and their respective attitudes towards Carthage. In describing the sunrise over the city, Flaubert simultaneously shows its effect on both the protagonists, with all that this entails for the development of the action. Spendius, motivated by avarice, lechery, and a desire for revenge, but recognizing his weakness and Mâtho's strength, is the tempter, while Mâtho, already believing that: 'la malédiction de Moloch pèse sur moi' will have his behaviour determined by the (obviously symbolic) flight of Salammbô.

The sunrise passage is, indeed, quite remarkable in its symbolism.[1] There is first the obvious parallel with the end of the book where the sun sets on Mâtho's death, as it is now rising on his strength and vigour. Secondly, we are shown Spendius, who is bent on using his new-found liberty in serving Mâtho, reacting with religious fervour to the rising of the sun: this is the first in a long series of parallels between Mâtho and Moloch. The metaphors and similes of the descriptions simultaneously reflect the preoccupations of both Mâtho and Spendius, and the situation and fate of Carthage. The mere fact that they are looking down on the city—dominating it as Emma dominated Yonville when she went riding in the woods with Rodolphe—is one reflection of this. But Spendius' chief aims are revenge, money, and women, and the water tanks are compared with 'boucliers d'argent', there is a 'pluie d'or', the bows of the ships 'étincelaient', there were camels loaded with merchandise, money-changers in the streets, people gathering gold in the very sand, storehouses overflowing with sacks of grain, peacocks in the cedars, courtesans in full business. The argument for an attack seems conclusive. But other, more sinister omens are also present: the 'pluie d'or' is part of an over-all 'rougeur épandue, car le dieu (the sun, Moloch-Mâtho), comme se déchirant, versait à pleins rayons sur Carthage la pluie d'or de ses veines', and the roof of Khamon 'paraissait tout en flammes' (cf. p. 399, where Mâtho, brought back to Carthage after his capture, opens his eyes: 'Il y avait tant de lumières sur les maisons que la ville paraissait tout en flammes'); they see not only the courtesans, but also that 'les fourneaux pour cuire les cercueils d'argile commençaient à fumer'; the sun is certainly shining on the Mercenaries' swords, but the

---

[1] For a different approach to this passage—its development from Flaubert's *Notes de Voyages* and his personal experience of a sunrise over Tunis—see Bart, op. cit., pp. 43–7, and Appendix B, pp. 58–60. Bart does, however, stress that the final description includes only details which have psychological or structural relevance to the book, and notes how purely decorative elements were omitted.

Mercenaries are in no condition to use them, and are already surrounded by death and devastation:

> Les soldats ivres ronflaient la bouche ouverte à côté des cadavres; et ceux qui ne dormaient pas baissaient leur tête, éblouis par le jour. Le sol piétiné disparaissait sous des flaques rouges. Les éléphants balançaient entre les pieux de leurs parcs leurs trompes sanglantes.

There are valuable trees like cedars, but many have already been destroyed. There are great quantities of grain, but much of it has already been wantonly wasted. And above all, the one thing which could make Mâtho want to attack—Salammbô—is well on the way to Utique.

The next, very brief, occurrence of the double point of view of Mâtho and Spendius expands this symbolism, and also introduces a contrast with the Carthaginian point of view (p. 32). The Mercenary army has been persuaded to move away from Carthage (the two protagonists are temporarily escaping their destiny) and they are marching by moonlight (i.e. Tanit—gentleness, in contrast with the last scene). 'Au loin, des troupeaux réveillés bêlaient, et quelque chose d'une douceur infinie semblait s'abattre sur la terre.' This peaceful state is partly conditioned by the heroes' pride and security in the never-ending procession of their soldiers—the same sight which had so recently caused the Carthaginians terror, and no small relief at their departure (pp. 27–9). But of course the tranquillity is very brief, for it is not long before both men return to their normal preoccupations: for Spendius 'Des espoirs de vengeance, revenus, le transportaient', and 'Mâtho était retombé dans sa tristesse'.

Mâtho and Spendius' clandestine entry into Carthage and their stealing of the sacred veil (pp. 86–102) is by far the most extensive example of the double point of view, which is carefully adhered to from the moment the two men begin to climb the aqueduct. As in the scenes where the Barbarian point of view is used to describe Carthaginian civilization, the passage limits itself mostly to facts, to those aspects which both can see, or to those fairly basic feelings which both experience simultaneously; and what they see is important not only to their immediate preoccupations (finding their way from the reservoirs to the temple and the veil), but also to the reader, who is thus introduced to yet more aspects of Carthage—the construction and design of the reservoirs, the exterior of the temple, then its complex internal organization, with its inhabitants, its decorations, and finally the inner sanctum with the veil. Some of this information, particularly the new aspects of the religion of Tanit, is intended for comparison with details in other scenes. It is here that we discover how important is the sexual basis of this religion, and are treated to some of the 'simulacres obscènes' of which Salammbô is so far ignorant (cf. p. 61). Now it is precisely this sexually-based knowledge which the Carthaginian virgin is seeking (see particularly p. 64, and infra, p. 223), although of course she does not quite realize it: her religious aspirations are as clearly intertwined with sexual desires as are Emma Bovary's. It is appropriate that the reader, as well as Salammbô, should be introduced to these mysteries through Mâtho, since the Mâtho-Moloch identification and the Moloch-Tanit relationship are so vital to the book's tragedy, on both the national and the personal level.

Flaubert has so much significant information of this sort to give us, and the contents of the temple are so numerous, that he resorts to the expedient of making his heroes lose their way and leave by a different exit, so that they do not look too much as if they are a mere set of peripatetic eyes. Not that the description is unrealistically presented: given the heroes' state of mind, with Mâtho expecting to be struck dead by an offended deity at any moment, and Spendius ready for the more probable, but, for him, no less terrifying, appearance of armed priests; given also their natural curiosity, the strangeness of their surroundings, and the fact that they have no idea where they are going or where they will find the veil, it is understandable that they should scrutinize every detail on their way. Their point of view is eminently suitable for presenting all this new archaeological information. Besides, there is more to the description than this. It is of very great importance that the interior of the temple should be seen only by Spendius and Mâtho: no one penetrates into such sanctuaries with impunity, as they both well know. And on a

symbolic level, the characters' wanderings are a re-enactment
of the labyrinth myth: they are part of the over-all pattern of
symbolism which will be discussed later.[1] The episode is at the
same time an illustration of the lengths to which both men will
go to achieve their respective aims, and both an omen and a
miming of their final failure and death. And since in their failure
they also drag down with them thousands of their companions,
it is obvious that within the context of the whole book this
episode deserves the prominence it is given.

The episode also gives the reader further insight into the
characters of Mâtho and Spendius. With only two characters,
it is easy for Flaubert to individualize them both, through direct
and indirect dialogue and by occasionally showing their thoughts.
Thus when they emerge from the reservoirs, Mâtho's first
thought is to find Hamilcar's palace, but Spendius, uninterested
in Salammbô, discloses his own plan to weaken Carthage by
stealing the veil. It is noteworthy that Spendius does not himself believe in the power of this veil, but he knows that Mâtho
does, and he also knows the psychological influence its loss will
have on the Carthaginians. To this extent he is intellectually
superior to the other characters; but, ironically, his own death
will be caused by the veil's influence. Not that he was wrong
in denying its power: he simply underestimated the psychological
influence which he is the only one to recognize, and the despera-
tion with which Carthage would fight to get it back. Mâtho,
on the other hand, believes that he is committing sacrilege, and
is therefore convinced that sooner or later divine punishment
will obliterate him; and when he later loses the veil back to
Carthage as well, he cannot suppress the idea that he is doomed.
This conviction is instrumental in ensuring that he is in fact
doomed. The psychological and structural importance of this
episode can be gauged by the fact that these two basic attitudes,
which run right through the book, are firmly established here.
Every time Flaubert mentions the individual feelings of the two
men, it is to emphasize the differences in their attitudes, with the

---

[1] I am indebted to Ross Chambers, of the University of New South Wales,
for this observation.

latent irony that they both ended up dead, for substantially the same reasons. Thus Mâtho advances slowly and timidly, while Spendius urges him on; he is terrified by the sight of a certain grille, while Spendius nonchalantly explains that he has seen the same thing elsewhere; at the first real obstacle Mâtho wants to turn back, while Spendius is forecasting the effect of their crime on Carthaginian morale; at the sight of the sleeping women and their exotic perfumed surroundings, Mâtho's attention turns to Salammbô (whom he is beginning to identify with Tanit, just as she identifies him with Moloch), while Spendius is calculating what the women and their jewels would be worth on the open market; Mâtho prostrates himself before the door to Tanit's inner sanctum, while Spendius looks for a way in. When they reach the veil, a strange reversal of roles occurs. Once the sacrilege has been committed and Mâtho has satisfied himself that he has not dropped dead, he begins to believe what Spendius had told him earlier, namely that he is now invincible. This does not make him want to rush off and destroy Carthage as Spendius had hoped, for he had in any case wanted to do this only as a means of getting to Salammbô. But now he has the veil, such a course would be tedious: he feels he can reach her by more direct means. He is mistaken, as we shall soon see.

The fact that he now takes over the dominant role, as if by magic, is not a change of personality due to the influence of the veil. It appears to be so to Mâtho and Spendius, and therefore to the reader; but in fact we are shown elsewhere that Mâtho is by nature a leader and a powerful personality, while Spendius is by nature an opportunist and a sycophant.[1] Spendius has so far been able to impose himself because Mâtho *believed* he was under the influence of Tanit (see pp. 38–42); henceforth he *believes* he now controls this influence, so master and slave return to their true roles. None of this is obvious in the actual words of the passage under consideration. It can be inferred only by reference to other passages from other points of view and in different

[1] Mâtho was already a leader when we first met him—p. 17, he was sitting at the leaders' table, opposite Narr'Havas, who is a prince. See also pp. 18–19, 32, 37. For Spendius, see especially p. 371.

circumstances. We are again face to face with Flaubert's favourite
theme of appearance and reality: and once more, because of the
point of view technique, the appearance is stated as if it were
reality, while the 'real' reality is to be found elsewhere.

   The other important passage where two basically different
witnesses are used simultaneously is the one showing Salammbô's
journey from Carthage to the Barbarian camp (pp. 251–8).
Salammbô is of course the principal character, but she is accompanied by a guide. This latter is of no importance whatsoever—
he is not a character at all in the ordinary sense—yet he does
serve a purpose. Considering that this passage leads to the central
crisis of the book, the possession of Salammbô by Mâtho, its tone
is remarkably neutral, almost off-hand. Salammbô is aware,
through both her own intuition and the behaviour of Schahabarim and Taanach, that she is being led to some event of the
utmost importance. Yet in these pages we do not once penetrate
her thoughts, we are never told how she feels about whatever it
is which is to confront her. We are given no more than a few
semi-physical reactions of minimal importance, such as: 'Malgré
tous ses voiles, Salammbô frissonnait sous la fraîcheur du matin;
le mouvement, le grand air, l'étourdissaient', 'Salammbô rêvait
sous ses voiles, et malgré la chaleur, ne les écartait pas, dans la
crainte de salir ses beaux vêtements.' These passing references,
combined with the progressive nature of the description, and
the fact that the reader never goes outside the experience of the
characters, are sufficient to show that the passage is indeed from
Salammbô's point of view; but it does seem strange that her
reactions are not given more fully.

   If what we have conjectured about the 'double' point of view
is correct, one reason for this becomes apparent. Flaubert can
heighten the reader's expectancy, and enhance the effect of the
tent scene, by withdrawing from his heroine in this preparatory
passage, so that our main attention is diverted from her to the
countryside, and the description is almost completely factual.
This is the technique used frequently by Flaubert in combined
point of view passages, and in the one concerning Spendius and
Mâtho just considered. It would seem that the presence of the

slave, converting the point of view into a double one, has provided Flaubert with a reason for *not* penetrating Salammbô's thoughts, but for looking objectively at the devastation caused by the war. Since Salammbô and the guide have not been taking part in the fighting, and had not previously been outside Carthage, they are neutrals, as it were, and *their* view of the destruction is therefore of importance. Other parts of the book show the Barbarians suffering, and horrified at Carthaginian destruction and atrocities, and vice versa; but such sights are normally presented in relation to the feelings of the group on the receiving end, and are intended largely to show how they aggravate wrong feelings and thereby perpetuate the war. Only here are we shown these horrors in the absolute, with no attempt to lay more blame on one side than the other. It is given only to Salammbô and her guide, removed from the conflict and viewing the results after the heat of battle emotions has passed, to see that destruction and slaughter are in themselves bad, regardless of who may have been to blame: no one else in the book meets the old woman who 'marmottait des paroles de vengeance contre les Barbares *et* contre les Carthaginois'. For once Flaubert wants actually to divorce the scene from his characters' reactions to it.

This naturally does not mean that the descriptions have no relevance to Salammbô's immediate situation—Flaubert's ability to make one scene serve several purposes is well known. On a symbolic level, the scene of devastation, the frequent references to death, corpses, blood, ruins, blackness, emptiness, things broken and torn, if seen in relation to Salammbô's lack of reactions, are so many portents of her destiny, and of her fatalistic acceptance of it. One short example will suffice: 'Puis le soleil se leva; il la mordait sur le derrière de la tête; involontairement elle s'assoupissait un peu.'

Hamilcar

We must now turn to those parts of *Salammbô* which are presented from the point of view of a single character, in the manner which in *Bovary* occurred more frequently than other techniques. That this method is used in less than half of *Salammbô* has already been explained; but its importance is still very great, for the passages where it is used are the ones in which the characters come to life as individuals, and the huge impersonal struggle is reduced to human terms.

In terms of volume, Hamilcar's point of view is the most important. There are, however, two better reasons for dealing with him first: in some ways his point of view is used for presenting information similar to that given in passages already examined, and Flaubert himself, in his letter to Sainte-Beuve, made some relevant comments on his presentation of Hamilcar.

Most of Chapter VII ('Hamilcar Barca', pp. 138–87) dealing with Hamilcar's return to Carthage, is from his point of view. After two passages showing the approach of his ship, seen by the people of Carthage (and, incidentally, the joyful welcome which they here give Hamilcar is to be compared with other passages showing their feelings towards him; some of these have already been commented upon), we follow Hamilcar to his official house, and into the Carthaginian equivalent of a chapel, which is duly described. After his personal devotions,[1] we follow him on to the terrace, to a conference with his supporters, the meeting with the Ancients, the conversation with Salammbô, and the review of his personal losses.

In some parts of this long chapter Flaubert is clearly using Hamilcar's point of view partly as an excuse for presenting yet more Carthaginian civilization—particularly in the descriptions of the temple of Moloch, and of Hamilcar's cellars, stacked with fabulous riches. Yet both descriptions are, for various reasons, necessary to the novel's development: even those who, following Sainte-Beuve, would prefer them to be shorter and faster-moving usually concede as much. Granted this, it will then readily be admitted that Hamilcar's point of view is particularly appropriate for two reasons: he has just returned after a long absence (the

---

[1] Which, among other things, give the lie to the Ancients' allegations that he is sacrilegious, and show that within the limits of his civilization, he is very devout, trying to go farther than the common herd in his quest for truth. Hence, no doubt, the animosity of the priests.

stranger's eye), and he has an intense personal interest in both the meeting in the temple, and in what the Barbarians have cost him in his own house. Seen in this light, the apparently tiresome detail begins to have some psychological validity. A person of Hamilcar's character, in a situation of such vital concern to him, would not let the tiniest detail escape him, and conversely, one so acute would have to be such a character in such a situation. Besides, why should one read a book merely to enjoy an uninterrupted flow of narrative?

These two descriptions do differ somewhat in their emphasis. That of the temple of Moloch is more concerned with the character of Carthage, the second with the character of Hamilcar (although each of them shows both to some extent). In other words, the temple scene is in the category of archaeological information, so that Hamilcar's point of view tends to be fused with the collective one. As with the scenes concerning Salammbô's religion and Mâtho and Spendius' penetration into the temple of Tanit, the normal collective point of view is impossible here, since the populace is again excluded. An alternative would be to use the point of view of all the Ancients. It may perhaps be argued that this is what has been done, for it is *on* rather than just Hamilcar who proceeds to the interior of the temple, and examines the layout, the decorations, and the rites. It is noticeable, too, that references to Hamilcar's feelings, although present before and after this scene, are infrequent (cf. Salammbô's journey to the Barbarian camp). But of all the people present only Hamilcar would look at details with the stranger's eye. That his long absence has increased his perception of what for others are quite ordinary objects, thereby making him a better witness, has in fact already been stated: 'A chaque pas il retrouvait des armures, des meubles, des objets connus qui l'étonnaient cependant, . . .' (p. 141). Besides, it is *his* future that is at stake; he knows, more clearly than anyone else, that the future of Carthage is equally in the balance; and it is here that he is told of the relationship between Salammbô and Mâtho, which, though non-existent for the moment, determines much of his subsequent behaviour. Had Flaubert wanted only to provide a picture of the temple, he

could have done so earlier, during the meetings of the Ancients
mentioned on p. 119. The description is more apposite here,
where the stormy debate—which could not have taken place
were Hamilcar absent—seems to reflect the anger of Moloch
himself, where Hamilcar actually offers himself to Moloch.[1]
The sinister importance of the temple to Hamilcar and to Carthage,
and a portent of the damage it will eventually cause, are implicit
in the first paragraph of its description, and only Hamilcar could
see it in these terms:

> Le temple de Moloch était bâti au pied d'une gorge escarpée, dans
> un endroit sinistre. On n'apercevait d'en bas que de hautes murailles
> montant indéfiniment, telles que les parois d'un monstrueux tombeau.
> La nuit était sombre, un brouillard grisâtre semblait peser sur la mer.
> Elle battait contre la falaise avec un bruit de râles et de sanglots ...
> (p. 146).

This piece of 'archaeological' description is thus rather special
because its occurrence is determined by the point of view of an
individual. It is another good example of Flaubert's concern for
balance and significant description—and also, whatever one
might at first feel, his desire not to overload his book, to include
only details of direct relevance to the fate of his characters. He
does not, for example, describe the temple of Eschmoûn, where
the *assemblée des Riches* takes place the following night (see pp.
161, 187). That he should give prominence to those of Moloch
and Tanit is justifiable in itself, given that part of the subject of
the book is the alternating influence of these deities. Their descriptions are further justified by the fact that they are presented in
relation to major characters, and when the action is taking a
decisive turn. That Flaubert was also displaying his erudition,
teaching his readers some of the more sensational aspects of

---

[1] Ironically, for this empty act, the result of a fit of anger, symbolically makes
him the servant of Mâtho, who is to destroy his daughter; and on a factual level
Hamilcar does help to bring this destruction about, by the way he has brought
her up in ignorance, and his determination not to discuss Mâtho with her. Ironically, too, because it points forward to his very different reaction when a real
offering to Moloch, in the form of his son, is required.

ancient history, and indulging his personal tastes, is surely of minor critical importance.

When Hamilcar returns to his palace, the well-known inspection of his riches begins. It is worth quoting Sainte-Beuve's objection to this passage in full, since it constitutes one of his basic criticisms of the whole book:

C'est au sortir de là qu'Amilcar se met à visiter sa maison qu'il a depuis si longtemps quittée, et ses magasins, ses entrepôts, ses cachettes secrètes, les caveaux où gisent accumulées des richesses de toute sorte qui nous sont énumérées avec la minutie et l'exactitude d'un inventaire: exactitude est trop peu dire, car nous avons affaire ici à un commissaire-priseur qui s'amuse, et qui, dans le caveau des pierreries, se plaira, par exemple, à nous dénombrer toutes les merveilles minéralogiques imaginables, et jusqu'à des escarboucles 'formées par l'urine des lynx'. C'est passer la mesure et laisser trop voir le bout de l'oreille du dilettante mystificateur. Dans toute cette visite à des magasins souterrains, le but de l'auteur n'est pas de montrer le caractère d'Amilcar, il n'a voulu que montrer les magasins. Mais ils ont beau renfermer des couloirs, des portes masquées, des surprises sans nombre, comme il paraît qu'on en rencontre dans les sépulcres des rois à Jérusalem, l'architecture, même avec tous ses dédales, ne saurait être un ressort de roman ni de poème. Amilcar, le grand homme d'Etat, le père d'Annibal, ne gagne pas à cette visite où il est présenté comme un violent et un cupide, ne se possédant pas, à tout moment hors de lui-même. Si l'on voulait personnifier en lui le type du grand marchand très-dur, il ne fallait pas que ce côté fût pris et taillé en charge aux dépens du reste du caractère.[1]

In reply, Flaubert stated (v. *supra*, p. 153) that he had on the contrary kept the actual description in the background, and that the main point was the *progressive* anger of Hamilcar as he discovers the damage. The debate remains open, although it is not difficult to find reasons for supporting Flaubert's view. Hamilcar's anger had begun to build up long before this: the sight of the neglected triremes which he sails past on his arrival (p. 140) was the first step, and he has just returned from the meeting of the Ancients and spoken to Salammbô—an interview which, because of a misunderstanding of the type which occurs frequently in

[1] Sainte-Beuve, op. cit., pp. 214–15.

Flaubert's works, has convinced him that she has succumbed to
Mâtho, as the Ancients had maliciously suggested. It is not entirely unreasonable that he should be a little short-tempered
when he finds that he has been robbed as well! Sainte-Beuve
states that this passage is not intended to show Hamilcar's character, but only his riches. Yet surely it reveals that Hamilcar is a
true Carthaginian, with the same commercial spirit as prompted
the Council not to use the hair of their female slaves even to
save their own lives. Hamilcar is angry when he begins his review, but (p. 166) 'en apercevant l'accumulation de ses richesses,
il se calma; sa pensée, qu'attiraient les perspectives des couloirs,
se répandait dans les autres salles pleines de trésors plus rares'.
His avarice is underlined again several times: his insistence on
knowing exactly what he had lost, his approval of the Intendant's
understating his income for tax purposes, his desire to corner
grain in preparation for the hard times ahead, his noticing three
empty money-jars among all the thousands of full ones, his
idiotic pleasure at the sight of his precious stones, the falsification
of the perfumes he was exporting, and so on. Other passages
show his mounting anger against the Barbarians—the motivation
for his accepting the command of Carthage's army—and his
unfeeling cruelty (as Flaubert pointed out, the punishment of
his slaves prepares the way for his later atrocities—and also,
incidentally, further underlines the fact that he is a real Carthaginian). The long presentation of objects is, moreover, in itself
a reflection of Hamilcar's character. It is *things* which are important to him: like most Carthaginians, but unlike Salammbô,
he is a materialist. He takes enormous pleasure in his vast possessions, and he loves to feast his eyes upon them. But just as the
war broke out because Carthage could not bear to hand
over some of its vast wealth to the Barbarians who had legiti-
mately earned it, so Hamilcar's anger mounts as he discovers
that someone has removed a small proportion of his riches. He
will continue the war for the same reasons as those for which it
was begun.

     Hamilcar is, moreover, an important character in that he
forms a link between Salammbô and Carthage—between the

individual and the social aspects of the novel. Now at the end of the Council meeting, we know almost nothing about him except that he has a violent temper, and has just stated his apparently irrevocable decision not to lead his country against her attackers. Within a few hours he has altered the course of history by changing his mind. No reader could accept such a momentous reversal of attitude without being shown how it occurred, so Flaubert must first show Hamilcar's character, and secondly explain what new factors, acting upon this character, can affect it so radically. He does both in twenty-five pages. When one considers that Proust, for example, might well have taken five times as long to lay the foundations for such an important change, the fact that Hamilcar is also shown to be so thoroughly a product of his race, and that we are given a catalogue of what the fashionable Carthaginian regarded as wealth, might almost be regarded as a bonus!

In this description we again see some of the extra benefits of using the point of view technique. As in *Bovary*, characters are apt to accept beliefs or impressions as facts, usually with undesirable consequences. Hamilcar is less prone to this malady than Salammbô or Emma, perhaps because he *is* such a materialist, so unreceptive to spiritual values. But his attitude to Salammbô is based on two misapprehensions, first that a daughter was a sign of displeasure from the gods (p. 164), and secondly that 'elle avait failli dans l'étreinte d'un Barbare' (p. 166). The latter, which is given credence by the Intendant's revelation that Salammbô had ordered the vast expense for the Mercenaries' feast (p. 173), is exacerbated by being identified in his mind with his financial losses:

... malgré ses efforts pour les bannir de sa pensée, il retrouvait continuellement les Barbares. Leurs débordements se confondaient avec la honte de sa fille, et il en voulait à toute la maison de la connaître et de ne pas la lui dire (p. 179).

A chaque pas il découvrait quelque désastre nouveau, une preuve encore de cette chose qu'il s'était interdit d'apprendre (pp. 180-1).

An event which has not yet taken place is partly responsible for the sufferings of Carthage.

Like Salammbô's shame, but on a lesser scale, other 'facts' are stated in the course of this description. Hamilcar's acceptance of Carthaginian myths and traditions, implied by his point of view, emphasizes the extent to which he is bound to his milieu. The origins and magical properties of some of his treasures are presented thus:

C'étaient des callaïs arrachées des montagnes à coups de fronde, des escarboucles formées par l'urine des lynx, des glossopètres tombés de la lune. ... Les céraunies engendrées par le tonnerre étincelaient près des calcédoines qui guérissent des poisons. Il y avait des topazes du mont Zabarca pour prévenir les terreurs, des opales de la Bactriane qui empêchent les avortements, et des cornes d'Ammon que l'on place sous les lits afin d'avoir des songes (p. 176).

Later (p. 178) there is a reference to 'gigantesques morceaux d'ambre, matière presque divine formée par les rayons du soleil', while his perfume makers are described as 'des Cyrénéens de mœurs infâmes'(!) Some at least of Hamilcar's 'wealth' has the same objective worth as native shell-money or a rare postage stamp.

The question of the origin of the 'escarboucles' was raised by Sainte-Beuve, and in reply Flaubert merely quotes his source for this piece of information (Theophrastus): he does not explain or justify his use of it. But it obviously does not follow that because Flaubert found it in an ancient writer, he believes it to be true, nor is Sainte-Beuve's postulation of a 'dilettante mystificateur' very likely. Flaubert is simply saying that since the ancients believed this to be the source of the stone, he is justified in portraying Hamilcar as believing it, so that the modern reader is placed with the author on a superior level to the character. Like the whole Carthaginian populace, Hamilcar is bound by the exotic *idées reçues* which we have already mentioned.[1]

---

[1] Bertrand (op. cit., pp. 150–2) insists on the psychological, in addition to the historical and archaeological, value of all the descriptions in *Salammbô*. His comments on this passage strongly recall the letters by Sainte-Beuve and Flaubert, although he does not mention either; and this is the only example he cites to support his statement about the whole book. Mason (op. cit., p. 124) takes six lines to dismiss the whole episode as superfluous.

Hamilcar's point of view does not recur to any significant degree until the priests come to claim Hannibal for the sacrifice to Moloch (pp. 335-40). As his attitude to his son is essentially self-centred (p. 186: Hannibal is 'un prolongement de sa force, une continuation indéfinie de sa personne'), it is a psychological necessity that he should not sacrifice the boy, even though he had subscribed to the principle of a sacrifice. When he realizes that the slave, whose son he has substituted for Hannibal, may think the same way, he almost falls victim to a human feeling; but he quickly masters this weakness, and treats the slave's reaction as an insult instead (pp. 337-8). He would, indeed, have punished this insolence by death, were he not afraid of the vengeance of the gods (p. 339). Finally, when he is certain no one can see him, he does give vent to some paternal joy; but for the reader who remembers the reasons for his love, this joy is as empty as his simulated grief when he hands over someone else's son. The whole passage so clearly emphasizes the dominating traits of Hamilcar's character—and of Carthage—that it requires no further comment.

Subsequent passages from Hamilcar's point of view add little to the picture we now have, nor do they represent anything startling in technique. On two occasions he is used as a 'mirror' by which we see others—the Barbarian ambassadors from the *Défilé* (pp. 370-2), and the thirty crucified Ancients, including Hannon (pp. 387-8). The Barbarian ambassadors had to be seen by an outsider to complete the picture of the effects of the *Défilé*, since the Barbarian point of view could not reveal the slow physical changes which were taking place in all of them; and it is particularly appropriate that it should be Hamilcar who is chosen to view the effects of his own plot: the condition of these ten ambassadors symbolically underlines the disintegration of the Barbarian resistance, which this scene portrays on a literal level. Similarly, the crucified Carthaginians, whom, significantly, Hamilcar can see more or less at the same time as the walls of the city, represent the imminent downfall of all he has been fighting for. Again Hamilcar is the appropriate witness, especially since the bulk of the passage describes the quite literal disintegration of Hannon. In itself, this could be nothing but a source of pleasure to Hamilcar—the more so in that this is the fate with which Hannon had threatened him (p. 161)—but he cannot fail to realize that the end of so many leaders must soon mean the end of Carthage. Finally, the dreadful disease with which Hannon is afflicted has recurred several times through the book, each time at a more advanced stage. This, too, is a symbol: Hannon's rival, Giscon, who was morally and physically healthy, was captured at an early stage of the war, and entirely through the cowardice and underhand dealings of the diseased Hannon and his party (pp. 83–4). After this, it is the diseased party which ruled Carthage until Hamilcar's arrival, and then unceasingly did its best to obstruct him.[1] Hannon's death on the cross represents the end of a state which died because of its corruption.

Salammbô as object

It was remarked earlier that the actions and feelings of individual characters are frequently included in the description of the group to which they belong, even though the individuals may not be specifically mentioned. This applies in particular to Mâtho, who is on the scene from the beginning of the book, but is not individualized until after the liberation of the slaves and the appearance of Salammbô. This order of events serves to emphasize that anything which is said of the Barbarians is equally true of Mâtho, unless there are specific indications to the contrary. Thus although the liberation of the slaves by 'des soldats', and the appearance of Spendius, are quite clearly presented from the collective point of view of the Mercenaries, we subsequently discover (p. 20) that Mâtho had been directly involved. Similarly the appearance of Salammbô is from the point of view of all the Mercenaries, with little to indicate at the time that Mâtho was more impressed than anybody else; that he alone was totally under her spell is revealed later (on p. 41 he even quotes some of the words she sang, although these were said to be in a language

[1] e.g. see pp. 290–1, and p. 383: 'Hannon, par désir d'humilier son rival, ne balança pas'. This is why he was finally captured.

which none of the Barbarians could understand). And any possible doubt about Mâtho's being one with the Barbarians is dispelled by the first description of him: 'Des éclaboussures de sang lui tachetaient la face', which apart from containing a symbolic portent shows that Mâtho had been enjoying some of the less attractive activities of the feast.

The interplay between the individual point of view of Mâtho and the collective one of the Barbarians continues throughout the book: the collective point of view is frequently interrupted by a brief passage showing Mâtho's thoughts on the matter in hand.[1] These passages have the effect of rim lighting—they make Mâtho's form stand out against the background mass, by insisting on his *idée fixe*, showing how his personal reasons for wanting to destroy Carthage provide him with a special force which he is continually communicating to his followers. But his general reactions—particularly his brutality, his superstitions, and his mistaken ideas about the truth of the situation—are those of all the Barbarians, which is why they are almost invariably shown within passages giving the collective view. Indeed, some passages, such as the one on pp. 327-9 showing his incredible single-handed butchery, seem to have little purpose beyond this moral link. Mâtho is not different from the other Mercenaries; he has all their attitudes, plus a few individual ones. Flaubert has developed a method of character presentation which was barely hinted at when, during the *Comices*, he implied that Rodolphe and Emma were to be identified with *on*. This method is very economical, in that when he comes to Mâtho's personal story, he has no need to develop at length the determining factors of his behaviour, but can concentrate on those rare elements which Mâtho does not share with the other Mercenaries. It has the added advantage of helping the unity of the novel, by binding

[1] e.g. when the Barbarians are examining Carthage (pp. 68-70), Mâtho is looking at Hamilcar's palace, with the great door symbolically closed (it first closed as Salammbô fled from him, p. 19): he is jealous of Carthage because it protects Salammbô. Other examples pp. 38-9, 85, 123-5, 218-19, etc. At these points Spendius' point of view also occurs fairly often, to show Mâtho's external appearance as well: in fact this seems to be the prime reason for using Spendius at all.

together the individual and the mass aspects of the story. Its main disadvantage is that the protagonist is not clearly drawn in his own, individual, terms, and tends to be what has been called a 'flat' character. But since this appears to be one of the points of the book—that real individuals in such a milieu are rare—it is difficult to see how Flaubert could have avoided this without upsetting what he regarded as the historical truth of the situation.

Several of the passages cited above do show, however, that when Flaubert wants to individualize Mâtho's character, he uses the same method as in *Bovary*: he shows his character viewing a scene of personal importance, on which is imposed a meaning and a validity which it would not have for a disinterested person. This is true, for example, of the description of Carthage on pp. 68–70, already twice referred to. Mâtho's view of the city is different from that of the other Barbarians; and their view of it is in turn different from that of an ordinary tourist, or from that of an omniscient narrator. In the same way, the description of the countryside stretching out before Mâtho (pp. 123–4) is conditioned by his preoccupation with Salammbô: one notes the similes referring to gold and precious stones, the tranquillity and sweetness of the evening breeze, the fertility of the countryside, and the pyramid-shaped island (the cone is one of the sacred forms which Mâtho encountered, and worshipped, in the temple of Tanit, pp. 93, 99, and the shadow of Salammbô's palace is likened to a 'monstrueuse pyramide', p. 101).

Mâtho's attitude towards Salammbô herself best shows this exotic *Bovarysme*. It is sufficient to compare the various descriptions of the heroine, and to consider them in relation to whichever person happens to be the witness. We have already seen how the assembled Mercenaries were moved to note particularly the richness of her costume and the influence of the moongoddess.[1] It gradually becomes apparent that Mâtho was impressed

---

[1] pp. 13 et seq. There is in addition a remarkable similarity in the over-all impression created by this first view of Salammbô and that of Hannon (pp. 44–5) —a parallel rendered more striking by the fact that the Mercenaries are the witnesses in both cases. It is an impression of extreme pallor in the midst of excessive

especially by the latter; and when she is next described, in a conversation between Mâtho and Spendius, the emphasis is therefore quite different (p. 41). Instead of wealth and the vague influence of the gods, the picture is now one of desirability and direct menace from the gods. It is the difference between Mâtho's personal point of view and that of the massed Barbarians—but there are still enough similarities to remind us that Mâtho is also a Barbarian.

Mâtho does not see Salammbô again until, after having stolen the veil and gained confidence, he enters her room (pp. 103–6). The mood is now one of mystery, softness, and gentleness, as befits the abode of the representative of Tanit; and it is fostered by the witness, who is convinced it must be so. It is also helped by the darkness, which ensures that the description must be both progressive and impressionistic, as Mâtho gropes his way towards what he is seeking. In both atmosphere and technique, the passage recalls the hero's visit to the prostitute in *Novembre*, but with the moon-sun symbolism superimposed. Mâtho's first discoveries are 'des senteurs exquises' and 'la trace d'un pas humide' (an echo of the 'rosées fécondes' and the fertility of the 'obscures profondeurs de ton humidité' in Salammbô's hymn to Tanit on p. 58, and the Carthaginian belief that 'l'eau est enfantée par la lune' on p. 352). Salammbô's bed is 'un grand carré d'azur se tenant en l'air par quatre cordes qui remontaient'—the bed is suspended from the ceiling and the mosquito net is blue. Mâtho makes his way to the bed, but 'la lumière s'arrêtait au bord; et l'ombre, telle qu'un grand rideau, ne découvrait qu'un angle du matelas rouge avec le bout d'un petit pied nu posant sur la cheville'. Only when Mâtho brings the lamp over can he really see Salammbô, and only then is she described; not surprisingly, she is presented in terms suggesting the same mystery, but also the

---

wealth and ornamentation. Both people are symbols of Carthage. Salammbô's pallor is attributed to Tanit, which we know to be false; Hannon's to leprosy, which we know to be a fact. Could Salammbô's pallor be a symbol of the moral leprosy of Carthage—one of those symbols which, as we remarked in the chapter on *Bovary*, escape the notice of those very characters who constantly look for symbols?

same gentle, domestic femininity, as were evident in the description of her room. Mâtho's physical desire is not actually mentioned at this point, but as the sight of Salammbô prompts him to set fire to the mosquito net, it is presumably not absent. Additionally, the blue net, the bed suspended from the roof, the white clothing, all place an almost embarrassing emphasis on the Salammbô-Tanit parallel: 'Les courtines, perpendiculairement tendues, l'enveloppaient d'une atmosphère bleuâtre, et le mouvement de sa respiration, en se communiquant aux cordes, semblait la balancer dans l'air ' (p. 104). That Mâtho should then appear, as it were, in a flash of fire as she wakes, and that the sunrise should be mentioned in the same paragraph as the words 'Salammbô s'appuyait *en défaillant* contre les coussins du lit', gives more than adequate prominence to the other half of the symbolism.

This weighty significance, and Flaubert's obvious revelling in descriptions of still more wealth, should not lead us to forget that on another level this scene remains realistic, in accordance with Flaubert's normal habits. The exotic riches which the reader, following Mâtho, sees surrounded by such mystery are nothing more than the trappings one might expect to find in a Carthaginian princess's bedroom. Salammbô is a young woman in her ordinary domestic surroundings. She has left clothes lying about, her slippers are lying on the floor where she took them off to wash her feet, many of the objects mentioned are utilitarian. At bottom, we are watching an enflamed male paying an illicit nocturnal visit to a lady's bedroom. Like most of Flaubert's characters, Mâtho has built up an elaborate superstructure, in the reality of which he believes completely, over his real motives. It is this superstructure which is presented to the reader through the character's eyes.

Salammbô next appears when she welcomes Hamilcar back to Carthage (pp. 163–6). The witness is her father, who will not be impressed in the same way as the Barbarian horde, even though the grand opera atmosphere is maintained by her usual extravagant retinue. The tone is set by the paragraph (p. 164) which shows Hamilcar remembering his bitter disappointment that his first surviving child was a girl. The description of her person follows. Although it is on the whole as factual as the earlier one, suggesting that Flaubert is 'placing' another rich Carthaginian costume, it ends on a completely different note. It is the cold, not Tanit, which Hamilcar sees as the cause of her pallor. There is none of the mystery Mâtho had seen, for her father is not 'ébloui par les splendeurs de sa tête' (p. 106). But there is more Flaubertian double-barrelled irony here. Although the Mercenaries are mistaken in assuming Salammbô to be under Tanit's influence, through a combination of circumstances (not least of which is everybody's belief, including her own, that this is true), the outcome is the same as if she were so. If Mâtho is deceived in ascribing her pallor to the moon, Hamilcar is equally deceived in blaming the temperature.

Salammbô's appearance in the costume which she wears to her rendez-vous with Mâtho is presented through three separate witnesses—an indication, through form, of the centrality of the tent scene, and an excellent opportunity to gauge the effect of change in point of view. First, Salammbô is dressed by Taanach, an operation which reveals what the well-dressed Carthaginian princess would wear for an important event. This part of the description is factual: as the point of view is that of both Salammbô and Taanach, the part played by personal feelings and aberrations is minimized. Nevertheless the reader, already accustomed to degrees of symbolic meaning which can be present whether or not the characters are aware of them, will not fail to notice the colours of the clothes. There is a 'couleur vineuse', the deep red worn by the priests of Moloch at the sacrifice of the children (p. 348) and at the meeting of the Ancients (p. 150; cf. p. 407), by Salammbô when Mâtho falls under her spell (p. 14), by Mâtho when he meets her at the Mercenaries' camp (p. 257); and when he breaks into her room, the dawn throws 'une couleur vineuse' on to the walls (p. 105). There is blue with silver stars, an obvious reminder of Salammbô's relationship with Tanit; blue is also worn by the priests of the fertility cult of Cérès (p. 344; cf. p. 342), and is the colour of the curtains of the temple of Eschmoûn

(p. 341), another Carthaginian sun and fertility god (see pp. 320, 406–7. The python is the symbol of Eschmoûn). There is white, the colour of the priests of Tanit, worn by Salammbô when her personal preoccupations are first presented (p. 58), when Mâtho breaks into her room (p. 104) and at her short-lived triumph at the end of the book (p. 406).[1] There is red again, and finally black, the colour worn by those seeking children for the sacrifice to Moloch (p. 334).[2]

The dressing completed, Salammbô, like Emma Bovary, admires herself in a mirror and removes the last tiny imperfection (p. 248). This is the signal for a second description, this time splendidly impressionistic, a feast of light, consonant with the coquetry suggested by Salammbô's first action and the womanly vanity which temporarily overshadows the portents: '. . . et Salammbô, debout à côté de Taanach se penchant pour la voir, souriait dans cet éblouissement'.[3] Only one apparently innocent

---

[1] The question of colour symbolism in *Salammbô* is very complex. It has been touched on by Bieler: 'La Couleur dans *Salammbô*' in *The French Review*, vol. xxxiii, no. 4, 1960, pp. 359–70, who counts the number of occurrences of each colour, and notes that the sombre tones of black and red are most frequent. But when he says black symbolizes Tanit and red Moloch, he is, I believe, mistaken. Both red and black represent Moloch (ferocity), while blue and white (with silver) stand for Tanit-Eschmoûn (gentleness and fertility). Combining the colours in this way gives (from Bieler's table) 199 symbols of ferocity and 101 of gentleness; no other colour is used nearly so often. This proportion is consistent with the over-all meaning of the book, even though this over-simplifies the question.

[2] Heuzey: 'Le Costume de Salammbô' in *Bulletin des Amis de Flaubert*, no. ii, 1951, p. 13, criticizes the presentation of this scene on the grounds that an observer looking at Salammbô would not be able to see the various layers of garments described here, since they are all covered by a cloak. He continues: 'la description reste confuse, sans vue d'ensemble ni raccourci évocateur. Elle semble plus d'une habilleuse que d'un peintre. Tout se passe comme si l' écrivain . . . s'était identifié avec le personnage de la vieille servante et décrivait les différentes pièces de l'habillement au fur et à mesure qu'il en revêtait le corps de son héroïne.' If my argument is correct, this is precisely what Flaubert wanted to do.

[3] The vanity is a little surprising here, but is consistent with Flaubert's rather brutal theories about female 'idealism'. In spite of portents and premonitions, Salammbô feels in a confused way that it is important for her to look her best for this interview with Mâtho—cf. p. 255, during her journey to the Barbarian camp: 'Salammbô rêvait sous ses voiles, et malgré la chaleur, ne les écartait pas, dans la crainte de salir ses beaux vêtements'.

simile remains to remind the reader, if not Salammbô, of the purpose of her splendour: 'le miroir, comme un soleil, lui renvoyait des rayons'. Both in the physical world and, symbolically, in Carthaginian cosmogony, the moon's glory and influence depend upon the rays of the sun.

At the Barbarian camp, the key changes. Mâtho first sees Salammbô in terms of mystery and moonlight, a 'forme vague se dressant comme un fantôme dans les pénombres du soir' (pp. 256–7). The picture is, of course, *truqué*—the circumstances of their meeting, particularly the moon rising behind her and her many flowing clothes, have been carefully arranged so that the witness *must* see her in a certain way; and since this view is so appropriate to his ideas of her, it reinforces them considerably. The scene takes on a significance, both for Mâtho and for the reader, which the individual facts do not in themselves allow—just as the entirely domestic and realistic detail of the wet footprint on the floor became meaningful through the circumstances surrounding it.

In the tent, Salammbô is for the first time close enough to become something real, something more than a mysterious and elusive symbol. Only at this point does Mâtho really begin to examine her (pp. 259–60). But the mind works slowly when it has to reverse a long habit of deification. Mâtho's physical desire takes some time to gain the upper hand, and the process begins with a rather impressionistic picture of Salammbô as an extension of her ornamentation, not yet a woman. Practical considerations partly determine this order of events, for the delay allows Flaubert to describe more jewels, and to complete the details of her costume. If he had concentrated all this magnificence into one long description, rather than interspersing it with the action and spreading it over three shorter attacks, Sainte-Beuve's reproach of 'chinoiserie' would have been even more justified. But more than this, the picture we are given here retrospectively underlines the salient features of two previous ones. The Mercenaries' first view of Salammbô was one of bejewelled splendour, which reinforced their ideas of Carthage's wealth and mystery. It is important that the idea should now be confirmed for Mâtho.

Secondly, while Salammbô was being dressed by Taanach, we noticed that the colours chosen provided links with other parts of the book. If these clothes are now seen as an inseparable aspect of Salammbô's person, the significance of the colours is reinforced, if not for Mâtho, at least for the reader. But the main purpose of the description is gradually to lead Mâtho away from his conviction of the untouchable nature of his 'goddess'. Following out the various aspects of the idea that her body and her clothing are as one, he reaches the point where he watches drops of liquid perfume moisten her bare shoulder (another symbol of the moon's fertility). The fascination of this simple phenomenon leads him to touch her, and the 'résistance élastique' of her skin quickly breaks the spell.[1]

But for the purposes of the whole book, it would not do for Salammbô's mystery to be dispelled completely. There is nothing Flaubert wants less than that she should be deprived of the halo which, in the eyes of most of the characters, and of the reader, surrounds her. For Mâtho she has become a woman; this 'realism' must be disguised again as quickly as possible. Mâtho's last words in this scene (p. 266) recall that he had almost identified her with Tanit; and although the imperfect tense implies that he has now rejected that identification, his words are a good base upon which to build. In quick succession the camp goes up in flames, Hamilcar attacks, Narr'Havas defects, and Salammbô disappears with the sacred veil. Now all these events have perfectly logical explanations. Hamilcar, in an apparently hopeless situation, surrounded by chance by the Barbarians (p. 222) and outnumbered ten to one (p. 224), had set fire to the Libyan camp as a last defiant gesture, merely for the sake of doing something; he had no idea that by its timing this action would create such havoc (p. 274). Narr'Havas, who had already changed sides more than once, was interested only in being with the winners, so that, seeing the unexpected military result of Hamilcar's gesture, he quickly

---

[1] Note the complexity of this capital scene in Flaubert's mind, and compare his intentions with the result: 'Mais juge de mon inquiétude, je prépare actuellement un coup, le *coup* du livre. Il faut que ce soit à la fois cochon, chaste, mystique et réaliste' (*Cor.*, IV, 406).

decamped (p. 273); in any case he heartily disliked Mâtho (pp. 19, 38). Salammbô, whose purpose in visiting Mâtho was to retrieve the veil, and who had been told by Schahabarim that submitting to Mâtho's wishes was an essential part of the strategy (pp. 240–3), would certainly have been shaken by the mysterious outbreak of fire (Moloch), and the imprecations of the now hideous Giscon (p. 269). Left alone in the confusion, she would naturally judge it prudent to remove the veil and herself from the area as quietly as possible. Mâtho, however, ignorant of all these circumstances, sees only their apparently cataclysmic results. He could hardly avoid reverting to his original idea of Salammbô as a terrible, superhuman being with a distinct personal dislike for him. This is confirmed for him—and for everybody else, Carthaginians and Barbarians alike—by Salammbô's reappearance with the veil before Hamilcar (pp. 274–5). Thus Salammbô is quickly replaced on her pedestal, and Mâtho is back where he started, with the important exception that Hamilcar is now fighting a war of retribution. This change is occasioned by the Barbarian torturing of their prisoners, and in particular by their needlessly aggressive gesture of throwing the head of Giscon (a personal friend and political ally of Hamilcar—see pp. 151–2) into the Carthaginian camp. From Mâtho's point of view, however, the new political situation is simply another confirmation of the general malediction under which he labours: on p. 284 he is 'écrasé par l'injustice des dieux'. For these reasons, his attitude towards Salammbô does not substantially change after the tent scene: she remains an absence, and so continues to obsess him. He does not see her again until he is at the point of death (p. 412).

If Salammbô is an absence for Mâtho, she is very much more so for Narr'Havas,[1] who was equally impressed by her at the Mercenaries' banquet, but has never managed to get so close to her. His desire, however, is uncluttered by metaphysics, just as his allegiances are free from inhibiting factors like loyalty. At Salammbô's first appearance he looks at her in a distinctly un-

---

[1] There is some irony in Narr'Havas' name, which one would imagine could be more properly applied to Mâtho: '*Nar-el-haouah*, feu du souffle' (*Cor.*, V, 78).

spiritual manner—'en écartant les narines, comme un léopard
qui est accroupi dans les bambous' (p. 18); and on the eve of the
final battle his thoughts are nothing if not mundane: 'Alors ses
angoisses disparurent, et il ne songea plus qu'au bonheur de
posséder une femme si belle' (p. 393). (Hamilcar showed some
acuity of judgement in forbidding Narr'Havas to go near
Salammbô until after their wedding (p. 355).) Salammbô, haun-
ted by Mâtho's associations with Moloch, has no interest in
Narr'Havas (pp. 355, 393). These attitudes are as truly reflected
by the point of view technique as those binding Salammbô and
Mâtho: Narr'Havas seldom has the opportunity of seeing her,
and when he does, he sees no mystery, no splendour, simply an
attractive but distant young woman. At their betrothal ceremony,
she is merely 'calme comme une statue, semblant ne pas comprendre' (p. 275). It is difficult to realize that she is dressed in the
same magnificent costume as when she was with Mâtho, and
now has the veil as well. But Narr'Havas is not interested in
this, any more than is Hamilcar, who notices only the broken
ankle chain. Later, when she receives Narr'Havas in the garden
of her palace, she has a veil over her face, so that he can distinguish
only her eyes—and even these are not described. Her lips and
her hands, although brilliant, remain closed in by the veil; she
makes no gestures, and she hardly speaks. When she does, it is
about Mâtho (p. 380), and this subject alone induces some sem-
blance of a human reaction. Only after he has been discussed
does a little of the habitual mystical symbolism creep in, for now
'les yeux de Salammbô, au fond de ses longues draperies, avaient
l'air de deux étoiles dans l'ouverture d'un nuage'. But at this
point Narr'Havas leaves her.

The stage is now set for the final scene, the splendid marriage
of Salammbô and the atrocious death of Mâtho—and how
perfectly the descriptions of this last chapter round off the original
Mercenary ideas about Carthage: wealth and terror. Salammbô
has certainly prospered, for it is her own people who, after considerable variation in their attitudes towards her (depending on
the fluctuating fortunes of the city), have now decided that her
recovery of the veil has saved the city, that she is almost a goddess

(p. 403). Flaubert's irony is again evident in this latest collective view of Carthage. There is no more logical justification for the present belief than for the earlier one that the veil had been lost through Salammbô's fault, or for the Mercenaries' idea that she was under the influence of Tanit. As in *Bovary*, the irony comes through the many changes in point of view: the reader, who can glean more factual information than any character or group in the book, is superior to all of them. Still, Carthage *believes* Salammbô is almost a goddess, and this allows her appearance to be both consistent with the present mood, and an echo of the beginning of the novel. Once more her personal attributes are neglected in favour of the splendid wealth of her costume and her jewellery. But now it is broad daylight: the mysterious atmosphere engendered by the light is therefore absent, and so, naturally, is the awesomeness resulting from it. Besides, the Carthaginians are not afraid of Tanit as the Mercenaries were: for the latter she was a foreign deity, and therefore fearsome; for the Carthaginians she is a beneficial goddess, the converse of the terror inspired by Moloch. Salammbô's identification with Tanit is on this occasion something in which to rejoice. Forebodings are absent, the relevant religious trappings are openly exhibited: the fertility symbols of the python of Eschmoûn and the crystal egg of Tanit, so placed that it is 'fertilized' by the rays of the setting sun (p. 407). The identification is an apotheosis, not a portent:

> Ayant ainsi le peuple à ses pieds, le firmament sur la tête, autour d'elle l'immensité de la mer, le golfe, les montagnes et les perspectives des provinces, Salammbô resplendissante se confondait avec Tanit et semblait le génie même de Carthage, son âme corporifiée.

Thus we can add another element to Mâtho's general confusion about Salammbô. Not only is he mistaken in believing that she had laid a curse on him, but his very assumption shows his ignorance of the nature of Tanit. Even if Salammbô were Tanit, she would not lay curses on people. Far from being a malevolent deity, Tanit is the one who labours under the curse of Moloch.

The secret of existence

If Mâtho is confused about Salammbô, she is equally confused about him. Flaubert must present certain parts of the book from her point of view, so that the reader can judge the effects of this. When we begin to look for such passages, an interesting fact emerges: with the possible exception of the arrival of Schaha-barim,[1] Salammbô's point of view does not occur to any extent until more than half-way through the book. We have seen her in private before this, and have heard her speak (pp. 56–65), so that we already know something about her; but we have hardly been permitted to see how she thinks, which can be shown with certainty only by following her point of view, by getting inside her mind.

The fact that Salammbô's point of view is so rare in the first half of the book will naturally influence the reader's concept of her character. If we know her only through what others think of her, it is inevitable, even if we are aware that we ought not to take these people's ideas as objective truth, that something of their attitude will be incorporated into our own. Flaubert wanted to present his heroine as a vague, mysterious being, and knew that if she were a real living person this atmosphere must be partly destroyed. The desired atmosphere could be achieved only by presenting his heroine as an image in other people's minds. *Salammbô* has frequently been criticized on the grounds that its heroine is not a flesh-and-blood character; but if she had been, she could not have had the same effect on a person like Mâtho, and the whole tone of the novel would have been completely different.[2] There seems little point in wishing that a novelist had written something else.

It is true that Flaubert confesses some dissatisfaction with the

---

[1] p. 62. This is in Chapter III, which is mostly presented by the narrator (v. *supra*, pp. 181–4) but the wording as Schahabarim arrives suggests a brief inter-polation of Salammbô's point of view. It would of course be particularly appro-priate that the only significant occurrence of her point of view in 230 pages should be a description of the high priest of Tanit. Besides, this description has its echo in the tent scene: 'Salammbô, accoutumée aux eunuques, se laissait ébahir par la force de cet homme [Mâtho]' (p. 263).

[2] See also Thibaudet, op. cit., pp. 137–41.

proportions of his novel: he admits to Sainte-Beuve that he made the pedestal too big for the statue, and that an extra hundred pages (!) relating to Salammbô herself would have improved the situation. One may doubt the validity of this statement, and even Flaubert's sincerity in making it. While he invariably found faults with his books after they had been published—so conscientious a writer could never be entirely satisfied—this very meticulousness prevented him from publishing until he had done what he believed at the time to be his best. The lack of a hundred pages could never have escaped him if he had really believed it was a fault. Moreover, he made it clear elsewhere in the same letter that he did not *want* to present Salammbô as a sort of Carthaginian Emma, torn by conflicting passions: 'Salammbô au contraire demeure clouée par l'idée fixe. C'est une maniaque, une espèce de Sainte Thérèse.'[1] As the book stands, any careful reader can see in the character of the heroine ample reason for her behaviour, and for this behaviour affecting that of the other characters. A more intimate knowledge of her mind is not necessary, as it is for Emma, and such a knowledge would destroy the sense of elusiveness and semi-divinity which Flaubert had so carefully built up by using the point of view of people like Mâtho.

Salammbô's point of view does not really begin, then, until Chapter X (p. 233). We are told she is insensible to the threatening attitude of the Carthaginian populace, because 'Elle était troublée par des inquiétudes plus hautes'—namely the illness of the python, which is first described in terms of Carthaginian beliefs, but soon brings her back to her own preoccupations, through the comparison of the snake and her own interior 'spiral'. It is interesting that the spiral image should occur here, when Salammbô's mind is groping after nothing less than 'le secret de l'existence universelle' (p. 234). Several of Flaubert's characters—notably Saint Antoine and Schahabarim, but on a more banal level, also Emma, Frédéric, Bouvard, and Pécuchet—have this problem, doubtless because the young Flaubert himself had. Poulet points out that spirals and related metaphors (e.g. the pebble thrown into a pool of water, which also creates circles

[1] *Cor.*, V, 57–8.

of ever-increasing radius) occur fairly often both in Flaubert's *Correspondance* and in his works, and usually indicate a desire for experience and knowledge outside the normal limits of the person concerned.[1] Flaubert had in fact planned a work called *la Spirale*, which would apparently have considered how far the ever-increasing circles of inner personal experience (through imagination and hallucination) could be removed from the starting point of the spiral (reality) without something really drastic happening, and what would happen if the process got out of control. For the hero of *la Spirale*, the answer proposed was complete madness as far as society is concerned, but absolute happiness for the hero himself.[2] (The similarity between this situation and that of Bouvard and Pécuchet—on a burlesque level—springs to mind.) This answer may have occurred to Flaubert as a result of his own experiences. If we can judge by the few direct statements on the matter in the *Correspondance*—and it must be remembered that they may be simply *littérature*—he seems to have experienced moments when he felt that he was just on the brink of some world-shattering illumination.[3] At these moments he was torn between great joy and a terror that it was all too big for his mind, that reality was escaping him completely, that he was, perhaps, on the verge of madness. But Flaubert was in some ways an exceptional being. Because of his theory of universality, the people he wrote about had to be more ordinary: the solution of joy in madness is not possible for normal people. With the exception of Saint Antony, then, Flaubert's characters do not experience ecstatic bliss at the end of their spiral, for they never get far enough from reality, which always intrudes sharply at the crucial moment. Besides, this reflects the other side of Flaubert's personal experience: he was abnormal enough only to see the *possibility* of the final illumination granted to Saint Antony and the hero of *la Spirale*. He never actually

[1] Poulet: 'La Pensée circulaire de Flaubert' in *NNRF*, juillet, 1955, pp. 30–52; see also Cellier: *Etudes de structure* (Paris, Archives des lettres modernes, no. 56, 1964), p. 15.

[2] See Durry, op. cit., pp. 21–2, and especially Dimoff: 'Autour d'un projet de roman de Flaubert: *la Spirale*' in *RHL*, octobre–décembre, 1948, pp. 309–35.

[3] e.g. *Cor.*, I, 220, 229–30; II, 4, 51, 461; III, 76–8, 146, 270; IV, 180–1; V, 350.

crossed the border into this territory: like other normal people, he always retreated in time. This fact seems to have brought him to the conclusion that for ordinary beings it is a delusion to believe that any real illumination about universal knowledge is possible—hence his 'accepter les choses comme elles sont' philosophy. Flaubert therefore provided most of his characters with the alternative, much more mundane, solution. For them, the spiral can be seen as a more concrete metaphor: a kite. The line is not an imaginary one disappearing to infinity, but a real one, whether one likes it or not, keeping the kite firmly attached to the ground, no matter how high it may soar; and when the wind drops, the kite comes back to earth with a thud—the higher it had soared, the bigger the thud.

The spiral metaphor concerns not the search for knowledge or experience, but the search for it through illuminatory—non-rational—means. By the time he was writing *Salammbô*, Flaubert had personally renounced this method of finding truth. His endowing Salammbô with the spiral constitutes an implicit criticism of her, and warns us that she is the victim of her own illusions, that the fall must come. Besides, Flaubert and the hero of *la Spirale* had tried *voluntarily* to transform the facts of existence, whereas with characters like Salammbô this effort of will is absent;[1] they ignore the facts simply because they do not know what the facts are; they accept as fact what appears to be factual. Salammbô's 'spiralling' feeling, already invalid as a method of achieving knowledge, is doubly invalid because it is not even a method, but occurs accidentally: it is itself a result of her illusions. Far from being a conscious metaphysical symbol, it is suggested to her mind by a real, concrete spiral before her eyes, that of the

---

[1] The difference between Flaubert's attitude and the one he gives to Salammbô is discernible in the following passage: 'Vous me demandez comment je me suis guéri des hallucinations nerveuses que je subissais autrefois? Par deux moyens: 1° en les étudiant scientifiquement, c'est-à-dire en tâchant de m'en rendre compte et, 2° par *la force de la volonté*. J'ai souvent senti la folie me venir. . . . Mais je me cramponnais à ma raison. Elle dominait tout, quoique assiégée et battue. En d'autres fois, je tâchais, par l'imagination, de me donner facticement ces horribles souffrances. J'ai joué avec la démence et le fantastique comme Mithridate avec les poisons. Un grand orgueil me soutenait et j'ai vaincu le mal à force de l'étreindre corps à corps' (*Cor.*, IV, 180–1).

sick snake which she has been contemplating. It is also ironic, therefore, that her spiral should be accompanied by the same mixture of expectancy and fear as Flaubert had experienced when he was consciously trying to escape from reality: this is all part of the anticlimax which he is preparing for her.

Meanwhile, the rest of this passage contributes in other ways to the coming anticlimax, because of the continued point of view presentation. We are informed of the immense psychological influence of the veil on Salammbô, simply by following her ideas, and the 'facts' she accepts concerning it: 'Un mystère se dérobait dans la splendeur de ses plis; c'était le nuage enveloppant les dieux, le secret de l'existence universelle, et Salammbô, en se faisant horreur à elle-même, regrettait de ne l'avoir pas soulevé' (p. 234). Then follows a description of how she spent her days, which is strongly reminiscent of Emma's boredom and lassitude at Tostes and Yonville. Where Emma sits all day with a book which she does not read (pp. 83–4), Salammbô sits all day with one leg in her hand, as a sort of Oriental equivalent; both have vague desires to do something unusual and a little spectacular for their respective religions, while neither questions for a moment the validity of these desires or their motivation.[1] Both wander listlessly about, allowing the very sight of everyday objects and actions to reinforce their feeling of boredom and futility.[2] Both have *crises nerveuses*.[3] And both, as a result of their lassitude, attach undue importance to one regular event.[4]

[1] Emma 'voulut devenir une sainte. Elle acheta des chapelets, elle porta des amulettes; elle souhaitait avoir dans sa chambre, au chevet de sa couche, un reliquaire enchâssé d'émeraudes pour le baiser tous les soirs' (p. 296). Salammbô 'voulait s'en aller dans les montagnes de la Phénicie, en pèlerinage au temple d'Aphaka, où Tanit est descendue sous la forme d'une étoile' (p. 234).

[2] Les améthystes et les topazes du plafond faisaient çà et là trembler des taches lumineuses, et Salammbô, tout en marchant, tournait un peu la tête pour les voir. Elle allait prendre par le goulot les amphores suspendues; elle se rafraîchissait la poitrine sous les larges éventails, ou bien elle s'amusait à brûler du cinnamome dans des perles creuses (pp. 234–5). Cf. *Bovary*, p. 88: 'Et elle restait à faire rougir les pincettes, ou regardant la pluie tomber.' See also pp. 89–91, 173–4, 399.

[3] *Bovary*, pp. 92–3, 150, 151; *Salammbô*, p. 93.

[4] Et Emma quotidiennement attendait, avec une sorte d'anxiété, l'infaillible retour d'événements minimes, qui pourtant ne lui importaient guère. Le plus considérable était, le soir, l'arrivée de l'*Hirondelle* (p. 294).

Naturally there remain very important differences between the presentation of the two states of mind, notably the fact that Emma's feelings change more frequently, and are more widely distributed over the book: Salammbô's are concentrated in one relatively short passage. Emma's feelings are given more prominence, and developed at greater length, and her thoughts are more explicit: Emma's problems are much more central to the subject of *Madame Bovary*. But the general sentiments of the two heroines do have similar manifestations, and are presented in much the same way. It may even be argued that the presentation of Salammbô's state of mind is more economical, *because* her thoughts are not developed so explicitly, but sufficiently indicated in her actions.

The passage concludes (p. 235) with a statement of Salammbô's feelings towards Schahabarim, which are important not so much as an aspect of the point of view presentation, as in preparation for her ideas about him after she has been with Mâtho. It is to be noted, however, that these feelings include a 'singulière volupté', engendered by his presence, and which she doubtless attributes to his knowledge of Tanit, and in general to his priestly functions. This is probably another aspect of her delusion, although no hint of this is given here, since we are following Salammbô's thoughts. He, too, has 'reconnu l'influence de la Rabbet' on his mistress, and his diagnosis is of the utmost importance in determining Salammbô's attitudes, for she believes him to be 'habile à distinguer quels étaient les dieux qui envoyaient les maladies' (p. 236).

The steps towards Salammbô's decision to retrieve the veil are now traced in a long passage in which dialogue, narrator

---

Au coucher du soleil, Taanach retirait les losanges de feutre noir bouchant les ouvertures de la muraille; alors ses colombes, frottées de musc comme les colombes de Tanit, tout à coup entraient, et leurs pattes roses glissaient sur les dalles de verre parmi les grains d'orge qu'elle leur jetait à pleine poignées, comme un semeur dans un champ (p. 235).

In both cases the unimportant event happens to have extra significance for the character, which will not be realized until later: the *Hirondelle* is soon to carry Emma on her weekly visits to Léon, and Salammbô's doves fly away just as she is preparing for her rendez-vous with Mâtho.

presentation and Salammbô's point of view are intermingled (pp. 238–45). It is here that her false assumptions from false premises are most clearly expounded—so clearly, in fact, that it hardly seems worthwhile to point them out in detail. The passage is crucial for explaining Salammbô's motives and behaviour, but it is not notable for its subtlety. Salammbô's literal-minded interpretation of her religion (which is strongly reminiscent of Félicité's) becomes very clear: '... elle prenait des conceptions pour des réalités; elle acceptait comme vrais en eux-mêmes de purs symboles et jusqu'à des manières de langage' (p. 238). The priest's exposition of religious principles and Salammbô's duty as regards the veil completes the confusion in her mind, so that she now firmly believes that Moloch and Mâtho are the same being, and that no good can result:

Une épouvante indéterminée la retenait; elle avait peur de Moloch, peur de Mâtho. Cet homme à taille de géant, et qui était maître du zaïmph, dominait la Rabbet autant que le Baal et lui apparaissait en-touré des mêmes fulgurations; puis l'âme des dieux, quelquefois, visitait le corps des hommes. Schahabarim, en parlant de celui-là, ne disait-il pas qu'elle devait vaincre Moloch? Ils étaient mêlés l'un à l'autre; elle les confondait; tous les deux la poursuivaient (p. 241).

The confusion is then developed in the symbolic terms in which they appear to Salammbô's mind. She sees circles of fire spinning before her eyes, which echoes the spiral and has similar significance, and also recalls the 'globules couleur de feu [qui] éclataient dans l'air comme des balles fulminantes' which describe Emma's hallucination as she returns to Yonville just before *her* fate becomes conclusive. The torches carried by the restless Carthaginians 'faisaient comme des soleils qui se roulaient par la ville'.[1] Salammbô is disturbed by the fact that her serpent is missing, but then finds it changing its skin; and gradually as her decision becomes firmer the serpent recovers from its illness,

---

[1] It is true that the view of Carthage is shared by two witnesses (Salammbô and Schahabarim), which one would normally expect to result in greater objectivity. But both these characters are in their own ways preoccupied with the manifestations of the sun god, and both are therefore predisposed towards this kind of symbolism: Schahabarim's apostasy, as well as Salammbô's fate, is foreshadowed in this image. The two subjective deformations coincide.

which of course convinces her that her decision is correct. The incidental mention of the snake's shedding is clearly to inform the reader of the real cause of its illness, which Salammbô had taken as a message from the gods; and its recovery, which she believes to be another message, is equally physiological.[1] Once again events having rational explanations are endowed with mystical virtues because of the point of view. So, too, the bird migration takes on extra meanings: for Salammbô, the pigeons are earthly representatives of 'les colombes de Tanit' (p. 235), so that their departure is distinctly ominous; but in addition they leave late in the afternoon, at a time when 'une couleur de sang occupait l'horizon' (p. 243). And since they are going to Sicily, they conveniently fly towards the sun: thus 'elles disparurent comme englouties et tombant d'elles-mêmes dans la gueule du soleil' (p. 243).

The famous snake dance now follows (pp. 244-6). While a good deal of this is also from Salammbô's point of view, that of Taanach intervenes so that we can view the over-all scene—in particular the references to the moon, and, once more, the wet footprints:'... elle se renversait sous les rayons de la lune. La blanche lumière semblait l'envelopper d'un brouillard d'argent, la forme de ses pas humides brillait sur les dalles, des étoiles palpitaient dans la profondeur de l'eau' (p. 246).

There are also several parallels with the tent scene, which the reader will realize retrospectively—even to the snake's being compared to 'un collier rompu dont les deux bouts traînent jusqu'à terre' (p. 246; cf. p. 265: 'la chaînctte d'or éclata, et les deux bouts, en s'envolant, frappèrent la toile comme deux vipères rebondissantes')[2] and to the fascination of the snake's eyes, 'plus brillants que des escarboucles', which recall those of Mâtho,

---

[1] See, for example, Pope: *The Giant Snakes* (London, Routledge and Kegan Paul, 1962), pp. 68-9 for the physical changes which occur in a python just before shedding: languidness, lack of appetite, loss of contrast in colour pattern, change in over-all colour, changes in the colour of the eyes; also pp. 73-4, on the manner of disengaging itself from its old skin. All these details are faithfully recorded for Salammbô's python.

[2] This parallel, as well as the symbolism of the disappearing doves, mentioned above, has been pointed out by Demorest, op. cit., pp. 489 and 491 respectively.

'comme deux charbons dans la nuit'—remembering that *escarboucle* comes from the Latin *carbunculus*: *petit charbon*. Again Flaubert has so arranged his details that these two impressionistic descriptions could be based on reality and yet symbolically echo each other: already on p. 234 we had been told that the snake's eyes contained 'de petits points rouges', and now the closeness of the python's head to Salammbô's eyes could do the rest simply because of the laws of perspective; and in Mâtho's tent there are great flashes of lightning alternating with almost complete darkness, during which the flickering lamp in the tent could easily be reflected by Mâtho's eyes (p. 263).

When Salammbô crosses the Barbarian camp with Mâtho, an opportunity for mentioning more fires is provided: 'leurs reflets empourprés, illuminant certaines places, en laissaient d'autres dans les ténèbres, complètement' (p. 257). In these words the result of Salammbô's visit is precisely foretold—she does not find the secret of universal knowledge, but she does discover another sort. She also notes that Mâtho has become 'le véritable, le seul chef des Barbares' (pp. 257-8) and passes by the ditch in which the Carthaginian prisoners are held: Giscon's unexpected appearance and malediction are prepared, and also, because of the impressionistic nature of the description, his fate is unmistakably foreshadowed: 'il lui sembla que des visages posaient contre le bord, au niveau du sol, comme eussent fait des têtes coupées' (p. 258).

The confusion of the two protagonists about each other, and indeed about themselves, reaches a climax in this scene. Mâtho admits that he had identified Salammbô with Tanit, and the outcome of this interview does not dispel his delusion; but in addition, because of the words of Salammbô, Mâtho begins to regard himself as a god too (p. 261). At the same time, Salammbô both identifies him with Moloch (see especially the 'Moloch, tu me brûles!' p. 265, but there are several other indications), and regards herself as the chosen servant of Tanit: 'Elle se sentait comme appuyée sur la force des dieux; et le regardant face à face, elle lui demanda le zaïmph; elle le réclamait en paroles abondantes et superbes' (p. 259; cf. p. 262).

We need not follow out the Wagnerian accompaniments of this scene: the storm, at which Sainte-Beuve scoffed, and which Flaubert disingenuously defended by remarking how frequent storms are in Tunisia at the end of summer; the broken ankle chain; the veil falling on Salammbô at the critical moment; the reappearance of the moon, and so on. We should note, however, that even now Salammbô is convinced she is doing the will of the gods (p. 265)—this attitude is soon to change. We should note, too, the double anticlimax which Salammbô experiences: 'C'est donc là, songeait-elle, cet homme formidable qui fait trembler Carthage!' (p. 266) and 'Alors elle examina le zaïmph; et quand elle l'eut bien contemplé, elle fut surprise de ne pas avoir ce bonheur qu'elle s'imaginait autrefois. Elle restait mélancolique devant son rêve accompli' (p. 268). One can compare these sentiments with those of Flaubert's other 'fallen' characters. For example, Emma: '... et elle ne pouvait s'imaginer à présent que ce calme où elle vivait fût le bonheur qu'elle avait rêvé' (p. 55); 'Emma retrouvait dans l'adultère toutes les platitudes du mariage' (p. 401); Frédéric: 'Alors Frédéric se rappela les jours déjà loin où il enviait l'inexprimable bonheur de se trouver dans une de ces voitures, à côté d'une de ces femmes. Il le possédait, ce bonheur-là, et il n'en était pas plus joyeux' (p. 299). This is the end of the spiral, the return of the kite, the point where reality intrudes; or is it? We are still following Salammbô's point of view, and 'disillusionment' appears in the *Dictionnaire des idées reçues* as a bourgeois trait.[1] It is possible that she was as deluded in her disillusion as in her illusions. Since this scene appears to put an end to her hopes, this is a good point at which to recapitulate, to try to find the reality under the illusion.

Salammbô's original vague desires and frustrations are clearly sexually based (see in particular pp. 60, 64), and exacerbated by surrounding physical conditions, such as strong perfumes, fasting, and other religious rites.[2] She, of course, believes them to be

[1] ILLUSION—(Affecter d'en avoir beaucoup), se plaindre de ce qu'on les a perdues.
[2] See pp. 61, 247, and Flaubert's statement in his letter to Sainte-Beuve that this was part of his intention: 'On les empoisonnait de parfums, littéralement.

caused by the influence of the moon, and so do those around her, so that, no matter whose point of view we follow, this is the idea which predominates. Now she knows that Schahabarim has not told her everything about Tanit, and, aided by his hints, she imagines that what he is hiding is of supreme importance— 'le secret de l'existence universelle'. Already the irony is beginning, for the only 'secret' the priest is withholding is the sexual aspect of the deity (pp. 61, 64), and this is hardly as important as it is made to sound. It is, however, extremely important for the eunuch priest (pp. 65, 237, 239), but, because he has been forbidden by Hamilcar to instruct Salammbô in these matters (pp. 61, 63), he can speak about them only in religious and symbolic terms, thereby connecting them with a weighty cosmogony. He thinks he is thus turning Salammbô's attention away from them (p. 64), but, since she is predisposed to give great attention to them, since, not knowing this herself, she consciously turns all her thoughts to religion, and since in any case she takes literally what is primarily intended to be metaphorical (p. 238), the only result is her increased preoccupation with them.

Against this background Mâtho appears. Although the first time Salammbô sees him the point of view is not hers but that of the Mercenaries, it must be remembered that during this first scene he displays great strength (by throwing a loaded table at Narr'Havas) and a savage, animal-like temper (p. 19). This inevitably created an impression in the heroine's mind, and we discover during the tent scene (p. 261) that she believed this

---

C'est ce que j'ai eu soin de dire au commencement, dès qu'il a été question de la maladie de Salammbô' (*Cor.*, V, 64). Cf. this letter, quoted by Thibaudet, op. cit., p. 137: 'Il faut avoir le tempérament robuste pour monter sur les cimes du mysticisme sans y perdre la tête. Et puis, il y a dans tout cela (chez les femmes surtout) des questions de tempérament qui compliquent la douleur. Ne voyez-vous pas qu'elles sont toutes amoureuses d'Adonis? C'est l'éternel époux qu'elles demandent. Ascétiques ou libidineuses, elles rêvent l'amour, le grand amour; et pour les guérir (momentanément du moins) ce n'est pas une idée qu'il leur faut, mais un fait, un homme, un enfant, un amant. Cela vous paraît cynique. Mais ce n'est pas moi qui ai inventé la nature humaine. Je suis convaincu que les appétits matériels les plus furieux se formulent *insciemment* par des élans d'idéalisme ...' (*Cor.*, IV, 313).

violence to be directed at her. The irony is apparent: the fight had started because Narr'Havas believed Salammbô was offering Mâtho her bed. Mâtho was indeed chasing Salammbô, but by no means to kill her. With the beginning of the war, Salammbô identifies her own terror with that of Carthage—and again she is wrong—and blames all on Mâtho. Her suspicions seem to be confirmed when Mâtho appears in her room with the veil: obviously he has stolen it in order to dominate and destroy Carthage—for Schahabarim had told her the veil was the soul of the city (p. 64)—and he intends to begin with her, as he had apparently threatened to do the first time she saw him. The truth is that Mâtho had no desire to attack Carthage, that he had stolen the veil, much against his better judgement, in order to lay it at her feet, and that had she yielded to him—as she was tempted to do, moreover, in order to discover the 'secret' which Schahabarim had withheld (pp. 106, 234)—the war would probably have stopped there and then. Meanwhile, Schahabarim is having grave religious doubts, and beginning to wonder whether Moloch is not after all superior to Tanit. At the crucial stage in Salammbô's emotional development he tells her that Moloch dominates Tanit (p. 239), so naturally Salammbô identi- fies Moloch with Mâtho, who certainly seems to be dominating Tanit at the moment.

The irony of the tent scene is now fully prepared. Salammbô is convinced that she must rescue Tanit from Moloch, and that in doing so she will discover the secret of Tanit; but because this is sacrilege, she must die, as Schahabarim had warned her (p. 64). But who will cause her death—Tanit, for discovering the secret, or Moloch, who has wished her ill right from the beginning? That it should be neither is an important factor in Salammbô's subsequent behaviour, and is part of her two-fold anticlimax.

The question is still more complex. In the tent Salammbô finds the knowledge (sexual) which she had been seeking. It is ironic that, not knowing this is what she had been seeking, she should find this knowledge incidentally, as it were: she did not (consciously) come to the tent for this, and having found it, does not realize that she has achieved her unconscious desire. Because of her upbringing, she attaches far more importance to her broken ankle chain (p. 266) than to the sexual act (p. 318); she does not even know that she has been taught to fear the broken chain because of what it symbolizes, not in itself. She has unwittingly discovered the secret of Tanit, and therefore does not understand why the terrible 'Moloch' can behave like a harmless child. From this behaviour on his part she concludes that he is not so fearful after all. This conclusion is just as mistaken as her earlier one: she has not discovered his 'real' nature, but only another aspect of it. Her conclusion that she was previously mistaken is correct, but her belief that she has now corrected her mistake is wrong.

Now what of the veil? Salammbô believed she was seeking not sexual fulfilment, but unification with the Goddess (p. 60), 'le secret de l'existence universelle'. She believed that the veil would permit this, but of course it cannot; when she finally contemplates it, she feels frustrated 'devant son rêve accompli' (p. 268). The veil, then, did not hide what she expected, but did hide what she really needed, and did in fact indirectly reveal its secret to her (through Mâtho). She had been mistaken all along in her ideas about the veil, and is now equally mistaken in feeling disappointed with it. The end of Salammbô's spiral is not, after all, the return to reality, but merely the return to apparent reality. Her new 'truth' about her two favourite illusions—the veil and Mâtho—is only partial truth, just as her old one was.[1]

We saw that this climactic scene provided the possibility for Mâtho to cease regarding Salammbô as a goddess, but that by a complex coincidence of circumstances this did not happen. In Salammbô's case, the de-mystification of Mâtho, and of herself, does take place. She rejects the magical qualities of both Mâtho

[1] Demorest, op. cit., pp. 484 et seq., lists in some detail the occurrences of the major symbols of *Salammbô*, especially those concerned with the sun and the moon, water and the serpent. He also mentions Salammbô's disillusionment. But he fails to see that all these symbols are ironic because they depend upon a false view of reality, the characters' delusions about themselves and others. Nor does Demorest point out the irony of Salammbô's disillusionment, and its connections with the falsity of the symbols. This seems to me to be the most important aspect of all.

and the veil: 'Les angoisses dont elle souffrait autrefois l'avaient abandonnée. Une tranquillité singulière l'occupait' (p. 316). As a result, she also rejects the domination of the priest, her concern for the python, and her religious fasting (p. 316). She now spends her time looking across at the Barbarians, just as Mâtho had been continually drawn towards Carthage; for Salammbô's old preoccupation with Tanit and Moloch has been replaced by a new, sharply contrasting one, which is expressed in the simplest, most straightforward language: 'Elle aurait voulu, malgré sa haine, revoir Mâtho. De tous les Carthaginois, elle était la seule personne, peut-être, qui lui eût parlé sans peur' (p. 317). Mâtho is a man, but a man she would like to see again. The 'hate' which is mentioned need not be taken too seriously: Salammbô had had an opportunity of killing Mâtho (p. 267) which she did not take, and now (p. 318) she does not want to mention this, because she knows she ought to have killed him.[1] In any case this hate progressively diminishes as she comes to realize her true feelings towards Mâtho the man. There are only three more passages before the final chapter in which we are told Salammbô's inner feelings, and all are intended primarily to show this evolution. Thus p. 355: 'Bien qu'elle demandât, tous les jours, à Tanit, la mort de Mâtho, son horreur pour le Libyen diminuait. Elle sentait confusément que la haine dont il l'avait persécutée était une chose presque religieuse . . .' (Note that although she is becoming clearer about her own motives, she is still scarcely aware of his); p. 380, while she is talking with Narr'Havas: 'Le souvenir de Mâtho la saisit; elle ne résista pas au désir de savoir ce qu'il devenait.' At this point we cease to look at Salammbô from the inside, and her subsequent reactions are presented from Narr'Havas' point of view, which allows some ambiguity. We are told that she *seemed* to be pleased that Mâtho would soon die; she even asks Narr'Havas to kill Mâtho; but when the latter replies that he will certainly do so and then marry her himself, 'Salammbô

---

[1] Thus for the second time she has let slip an opportunity of ending the war, and on this occasion it is not through ignorance but through selfishness. These two lost opportunities add an extra piquancy to the final scene, in which the whole of Carthage bows down to her as the saviour of the city.

tressaillit, et elle baissa la tête'. The reader can no doubt accurately guess her deepest sentiments, but the fact that they are not explicit, because of the method of presentation, does serve to emphasize the ambiguity of her attitude. She may be sincere, on a conscious level, when she says she wants Mâtho killed. Her true feelings may still not be absolutely clear to her, so that her point of view would not help here. It is her physical reactions, not her thoughts, which betray her to the reader. This hypothesis is confirmed by the third very brief passage, p. 393: 'Le souvenir de Mâtho la gênait d'une façon intolérable; il lui semblait que la mort de cet homme débarrasserait sa pensée, . . .' She does think she wants him to die, but only to rid herself of her obsession; yet obviously if she is obsessed by him she does not want him to be harmed at all. She is still deluding herself, both in her desire for his death and in her theory that this will cure her. Her delusion is also indicated by the analogy she draws—an analogy which is manifestly also false, a Carthaginian *idée reçue*: '. . . comme, pour se guérir de la blessure des vipères, on les écrase sur la plaie' (p. 393).

The final passage from Salammbô's point of view (pp. 412–13) brings this evolution to an end. With the other Carthaginians, Salammbô has watched Mâtho being tortured, and at the end of the ferocious obstacle race, the final description of him is presented through her eyes. The real nature of her preoccupation and the real nature of his feelings towards her, become clear as she looks at what is left of him:

> . . . et la conscience lui surgit de tout ce qu'il avait souffert pour elle. Bien qu'il agonisât, elle le revoyait dans sa tente, à genoux, lui entourant la taille de ses bras, balbutiant des paroles douces; elle avait soif de les sentir encore, de les entendre; elle allait crier. Il s'abattit à la renverse et ne bougea plus.[1]

---

[1] pp. 412–13. The text quoted is that of the last edition corrected by Flaubert (Lemerre, 1879); the original edition (Lévy, 1863) contained the following extra words after 'entendre', which underline still more the presence of Salammbô's point of view in this passage: 'elle ne voulait pas qu'il mourût! A ce moment-là, Mâtho eut un grand tressaillement: elle allait crier . . .'. See *Variantes*, Conard edition, p. 501, and Pléiade edition, p. 1027, which follows the text of the original edition.

Illumination comes to her, as to Emma, when it is too late. To add to the blow, the priests rush round her and congratulate her on Mâtho's death: 'c'était son œuvre'. Another statement showing the ramifications Flaubert can give to a situation. The priests believe that Salammbô had caused Mâtho's death by wresting the veil from him; we know his death was caused by a long chain of events, some of which were chance, some avoidable. On the other hand, if Salammbô did not actually bring about this death, she was, simply by being what she was, indirectly the cause of it. Like most other characters in the book, the priests are both wrong and right.

Salammbô's own death raises a similar question. For the people of Carthage, who have once more turned from Moloch to Tanit (now that the danger has passed), and whose point of view triumphantly ends the book, its cause is perfectly simple: 'Ainsi mourut la fille d'Hamilcar, pour avoir touché au manteau de Tanit'. This is patently not the view of Flaubert. Given Salammbô's psychological evolution and the fact that every 'supernatural' event which we have discussed has an ordinary physiological or psychological explanation, it is much more reasonable to conclude that her death came from severe emotional shock, some signs of which are already evident on p. 413. The priests' congratulations probably contributed: if Mâtho's death were not directly her doing, she had certainly wished for it, and her flash of illumination had just shown her how she had morally contributed towards it: 'la conscience lui surgit de tout ce qu'il avait souffert pour elle'. She then has to witness the extraction of his heart, its offering to Moloch, and the huge sadistic joy of her compatriots. It is not surprising that she was unable to withstand all this. And yet she *did* touch the veil, and circumstances were such that this fact did eventually cause Mâtho's death, and therefore her own. Again the irony is double: Carthage is wrong in ascribing such powers to a piece of cloth, but because so many people believed in it, events occurred *as if* the cloth had had these powers. One is reminded of Jack, in Swift's *Tale of a Tub*, who walked along the street with his eyes closed, and when he struck his nose against a post was satisfied that this was a case of predestination. To the very last sentence Flaubert uses point of view to show people confused because they are unwilling or unable to look at facts.

Logic disguised

In summing up, we could quote another passage from the letter to Sainte-Beuve, which answers the critic's sceptical remarks about the power of the veil in a manner which implies the intentions we have been examining:

> Pourquoi ne voulez-vous pas non plus que *la disparition du Zaïmph* ait été pour *quelque chose* dans la perte de la bataille, puisque l'armée des Mercenaires contenait des gens qui croyaient au Zaïmph? J'indique les causes principales (trois mouvements militaires) de cette perte; puis j'ajoute celle-là comme cause secondaire et dernière (*Cor.*, V, 64–5).

Everywhere this principle is seen to be operating. Not only do the fortunes of the war tend to vary according to who has the veil, not only are Salammbô and Mâtho confused about each other's real nature, and sometimes their own, and the Carthaginians confused about both; even in smaller details, like the illness of the serpent, the death of those who killed the sacred fish, the thunderstorm following the sacrifice to Moloch, Salammbô's premonitions about her death, Schahabarim's defection to Moloch, and so on, there is a logical cause-and-effect sequence disguised by the use of point of view (either individual or collective), but made available to the reader through the judicious changing of the point of view. By doing this, Flaubert also makes the valid point, widely accepted in such diverse fields as psychosomatics and biblical studies, that very strange things can happen if people believe strongly enough in their possibility. The power of the veil becomes real because so many people believe it to be real: *Salammbô*, far from being merely an escape into the magic of the past, is also, like *Saint Antoine*, the work of a faithful nineteenth-century rationalist. But principally Flaubert is again using point of view to show not only the almost continuous conflict between appearance and reality, which is perhaps a little banal, but also, by arranging a dynamic situation, a much more involved conflict. What is illusion when the characters think it is reality tends to become reality just at the time the characters think they have found it to be illusion, and vice versa. And he does this not for one or two protagonists, but for almost every individual in the book, and for two whole nations as well. The ramifications of the subject may be even wider-reaching than those of *Bovary*, and the aspects of human behaviour treated, while different, are at least as important. To bring this complex mass of detail together into one unified volume was an enormous undertaking, and the present study has done little more than introduce one element of it. As with all of Flaubert's works, the more one studies it the more one realizes how much there is to be studied. But it is truer of *Salammbô* than of any other work by Flaubert that it has not been studied nearly enough— otherwise the book would not be discreetly ignored as at present. Even those critics who see in it Flaubert's greatest work, his most typical work, his most profound work, his most philo- sophical work, his most learned work—all of which appellations are in any case doubtful—still treat it superficially. We have yet to see an adequate critical treatment of it.

V

L'EDUCATION SENTIMENTALE

The unworthy witness

AN increasing body of opinion regards *l'Education sentimentale* as Flaubert's best work, and one of the greatest monuments of nineteenth-century fiction. It is a judgement which contrasts sharply with the blank incomprehension which, when the book appeared, overwhelmed the applause of Flaubert's friends and the wild enthusiasm of some young Naturalists. Such incomprehension is not difficult to explain, for as a rule only two sorts of novel had much appeal for the public, then as now. The first category, by far the larger, consisted of novels which were simple-minded like the public itself, and simply and clearly served it the tepid ideas and prejudices to which it was accustomed. The second could indeed contain something new and valid, but seldom made headway unless it had the benefit of a considerable scandal, sometimes skilfully manipulated by the author and/or his friends. *Madame Bovary* belonged to the second category. To a certain extent, it also belonged to the first, for it is a novel which readily appeals to the uninitiated at a first reading. Alone among Flaubert's published works, it has a clearly developed story presented in an apparently fairly conventional manner, its irony and comic effects are in several passages unsubtle enough for almost anyone to grasp, it has the requisite love interest and an oppressed heroine, and characters like Emma, Homais, and Bournisien can be said to be 'real' in the sense in which this term is used by those who do not feel bound to consider what they mean by it. It is sufficiently straightforward to maintain interest and enjoyment, and to provide at least an inkling of its various messages during a fairly cursory first reading. Of course, it is in addition a novel which reveals new depths every time it is re-read; but those who are primarily responsible for the success of a book, in terms of sales and immediate reputation (and I am convinced that these elements influence a book's subsequent reputation and 'value' more deeply than many critics are willing to allow), are precisely those who seldom re-read a novel: the journalistic critics and the general public. *L'Education sentimentale* is more difficult. It, too, at first appears orthodox in its presentation, but it soon fails to live up to the expectations of a reader who wants to grapple with it in these terms: he is likely to experience boredom and confusion at his first attempt. Neither the minor characters nor the mass of theories and ideas which are bandied about seem to fall into any clear pattern or any stable individualized mould. Uneasiness and a sense of being cheated frequently follow. It is plain that Flaubert is 'getting at' someone and something, but who and what, and why?[1] From here it is but a short step to one of two conclusions: either he was getting at everyone and everything, he is therefore a pessimist and a misfit and life isn't really like that at all, so we can ignore this book and settle back to read *edifying* or *exciting* literature; or if the book was any good it would have told us quite clearly who and what it was getting at so we could agree or disagree for a moment and then settle back. ... A glance at the critical comments on *l'Education sentimentale* will quickly confirm the presence of one or other of these attitudes in a surprising number of cases, even among those critics who appear to be sincere.[2] In many (but not all) cases they clearly stem from a superficial knowledge of the book and its aims.

It can, of course, be argued that one of the signs by which great works can be recognized is precisely that a first reading inspires a desire to try again; that, like *Bovary*, they immediately reveal enough of their greatness to convince the reader that it

---

[1] See Cortland: *The Sentimental Adventure* (The Hague, Mouton and Co., 1967) pp. 128 et seq. for an interesting attempt to analyse reader reactions to Flaubert's novels more fully.

[2] For examples of the early critical reaction to this novel, see the Appendix to the Conard edition, pp. 693 et seq., and Dumesnil: *l'Education*, op. cit., pp. 167 et seq.

will be worth while to look for deeper-buried treasures; and that if everything had to be read several times, on the chance that it *may* be a *chef-d'œuvre* in spite of appearances, we should quickly fall several decades behind the printing presses. While one may subscribe to all this on a practical level, and may frequently be guilty oneself of rejecting works without giving them sufficient chance to reveal themselves, practical considerations and personal inadequacies cannot alter the fact that a great work remains great whether or not its greatness is immediately apparent. We return to the starting-point: that *l'Education sentimentale* should not have had the recognition accorded to *Bovary* is understandable, but the reasons for it are largely extra-literary.

I do not propose to argue, however, that re-reading *l'Education* many times will automatically reveal that Flaubert's more mature uses of point of view make this a greater novel than *Bovary*. In spite of the opinion of several modern critics, and the preoccupations of twentieth-century novelists, it is not at all certain that the two are necessarily connected.[1] The purpose of this study is to examine the evolution of a technique in a writer who is assumed to be great, without any systematic attempt to prove his greatness. There will be no attempt, either, to prove that *l'Education sentimentale* is greater than *Bovary*: this must remain a personal opinion. However, it will occasionally be possible to dismiss certain arguments against *l'Education* as invalid or irrelevant, and to suggest that some of them may arise from a misunderstanding of Flaubert's use of point of view. Apart from this, our study of the technique should give an example of how much a close reading of this book can yield, however one approaches it. To this extent its greatness will at least be indicated.

Superficially, *l'Education* and *Salammbô* may appear to have a good deal in common, for both concern a group of individuals trying to work out their relationship to a society in turmoil. But we should not expect these similarities to go very deep, nor, as a result, will they necessarily be reflected in similar

---

[1] See Friedman, loc. cit., who does concede this point in the conclusion of his article, p. 1182.

techniques of presentation. *Salammbô* could not be undertaken without presenting a complete factual picture of the society concerned, from both the material and the spiritual standpoints. It was impossible for Flaubert to begin by creating individuals and then try to fit them into their social background. Besides, we have argued that it was part of the point of that book not to have individuals, but to present each character as little more than a separate manifestation of a mob society.

The few surviving plans of *l'Education*—those very early ones published by Mme Durry[1]—reveal a basically different intention and emphasis. From the very beginning, Flaubert struggled to find a simple story concerning the interrelationships between a very small number of individuals, and to work from there. This concern lasted for several months at least, for in the whole of the *Carnet 19* there are only two vague hints that the subject of his book might be expanded to include wider social questions.[2] Flaubert was of course aware of the increased potential significance of a more broadly-based work. About the time he finally settled on the Schlésinger plan, he referred to his novel as 'une série d'analyses et de potins médiocres', 'des couillades usées'; but by the time he is ready to begin writing it has become 'l'histoire morale des hommes de ma génération'.[3] But this broadening never weakens the original intention to deal with the subject by following individual destinies: 'Bien que mon sujet soit purement d'analyse', he says in 1867, 'je touche quelquefois aux événements de l'époque. [!] Mes premiers plans sont inventés et mes fonds réels'; and even when he seems most worried that his individuals may be lost in the background material, he is still quite firm about his priorities: 'Je veux représenter un état psychologique.... Je suis donc obligé de reculer à un plan secondaire les choses qui sont précisément les plus intéressantes [i.e. the historical facts and personalities]'.[4]

---

[1] *Flaubert et ses projets inédits.* Two thousand pages of poems, notes, and manuscripts were sold in 1931 and have apparently not been seen since.

[2] Durry, op. cit., pp. 187, 192.

[3] *Cor.*, V, 92; X, 319 (both these letters seem to date from March 1863); *Cor.*, V, 158 (October 1864).

[4] *Cor.*, V, 327; XI, 65; V, 363.

Keeping one or more individuals at the centre of the book can solve some of the problems of structure and unity which were inherent in the subject of *Salammbô*. Flaubert adopted a combined point of view there for two main reasons: it minimized the possibilities of subjective aberrations, and was therefore useful for the resuscitation of a forgotten society, and it placed the emphasis on the crowd. But it did cause problems, for in some scenes it could not reasonably be used. In addition, Carthage was facing an attack from outside, and the attackers, too, had to be presented to the reader. All this resulted in a complex series of changes of point of view, which must have been very difficult to handle. Such considerations may have influenced Flaubert in working out his new subject; at any rate, his final decision was such that this type of difficulty was largely overcome before he began writing. As in *Bovary* the society concerned was well enough known by his readers for the background to be introduced without the necessity for careful objectification. The social crisis was to come from within, so that it would be possible for a single observer to be used for all sides of the conflict. If the social status of this observer was carefully chosen, he could, without offending verisimilitude, be made to move in circles above, below and within his own, and thus observe a great variety of habits and attitudes, as well as typical manifestations of the crisis. If the emphasis is to be on individuals, the same point of view can be used to observe both private and public signs of the unrest. Finally, a return to the individual point of view, as used in *Bovary*, would give more freedom to dramatize again the disorders arising from the perennial conflict between what life is and what people would like it to be. An added advantage would be that at least a certain measure of unity would be automatically assured by having as a constant one observing character at the centre of the action.

Such reasoning would seem to be confirmed by changes in Flaubert's early plans.[1] Flaubert's decision to transfer the centre of interest from the married woman to the aspiring lover coincides with his decision to expand the original simple parallel

---

[1] Durry, op. cit., pp. 155–6.

between the *Bourgeoise* and the *Lorette* into a parallel between two societies, each with a satellite group of secondary characters —this is the first step towards broadening the scope of the novel. Obviously the *Bourgeoise* cannot penetrate into the world of the *Lorette*, but the husband and the lover can, and they can also serve as a link between the two societies. The interests of point of view, unity, and balance can thus be made to coincide. From here the principle can be extended almost indefinitely: make the young man a student, and he can easily meet representatives of every shade of thought among contemporary youth; make him a provincial, and the bourgeois society of the provinces can be satirized; make him intermittently rich and ambitious, and he can meet people like Dambreuse and a whole new social group. Finally, invent a series of possible interrelationships, such as Arnoux's dealings with Rosanette, Roque's with Dambreuse, and so on, so that not only the central figure, but almost everyone else, can be seen moving in at least two different social circles, and presenting a different face in each, and the structural patterns can become so tightly interwoven that they appear almost miraculous.

Most of these possibilities were still very much in the future when Flaubert decided that Frédéric would be the pivot of the novel, but the decision remained firm. About 70 per cent of the finished work is presented from Frédéric's point of view, and if one includes scenes in which he is present although the point of view is not his alone, this rises to over 80 per cent. This is a considerably higher proportion than is granted to the central figure of Flaubert's previous works, and must necessarily have a bearing upon our interpretation of *l'Education sentimentale*.

It should be said at the outset that Flaubert's correspondence contains only one passage suggesting that he may intentionally have arranged his novel about a significant use of point of view. In a letter to Tourgeneff, apparently in reply to a criticism by the latter about the range of Mme Arnoux's voice, he says:

Sans doute, le passage en question n'est pas très fort. Je le trouve même un peu coco. Cependant, une voix de contralto peut faire des effets de *haut*, témoin l'Alboni; et au fond vous me paraissez sévère. Notez, pour me disculper, que *mon héros n'est pas un musicien* et que mon héroïne est une personne médiocre.[1]

Apart from the slighting reference to Mme Arnoux, which should not go unnoticed, Flaubert contends that whether or not such a musical effect is possible, he is justified in saying that it occurred, because Frédéric thought it occurred. The passage does at least show that considerations of point of view were not unknown to him.

The *Correspondance* may be silent, but an examination of the novel itself from this angle offers so many subjects for discussion, that there is no hope of dealing with them all in a single chapter. One can do no more than treat a few precise topics fairly exhaustively. I intend to concentrate on various types of descriptions, and on a few other matters of relevance to the usual critical approach to this novel.

It would be tedious to begin once more by establishing that a limited point of view technique does in fact occur in *l'Education sentimentale*. If my remarks about the earlier works are accepted, there will be no difficulty in agreeing that basically the same methods are employed here. This can quickly be verified by opening the book almost at random. Most frequently it will be found that the conditions outlined earlier are all present, and that moreover the witness is almost invariably Frédéric himself. This chapter will be concerned with the significance of this fact, by relating it to our interpretation of the characters and of the book as a whole, and to Flaubert's avowed aims in the writing of any novel.

If Frédéric is to be almost constantly our witness, the first essential is plainly to establish his reliability—a task not remarkable for its difficulty. We know, first of all, that in general Flaubert was not proposing his hero as a model whose behaviour might be copied. He never did this, of course, but in this case he recorded

---

[1] *Cor.*, XIII, 278; italic mine.

his attitude in a note on the first copy of the novel he received: 'Frédéric Moreau, homme de toutes les faiblesses' (a quotation from the novel itself). He also added a 't' to the sub-title, to make it read: 'Histoire d'un jeune hommet'.[1] The *faiblesses*, which we might interpret as an inability to resist suggestions and temptations, are expressed in the novel by an exasperating mobility of attitudes, these attitudes being conditioned more by immediate circumstances than by a cool and logical consideration of the facts. One of the themes which we have followed in Flaubert's previous works is again evident.[2]

Frédéric's mobility is very striking in his relationships with other people, and one manifestation of it is important to the present argument. The two scenes on pp. 59–61 provide a simple example as a starting-point. Pellerin, who has recently suffered from Arnoux's doubtful business methods, condemns the latter in most violent terms. Frédéric suggests, at first only timidly, that Pellerin is exaggerating; but in the face of the latter's violent reaction, gradually comes to defend Arnoux in more definite terms, and in doing so convinces himself that Arnoux is a better person than it had ever occurred to him to think: 'Dans l'échauffement de son éloquence[3] il fut pris de tendresse pour cet homme intelligent et bon, que ses amis calomniaient et qui maintenant travaillait tout seul, abandonné. Il ne résista pas au singulier besoin de le revoir immédiatement'. Patently an example of *style indirect libre*: it follows Frédéric's thoughts *of the moment*. Frédéric returns to Arnoux's shop to find him engrossed in his work, not feeling in the least 'abandonné'. He is welcomed very casually and is offended by Arnoux's light-hearted banter, which does not fit his own mood of sentimental friendliness. As a result:

Frédéric se sentit de plus en plus irrité par son air de méditation, et

[1] Quoted by Dumesnil, Belles Lettres edition of *l'Education sentimentale*, Introduction, p. cvii.

[2] This mobility is equally evident in most of the other characters as well—which is one of the methods by which Flaubert underlines the universality of his theme.

[3] Cf. p. 318: 'Frédéric se mit à défendre Arnoux. Il garantissait sa probité, finissait par y croire, inventait des chiffres, des preuves'; and Cortland's remarks on the farewell scene, op. cit., pp. 98–100.

surtout par ses mains, ... de grosses mains, un peu molles, à ongles plats. Enfin Arnoux ... lui passa la main sous le menton, familière-ment. Cette privauté déplut à Frédéric, il se recula; puis il franchit le seuil du bureau, pour la dernière fois de son existence, croyait-il. Mme Arnoux, elle-même, se trouvait comme diminuée par la vulgarité de son mari.

Several more emotive words, this time in the opposite direction —it is difficult to believe we are talking of the same man. Just as the insignificant anger of Pellerin made Frédéric warm to Arnoux, so the insignificant behaviour of Arnoux makes him change his mind. There is nothing about Arnoux's hands, for example, which could possibly have turned Frédéric against him—if there were, it would certainly have happened long ago. There seems nothing outrageous about a friend behaving 'familièrement', and little reason to be displeased by the 'privauté' in question. Arnoux is the normal Arnoux: only Frédéric's point of view transforms him. There is, in short, no justification for accepting Frédéric's view—favourable or otherwise—as either an objective fact or as a judgement by the author. The two scenes tell us more about Frédéric than about Arnoux, and in this Flaubert differs from other nineteenth-century novelists, who more frequently use their main characters to inform the reader of traits of character in other people.[1]

Flaubert's impersonality can also be seen at work. In both scenes he unerringly reports the attitude of his character, even to using many of the actual words which must have been passing through his character's mind. But he does not *say* he is doing this, nor does he indicate in any way that he is pointing out the

---

[1] Cf. our remarks on the description of Mme Renaud's hands and eyes, *supra*, p. 69. There the hero used several emotive words, but his impressions were nevertheless patently approved by the author: they have to be regarded as ob-jectively true. In *Bovary*, the colour of Emma's eyes is not an objective fact, but a series of impressions; the description of her hands is included not for its objective validity, but because of its importance to Charles—yet it still tells us something about Emma's character, in that it reveals that she did not work on the farm as she said she did. The present description of Arnoux's hands represents a further step: the emotive terms now reveal nothing of interest about Arnoux, but only about the witness; and they now serve to separate the author from his character rather than showing the two in agreement. See also *infra*, pp. 252 et seq.

contradiction between the hero's two attitudes. There is not even any suggestion of irony in the language—the irony comes solely from the juxtaposition of the two scenes. Now all these points are obvious in the example in question, simply because the two scenes occur so close together. Commentary would have been superfluous, except to emphasize that this same principle operates in many parts of the book in a less convenient manner. The scenes are sometimes so far apart, and the conflicting attitudes mentioned so casually, that it can be most difficult for the reader consciously to make the required comparison, because of the unreliability of his memory. We are again confronted with the necessity of reading this novel many times over before we are in a position to appreciate it.[1]

In the light of this, consider some of Frédéric's other attitudes —for example, his constantly changing feelings about Rosanette. When he first calls on her he barely notices her exaggerated pre-occupation with small amounts of money (p. 189), which ought to have told him something very important about her character; he is more interested in the 'façon câline, presque amoureuse' (p. 190) in which she looks at him. On the strength of this alone, which he may very well have imagined, 'Il était léger en sortant de là, ne doutant pas que la Maréchale ne devînt bientôt sa maîtresse' (p. 191)—he is even able to close his eyes to her most unsubtle reaction to his timid gallantries: 'Oh! faites! ça ne coûte rien!' (p. 191). Having ensured that Arnoux makes her the present he had promised, he takes her obviously interested effusions of thanks as an advance (p. 212), in spite of having found Delmar with her in embarrassingly intimate circumstances; and when he is skilfully dismissed, he suddenly discovers he does not like Rosanette after all: 'Elle commençait, du reste, à l'agacer fortement'—and there follows a list of her faults, centred in

[1] For another simple example of the process, important because it shows Frédéric's waverings in regard to Mme Arnoux, compare p. 139 (as he is becoming resigned to living in the provinces) and pp. 139–40 (on the news of his inheritance): '... Mme Arnoux était pour lui comme une morte dont il s'étonnait de ne pas connaître le tombeau, tant cette affection était devenue tranquille et résignée'. '... et une joie frénétique le bouleversa, à l'idée de revoir Mme Arnoux. Avec la netteté d'une hallucination, il s'aperçut auprès d'elle, ...'

particular about the mobility of her character! (p. 213). His desire continues, however, and Rosanette's attractiveness increases with his apparent chances of success: when she speaks of dismissing her latest protector, the rich but senile Oudry, 'Frédéric fut charmé de ce désintéressement' (p. 218). The reader will already have made up his own mind on that. The extra irony is that Frédéric believes in the purity of her motives only because he himself is not disinterested: he imagines she is doing it for him. Hence his joy when Rosanette writes to announce Oudry's disgrace: 'Rien de plus! Mais c'était le convier à la place vacante. Il poussa une exclamation, serra le billet dans sa poche et partit' (p. 223). Even after discovering that he was not, after all, at the head of the queue (Delmar is already in the bus) he cannot admit that he had misinterpreted Rosanette's conduct and motives. It is in his nature to blame others rather than himself: 'Frédéric descendit l'escalier, lentement. Ce caprice-là dépassait tous les autres. Il n'y comprenait rien' (p. 233) and 'Cette perfidie de Rosanette lui semblait une chose anormale, injuste' (p. 235).

But it is also in Frédéric's nature not to learn from his mistakes. He is taken in by her next apparently inviting letter as well, in the fond hope that 'on ne se moque pas deux fois du même homme à propos de rien' (p. 288). So at the races[1] Rosanette has '(de) jolis yeux, à la fois tendres et gais' (p. 289)—as she had had last time he had hoped (p. 211)—and the news of Delmar's fall from grace effaces all previous misfortunes from his mind (p. 290): he carefully ignores the casual context of her 'Je t'aime, mon chéri', and 'ne douta plus de son bonheur; ce dernier mot de Rosanette le confirmait' (p. 293). The pattern repeats itself exactly. In the midst of this beatific state, Frédéric suddenly

---

[1] It will be recalled that this adventure is motivated partly by a desire to make Mme Arnoux jealous (p. 288), even though he had just been highly vituperative about her, and sworn to dismiss her from his mind (cf. *infra*, p. 290). Then when Mme Arnoux does see him with Rosanette, he feels that 'une chose irréparable venait de se faire et qu'il avait perdu son grand amour' (p. 297). Even the presence in his carriage of 'l'amour joyeux et facile' can barely console him—and he does not yet know that his certainty of even this love is soon to vanish. The way in which Frédéric's inconsistencies cut across his relationships with the various women is one of the most complex and most highly-finished aspects of this book.

comes face to face with Rosanette's 'désintéressement', for she is now wearing a different bracelet from the one she had on when she left home (pp. 291, 305). She goes off with Cisy, who had effected the change, and Frédéric, once again caught in the web of illusion which he had been spinning about himself, is forced into another series of rationalizations to protect him from facing the truth:

> Quant à la Maréchale, il se jura de ne plus la revoir; d'autres aussi belles ne manquaient pas; et puisqu'il fallait de l'argent pour posséder ces femmes-là, il jouerait à la Bourse le prix de sa ferme, il serait riche, il écraserait de son luxe la Maréchale et tout le monde (p. 307).

But Frédéric immediately answers Rosanette's next bidding, as if he had not sworn never to see her again, nor to dazzle her with his riches (while never seeing her again) (p. 363). And so it goes on. Whenever Frédéric needs to turn to her because something else has upset him, she seems to have all the virtues, both physical and moral. He even goes so far at one point as to place her on a pedestal similar to the one on which Mme Arnoux is precariously balanced:

> Il ne doutait pas qu'il ne fût heureux pour jusqu'à la fin de ses jours, tant son bonheur lui paraissait naturel, inhérent à sa vie et à la personne de cette femme. Un besoin le poussait à lui dire des tendresses. Elle y répondait par de gentilles paroles, de petites tapes sur l'épaule, des douceurs dont la surprise le charmait. Il lui découvrit enfin une beauté toute nouvelle, qui n'était peut-être que le reflet des choses ambiantes, à moins que leurs virtualités secrètes ne l'eussent fait s'épanouir.[1]

But when Frédéric has his sights on someone else, or when Rosanette disagrees with him or ruins his plans or turns to other men, she becomes a *catin*, lazy, avaricious, ignorant.[2] He discovers all the faults which had been typical of her from the very beginning, but which it had suited him not to notice.

It has been necessary to follow these changes through in such detail—and even so, I have not mentioned all of them—in order

---

[1] pp. 469–70; cf. pp. 443, 447–8, 461–2, 507, 516.
[2] pp. 445, 489–90, 515, 518, 561.

to show quite clearly their extent and importance. While it is generally agreed that this mobility *is* a trait of Frédéric's character, it is perhaps not so widely recognized that the whole structure of the novel, and therefore our interpretation of it, is totally dependent upon the fact. Almost every one of Frédéric's attitudes either contradicts something which he had previously established, or establishes something which is destined to be contradicted later. This statement holds true in every area of Frédéric's experience: his beliefs about the political events, his artistic and financial ambitions, Louise Roque, Madame Dambreuse, people like Deslauriers or Sénécal, Arnoux and also Mme Arnoux, reveal the same constantly shifting standards.[1] Even very minor characters often change their appearance and value according to the circumstances and Frédéric's mood: at Arnoux's shop Burrieu, Lovarius and Dittmer all seem uninteresting and 'bourgeois', for 'aucun ne répondait aux préjugés de l'étudiant' (p. 48). But when these same people appear round the Arnoux dinner-table, we find that 'la compagnie, les mets, tout lui plaisait', and that 'la causerie surtout amusait Frédéric. Son goût pour les voyages fut caressé par Dittmer, qui parla de l'Orient. ... Puis, une discussion entre Lovarius et Burrieu, sur l'école florentine, lui révéla des chefs-d'œuvre, lui ouvrit des horizons, et il eut mal à contenir son enthousiasme quand Pellerin s'écria ...' (pp. 66–7).

Frédéric, then, cannot avoid seeing events, no matter how trivial, in relation to himself. If they can be twisted in his favour, they will be. If this reinterpretation results in his hopes being dashed, he again reinterprets the events so that his lack of perspicacity can be ascribed to someone else's capriciousness. (He is not, of course, always wrong in this. Most of the other characters are quite as capricious as he is, and equally inclined to lay the

[1] Frédéric is thus an embodiment of Jules's conclusion, towards the end of the first *Education*, that 'l'inconséquence est la conséquence suprême, l'homme qui n'est pas absurde aujourd'hui est celui qui l'a été hier et qui le sera demain' (*Œuvres de jeunesse*, III, pp. 279–80); cf. *supra*, p. 77. The conclusion is naturally no longer explicit; but it certainly remains, and underlines the affinities between the two *Education* and the consistency of Flaubert's attitudes towards humanity and towards his heroes.

blame on others.) He is incapable of a disinterested appraisal—
another Flaubert 'hero' displays one of the cardinal sins. Unlike
Emma, however, he shows a remarkable adaptability to circumstances, particularly as regards the various women in his life.
Whether it be Rosanette, Mme Arnoux or Mme Dambreuse,
he quickly resigns himself to making the best of what is available.
Elaborate rationalizations always satisfy him that the unavoidable
alternative to his original plans is after all the one he wanted all
the time. His mental state reflects a precarious balance which
will always be disturbed immediately circumstances change in such
a way that the accepted alternative is no longer the only necessary
one. Given his monumental egotism and lack of self-criticism—
the two frequently go hand in hand—he is unaware of these
processes, and therefore of the consequent contradictions in
thought and behaviour. There is thus little possibility of his ever
correcting the tendency, and this fact, too, will be relevant to
our interpretation of the novel.

The basis of Frédéric's rationalizations is purely emotional.
He reacts to a situation according to his mood, what he imagines
to be his interest, and, in the case of the women, his chances of
success (almost invariably sexual). This is emphasized by the high
proportion of emotive words in the passages quoted, and applies
equally to his favourable and his unfavourable reactions. Since
Frédéric is unaware of this, his emotional reactions, however
shaky, are stated entirely in his own terms—that is, as unquestion-
able facts. The novel is full of these dogmatic, apparently immutable generalizations about people and events, which have
no objective validity. Frédéric's inability to see facts is thus
matched by his readiness to 'conclude'. Hence he displays a
second Flaubertian cardinal sin, so that for two reasons the
apparently guileless reporting of his reactions, even in his own
terms, constitutes a constant implicit criticism of him, and,
through him, of people in general.

As in Flaubert's other books, the double invalidity of Frédéric's
conclusions—through both the flagrant contradictions they display, and the method by which they were reached—remains
constant whether any particular conclusions happen to be

objectively valid or not, or whether any happen to correspond with what we know to have been Flaubert's personal views. It is impossible to sort out the valid conclusions from the others, simply because all are arrived at in the same suspect manner. We return to Flaubert's concept of impersonality: although he approved of some of the attitudes of Frédéric and the other characters, the only valid comment we can make (without reference to external material, such as the *Correspondance*) is that *all* attitudes are suspect, and that none can be imputed to the author.[1]

In the passages quoted, Frédéric's attitudes are expressed by means of direct, indirect and free indirect speech. As in Flaubert's earlier books, but to an even greater extent,[2] this last is of particular interest. It is often unclear, when the passage is read in context, whether we are faced with free indirect speech or traditional third-person narration. But when such passages are compared with others showing other attitudes of Frédéric, as they were certainly intended to be, we again realize that we must not ascribe to the narrator statements which reflect the erratic workings of Frédéric's mind. The need for such caution is more pressing

[1] It follows that attempts to define the extent of Flaubert's 'identification' with his characters, and therefore his sympathy for them, appear both inadequate and irrelevant. That Flaubert 's'acharne sur lui-même' in depicting Emma's weaknesses (Thibaudet, op. cit., p. 102), that both Emma and Frédéric, for all their foolishness, are superior to their fellows because they have an ideal and a poetry which was Flaubert's own (Giraud: *The Unheroic Hero* (New Brunswick, Rutgers University Press, 1957), pp. 148 et seq.)—such statements are doubtless true. But ideals, like Homais's intelligence, are worth little if they are misguided and mishandled: here Flaubert decisively separates himself from both his heroes and his former self. Only this critical separation, the ability to judge even what was dearest to him, makes his novels possible. The 'sympathy' with which he presents these ideals is partly illusory, having two main sources: the point of view presentation, and the confused, nostalgic feelings of the reader that *he* once had these ideals (and probably still pays lip service to them) and that they were the finest part of him, too—a Paradise Lost. But this should not cloud the main issue: *within the books*, the ideals are on the same footing, and just as suspect, as the secondary characters' more mundane preoccupations.

[2] Ullmann, op. cit., pp. 114–17, looks only briefly at the use of the device in this novel, but makes two points relevant to our argument: it occurs nearly three times as often as in *Bovary*, and it has become more elliptical: 'transitions are often abrupt and unprepared, leaving it to the reader's ingenuity to supply the missing link' (p. 116).

here than previously, since the point of view in *l'Education* is more nearly restricted to that of Frédéric alone. 'Narrator' passages, which could help us correct Frédéric's one-sided appraisal, represent only about 11 per cent of the total book, and even this small figure includes passages which reflect the sentiments of *on*—merely a different type of *style indirect libre*. Further, passages—and even single sentences—containing such disguised examples of *style indirect libre* can occur at any moment, and not necessarily within a scene, or in a 'picture' of Frédéric's mind resulting from a scene, as most frequently happened in *Bovary*. They can sometimes be isolated comments in a summary of a series of actions, or mentioned in passing in the most unobtrusive manner possible. For example, at the beginning of a description of one of the regular Saturday meetings of Frédéric and his friends, there occurs a very simple sentence: 'Tous sympathisaient' (p. 80). Neither before nor after this occasion was there much love lost between Frédéric and, say, Martinon or Sénécal, and at various times he also intensely dislikes Regimbart, Pellerin, Hussonnet, Cisy, and even Deslauriers, many of whom also have quarrels among themselves. The idea expressed in these two words is relevant only to its immediate context, and for most of the book has no validity whatsoever. It is not narration, but *style indirect libre*.

All this tends to upset the categories established by Friedman, who attempts to define the various possibilities of relationship between the author and his work.[1] At first sight, one would expect to be able to class Flaubert's method as that of 'Neutral Omniscience', the distinctive features of which, says Friedman, are an 'absence of direct authorial intrusions', with the author speaking impersonally in the third person, with scenes, as opposed to narration, occurring frequently, but not exclusively. In such scenes, the characters are permitted to act and speak for themselves, but are described and explained in the author's voice, not in that of one of the characters. So far, the explanation would seem to fit both *Bovary* and *l'Education*. But by way of further explanation, Friedman quotes a passage from *Tess of the d'Urbervilles*;

[1] Friedman, loc. cit., pp. 1160–84.

then, to distinguish this method from ones which he regards as
more modern and more highly developed (what he calls 'Multiple
Selective Omniscience', or 'Selective Omniscience', as typical
exponents of which he regards Virginia Woolf, James, and
Joyce), he re-writes the passage so that it occurs 'within Tess's
sensory frame'. This operation consists largely in adding words
of perception—'she saw', 'she noticed', 'she sensed'—and the
result is very similar to Flaubert's normal mode of description.
It would therefore appear that Friedman would place Flaubert
in this later category of 'Multiple Selective Omniscience', which
he says differs from the previous one in that thoughts, motives
and so on are *shown* consecutively and in detail as they pass
through the character's mind, not summarized and explained
after they have occurred; as a result, this method is almost entirely
scenic, with very little narration. But in these terms Flaubert
would not fit here either, for he does quite frequently summarize,
and none of his novels is anything like completely scenic. Even
allowing for the fact that Friedman has attempted to convey a
great deal of information in a very small space, it is clear that
he does not provide for all the possibilities. The difficulty stems
from the fact that, apparently following Lubbock, he makes too
definite a distinction between scene and narrative—a distinction
which Flaubert, in the interests of unity of tone, did his best to
minimize in his later novels. While it is true that Flaubert does
explain actions and thoughts in his own style in scenes, he still
places them within the sensory frame of a character; on the other
hand, while it is true that there are many passages of summarizing
in his works, these too tend to remain largely within the 'sensory'
frame of the character—especially in *l'Education*—in the sense
that no matter how 'un-scenic' the passage, no matter what
length of time passes in the course of the brief summary, it is
still presented largely in terms of the attitudes and thoughts of
the character, not those of the author. No better example of this
could be had than the celebrated beginning of Chapter VI of
Part III:

Il voyagea.

Il connut la mélancolie des paquebots, les froids réveils sous la tente, l'étourdissement des paysages et des ruines, l'amertume des sympathies interrompues.

Il revint.

Il fréquenta le monde, et il eut d'autres amours encore. Mais le souvenir continuel du premier les lui rendait insipides; et puis la véhémence du désir, la fleur même de la sensation était perdue. Ses ambitions d'esprit avaient également diminué. Des années passèrent; et il supportait le désœuvrement de son intelligence et l'inertie de son cœur (p. 600).

Although this passage appears to be nothing more than a necessary bridging of time (it covers sixteen years), several statements, if read in conjunction with other parts of the book, reveal the irony and contradictions it contains. In the first place the over-all tone, one of boredom and futility, of actions not worth performing and of events not worth reporting, is the one which occurs wherever Frédéric experiences a 'down' period. This strongly suggests that even here we are not dealing with something objectively valid, but with Frédéric's personal distorted view. We are told, too, that 'il connut . . . l'amertume des sympathies interrompues': he had not learnt from experience that not one of the people with whom he at first felt 'sympathie' ever lived up to his expectations (because of his egotism and theirs); and that he had seldom in the past regretted breaking off relationships with people. We are told that he had other loves, but that 'le souvenir continuel du premier les lui rendait insipides'; yet never, even in his most passionate period, was there any such thing as a constant preoccupation with his great love: he had spent considerable periods without even thinking about Mme Arnoux, he had sometimes forgotten about her completely until she re-entered the orbit of his experience by accident,[1] and on occasions he actively wished not to see her any more.[2] This statement is as much a part of Frédéric's view of himself, and as much a lie (albeit an unconscious one), as the ones he invents so readily in the 'tender' good-bye scene which follows (in which we are actually informed that Frédéric has not changed: 'Frédéric,

---

[1] e.g. pp. 29, 37, 139, 191–2, 373, 489.
[2] e.g. pp. 132, 157, 265, 287, 366, 384, 405, 491.

se grisant par ses paroles, arrivait à croire ce qu'il disait' (p. 604)). Further, we are told that 'la véhémence du désir, la fleur même de la sensation était perdue'; yet one of the major traits of Frédéric's character is that he never had very active desires, sexual or otherwise, and in any case what he had was already lost by the time his liaison with Mme Dambreuse was beginning to bore him (p. 536). Similarly, 'Ses ambitions d'esprit avaient également diminué'—which they had already done on several previous occasions—and 'il supportait le désœuvrement de son intelligence et l'inertie de son cœur'—which he had been doing, on and off, ever since the beginning of the novel. No matter how brief and off-hand this summary may appear, it is a resumé of Frédéric's whole attitude towards himself and towards life: as with so many other passages, it recounts what he *believed* happened in these sixteen years. By comparing it with other parts of the book we can see that it does not really square up with the facts. Even here the point of view is Frédéric's, and is as unreliable as usual.[1] The consequences of using Frédéric's point of view so frequently are likely to be far-reaching.

Idle pursuits

In the nineteenth-century novel, physical descriptions of characters were traditionally very informative about mental states and attitudes. Even authors who were not as naïve as Balzac about physiognomy and phrenology usually made their descriptions significant in this way. Some Romantics favoured either beautiful heroines and handsome heroes, or as a variation, heroes who were deformed and monstrous, but who had all the best human feelings—or at least would have had, if they had been given the opportunity by a wicked society. The Realists and the Naturalists continued the tradition in their own way: Champfleury and Duranty like to present the bourgeois as fat and ugly to match his mind, but sometimes with a beautiful daughter who temporarily has more noble sentiments; and Zola and the

---

[1] See also Cortland, op. cit., pp. 94–6, who makes similar, but less detailed, comments on these passages.

Goncourt are usually at pains to make their characters' appearance reflect at least their social status and the physical effects of their environment. Flaubert, too, frequently followed these traditions. Most of the characters in his early works belong to one or another of the commoner romantic types, and the initial descriptions of Charles Bovary and his hat, or Homais, with his green slippers and his small-pox, are plainly intended to reveal both character and social status. At the same time, descriptions of people in *Bovary* can serve other purposes: those of Rodolphe and Léon invite comparisons with Charles in Emma's mind, Charles notices different things about Emma from Rodolphe, Emma in distress notices different aspects of Bournisien's appearance from those presented by the narrator, and Charles himself has both good and bad points, which are noticed by Emma according to her mood. In the same way, the emphasis on different aspects of Salammbô's appearance varies according to whether she is being viewed by Mâtho, by Hamilcar, or by the people of Carthage.

That Flaubert is indeed moving away from the orthodox view of the connection between external appearance and internal reality is emphasized in one very striking way in *l'Education sentimentale*. There is no description of Frédéric himself. We are told on page two that he was 'un jeune homme de dix-huit ans, à longs cheveux et qui tenait un album sous son bras', but that is all. This fact, noted by Faguet but largely ignored since, constitutes another link between Flaubert and several twentieth-century writers, who have realized that people's appearance has little bearing upon their relationships with others, providing it is within the very broad limits of what can be regarded as 'normal'. It also fits the point of view scheme: if the point of view is Frédéric's, or includes Frédéric's, in every scene of the book in which he is present, a description of his appearance is not easy to arrange.

What of Frédéric's views of others? Physical characteristics, as noted by the hero, will usually be objective—what he thinks is black hair, for example, will be black in fact, and will therefore tell us something about the person being described; but these details will lose much of their objectivity by the way they are presented, in what circumstances it occurs to the observer to notice them, and so on. In particular, their objectivity will be weakened by the emotive words combined with them: it will be the emotive words, and not the actual characteristics, which will influence the reader's attitude to the person in question. This has in fact always been so: when writers wish, for example, to convey the idea that their heroine is beautiful, no amount of purely objective description can ever achieve this—the author has either to *say* that she is beautiful, or to keep his description within a widely-accepted convention of beauty—for example, by pointing out the perfect oval of her face, by giving her blue eyes and blond hair, or black eyes and blue-black hair. The mature Flaubert differs from his predecessors not in this, but in the fact that other novelists expected the reader to accept these emotive words and these conventions on trust. When Stendhal tells us that Mme de Rênal had naïve charm, grace and vivacity, or that Mathilde de la Môle had a 'port de reine', or when Balzac tells us that Charles Grandet was a handsome and elegant young man with aristocratic manners, the reader must accept these judgements as facts. On the other hand, when we are told that Mme Arnoux was breathtaking in her beauty, with her black eyes and hair, we can assume only that she appeared beautiful to Frédéric; indeed, the very fact of her having such conventional attributes, showing the attraction of literary *idées reçues* for Frédéric, is an implied criticism. Frédéric idly wonders why no one else on the boat appeared to notice his goddess; and his self-indulgent musings on her 'beauty' lead him to think she may be Andalusian (i.e. exotic and romantic, but in the most conventional manner), or perhaps, in view of the negress accompanying her, even Creole (more exotic, more romantic, equally conventional). Her birthplace is Chartres (p. 91).

Almost without exception the characters of this book are presented within the orbit of Frédéric's direct experience. There is very little of the technique by which, in *Bovary*, several important characters, including Léon and Homais, are introduced before the heroine arrives. No character is described until Frédéric actually meets him (although some, such as Louise and M.

Dambreuse, are referred to before this happens), and in nearly all cases the reader knows no more about him than does Frédéric. This applies even to the characters' names. Only after a long conversation does Arnoux, deciding that Frédéric is worth knowing, introduce himself to both the hero and the reader; Mme Arnoux remains anonymous throughout the first descriptions and the saving of the shawl, until Arnoux arrives and calls her 'ma femme'. Rosanette and La Vatnaz, who are first glimpsed at the opera (p. 35), are nameless until they are identified by Frédéric, the latter at Arnoux's shop (p. 51), and the former when Arnoux introduces him, some four and a half years and 130 pages later (p. 164).[1] Hussonnet is a 'jeune homme blond' (p. 38) until, having followed Dussardier to the police station, they 'déclinèrent leur nom avec leur qualité d'élèves en droit'.[2]

If almost all our knowledge of the characters comes to us through Frédéric, an important aspect of the novel's technique is the extent to which the reader's attitude can (or should) be determined by the vagaries of Frédéric's character. By examining in detail the physical descriptions of the three Parisian women, we can see how Frédéric's involvement, and his humour of the moment, affect both the extent and the validity of the description, and hence help to reveal Flaubert's message.

The first appearance of Mme Dambreuse provides a classic example of Flaubert's methods of presentation—first, because she is introduced well in advance of the time when she begins to play an active part in the novel, and secondly because the subjective point of view technique is so clearly present:

Un coupé bleu, attelé d'un cheval noir, stationnait devant le perron. La portière s'ouvrit, une dame y monta et la voiture, avec un bruit sourd, se mit à rouler sur le sable.

Frédéric, en même temps qu'elle, arriva de l'autre côté, sous la porte cochère. L'espace n'étant pas assez large, il fut contraint d'attendre. La

---

[1] Castex, op. cit., p. 57, considers that this example demonstrates an unjustifiable confidence on Flaubert's part in the reader's attention.

[2] p. 43. Incidentally, this is another case of a very elliptical form of *style indirect libre*. Hussonnet is not a law student, but knew that the police would ask many more questions if he revealed that he was a journalist. Flaubert reports the 'facts', the reader deciphers them.

jeune femme, penchée en dehors du vasistas, parlait tout bas au concierge. Il n'apercevait que son dos, couvert d'une mante violette. Cependant, il plongeait dans l'intérieur de la voiture, tendue de reps bleu, avec des passementeries et des effilés de soie. Les vêtements de la dame l'emplissaient; il s'échappait de cette petite boîte capitonnée un parfum d'iris et comme une vague senteur d'élégances féminines. Le cocher lâcha les rênes, le cheval frôla la borne brusquement, et tout disparut (p. 28).

Because of the attendant circumstances (in themselves perfectly realistic), Frédéric sees nothing of Mme Dambreuse, but only a vague picture of wealth and elegance. As usual, the reader is not permitted to have more factual knowledge than the character, although he is free to interpret it differently—having once read the book, he has the advantage of being able to see the passage in relation to the future. He can therefore see, from the terms in which this fleeting vision is presented, that it is a record, not of what Frédéric could see, but of what Frédéric, given his character and his present preoccupations (see pp. 26–8), actually noticed. Nothing is described which does not contribute to the idea of luxury: the concierge and the coachman, whom Frédéric could presumably see quite clearly, are barely mentioned. The passage tells us precisely nothing about Mme Dambreuse, but a good deal about Frédéric. There is, too, a symbolic level of meaning which is also a direct result of the way the passage is presented. For this is a picture of unattainability: what little Frédéric has seen quickly disappears. This is the beginning of a search, an attempt to grasp the inaccessible, which is paralleled in the case of the other two Parisian women. They, too, are first presented in similar terms—Mme Arnoux is an impassive receding picture on the departing boat (p. 11), and Rosanette, having asked him to dance, 'dit "Bonsoir!" fit une pirouette et disparut'.[1] It would seem that it is precisely this unattainability which renders the three women interesting in Frédéric's eyes:

---

[1] p. 167. These 'disappearances' are emphasized, in the case of Mme Arnoux, by the vision of quiet romantic happiness which Frédéric imagines on the banks of the Seine: 'A ce moment, une jeune dame et un jeune homme se montrèrent sur le perron, entre les caisses d'orangers. Puis tout disparut' (p. 10).

only Louise stands and stares when they first meet, only she seems to be an authentic possibility, yet only she is rejected. Moreover, when in the case of Mme Dambreuse and Rosanette the 'unattainable' is in fact achieved, it soon becomes little more than a painful duty. Surely the implication would be that had Frédéric had a real opportunity to compare the reality of Mme Arnoux with his ideal of her, the same disillusionment would have followed. These symbols of unattainability work on two levels: the women first appear unattainable, in the purely social and materialistic sense, to the naïve provincial; he subsequently discovers that for two of them (and no doubt for the third, if circumstances had been different) the symbol is false at this first level; but it then becomes clear—and this should have been part of Frédéric's 'education', were he not so obtuse—that on this plane attainment is nothing, that communication does not necessarily follow, that the women remain as unattainable, in the deepest sense, as ever. The symbol is in the long run distressingly authentic. Like Salammbô, Frédéric does not know what he is looking for, which partly explains his sense of emptiness when, with Rosanette and Mme Dambreuse, he finds what he *thought* he was looking for.

At the time of his first sight of Mme Dambreuse, Frédéric, spurred on by Deslauriers, could see her as part of his brilliant future in Paris: luxury was therefore what he wanted to see. But true to form, having received no response to his New Year card, he lets the matter drop. Were it not for a chance meeting at the theatre some *three years* later (pp. 126–7), Mme Dambreuse, one might suppose, would have disappeared from Frédéric's life. Flaubert very cleverly uses this encounter both to present the Dambreuse fairly objectively, and to indicate in advance another series of lapses in Frédéric's judgement. At this point the hero's future in relation to Mme Arnoux appears relatively bright (pp. 124, 126). He feels emotionally fulfilled (or, rather, about to be), so that he is not seeking, he is not *disponible*. He goes to the theatre 'par désœuvrement', and takes no interest in the programme;[1]

---

[1] The description of what he saw reflects this faithfully. The play is dismissed with a brief and confused summary, contrasting strongly with the long exposi-

as a result he takes a half-hearted interest in the audience instead. He casually notes a couple who are remarkable only because they seem out of place. It is because Frédéric has no personal interest in these people that he (and the reader) can see them for what they are: tired, bored with each other, the wife considerably younger than her husband, and possessing no outstanding physical characteristics: 'ni grande ni petite, ni laide ni jolie'. Both are the embodiment of mediocrity. This brief description, one of the very few 'true' ones in the whole novel, contrasts strongly with, say, those of Mme Arnoux, or the first one concerning Mme Dambreuse; it is paralleled by the first description of Louise, for much the same reason: the witness is not interested.

But he soon becomes interested. When he realizes who they are and begins to talk to them, a transformation takes place in Mme Dambreuse:

> ... l'aménité spirituelle de son visage contrastait avec son expression chagrine de tout à l'heure. ... Frédéric, habitué aux grimaces des bourgeoises provinciales, n'avait vu chez aucune femme une pareille aisance de manières, cette simplicité, qui est un raffinement, et où les naïfs aperçoivent l'expression d'une sympathie instantanée (p. 127).

The sudden occurrence of a series of favourably-inclined emotive terms can be partly explained by the fact that Mme Dambreuse's boredom leads her to 'put on an act' in the presence of any presentable young man. More important is Frédéric's sudden identification of the unknown uninteresting female with the elegant and mysterious lady in the carriage, which coincides with M. Dambreuse's excuses for past negligence and compensatory overtures. This woman has now become a 'possibility' again (Deslauriers's reaction is 'Fameux!'), so Frédéric must quickly rebuild his earlier colourless image. But for the reader it is too late: the valid judgement was made when Frédéric was caught off guard, and any subsequent ones—either for or against

---

tion of Lucia in Madame Bovary. Flaubert follows his character's point of view even in what he does not describe. Cf. the occasion when Frédéric sees Arnoux at the theatre, and is so interested in the two women with him that we are not even told what the programme was (p. 36); and also the description of his visit to the opera on the night preceding his duel with Cisy (p. 324).

—are to be measured by this standard. And for once the narrator intervenes briefly to emphasize his point: it is only for the 'naïfs' of this world that the manners of a Mme Dambreuse are 'l'expression d'une sympathie instantanée'.

When Frédéric is actually invited by Mme Dambreuse, however, the apparent promise of the meeting at the theatre seems far from being realized. It is *jour de réception,* and although he is suitably impressed once more by the luxurious surroundings (p. 185), the people, including Mme Dambreuse herself, disappoint him by their banality: '. . . et la misère des propos se trouvait comme renforcée par le luxe des choses ambiantes; mais ce qu'on disait était moins stupide que la manière de causer, sans but, sans suite et sans animation. . . . ils s'en tenaient aux lieux communs les plus rebattus' (p. 186). This passage, which may be compared with Bouvard and Pécuchet's reaction to the Comte de Faverges, is usually taken as an open comment by Flaubert on the inadequacies of the *bourgeois.* But the matter is not quite so simple. While these words do no doubt reflect Flaubert's views, to accept them at face value is to misunderstand his novel technique, and what he is trying to tell us about Frédéric. The whole of this scene is presented as Frédéric's experience; for the purposes of the novel the comments must be regarded as Frédéric's. The importance of this will emerge in due course—for the moment, it is sufficient to be aware that the severity of Frédéric's judgement reflects the fact that he has not been received as he would have wished. Mme Dambreuse receives him with 'un mot aimable . . . mais sans paraître surprise de ne l'avoir pas vu depuis longtemps'. This hurts his pride, as we are informed later: '— Tous les mercredis, n'est-ce pas, M. Moreau? rachetant par cette seule phrase ce qu'elle avait montré d'indifférence.'

For the same reason, Mme Dambreuse is here seen as little more than a manifestation of her unsympathetic milieu (p. 186). While she is no longer entirely uninteresting—Frédéric now has the leisure to examine her more closely, and the description must after all represent some advance on the previous one—she is certainly not the mysterious being of the carriage. The details noted suggest cold, correct reserve: the 'fraîcheur sans éclat',

especially when reinforced by the image of a 'fruit conservé';
the 'gestes délicats', which recall the 'aménité spirituelle' of the
previous encounter, but, because of their context, on a less wel-
coming plane; and the clothes: 'Elle portait une robe de moire
grise, à corsage montant, comme une puritaine.' Her good
points—her hair, her eyes, her hands—being surrounded by less
favourable elements receiving more stress, are not yet given
their full emotive value, even though it is important that they
are noted here. The over-all impression corresponds with
Frédéric's mood, especially in the final image of the puritan,
which has the force of a summary of the whole person. For this,
too, is a symbol of unattainability, echoing the earlier one of the
coach. Frédéric has now discovered—or so he believes—that
Mme Dambreuse is unattainable not because of her exciting,
elusive mystery, but because of her cold, empty surroundings.
The image also looks forward to a later description, which we
shall examine in due course.

Frédéric next sees Mme Dambreuse at her ball. He believes
at this moment that two courses of action are open to him: M.
Dambreuse can advance his worldly ambitions (p. 222), and
Rosanette has just announced that she has dropped M. Oudry
(p. 223). His two major desires are pulling him in opposite directions. The apparently difficult conquest of Mme Dambreuse
seems the less promising method of fulfilling his sexual needs.
She and the other women are at first presented, therefore, in the
same ambivalent, but on the whole only slightly less uninviting,
manner as on the previous occasion. Mme Dambreuse now has
a dress embellished with lace, her hair has received more attention;
but the puritan image remains in her lack of jewelry, and her
coldness in her difficulty in conversation (p. 224). And although
'les seins s'offraient aux regards dans l'échancrure des corsages',
although 'on croyait quelquefois, à certains frissonnements, que
la robe allait tomber', although 'un courant d'air parfumé circu-
lait sous le battement des éventails', nevertheless 'la décence des
figures tempérait les provocations du costume; plusieurs même
avaient une placidité presque bestiale' (pp. 228–9).

Nevertheless, Mme Dambreuse can offer something more

than sexual satisfaction. With the glimmerings of financial ambition comes a more attractive view of her. Her faults remain, but are now minimized: this time her better points begin to emerge. Favourable emotive words appear, and the mention of her hair—the fourth—is for the first time accompanied by words explicitly linking it with sexual attractiveness (p. 299: 'une langueur passionnée'). The 'fraîcheur sans éclat' of her complexion has given way to 'son front couleur d'agate', which, moreover, 'semblait contenir beaucoup de choses et dénotait un maître' (p. 230). Her very colour has changed in emotive value.

It is not until after Frédéric has arrived home that some of his attitudes, already implicit in the descriptions of the evening, are specifically stated (pp. 232–3). For the first time, he now consciously considers Mme Dambreuse as a possible mistress, and the idea is associated in his mind with his new prosperity and the possibility of yet more wealth through M. Dambreuse. It does not occur at a conscious level until, because of his new position, the difficulties appear to be partly overcome. Frédéric had gone to the ball full of hope of an easy financial success with M. Dambreuse, and an easy sexual success with Rosanette. Because of this basically optimistic mood, which nothing during the evening had interfered with, he has come away even more optimistic, with the hope of sexual success with Mme Dambreuse as well—even though Mme Dambreuse had done nothing to encourage this change of attitude. Henceforward the unattainability symbols relating to Mme Dambreuse cease, or at least cease to have any validity in Frédéric's eyes. He has exorcised them by his 'Peut-être qu'elle n'était pas si difficile?'

That Mme Dambreuse was completely indifferent towards Frédéric, in spite of his hopes, is amply demonstrated by the fact that he receives no more invitations, and has very little more to do with her, for some time. He does not feel this very deeply since he is busy discovering that both Mme Arnoux and Rosanette are as far out of reach as they ever were. When all hope with them again disappears, and at the same time he makes some unexpected financial gains, he returns to one of Mme Dambreuse's

soirées, 'pour montrer que rien ne le gênait' (p. 337). His bravado,
coupled with his earlier rejection of the idea that she is unattainable, and with his failing fortunes with Mme Arnoux and Rosanette, will make Mme Dambreuse seem more attractive than
ever before. The setting also contributes to the mood, although
readily explainable on a realistic plane: this is a 'soirée ordinaire',
so there is much less light and noise than on the afternoon of the
first visit, or the evening of the ball. The few lamps in the corners
of the room, the complete darkness outside, and the 'murmure
de voix discrètes', heighten the effect of the one large lamp under
which Mme Dambreuse is sitting, like an ornamental centre-
piece. Both her attitude (casually leaning back in a rocking-chair)
and her clothes (lighter colours, much more ornamentation, and
of a softer, more feminine nature), can also be explained by the
circumstances and the season; but Frédéric notices them because
they coincide with his mood. Far from reminding him of a
'puritaine', she now appears 'tranquille comme une œuvre d'art
pleine de délicatesse, une fleur de haute culture'.

But this time developments are not nearly so encouraging.
Through a series of unfortunate coincidences, Frédéric is gently
reprimanded by M. Dambreuse, apparently accused by Mme
Dambreuse of being Rosanette's lover, then Mme Arnoux's—
accusations which are particularly crushing to his *amour-propre*
because he had been trying so hard, but without success, to make
them true. He sees the newspaper containing the article by
Hussonnet making him appear so foolish, is forced to admit that
he is acquainted with that evil political conspirator Sénécal,
expounds ideas which he knows to be both ridiculous and, in
the present company, heretical, and, final blow to his pride,
believes that he has failed to impress any of the women present!
Small wonder that he should be very angry—anger being a
defence mechanism which relieves him of the responsibility of
examining how much his conduct has contributed to his dis-
comfiture. Small wonder, too, that he should now be so ill-
disposed towards Mme Dambreuse: having spent the early part
of the evening seeing her as more attractive than ever before,
she has had the bad grace not to return the compliment in un-

equivocal terms; and now, 'déterminé à ne jamais revenir dans cette maison, à ne plus fréquenter tous ces gens-là', he is left with a laboriously created image of feminine desirability for which he has no further use.

The Dambreuse soirée also echoes the ball scene in that Frédéric's attitudes and fortunes develop in similar ways, but in the opposite direction. In the ball scene, he arrives with great optimism, but little immediate interest in Mme Dambreuse; in the course of the evening, what he imagines to be his success influences him to want more success, and gradually to see Mme Dambreuse as a worthy victim of his charms; this in turn increases his original optimism. In the present scene, he arrives with little hope on any of the fronts of his war with society, but with considerable interest in Mme Dambreuse; in the course of the evening, what he imagines to be his failure brings him to even more resounding failure; and this in turn intensifies his original pessimism. The two scenes are parallel in another, more amusing way: through all these variations in attitude towards her and her milieu, Mme Dambreuse herself does nothing to justify any of them. Nowhere in the ball scene does she encourage Frédéric; and in the soirée scene there is little to show that either she or her husband is really displeased with his behaviour. All the things he *believes* have made them displeased are figments of his imagination. M. Dambreuse mentions the financial deal only in passing, and easily allows the subject to be changed—he is, of course, utterly indifferent whether or not Frédéric takes the position offered. So, too, no doubt, is Mme Dambreuse when she seems to be making reference to Rosanette as his mistress. It is not even certain that she *is* making such a reference— Frédéric's mental 'l'allusion était claire' (p. 340) presupposes the massive weight of his egotism. And if there were any doubts about Flaubert's intentions in this sentence, the following one would surely dispel them: 'Il sembla même à Frédéric que toutes les dames le regardaient de loin, en chuchotant'. He is wrong: they, like everyone else, are totally unconcerned about whatever Frédéric may do or say. It is this truth above all which it would never occur to him to face. He must build an image of himself inspiring positive feelings; and these feelings he sees as either favourable or otherwise according to his own humour.

At the Dambreuse dinner party (pp. 488–501), similar principles apply. Frédéric, sure of success, is identifying himself with these people—a crushing comment upon him, especially as the sole cause of the fellow feeling is that he is no longer being ignored. The change in situation is particularly ironical because it is on this occasion, and not the previous one, that the story of his dealings with Rosanette, Pellerin, and Cisy is brought into the open—and his reputation does not appear to suffer at all. For the first time, Mme Dambreuse appears really to be paying attention to him, so the description of her, although brief and retaining several of the elements of previous ones, reflects this (pp. 498–9). Her 'coquetteries', and the colours mentioned, represent the climax of a development. Her dresses have changed from grey (p. 187) to mauve (p. 224) to lilac with large quantities of lighter-coloured muslin (p. 337), and now finally to white with infinitely varying reflections of brightly-coloured lights. Concurrently, Frédéric 'se rappelait l'autre soirée, celle dont il était sorti, le cœur plein d'humiliations; et il respirait largement; il se sentait dans son vrai milieu, presque dans son domaine, comme si tout cela, y compris l'hôtel Dambreuse, lui avait appartenu'. Entirely satisfied with himself, Frédéric judges both Mme Dambreuse and her milieu in the kindest possible terms.

It is his self-satisfaction (combined with the fact that he has once more lost hope with Mme Arnoux and that because this was Rosanette's doing he is also turning against her) which finally crystallizes into a wholly sympathetic picture of Mme Dambreuse's character and behaviour:

Ce fut un soulagement pour lui, quand les soirées de Mme Dambreuse recommencèrent.

Celle-là, au moins, l'amusait! Elle savait les intrigues du monde, les mutations d'ambassadeurs, le personnel des couturières; et, s'il lui échappait des lieux communs, c'était dans une formule tellement convenue, que sa phrase pouvait passer pour une déférence ou pour une ironie. Il fallait la voir au milieu de vingt personnes qui causaient, n'en oubliant aucune, amenant les réponses qu'elle voulait, évitant les périlleuses! Des choses très simples, racontées par elle, semblaient des confidences; le moindre de ses sourires faisait rêver, son charme enfin, comme l'exquise odeur qu'elle portait ordinairement, était complexe et indéfinissable. Frédéric, dans sa compagnie, éprouvait chaque fois le plaisir d'une découverte; et cependant, il la retrouvait toujours avec sa même sérénité, pareille au miroitement des eaux limpides (p. 519).

The emotive terms have now overwhelmed the descriptive ones, which are totally lacking. There is real truth in this: once a man decides that a woman attracts him, considerations of physical beauty cease to have any relevance as long as the attraction lasts. In addition, the 'reasons' given here for Frédéric's attraction, while sincere as far as he realizes, are quite false: several of the 'good' points he now sees in Mme Dambreuse are precisely those which, in less optimistic moods, he had regarded as faults or as barriers; and those he cannot hide, like the 'lieux communs', he at least interprets charitably. The more self-satisfied he becomes, the more he ignores (pp. 522, 523, 534). It is no longer Mme Arnoux, or even Rosanette, who can lead him to 'une autre vie, qui serait plus amusante et plus noble' (p. 521): Frédéric will be idealistic about anybody, when he has to be.

He also amuses himself, now that he knows Mme Dambreuse more intimately, by comparing her public and her private behaviour (pp. 534–5), thereby actively destroying, as it were, the early puritan symbol of unattainability. But his 'destruction' is ironic, for, as we noted earlier, the symbol is authentic and indestructible. Almost immediately, Frédéric's inevitable dissatisfaction begins to develop, and with it a recurrence of Mme Dambreuse's faults. When she calls on him in a ball-dress, 'son corsage ouvert découvrait trop sa poitrine maigre'.[1] When she begins to 'spy' on him, we are given a long list of moral faults, which parallel those he ascribes to Rosanette when *she* ceases to please him, which are logically just as invalid, which in any case must have been obvious all along, and which sometimes piquantly

---

[1] Besides being a statement of a physical inadequacy which is ironic because it took Frédéric so long to discover it, this is an expression of Frédéric's displeasure that the non-existence of the 'puritan', which he discovered so slowly, is being made very clear to others.

recall those of Frédéric himself. That he, of all people, should criticize someone because 'ses yeux restaient secs devant les haillons des pauvres', or because she was egotistic! (p. 559).

We must not leave Mme Dambreuse and her milieu without returning to Flaubert's method of satirizing the bourgeois. On Frédéric's first visit to the Dambreuse, when he was disgruntled by his reception, he made slighting mental remarks (which correspond with Flaubert's own sentiments) about the 'misère des propos' and the 'lieux communs'. But at the ball, when he had a greater chance of being accepted, he is disposed to judge these same people much more kindly (p. 232). All the satire on the bourgeois in this scene—and some of it is quite ferocious—is provided by letting them speak for themselves, by recording their conversation in direct speech, without any extra comments (pp. 226–8). The same distinction can be seen at the soirée. At the beginning, when Frédéric is more or less kindly disposed, he has no strong feelings about the political and social questions being discussed: the conversation of the bourgeois is presented in their own terms, bare of commentary (pp. 338–40); the same is true of the dinner party (pp. 488–501). But when Frédéric has experienced his imagined embarrassments and has become angry and reckless, open comment begins again:

La pourriture de ces vieux l'exaspérait, . . . (p. 343).

La plupart des hommes qui étaient là avaient servi, au moins, quatre gouvernements; et ils auraient vendu la France ou le genre humain, pour garantir leur fortune, s'épargner un malaise, un embarras, ou même par simple bassesse, adoration instinctive de la force. Tous déclarèrent les crimes politiques inexcusables. Il fallait plutôt pardonner à ceux qui provenaient du besoin! Et on ne manqua pas de mettre en avant l'éternel exemple du père de famille, volant l'éternel morceau de pain chez l'éternel boulanger (p. 342).

The more involved he becomes with Mme Dambreuse, the less the bourgeois are criticized: her milieu, like her other faults, fades into insignificance. With his decreased interest in Mme Dambreuse comes another critical picture of the political and social ideals of the class she represents (pp. 559–60). His attitude is kindest when his sympathy for her is at its height. Although he is never completely blind to the monstrous self-interest of these people, 'il était fier de les connaître et intérieurement souhaitait la considération bourgeoise' (p. 522), and 'sa joie de posséder une femme riche n'était gâtée par aucun contraste, le sentiment s'harmonisait avec le milieu' (p. 534). Obviously, their self-interest is really monstrous only when it conflicts with his.

It is quite clear, then, that explicit outbursts against the bourgeois must be seen as Frédéric's and not Flaubert's. While Flaubert would undoubtedly endorse them, they are entirely dependent on Frédéric's humour and chances of success: they have no more logical justification than his judgements of Mme Dambreuse herself. They are not authorial intrusions, but are intended to emphasize Frédéric's inconsistency. They also provide another example of Flaubert's impersonality at work. He wanted to satirize the bourgeois, of course, but only within the limits imposed by the wider implications of his novel. When his hero's views happen also to be his, he takes the opportunity of speaking through his hero's mouth; when his hero's views change he both records the change and expresses his own views by another method—direct speech. And he never tells us what he is doing.

As for Mme Dambreuse, so for Rosanette: there is an almost mathematical correlation between Frédéric's passing moods and the various pictures we are given. The emotive takes precedence over the descriptive in a manner which always reveals the nature and the extent of his involvement.

Our first view of Rosanette is when Frédéric sees her at the theatre with Arnoux (p. 36). It is the fact that she is with Arnoux that intrigues him most, and he notes only that she is 'une jeune fille blonde', and is not richly dressed. Since Frédéric has other preoccupations, the reader is deprived of more details. This first view parallels that of Mme Dambreuse at the theatre, not only in the circumstances of the meeting, but also because there is no indication that the young woman is either beautiful or interesting.

Rosanette makes more impression when Arnoux takes Frédéric to her ball, but, given his timidity and the nature of the occasion, she impresses more as a type than as a person: the thirst which the evening awakes in him is 'celle des femmes, du luxe et de tout ce que comporte l'existence parisienne' (p. 183). Hence his dream, which begins with a composite image of female desirability, consisting of the most alluring attributes of several of the women he had seen. At the ball itself Frédéric had been impressed by the scene as a whole: he would have been happy to sleep with any or all of the women present, independently of their beauty, simply because of what they represent to his naïve mind. Nevertheless Rosanette is a little more real then the others, and it is she who is finally the subject of his dream, the content of which reveals what she stands for. Her golden spurs—her costume, and by extension, the money she needs to buy such frivolous luxuries—form the central element.[1] On looking back, we find that it is Rosanette seen in relation to her costume which has been the subject of the descriptions. In the whole scene, the only two attributes mentioned which are specifically hers are her eyes—which are described simply as 'clairs, d'une indéfinissable couleur' (p. 175)—and her long blond hair, which even so is seen in relation to her costume (p. 181). Her description is certainly not objective or 'realistic'.

Even after Frédéric has lost some of his naïvety, his initial view of Rosanette as a sexual exotic, gay and carefree, remains to colour his subsequent attitudes. Now just as Mme Dambreuse ceased to be described physically when *she* came to be a real sexual possibility, so we have no physical details of Rosanette as long as she continues to be no more than this. We are given many details of her behaviour, we are even told that she dressed in front of him, and also that she was beautiful (pp. 205–6). We have the strongest impression of her attractiveness when Frédéric judges (wrongly) that he is nearest to being her lover; but even here we are told almost nothing of what she actually looked like: 'Ses jolis yeux tendres pétillaient, sa bouche humide souriait, ses deux bras ronds sortaient de sa chemise qui n'avait pas de manches;

---

[1] Leaving aside the sadistic element, which needs no explanation.

et, de temps à autre, il sentait, à travers la batiste, les fermes contours de son corps' (p. 211). Only a few minor details about Rosanette's physical charms can be gleaned in this way, with the facts subordinated to expressions of Frédéric's desire, right up to his final success, and the beginnings of their life together.[1]

It is at this point that a change begins to take place. For one thing, the original attraction, primarily sexually-based, could not be expected to last long after its initial fulfilment: if it is not supplemented with something else, it must die. Frédéric's egotism is such that he must have even a Rosanette all to himself. Normally this would be a vain hope (witness Arnoux's signal lack of success), but it happens that because of the Revolution her current protector has abandoned her (p. 448). In spite of his misgivings, Frédéric takes over her financial burdens, but, incapable of seeing himself and his mistress in this purely mercenary light, 'il éprouvait la joie d'un nouveau marié qui possède enfin une maison à lui, une femme à lui . . .' (p. 448). He soon discovers that this is not quite so, for he is sharing Rosanette with Arnoux; so he forces her to 'prove' she loves only him by going to Fontainebleau.

This she naturally does: since Arnoux is paying nothing (p. 450), she cannot afford to alienate Frédéric. Because such reasoning does not occur to Frédéric, the Fontainebleau episode becomes a romantic honeymoon, during which Rosanette rises in his estimation to something approaching his ideal of the dispenser of eternal felicity, a role usually reserved for Mme Arnoux. He is now the 'protector' in the best sense (p. 468), and for the first time the description of Rosanette both gives more detail and suggests a purer, non-sexual, idealized beauty; for the first time, too, her dress is quiet and natural, contrasting with the exotic, suggestive costumes we have previously seen her wearing:

Le sérieux de la forêt les gagnait, et ils avaient des heures de silence où, se laissant aller au bercement des ressorts, ils demeuraient comme engourdis dans une ivresse tranquille. Le bras sous la taille, il l'écoutait

[1] pp. 212, 289, 290–1, 300, 301, 304, etc. The most important case is pp. 370–3, where Rosanette tries unsuccessfully to seduce Frédéric. Again it is particularly her exotic costume and attitudes which he notices.

parler pendant que les oiseaux gazouillaient, observait presque du
même coup d'œil les raisins noirs de sa capote et les baies des gené-
vriers, les draperies de son voile, les volutes des nuages; et quand il se
penchait vers elle, la fraîcheur de sa peau se mêlait au grand parfum
des bois. ... et il contemplait son petit nez fin et blanc, ses lèvres
retroussées, ses yeux clairs, ses bandeaux châtains qui bouffaient, sa
jolie figure ovale. Sa robe de foulard écru collait à ses épaules un peu
tombantes; et, sortant de leurs manchettes tout unies, ses deux mains
découpaient ... Un besoin le poussait à lui dire des tendresses. Elle y
répondait par de gentilles paroles, de petites tapes sur l'épaule, des
douceurs dont la surprise le charmait. Il lui découvrait enfin une beauté
toute nouvelle ... (pp. 468-9).

A sentimental idyll with a *cocotte*, recounted with the utmost
seriousness! No wonder Rosanette decides it is Frédéric she
would like to marry: among her male acquaintances, she is unlikely to find anyone else so easily hoodwinked.

There are very few further physical descriptions of Rosanette,
and none of any importance until Frédéric begins to lose interest
in her because she has ruined his chances with Mme Arnoux,
and because his attentions are transferred to Mme Dambreuse.
By this time, she has definitely changed: she dreams of marriage,
she wants a *salon*, she receives many of her previous lovers (pp.
560-1)—in short, the liaison is breaking up. The final picture of
her shows Frédéric unimpressed and disillusioned by what he
had thought at Fontainebleau to be real qualities, and therefore
reverting to his original idea of her as merely a sexual possibility
—which, however, he now finds equally illusory:

... et à mesure que le fond même de sa personne l'agaçait davantage,
un goût des sens âpre et bestial l'entraînait vers elle, illusions d'une
minute qui se résolvaient en haine.

Ses paroles, sa voix, tout vint à lui déplaire, ses regards surtout, cet
œil de femme éternellement limpide et inepte. Il s'en trouvait tellement excédé quelquefois, qu'il l'aurait vue mourir sans émotion. Mais
comment se fâcher? Elle était d'une douceur désespérante (pp. 561-2.)

His relations with Rosanette, like those with the other women,
are finishing *en queue de rat*.

The graven image

We must now consider Mme Arnoux's appearance in relation to Frédéric's attitudes. Logically, we would expect to find a basically similar situation: the witness is the same, even if the woman is not. But the task will be more difficult, partly because Frédéric is much more preoccupied with this woman, and partly because it is so widely accepted that she is presented as a beautiful, idealized, romantic heroine. I believe that within the novel the importance of Mme Arnoux is a function, not of Flaubert's feelings, but of Frédéric's character and experience. She is by no means always idealized; and even when she is, this idealization can be seen as part of the over-all intention of the novel. It is just as surely a result of presenting the book from Frédéric's point of view, with just as many suggestions that this point of view is devoid of objective validity, as Frédéric's ideas about the other women.

Mme Arnoux, like the other characters, is seen almost exclusively through Frédéric. Flaubert's previous novels allowed us to compare differing points of view in order to gain a more objective picture, but this aid is scarcely available to us here: it is almost impossible to obtain a clear idea of what people other than Frédéric think of Mme Arnoux, except by implication. We can recall that no one else in the river-boat seemed to think she was remarkable (p. 9). Hussonnet is completely noncommittal, for when Frédéric asks him whether he often sees Mme Arnoux, he replies simply: 'De temps à autre' (pp. 45–6)—at any rate, he is not enthusiastic about her qualities. Pellerin, who is garrulous enough on most subjects, does not seem very interested in her either, but when pressed he does say she is faithful to her husband (p. 54)—it does not occur to Frédéric that she may be uninteresting to other men *because* she is faithful, and that this bodes ill for his chances. Louise Roque, it is true, finds her appealing because of her simplicity (p. 499). Regimbart 'faisait grand cas de Mme Arnoux' (p. 583)—but this is because she is 'vertueuse', and therefore, in his eyes, a help to Democracy; besides, even were his reason a little more cogent, Regimbart's judgement scarcely inspires confidence: he regards Arnoux as being 'plein de cœur et d'imagination' (p. 246). The other people who give an opinion of Mme Arnoux are as much motivated by self-interest as Frédéric, so that their judgements will also be suspect. Arnoux is full of praises for her, both morally and physically.[1] Mme Dambreuse concedes, sarcastically, that 'elle passe pour être très jolie' (p. 261). Deslauriers, probably with malicious intent, 'la trouvait "pas mal, sans avoir pourtant rien d'extra-ordinaire"' (p. 85). Rosanette is understandably vitriolic when Frédéric is leaving her for Mme Arnoux.[2] And Cisy, drunk and angry, casts aspersions on her morality mainly to annoy Frédéric.[3]

These details, while not particularly informative in themselves, at least show that Mme Arnoux is not the object of universal adulation. For further enlightenment, we have no choice but to return to Frédéric. We can begin by giving one further example of the way his mind works, and the way this affects the presentation of the narrative. Frédéric is attracted to Arnoux's shop because he assumes that by going there he is closer to his idol. He even spends his evenings standing in the street looking longingly up at the windows, in true romantic style:

> Au-dessus de la boutique d'Arnoux, il y avait au premier étage trois fenêtres, éclairées chaque soir. Des ombres circulaient par derrière, une surtout, *c'était la sienne*; et il se dérangeait de très loin pour regarder ces fenêtres et contempler cette ombre.[4]

But one day he accidentally discovers, to his horror, that Mme Arnoux does not live in this building at all, and: 'Le charme des choses ambiantes se retira tout à coup. Ce qu'il y sentait confusé-

---

[1] pp. 247, 264, 454. In Arnoux's case, this praise is tempered by criticism of her temper, her stubbornness and so on when he is in marital difficulties (e.g. pp. 241, 247); Frédéric himself cannot avoid noticing this aspect of her character on occasions (pp. 243, 249). It will be recalled that the early plans allowed for these less attractive qualities. See Durry, op. cit., p. 163; *infra*, p. 286.

[2] p. 589. Note that what Frédéric sees as her 'peau ambrée d'Andalouse', Rosanette sees as her 'teint couleur de réglisse'! As usual, there is no way of telling who is right: we can only conclude that both probably exaggerate.

[3] p. 318. In fact, Cisy is speaking of a *Sophie* Arnoux, showing either that he does not know Frédéric's heroine at all, or that he is confusing her with someone else. They become involved in their ludicrous duel for an even more ludicrous reason.

[4] p. 32. Italic mine; cf. p. 49.

ment épandu venait de s'évanouir, ou plutôt n'y avait jamais
été' (p. 58). The text had quite plainly suggested on two occasions
not only that these feelings were inherent in the building, but
also that they were based on indisputable facts. There could not
be a clearer warning.

In considering the early descriptions of Mme Arnoux, we
must also take into account the note in Flaubert's plan which
states that his first view of her 'occupe l'adolescence & se mêle
à sa floraison'.[1] Here is our first view of the heroine:

> Ce fut comme une apparition:
> Elle était assise, au milieu du banc, toute seule; ou du moins il ne
> distingua personne, dans l'éblouissement que lui envoyèrent ses yeux.
> En même temps qu'il passait, elle leva la tête; il fléchit involontairement
> les épaules; et, quand il se fut mis plus loin, du même côté, il la regarda.
> Elle avait un large chapeau de paille, avec des rubans roses, qui
> palpitaient au vent, derrière elle. Ses bandeaux noirs, contournant la
> pointe de ses grands sourcils, descendaient très bas et semblaient presser
> amoureusement l'ovale de sa figure. Sa robe de mousseline claire,
> tachetée de petits pois, se repandait à plis nombreux. Elle était en train
> de broder quelque chose; et son nez droit, son menton, toute sa per-
> sonne se découpait sur le fond de l'air bleu. . . .
> Jamais il n'avait vu cette splendeur de sa peau brune, la séduction
> de sa taille, ni cette finesse des doigts que la lumière traversait. Il con-
> sidérait son panier à ouvrage avec ébahissement, comme une chose
> extraordinaire. Quels étaient son nom, sa demeure, sa vie, son passé?
> Il souhaitait connaître les meubles de sa chambre, toutes les robes
> qu'elle avait portées, les gens qu'elle fréquentait; et le désir de la pos-
> session physique même disparaissait sous une envie plus profonde,
> dans une curiosité douloureuse qui n'avait pas de limites (pp. 6–7).

The reader's attitude is predetermined by the accumulation
of emotive words for a whole paragraph *before* any description
is given. Such words continue throughout the description, and
in some places take precedence over it. The factual evidence of
Mme Arnoux's beauty is negligible: we have an impression, and
nothing more. There is ample indication too that this impression

---

[1] Durry, op. cit., p. 163. See Cortland, op. cit., pp. 25–6 for similar points
about this description.

is Frédéric's alone: the normal indications of visual perception are frequent, and those attributes which he has not yet been able to distinguish (e.g. her eyes) are not mentioned. Of course, we do not yet know how unreliable Frédéric's impressions are, and this fact contributes to our tendency to accept all this as the author's statements; but when we know the book well we should not be caught out.

Certainly it cannot be denied that the impression is a very strong one—the mere volume of it testifies to this, for this is the most complete initial description of any person in the novel. If we compare it with that of Arnoux on pp. 3–4, for example, it is easily seen that people who interest Frédéric less are honoured with a much shorter description, which is also more objective, with fewer emotive terms, and yet which tells considerably more about the character of the person being described. Mme Arnoux is presented as primarily a catalyst for Frédéric's dreams, and all his subsequent thoughts and actions—the incredible tip to the singer, his sentimental attitudes about parting for ever, his dreams of lasting happiness on the banks of the Seine, his fantastic notion that Mme Arnoux may have intended an 'ouverture indirecte' by scolding her daughter for impoliteness—all these are the result of his impression. They are an accurate enough exposition of adolescent psychology, but reveal nothing at all of the validity of the impression. Even the famous sentence: '. . . et le désir de la possession physique même disparaissait sous une envie plus profonde, dans une curiosité douloureuse qui n'avait pas de limites', which has been quoted as evidence of the idealization of Mme Arnoux, must be seen in this context. On close examination, it reveals sentimental emptiness.[1] Flaubert would argue

[1] Cf. p. 388, where Mme Arnoux reacts to the 'romantic agony' gambit by begging him to leave: 'Et Frédéric l'aimait tellement, qu'il sortit'. Another example of *style indirect libre* disguised as fact: almost immediately 'il fut pris de colère contre lui-même, se déclara un imbécile, et vingt-quatre heures après, il revint'. If his motive for leaving really were love, the subsequent reaction would hardly be possible—cf. Henry, and the arrangements for the rue Tronchet meeting, ostensibly so that they can walk together in the streets, 'sans crainte de sa [i.e. Mme Arnoux's] part, sans arrière-pensée de la sienne' (p. 395). This noble sentiment, too, is easily enough seen for what it is as Frédéric proceeds with

that unless a man is abnormal or deluding himself, his attraction to a woman is in the final resort sexual (as the development of Frédéric's feelings, and the explicit comments we gleaned from the first *Education* show): it is only people like Frédéric who dress it up in this way.

It must be emphasized that Flaubert is not criticizing Frédéric for having sexual feelings, nor is he trying to detract from the value of the experience itself. The youthful cynicism of the first *Education* is long past. What he does criticize is Frédéric's inability to recognize the basis of his experience, his delusions about his real motives. His aspirations are no less real or valuable for being sexually based; it is he, and not Flaubert, who by rejecting this possibility is implying that there is something reprehensible in it. Flaubert's attitude is stated unequivocally in a letter that has already been quoted in relation to *Salammbô* (p. 224, note, q.v.). It is important enough for the last part of it to be quoted again: 'Cela vous paraît cynique. Mais ce n'est pas moi qui ai inventé la nature humaine. Je suis convaincu que les appétits matériels les plus furieux se formulent *insciemment* par des élans d'idéalisme . . .'.

For the moment, then, Mme Arnoux is 'le point lumineux où l'ensemble des choses convergeaient', a notion which fits in with Frédéric's present uncritical literary sympathies,[2] and his pseudo-romantic way of speaking with Deslauriers (p. 23). A mere two months later, on his return to Paris, he had completely forgotten about this spectacular being, until by chance he sees Arnoux's name on a shop (p. 29). What, then, are we to think of the fanfares of the first chapter? It seems clear already that this all-consuming passion is suspect, something trumped up by

preparations for a copy-book seduction. When she fails to arrive, 'il se jura de n'avoir plus même un désir' (p. 405), and a few hours later tumbles into bed with Rosanette.

[2] Cf. p. 21; also Durry, op. cit., p. 109, this note which shows clearly Flaubert's intention: 'violence que doit avoir un amour renforcé par des types littéraires admirés dans la jeunesse — il y a coincidence de l'ideal & du Reel'. See also Durry's own comments on this note, pp. 144–5. It should be added, however, that the note does not hint at the subsequent forms such a love can take in the mind of a person like Frédéric.

a romantically-minded adolescent subconsciously acting the role
of a literary hero. When he has more important things to think
about, he forgets the tragic career he has mapped out for himself.
However, now that he has remembered it again, it will for a
while become a part of his daily thoughts—but only after he has
become disillusioned with the *Ecole de Droit*, Martinon and Cisy,
grown discontented with his lodgings and begun to lose hope
of an invitation from the Dambreuse. In other words, his lonely
life contributes to his idea of himself inherited from books, as a
figure of solitude; the tragedy of unrequited, idealized love is
obviously required to round off the picture. That Frédéric views
the whole affair in these mock-literary terms is again emphasized
by the 'novel' he tries to write about it; but such superficial
inspiration flags quickly, and when, after more than a year, he
has not seen her again, it is not surprising that 'sa grande passion
pour Mme Arnoux commençait à s'éteindre' (p. 37). The irony
of this statement is now apparent: the 'grande passion' is a figment
of Frédéric's adolescent imagination, and were it not for another
chance meeting (with Hussonnet) his burning ardour, in this
direction at least, would have fizzled out like a damp fire-
work.

Yet however fictitious this passion may have been in fact,
Frédéric was certainly sincere in his belief in it. Consequently,
as soon as he finds in Hussonnet an opportunity of reviving it
once more, he does his best to take advantage of it. This is indeed
the only course open to him, for having already idealized Mme
Arnoux, he cannot now admit to himself that he did not really
love her at all. In Frédéric's character self-delusion takes precedence over all else, and at times there is an almost desperate air
about his efforts to hide himself from himself. His original ideas
about Mme Arnoux, irrespective of their validity, necessarily
remain to colour his subsequent attitudes, provided only that
she does not completely fade from his life—and naturally Flaubert
takes good care that this does not happen. It is part of the irony
of the novel—achieved by a series of literary *trucs* in the form
of completely unexpected chances—that whenever Frédéric, in
spite of his efforts, is on the point of total failure (and has therefore

just convinced himself that it does not matter anyway (e.g. p. 61)), he is accidentally drawn back into the web.

So he makes contact with Mme Arnoux for the second time. Again Frédéric's point of view is clearly used. At first, because of the lack of light and her dark clothes, he can see only her head, and few details are given (p. 65); only when they are seated at the dinner table has he the leisure to examine her more closely (pp. 67–8). The conversation (specifically, the aesthetic buffooneries of Pellerin, no less) leads his attention back to her: 'Frédéric, en écoutant ces choses, regardait Mme Arnoux. Elles tombaient dans son esprit comme des métaux dans une fournaise, s'ajoutaient à sa passion et faisaient de l'amour' (p. 67). The stimulus of false literature has been replaced by that of false painting—by the end of the chapter Frédéric has found his vocation in this very field— but an external stimulus is still necessary.

Unfortunately, the seating arrangement is such that Frédéric can see Mme Arnoux only when she leans forward, so the reader continues to be deprived of physical details. Only a dimple emerges from the meal (pp. 67–8); later, he is too timid to look her in the face while she is talking to him, and when she begins to sing the only new detail is her contralto voice. A series of highly impressionistic descriptions have revealed nothing of the heroine.

In this long scene Flaubert does, however, take care to hint that Frédéric is still thinking and acting in a juvenile way. The clearest example is the parting handshake she gives him, just as she had to Dittmer and Hussonnet. As with her scolding of her daughter in the first scene, Frédéric is tempted to regard this as very important: 'Pourquoi cette main offerte? Etait-ce un geste irréfléchi, ou un encouragement?' (p. 70). Although he quickly realizes that this is ridiculous, the detail does underline once more the spontaneous workings of his mind. Again, consider his joy at having her converse with him, and the impression this makes: 'Chaque mot qui sortait de sa bouche semblait à Frédéric être une chose nouvelle, une dépendance exclusive de sa personne' (p. 69). He, and with him the reader, skims over what she actually said, in favour of the impression: it is in fact precisely the sort of futile small-talk to which Frédéric, in less optimistic mood at the Dambreuse house, so strongly objects. It may even be that the phrase about these banal words being a 'dépendance exclusive de sa personne' is another example of Flaubert's double-meaning irony. Perhaps Frédéric was right after all in this judgement. Perhaps these words *are* typical of Mme Arnoux—perhaps she is a bourgeoise being *forced* to pose as a sentimental heroine.

On a symbolic level, these descriptions yield another meaning which is not available to Frédéric. Mme Arnoux is 'enveloppée d'ombre' when he first sees her (p. 65), and she is wearing a black dress. If we are correct about the changing colours of Mme Dambreuse's clothes, it is likely that a significant comparison is intended here. At any rate, both the lighting and Mme Arnoux's dress echo the first scene on the boat, where she was dressed in white and surrounded by the clear blue sky—this image, it will be remembered, was carried off down the Seine, leaving Frédéric stranded on his provincial shore. In the dinner scene, the symbols of impossibility take another form, but they are still present. And the meal itself, where Frédéric is so placed that there are several people between him and Mme Arnoux, so that he can catch only brief glimpses of her, is a pantomime of their entire relationship. A similar intention can be seen in the simple statement: 'Au moment des liqueurs [i.e. the time when stiffness and formality cease] elle disparut' (p. 68). It is now clear that Frédéric's timidity while they are talking rounds off the meaning of the whole scene: 'il n'osait lever les paupières pour la voir plus haut, face à face' (p. 69). We have acquired very little real knowledge of Mme Arnoux, who remains an absence because Frédéric dare not look at her squarely. If he did, he may discover that the Mme Arnoux of his imagination is very definitely an absence—has not, in fact, ever existed.

Now that Frédéric's attitudes towards this woman have been defined, Flaubert relents a little. After all, he did believe that it was important in a novel to provide facts. Not that he launches into a full-scale description (which would be out of keeping with his methods in this work), but he does reveal one or two further small details (pp. 78–9). The passage, which is still from Frédéric's point of view, begins with the sort of phrase we have come to expect: 'Il ne parlait guère pendant ces dîners; il la contemplait'. Moreover, it fairly rapidly degenerates into senti-mental verbiage which brings us back to Frédéric, although ostensibly dealing with Mme Arnoux. But it differs from those already examined, in that it is a composite description, not the result of a single occasion but a combination of details gleaned by Frédéric over several dinner parties. The characteristics men-tioned, scanty as they are, are consistent with this situation, for we are given the results of a closer observation than Frédéric had ventured on the first evening: the exact position of a small mole, finer nuances of the colouring of her hair, an habitual gesture. This has the advantage for the reader of permitting him to imagine, with just a little more accuracy, a living being with individual traits, as well as a chance materialization of a romantic type. While remaining faithful to Frédéric's psychology and to the point of view presentation, the passage makes a small con-tribution to the depiction of reality.

Some eight months later, Frédéric is no further advanced. Mme Arnoux has returned from a real absence, but as Frédéric carries on a desultory conversation, she recedes into the gathering dusk: we are given no physical description at all (p. 96). Then she puts on a *black* mantle, and they go out together into cold fog, where 'on n'y voyait plus'; and although the fog 'puait dans l'air' (the warnings become melodramatic), 'Frédéric le humait avec délices' because he could feel Mme Arnoux's arm—but only through several thicknesses of padded clothing. A far cry from embracing an almost naked Rosanette in bed. And when the light of reality returns (in this case the bright lights of the boule-vard), Mme Arnoux leaves him.

There follows yet another passage showing the profound influence Frédéric's preoccupation is beginning to have on his life; and in the midst of all this idealization there is another state-ment which has been quoted to 'prove' the noble nature of his passion: 'Il ne pouvait se la figurer autrement que vêtue, — tant sa pudeur semblait naturelle, et reculait son sexe dans une ombre mystérieuse' (p. 99). Could this be why Frédéric so often sees Mme Arnoux surrounded by shadows? In any case, this remark, even taken literally, loses its authentic ring when considered in relation to one made only a page earlier: 'Quant à essayer d'en faire sa maîtresse, il était sûr que toute tentative serait vaine.' The psychology is crystal clear, and corresponds perfectly with Frédéric's character: his ideal is too pure to be defiled because she is too difficult a conquest. Léon deluded himself in precisely the same way when, but only as long as, Emma was distant.[1] The situation is merely expressed more subtly in l'Education, with the inevitable result that it is more easily misunderstood. Besides, even if Frédéric were sincerely idealizing Mme Arnoux, this is still a very long jump (although one traditionally taken with no signs of breathlessness) from Flaubert's idealization of Mme Schlésinger. This whole celebrated passage ('Les prosti-tuées qu'il rencontrait aux feux du gaz ... d'une façon brusque et insensible' (pp. 97–8)), admirably written and psychologically impressive though it is, represents a false attitude to reality which Flaubert would never condone. In context, it is plainly satirical: satirizing people like Frédéric who borrow their feelings in one piece from a certain type of limited artistic experience and try to apply them directly to life, and also satirizing the type of book from which such feelings come. Consider, by way of contrast, Flaubert's view of just such a book:

Et d'abord, pour parler clair, la baise-t-il ou ne la baise-t-il pas? Ce ne sont pas des êtres humains, mais des mannequins. Que c'est beau, ces histoires d'amour où la chose principale est tellement entourée de mystère que l'on ne sait à quoi s'en tenir, l'union sexuelle étant reléguée systématiquement dans l'ombre comme boire, manger, pisser, etc! Le parti pris m'agace. Voilà un gaillard qui vit continuellement avec une femme qui l'aime et qu'il aime, et jamais un désir! Pas un nuage impur ne vient obscurcir ce lac bleuâtre! O hypocrite! S'il avait raconté l'histoire vraie, que c'eût été plus beau! Mais la vérité demande des mâles plus velus que M. de Lamartine.[2]

---

[1] *Bovary*, p. 148. Cf. Henry and Mme Renaud's motives in the first *Education* (*supra*, pp. 73–6), and p. 245 of the 1869 *Education*, where Frédéric, calling his timidity 'une invincible pudeur', argues that Mme Arnoux is different from other women: '*Par la force de ses rêves*, il l'avait posée en dehors des conditions humaines'.

[2] *Cor.*, II, 397.

If Frédéric's obsession with Mme Arnoux constitutes 'un mode nouveau d'exister' (p. 97), it is one which is both illusory and temporary.

At Mme Arnoux's birthday party at Saint-Cloud, it is first her shoes which attract Frédéric's attention (p. 115). This presumably has something to do with the way women dressed in the period. A sight of a woman's shoes, being a relatively rare occurrence, would no doubt constitute a more interesting phenomenon, in sexual terms, than it would today. In the case of a woman like Mme Arnoux, it would be a 'stolen' and hence even more exciting sight, at least to the naïve Frédéric. Such at any rate we must believe to be the case, for already after the first scene one of the 'particularités plus intimes' which he remembers was the sight of her foot (p. 12), and in the farewell scene he says 'La vue de votre pied me trouble' (p. 605). Similarly, Mme Dambreuse's foot is mentioned twice (pp. 337 and 498), at times when *she* seems attractive to Frédéric, and after the puritan image has been exorcised. We can now see, too, the full effect of the impression which Rosanette's costume, in which he could see not only her feet but her legs as well, must have made on Frédéric's desires; and the golden spurs, as well as her 'pieds nus dans ses pantoufles' (p. 507), also become more significant. So, too, does the fact that among Frédéric's preparations for the seduction of Mme Arnoux at the hotel in the rue Tronchet is the purchase of a pair of satin slippers (p. 396), and the sacrifice which leads him to give them to Rosanette instead (p. 408). Again, in the 'idealized' passage about the women referred to above, satin slippers, which 'semblaient attendre son pied' (p. 97) are mentioned among articles of feminine embellishment which attracted Frédéric's attention in the shop windows.[1]

---

[1] We find a similar preoccupation in *Madame Bovary*: Emma warming her feet at the fire when Léon first sees her (p. 109), the movement of her feet in her slippers when she meets Léon in Rouen (p. 323), and later in the slippers he himself had given her (p. 367); one of the things Rodolphe notices when he first meets Emma is her 'pied coquet' (p. 180), and as he walks behind her in the woods, he 'contemplait entre ce drap noir et la bottine noire la délicatesse de son bas blanc, qui lui semblait quelque chose de sa nudité' (p. 221); Justin is fascinated by Emma's shoes, just as he is by her underclothes (pp. 260–1); and in an earlier version the

In the passage in question, then, the shoes—especially in view of their open design and their colour—'ce qui dessinait sur ses bas un grillage d'or'—must have been a highly encouraging sight for Frédéric. We are not, however, informed here, as in the case of Rodolphe, that this seemed like 'quelque chose de sa nudité', because even this small amount of explanatory comment would not be consistent with Frédéric's point of view. Less honest with himself than Rodolphe, he is still trying to reject the sexual basis of his interest.

Later in the day, Mme Arnoux is silhouetted against the sunset (p. 119). What light there is is a 'lueur d'incendie', announcing the approaching darkness, and she herself is already in darkness. There have been no real 'light' images since the one which was carried away down the river.

It is against a background of night once more that they begin to talk (pp. 119–20). But even so, Frédéric believes he is making real progress, for 'C'était la première fois qu'ils ne parlaient pas de choses insignifiantes.' Again a little reflection reveals the value of this statement. It is hardly likely that Flaubert would regard as worthwhile a discussion questioning whether it was preferable to be a great orator or a great writer, and even less likely that he would approve Mme Arnoux's preference for the orator. Nor would he take it as 'significant' that a woman should believe in dreams, or that she should dislike certain perfumes. Besides, this is not the first time, as the text claims, that Frédéric believed they were speaking of 'serious' matters. Frédéric's new enthusiasm: 'cette droiture d'esprit se rapportait si bien à la beauté régulière de son visage, qu'elle semblait en dépendre'; 'Il l'aimait sans arrière-pensée, sans esprit de retour, absolument' has as little basis as earlier statements of this nature. We still have no objective evidence of either her beauty or her moral and intellectual excellence. The same applies to the return from Saint-Cloud: although Frédéric imagines a profound communication

---

sight of her feet during the ceremony of Holy Unction gives rise to a decidedly erotic vision by Charles of the first time he had seen her bare feet (Pommier et Leleu, op. cit., pp. 122, 611). Even Bouvard palpitates at such a sight (*Bouvard et Pécuchet*, pp. 177, 235).

with her, because of her secretly throwing away Arnoux's flowers and because her daughter is lying between them (pp. 121, 122), they are still in the dark: 'un réverbère, çà et là, éclairait l'angle d'un mur, puis on rentrait dans les ténèbres', and the apparent promise has already been withdrawn: 'Les plis nombreux de sa robe couvraient ses pieds.'

Internal protestations notwithstanding, Frédéric now begins to feel (a) that he may after all succeed in making Mme Arnoux his mistress, and (b) that he would therefore like to do so: 'Mme Arnoux était maintenant près de sa mère, à Chartres. Mais il la retrouverait bientôt, et finirait par être son amant' (p. 124). His love, we noted, had been pure as long as he had no prospects of success. Ironically, he has no grounds for believing that the situation has changed: he is basing his conclusions on the last time he had seen her (at Saint-Cloud), when any hope he had was nowhere but in his imagination, and on his present mood of general optimism, resulting from his having passed his examinations and from the advances of M. and Mme Dambreuse. The casual way in which this bald statement is introduced is typical. It is incidental to the main subject of the passage (Frédéric's arrangements for a picnic), and is almost furtive in its appearance. This is how it would occur to Frédéric—only in off-guard moments does truth cheat his defence mechanism. When he is directly concerned with his great love, he submerges the truth in a great wave of sentimentality. The unwary reader is hoodwinked by the novel's rhetoric: when he thinks back over Frédéric's attitudes, he tends to remember those which were given prominence by being developed at great length—the dishonest ones. He is caught in the very web of illusion which it is the purpose of the book to show was the cause of Frédéric's failure. But the truth is there for those who, unlike Frédéric, will seek it out.

Frédéric's initial reaction to the news that he has lost his inheritance casts further doubts on whether Mme Arnoux is the centre of his universe. Having hinted to her that he was immensely rich, he can no longer face her. So much for the fiction of profound disinterested love: he did not even believe that

Mme Arnoux's purity was sufficient to prevent her feelings from being affected by wealth (p. 136). True, the opposite *lieu commun*, the thought of living in a garret with Mme Arnoux devoting herself to him in appreciation of his sacrifice, also occurs to him, but home comforts, even in the provinces, quickly dissuade him from this course of action (pp. 131–2). After a single week, he is resolved never to bother about Mme Arnoux again (pp. 132, 139).

But Fate is determined not to give Frédéric any peace. No sooner has he reached this comfortable conclusion, than his inheritance reappears, and with the idea of money comes flooding back the idea of Mme Arnoux (pp. 139–40): he rushes off to Paris at the first opportunity.[1] This last chapter of Part I has thus given us a complete summary, rather clearer than usual, of Frédéric's attitude to his great love. It is a love which is false, as much bound up with his youthful dreams and ambitions as his false loves for the other women in the book. It needs continuous encouragement or indications of success even to survive. The idealism in which it is dressed up is equally false, an intellectual concept rather than an inherent part of the love. It depends not on any objective attractiveness, whether moral or physical, which Mme Arnoux may possess, but on Frédéric.[2] It is subject to all the changes of this most changeable character.

The second part of the novel continues to demonstrate the nature of this ideal. Frédéric has at last admitted the connection between his love and his dreams of luxury and passion. When he next meets Mme Arnoux, after his epic search for Regimbart through the interminable cafés of Paris, even he cannot help noticing the immense gulf between his dreams and the bourgeois domesticity, struggling to maintain appearances in spite of economic setbacks, which constitutes reality (p. 156). He is so disgruntled by the difficulty he has had in tracking Mme Arnoux

---

[1] Similar points are made, for a somewhat different purpose, by Giraud, op. cit., pp. 163–5.

[2] The fact that Flaubert may be saying that *all* human love is like this must not be overlooked.

down, that he even compares her son with the son of one of the café proprietors. Astounded at what he finds, and of course unable to realize that he could have been wrong all along about Mme Arnoux's splendour, the only stratagem he can imagine is to conclude that 'les passions s'étiolent quand on les dépayse, et, ne retrouvant plus Mme Arnoux dans le milieu où il l'avait connue, elle lui semblait avoir perdu quelque chose, porter confusément comme une dégradation, enfin n'être pas la même'. Rationalizations play havoc with logic: if this conclusion is true, it retrospectively judges his earlier feelings: if they depended not on the woman but on her material surroundings, they can scarcely be the stuff of pure undying love.

An interesting aspect of this scene, where it is given to Frédéric to see another dimension in his heroine, is the simultaneous indication that Mme Arnoux's essential quality—her unattainability—remains constant. She is again sitting before the fire in semi-darkness, and this time she has in addition her eyes turned away from him, completely absorbed as she is in her domestic responsibilities. There is no reason to assume, as does Frédéric, that she has changed in any way. The recurring 'darkness' theme suggests that she is faithful to her past, that her domesticity had always been present, together with—and indeed part of—her unattainability. Even on the boat she had for a time been absorbed in maternal cares, and when Frédéric first had dinner with the Arnoux there were signs of this more domestic side of their household (p. 65). On these occasions Frédéric interpreted such signs more kindly: 'Et Frédéric se réjouissait d'entendre ces choses, comme s'il eût fait une découverte, une acquisition' (p. 7); 'C'était un endroit paisible, honnête et familier tout ensemble' (p. 65). The difference here is that Frédéric is extremely bad-tempered after his day-long search, and because it is Arnoux, not his wife, who is delighted to see him again. Thus Flaubert's irony is again working on several levels: he makes Frédéric notice a change in Mme Arnoux where there is none; he makes him ascribe this change to factors which, while not valid in themselves, nevertheless invalidate what Frédéric had previously thought; and from these non-valid arguments he makes him draw conclusions which, while logically untrue and likely to be changed at any moment, are yet truer in fact than anything Frédéric had previously concluded about Mme Arnoux: 'J'étais bien bon là-bas, avec mes douleurs! A peine si elle m'a reconnu! quelle bourgeoise!'[1]

The couple's next meeting (pp. 192–4) is again one of hope. These two pages are so full of false attitudes, implicit contradictions and ironies, that one can only marvel at the ingenuity and conciseness of Flaubert, who tells so much with apparently so simple means. It is Frédéric's (unfounded) hopes of sexual fulfilment with Rosanette which bring Mme Arnoux to mind. Although we are not actually told that Frédéric had the same hopes as regards Mme Arnoux, the process of thought association makes it clear enough, once again giving the lie to the fiction of purity and disinterestedness. Once the idea of Mme Arnoux occurs to him, he must find (for his own benefit) an excuse for visiting her—one which is both innocent of any sexual undertone and sufficient to justify the reversal of his theory that she was merely a 'bourgeoise'. His excuse is the confidential message Rosanette had given him for Arnoux (p. 191); but he does take care to call at a time when he knows Arnoux will not be there!

Because the hope engendered by Rosanette has been transferred to Mme Arnoux, he is undeterred to find his idol in precisely the same domesticated situation as last time. One false hope has inspired another, which inspires an optimistic conclusion as false as the pessimistic one so recently drawn from the same set of facts. His optimism is expressed in several ways. The first is that at least she remains in the light of the sun, surrounded by the light of reflections: there is no returning darkness, no question of the image being carried off down the Seine. Is this a sign that her so far unshakeable unattainability is trembling? We shall return to this question in a moment. The second indication of Frédéric's optimism is that we are given another highly subjective

---

[1] p. 157. Frédéric's search for Regimbart as the only means of obtaining the Arnoux's new address, and his subsequent disillusionment, are clearly intended to figure Frédéric's 'search' in life. When finally the chase is over, his disappointment is a prophecy in miniature of the probable result of deeper contact with Mme Arnoux, even if he were ever to achieve this.

description of Mme Arnoux. The third is that when he is leaving she shakes hands with him, and, as before, he takes this as 'un engagement, une promesse' (pp. 193–4)—but this time with no sign of the earlier rational afterthought of 'Allons donc! je suis fou!': Flaubert assumes that the reader is aware of that by now.[1] The fourth contains additional irony. Frédéric, having mentioned the evening when they were returning together from Saint-Cloud, assumes that Mme Arnoux's sadness is calculated to 'défendre toute allusion à leur souvenir commun'. The occasion referred to provides another opportunity of seeing how Flaubert, while not departing from Frédéric's point of view, manages to go beyond it. Several details, all noticed by Frédéric but not combined into a credible hypothesis by him (because they did not appear directly to affect his amorous preoccupations), provide the key. At Saint-Cloud Frédéric had unwittingly contributed to Mme Arnoux's discovery of her husband's philanderings, and had even innocently given the knife an extra twist.[2] Mme Arnoux's thoughts must have been very different indeed from his on that evening: the 'souvenir commun' to which he alludes is not one at all. And just as he was mistaken then about her thoughts, so he is mistaken now in interpreting her reaction to the memory of them. Once more his optimism is founded on false assumptions.

Let us return to the image of light mentioned above. In the past these symbols of light and darkness surrounding Mme Arnoux have been superimposed on Frédéric's point of view, and operate on a level beyond his comprehension. Even though the realistic details on which they are based are seen through his eyes, the symbols themselves do not coincide with his mood:

[1] Cf. p. 284, where Frédéric sees encouragement in the simple act of her taking his arm.

[2] By bringing Arnoux a confidential letter from La Vatnaz (p. 114) and by giving Mme Arnoux a 'replacement' sunshade for the one he had broken in Paris, but which was not in fact hers (pp. 90–1, 116). Frédéric makes matters worse by obligingly fetching Mme Arnoux's bouquet, which Arnoux had accidentally wrapped in La Vatnaz' letter. All this is amusingly ironical, for had he realized what was going on, he would certainly have used these incidents consciously to cause a breach between Arnoux and his wife (cf. pp. 245, 247)—and would probably then have bungled it.

Flaubert communicates with the reader above Frédéric's head. If such a scheme were rigorously applied, we should be forced to conclude that on this occasion, where no darkness enters the picture, the reader is being informed, still above Frédéric's head, that Mme Arnoux was ceasing to be unattainable. Is it possible that Flaubert, while showing that Frédéric's optimism was logically unwarranted, was also hinting that in fact a change *has* occurred in Mme Arnoux, independently of Frédéric's attitude or of anything he may or may not have done? Flaubert would certainly welcome such an opportunity to complicate things still further. We do know that eventually Mme Arnoux will reach the point where bad luck rather than 'virtue' prevents Frédéric from sleeping with her; the change must come somewhere. One of Flaubert's early plans provides some help, for we are now at the beginning of what it calls the '3° période intime dans la Maison',[1] immediately following the 'Laps en province'. This plan contains the following notes:

elle ne l'aime que lorsque ses enfants commencent à se détacher d'elle — opposition du caractère de la fille — opacité du fils qui devient St Cyrien.

Alors elle est *seule* (le mari la néglige de plus en plus menage querel-leur) [plutot de la part de la femme que du mari] & il est tout naturel qu'elle remarque qui fait attention à elle.

The parts concerning the children are obviously some time in the future, but we are on the verge of the domestic quarrels: the Saint-Cloud episode shows that they have been threatening for some time, since Mme Arnoux no longer has any illusions about her husband's affections. It seems that in this passage the reader is being warned of the first authentic chink in the heroine's armour, in the very midst of the doubtful chinks which Frédéric imagines.

Following a brief passage the main purpose of which is to point a direct contrast between Mme Arnoux and Rosanette,[2] we find Frédéric witnessing the first open quarrel between Arnoux

---

[1] Durry, op. cit., p. 163.

[2] pp. 206-7, which contains no new elements, but which again shows Frédéric perfectly content with the domesticated milieu at which he had so recently sneered, and with the idea of seduction still hovering about.

and his wife (pp. 236–9). As with the Saint-Cloud letter, Frédéric has been indirectly responsible, for he persuaded Arnoux to buy the shawl (the subject of the argument) for Rosanette. This argument seems to increase his chances, and therefore increases proportionately Mme Arnoux's apparent beauty; but again the reader is expected to take this beauty on trust. Frédéric, thinking he has never been closer to his goal, can also think in more open —albeit still rather timid—sexual terms. The passage is worth quoting at length, for it is one of the most explicit statements of Frédéric's real attitude in the whole novel:

… et, tout en la plaignant, il se réjouissait, se délectait au fond de l'âme. Par vengeance ou besoin d'affection, elle se réfugierait vers lui. Son espoir, démesurément accru, renforçait son amour.

Jamais elle ne lui avait paru si captivante, si profondément belle. De temps à autre, une aspiration soulevait sa poitrine; ses deux yeux fixes semblaient dilatés par une vision intérieure, et sa bouche demeurait entre-close comme pour donner son âme. Quelquefois, elle appuyait dessus fortement son mouchoir; il aurait voulu être ce petit morceau de batiste tout trempé de larmes. Malgré lui, il regardait la couche, au fond de l'alcôve, en imaginant sa tête sur l'oreiller; et il voyait cela si bien, qu'il se retenait pour ne pas la saisir dans ses bras. Elle ferma les paupières, apaisée, inerte. Alors, il s'approcha de plus près, et, penché sur elle, il examinait avidement sa figure … et ce muet échange de leurs pensées était comme un consentement, un début d'adultère (pp. 240–1).

Frédéric has admitted to himself that Mme Arnoux, whatever other charms she may have, attracts him sexually (p. 249). She is now like the other women: he no longer bothers to see her as a person, and her physical and moral characteristics are barely mentioned from now on. Sketchy as they were in the past, they now disappear almost entirely, in favour of references to the clothes she was wearing and the light surrounding her. These elements continue the symbolic pattern which has been present from the beginning. When she calls on him to ask for financial help (a visit which he interprets as a sexual overture),[1] she is

[1] pp. 268, 269, 273. This is in spite of the fact that as a result of his anger with Arnoux, he had so recently sworn never to see either of them again (p. 265).

dressed in brown and black (p. 266). When Frédéric visits her at Creil, she is in a dressing-gown, but quickly disappears, to return 'correctement habillé' (p. 278): and although he looks imploringly at her several times during the interminable tour of the pottery works, we are never told what he sees—until, having returned to her room, he sees an impassible being, nothing but discouragement. There is no fire, it is raining, the image of a sphinx appears, and Mme Arnoux's 'profil pur se découpait en pâleur au milieu de l'ombre'. Her clothes and the shadows now combine forces, and the barrier becomes more explicit: 'Cette robe, se confondant avec les ténèbres, lui paraissait démesurée, infinie, insoulevable; et précisément à cause de cela son désir redoublait' (pp. 285–6). Finally, both her children arrive as further reinforcement.

Through a combination of circumstances Frédéric now seems content to accept his defeat, and for a period concentrates his attack on more vulnerable adversaries. During this quiet period, Deslauriers secretly visits Mme Arnoux, who realizes, as if by revelation, that she is in love with Frédéric (pp. 355–6). This scene, of the greatest importance, is one of the very few which are presented outside Frédéric's point of view. Flaubert continues to load the dice against his hero with an almost perverse delight. All Frédéric's efforts to secure such an avowal have failed lamentably: when it finally comes, not only is he not responsible for it, but he does not even know it has taken place. Since it can make no difference to his subsequent behaviour, it might just as well not have occurred at all. When he returns to Paris, he is 'vertueux' (i.e. determined not to waste any more time on 'passions infructueuses' (p. 366)), and does not go to see the Arnoux (p. 373).

Whatever his decisions, he has no control over chance. It is not long before he meets Mme Arnoux in the street. And the secret symbolic language between author and reader returns, for she is again in a flood of light, and again wearing bright colours (her dress is of 'soie gorge-de-pigeon' (p. 373), the same material and colour as Emma's sunshade which so impressed Charles, and as the dress with which Mme Bordin begins to make an impression on Bouvard).[1] This time Mme Arnoux's appearance certainly reflects her attitude towards Frédéric. Moreover, Frédéric is not insensible to this new appearance—one might almost say apparition, as in the opening scene—and the word 'splendeur' occurs to him once more. But the very fact that Frédéric reacts to this meeting in much the same way as he did on the boat shows that he does not appreciate the significance of this new appearance, as indeed he could not. For him, Mme Arnoux is once again a splendid female whom he has encountered by chance, and who—this time aided by a flood of memories— precipitates a bout of adolescent-type love. (The fact that Frédéric is now about twenty-five years of age, instead of eighteen, further underlines the falseness of his situation.) Mme Arnoux is almost as much a stranger as she was at the beginning, their conversation is quite as banal, and she is rather less likely (being seven years older) to have much objective beauty. Frédéric's moon-struck attitude—given that he is not aware of Mme Arnoux's change— is even less justifiable than it was on the boat. Flaubert is using the same subject-matter to show that while Frédéric has not changed, Mme Arnoux has, that Frédéric has a greater chance of success than ever before.

Having obtained from Deslauriers some indication of his new prospects,[2] Frédéric makes several visits to Mme Arnoux, including one in which his ardour is controlled only by an unexpected interruption (pp. 384–6). There are no further physical descriptions—sex is still uppermost in Frédéric's mind.[3] But when, as a result of the idyll at Auteuil, Frédéric knows that she

---

[1] *Madame Bovary*, p. 23; *Bouvard et Pécuchet*, pp. 58 et seq.

[2] pp. 374–5; cf. pp. 384, 386, 388.

[3] Comic irony occurs again here: 'Il protesta de l'innocence de son amour. Le passé devait lui répondre de l'avenir' (p. 386). Frédéric is putting forward, not a record of honesty and respect, but his bumbling and shyness, which he has so often regretted, as a guarantee of Mme Arnoux's future safety at his hands. He thinks he is being Machiavellian, promising yet more schemes aimed at sexual victory: in fact, the future will be more like the past than he imagines, for his bumbling and shyness will continue to disrupt his plans. By using indirect speech, Flaubert has given 'devait' a double meaning—the sense Frédéric put into the corresponding present tense, and the specifically imperfect meaning of 'was to'.

is once more 'sûre de ne pas faillir',[1] mention is again made of her dark-toned, all-enveloping clothes. At the Dambreuse dinner-party (after the failure of the rue Tronchet rendez-vous and Frédéric's success with Rosanette), his great love has grown so weak that it takes Frédéric's jealousy of Rosanette to raise even a flicker of interest, although Mme Arnoux is this time sitting beside him (her dress is black) (pp. 490–1). After a half-hearted attempt at making conversation, he is content to dismiss her with 'Eh bien, va te promener!'[2] He does, however, return to see her (pp. 511–14), and again he is on the verge of success—so that the description of Mme Arnoux is limited to the two statements that she was pale, and that she had a 'beau visage'. This is the scene which is brought to an abrupt end by Rosanette, and although it consists largely of conversation, the reader is warned that Frédéric will be cheated once more. Mme Arnoux's very pallor, which recalls that of an earlier scene of hopelessness (p. 285), and contrasts so definitely with the 'splendeur de sa peau brune' (p. 7), the light which previously 'pénétrait d'un fluide d'or sa peau ambrée' (p. 192), and the sunshine surrounding her face (p. 373), is one such detail; and she is once more engaged in domestic duties, and the weather is unkind.

'Et ce fut tout.' The final interview, many years later, adds little to our picture of Mme Arnoux, but does round off the symbols which we have been following: after so many changes, they at least remain. Mme Arnoux is as much an absence as ever: 'Dans la pénombre du crépuscule, il n'apercevait que ses yeux

---

[1] p. 391; cf. pp. 388, 389. But Frédéric has not given up hope: 'Il tremblait de perdre par un mot tout ce qu'il croyait avoir gagné, se disant qu'on peut ressaisir une occasion et qu'on ne rattrape jamais une sottise. Il voulait qu'elle se donnât, et non la prendre' (p. 392). The echoes of *les Liaisons dangereuses* in this context undermine the whole scene: Frédéric's thinking in Valmont's terms is a master-stroke of bitter burlesque. As a picture of Eden-like beatitude, this episode is as false as the Fontainebleau one, with which it must be compared.

[2] Cf. pp. 285–7, where his *élan* is abruptly halted by Mme Arnoux's attitude and his own recurring diffidence: 'Il voulut être fort, et allégea son cœur en dénigrant Mme Arnoux par des épithètes injurieuses: "C'est une imbécile, une dinde, une brute, n'y pensons plus"'. And p. 394, where Frédéric 'hates' Mme Arnoux for taking seriously what he had intended as a piece of strategy: 'Il était bien entendu qu'ils ne devaient pas s'apartenir' (p. 389).

sous la voilette de dentelle noire qui masquait sa figure';[1] and their walk together in the streets echoes the tone of the earlier one (p. 96), and of several other passages which I have noted: 'La lueur des boutiques éclairait, par intervalles, son profil pâle; puis l'ombre l'enveloppait de nouveau ...' (p. 602). Back in full light, Frédéric is shocked by her white hair, the only thing about her which he notices (p. 604). There is more to this statement than a realistic reminder of the passage of time. The shock which Flaubert has administered is not so much that Mme Arnoux is an old woman—she was already at the 'mois d'août des femmes' (p. 391) when Frédéric, faithful to his earlier ideal, was still trying to get her to bed—as a brief revelation that Mme Arnoux is not the woman he had imagined her to be, and possibly never was, either physically or morally. Had Frédéric dared to look her in the face at that first dinner-party (p. 69), he may even then have seen someone different, and the entire illusion upon which his life was built might have been dissipated.

Or would it? Such considerations are academic when we are dealing with a Frédéric: his whole being depends on illusions. And in this final scene, Flaubert, having revealed the falseness of what has preceded, makes it clear that no amount of symbolic revelation, no amount of experience—of sentimental education —will prevent such people from building illusions. Almost immediately Mme Arnoux again has 'le dos tourné à la lumière', and Frédéric, 'se grisant par ses [propres] paroles, *arrivait à croire ce qu'il disait*' (p. 604). He swiftly rebuilds his image of sexual desirability, both intensified and rendered unattainable by his timidity and his prudence (pp. 605–6), in spite of the now overwhelming evidence against the possibility of such an image.[2] Nothing but his death could prevent the fruitless and soul-destroying cycle of illusion, and even his death will not prevent

---

[1] p. 601. Maynial, op. cit., p. 130 mentions the frequent (but not invariable, as he claims) occurrence of red in portraits of Mme Arnoux. I believe that this colour has not as much significance as the more sombre tones, and in any case Maynial merely wants to show that red 'semble lié pour toujours, comme une sorte d'appel sensuel, à l'image de la femme', in Flaubert's mind.

[2] Cf. Cortland, op. cit., pp. 98–100, who also comments on the falseness of this scene.

others—Emma, Salammbô, Saint Antoine, Bouvard and Pécuchet, most of us—from repeating the exercise in their own way until the end of time.

All the evidence, then, confirms our original hypothesis: however different from the other characters Mme Arnoux may appear, these differences result almost entirely from the fact that she occupies a central position in Frédéric's thoughts. While not disputing that she is more important to him than the other people with whom he deals, we must conclude that this importance is a false one, resulting from a series of accidental circumstances independent of her. She is presented according to the same principles, and following largely the same techniques, as the other women in the book, and it is not her personal excellence but Frédéric's view of her which results in her seeming so remarkable to the reader.[1] Even as a catalyst for Frédéric's escapist dreams, she is superior to the others only in that his greater preoccupation with her causes her to be the subject of them more frequently—when she is not immediately available, he is equally capable of dreaming thus about Rosanette (p. 469), Louise (p. 365), or Mme Dambreuse (pp. 526–7). Again, the idea of a journey to certain privileged places (especially on a honeymoon), as a symbol of bourgeois pseudo-romantic conformity in Flaubert's mind,[2] runs through the whole book, and Mme Arnoux is not excluded from it. Frédéric dreams of taking both Louise and Rosanette to Italy (pp. 365, 469), and Mme Arnoux to the Orient, Spain, or Switzerland (p. 245); Martinon takes Cécile to Italy for

---

[1] Tillett, op. cit., p. 58 comes remarkably close to the truth when she states in passing that the Arnoux are 'so lacking in precision as characters that they might almost be products of Frédéric's imagination'. However, she intends this as a criticism, a weakness of Flaubert's characters who, in contrast with those of Balzac, do not 'emerge as individuals with the warmth and fervour of true life' (p. 56). On three separate occasions (pp. 56, 68, 71) Tillett mentions the fact that almost the whole book is seen through Frédéric's eyes, but on the whole she fails to come to grips with what this entails.

[2] Cf. his remarks on his own sister's honeymoon journey—in company with the whole family (Cor., I, 164, 167–8); the conversations about Italy at La Vaubyessard and Switzerland at the Lion d'or; and the article Italie in the Dictionnaire des idées reçues.

their honeymoon (p. 524), and Arnoux had taken his wife there for the same purpose (p. 244). Nor does her character appear to be so very attractive or idealized on the rare occasions when it seems to be reflected objectively through her speech and actions. We have already had occasion to mention some of her subjects of conversation; other traits noted are that 'elle ne s'exaltait point pour la littérature' (p. 207)—it is difficult to imagine a more complete condemnation by Flaubert than this: she is apparently not even as far along the road to salvation as Emma! —her objections to Frédéric's romantic outpourings are, like those of Mme Dambreuse, based entirely on bourgeois morality, rather than their sheer stupidity,[1] and her defence is based on such considerations as 'devoir', 'religion' (p. 286), and even 'convenances' (p. 386), even after she has admitted her love to herself. She takes Arnoux's invitation to dine with him in a 'cabinet particulier', as a slight on her virtue (p. 249). She gives herself up to the same puerile dreams as Frédéric (pp. 390–2): we are even told that 'Leurs goûts, leurs jugements étaient les mêmes' (p. 390)! She distributes gloves and handkerchiefs (p. 391) and locks of hair (p. 606) in the finest bourgeois–romantic style, and even sits and dreams on what she has tenderly named 'le banc Frédéric' (p. 602). The final scene shows that she has as many illusions about their love as Frédéric, and, like Frédéric, grasps at any words, no matter how blatantly untrue, which will preserve these illusions. The fact that she does not succumb to Frédéric's dubious charms is as much due to accident as to any inherent virtue she may possess; this was already allowed for in some of the earliest plans, and is suggested no fewer than six times in the novel.[2]

Finally, we must not overlook the reasons for which Mme Arnoux fails to come to the rue Tronchet. The description of the child's croup (pp. 401–5) constitutes the only important passage from her point of view in the whole book. There must be a good

[1] pp. 285, 286, 386; cf. pp. 525–6.
[2] pp. 385–6, 387, 395, 404–5, 514, 601. This point has already been made by Pommier in his *Compte rendu* of Durry's *Flaubert et ses projets inédits* (RHL, janvier–mars, 1953, p. 111); but Pommier refers only to the intrusion of Rosanette.

reason for this. Critics who mention this scene appear to have been so impressed by the anecdote of Flaubert's compassion for the child whose case he observed in order to be able to make the description, and so anxious to prove thereby that he was both conscientious in his search for 'truth' (i.e. factual details) and full of deep human feelings,[1] that they tend to overlook what from the literary standpoint is most important: Flaubert went to all this trouble in order to show his heroine in a crisis. The description of the croup has no value other than an illustrative one. The scene is largely a rhetorical device, intended to disguise and render acceptable to the reader the bare statement already noted in the plans: 'il n'y a pas que sa vertu qui l'empêche mais une circonstance fortuite'.[2] Once again, Flaubert's 'realism' is not the basis of his work, but the trimmings, something added later to give external expression to the idea. It would hardly be sufficient, at such an important turning-point of the story, for this extraordinary chance occurrence[3] to be reported as a mere fact, say by a message from Mme Arnoux to Frédéric. Such a method would incur considerable 'reader resistance', and would be dismissed as a weakness in construction, a *truc* introduced irresponsibly merely to advance the story. As the novel stands, the weakness—if it is one—is just as surely present, but the reader is so skilfully initiated into Mme Arnoux's point of view that his attention is absorbed by her reaction to a distressing situation. There is no better way of identifying a reader with a character, and thus nursing his critical faculty to sleep, than by beginning with a dream (p. 401), especially one caused by a stimulus impinging on the consciousness from reality. Then when Mme Arnoux wakens, a liberal use of *style indirect libre* takes over the responsibility, and the rhetorical battle is won: possible objections about the validity of the situation itself are forgotten.

[1] e.g. Dumesnil, introduction to Belles Lettres edition of *l'Education*, vol. I, p. lxxxviii; Castex, op. cit., p. 40.

[2] Durry, op. cit., p. 187.

[3] Remembering that it is not only the child's croup which is involved—we had been prepared for this in advance (p. 394)—but also the fact that he recovers from an illness which in those days, according to Dumesnil, could normally be cured only by an operation.

There is more to the passage than this. If Flaubert had really wanted to idealize Mme Arnoux, the croup scene would have been superfluous. The simple fact of her not coming would have suggested her virtue and her principles to the reader (as it does to Frédéric), or would at least have left him in doubt about her motives and free to accept the hypothesis of virtue as one possibility. But by inserting the croup scene as the *only* important one from Mme Arnoux's point of view, Flaubert is drawing attention to the fact that total virtue is not a possible explanation of her motives. In doing this he was moreover remaining faithful both to his personal philosophy and to the spirit of this book: while there may be degrees of idealism and virtue, those who act entirely from pure motives are few indeed.[1] There is nearly always some self-interest, or, at best, self-delusion behind most thoughts and actions. In this case it is self-delusion. We can be certain that Flaubert himself would not imagine any supernatural causal relationship between the child's recovery and the failure to keep the rendez-vous with Frédéric. Rare as they may be, such recoveries were possible, and Flaubert is simply presenting a medical fact. It is Mme Arnoux who concludes: 'C'était un avertissement de la Providence. Mais le Seigneur, dans sa miséricorde, n'avait pas voulu la punir tout à fait' (pp. 404–5), and it is her distressed state of mind which takes the conclusion further, and decides that next time her son will not be so lucky. Although the scene is from Mme Arnoux's point of view, and therefore is apparently sympathetic, we know that for Flaubert this was mere superstition—even for a Christian such popular theology is of doubtful validity—and that by making Mme Arnoux think in these terms he is quietly but firmly classing her as a bourgeoise.[2]

---

[1] The only totally honest character in the book seems to be Dussardier, but he is equally given to deluding himself, because of his stupidity and his ignorance—and, indeed, because of his honesty. Remember also this statement of general intention: 'Pas de monstres et pas de héros!' (*Cor.*, VII, 281.)

[2] Critics who compare this scene with similar details in *le Lys dans la vallée* and *Volupté* (Vial: 'Flaubert émule et disciple émancipé de Balzac' in *RHL*, juillet–septembre, 1948, pp. 233–63; Vial: 'De *Volupté* à *l'Education sentimentale*' in *RHL*, janvier–mars, avril–juin, 1957, pp. 45–65, 178–95; Castex, op. cit., pp. 62–5; Durry, op. cit., p. 159) fail to make this clear, and therefore fail to

Besides showing the reader Mme Arnoux's real value, this scene, like the much shorter passage where Mme Arnoux admits her love for Frédéric, has an ironic purpose. The reader is admitted to a knowledge which is not available to the hero, who assumes that Mme Arnoux does not come because her virtue or her fear of being found out was too strong at the last moment. He therefore turns his attentions elsewhere, and in addition the idealistic image of Mme Arnoux which he had previously entertained is greatly strengthened. For the reader, however, this image is from now on (if it were not already) a false one, and there should be a constant contrast in his mind between what Frédéric thinks Mme Arnoux to be, and what the reader knows her to be.

This extremely detailed examination of the Frédéric–Mme Arnoux relationship has been necessary to demonstrate the weight of evidence against the commonly-held view of the central characters. It seems strange that so much of it is so consistently passed over in favour of an interpretation which, if true, would be unique in Flaubert's mature work. One is surely obliged to reconsider the view that Frédéric compensates for some of his more flagrant stupidities by the continuing nobility of his ideal passion for Mme Arnoux. In many ways, this passion *is* one of his more flagrant stupidities: it is the most thoroughgoing manifestation of Frédéric's personality, and is neither noble nor continuous.[1] One might argue that an ideal so false is, for an author as uncom-

---

recognize just how different this scene is from the earlier ones, in spite of superficial similarities. Vial, it is true, insists on the idea of 'disciple émancipé', on the element of ironic negation by Flaubert of the sentimentality of his predecessors; but he does not suggest that the 'Idol' herself, as well as the adoring adolescent, may be reduced in moral status.

[1] The intermittence of Frédéric's love has itself long been recognized (e.g. see Durry, op. cit., pp. 177–8), but is seldom given the importance it seems to deserve. One of the best expressions of it is Taine's: 'Tous êtres mixtes, parfois grossiers, parfois délicats, à la fois bons et mauvais, avec des vouloirs intermittents, rien de grand, de fort, ni d'arrêté, une sorte de briquetage et de cailloutis moral plaqué de torchis et de plâtre qui s'écaille, avec un certain vernis courant. . . . Les types très francs et très absolus sont faux, ils n'existent que dans l'esprit. Tout homme réel et vivant n'est qu'un à peu près, un hybride, un mélange de velléités et d'inconséquences. Faire vrai, c'est faire le monsieur que voici, et non le personnage énergique et grandiose que mon imagination aurait du plaisir à contempler' (quoted in Conard edition, p. 703).

promising on moral issues as Flaubert, no ideal at all. Yet it is impossible not to feel that there is a positive side to such a relationship. If my arguments seem to leave this out of account, it is not because I deny its existence, but that I believe that a fuller understanding of the novel's complexity can be achieved if the reader is not content to remain a Frédéric, if he admits *also* that the idealization of Mme Arnoux is the less than perfect effort of an ordinary man faced with an ordinary woman. Frédéric's feelings and aspirations are real enough, however reprehensible, in intellectual terms, their cause. No doubt it is true, as Cortland, for example, argues,[1] that Mme Arnoux did inspire some of the most valuable and noble inner experiences of Frédéric's rather tawdry life. The same probably applies to most of us. Flaubert, with the memory of his own intense adolescence, is ridiculing not the experiences, but the delusions. He would maintain that the experiences would not be any the less vital if Frédéric were capable of honestly admitting their source, of facing reality at the same time—as Flaubert tried to do, for example, with Louise Colet. Such feelings then have more chance of being creative.

The unreal city

Descriptions of places, like those of people, reveal a great deal about the mood and the personality of the witness. An examination of some of these in their context shows that whatever factual, realistic basis they may have (and this is as always considerable), they frequently have a structural and emotional function, which goes far beyond the relatively primitive stage of well-expressed observation of material objects. This has certainly not gone unnoticed in the past. The idea of the Seine as a symbolic *leitmotif* is fairly well known; as long ago as 1912 Ferrère pointed out how the rhythm of the sentences in certain descriptions can reflect the character's mood;[2] Mme Durry, in noting the changes in value and proportion between the definitive description of the

[1] Cortland, op. cit., pp. 19, 31, 46.
[2] See Thibaudet, op. cit., pp. 151–4; Demorest, op. cit., pp. 538–40; Ferrère, op. cit., pp. 206–8.

auction sale and notes taken by Flaubert when he visited a real one, mentions that the reason for these changes is that in the novel the sale is no longer observed objectively, but by a 'témoin déchiré';[1] more recently Cortland has made some interesting comments on the presentation of material objects, based on the assumption that Frédéric's point of view is paramount.[2] The present study will sometimes be more detailed, and will have a slightly different orientation; but it will tend to confirm the assumptions in the statements referred to.

Several of the descriptions of Paris fall naturally into groups, thereby inviting comparisons. The most obvious case is the two descriptions of the traffic along the Champs-Elysées, where the comparison is explicit (pp. 33-4, 298-9); but it will be noted that even the comparison is made in Frédéric's mind, not pointed out by the author: 'Alors Frédéric se rappela les jours déjà loin où il enviait l'inexprimable bonheur de se trouver dans une de ces voitures, à côté d'une de ces femmes. Il le possédait, ce bonheur-là, et n'en était pas plus joyeux' (p. 299). Once more we have to reckon with his point of view: we are looking only at what he notices. Some of these things measure his progress in worldly knowledge. For example, the earlier description is concerned with 'voitures' in general: the only two types specifically mentioned are 'calèches' and 'coupés'. In Frédéric's present state the very fact of being in a carriage, of whatever sort, would in itself be a luxury beyond his reach. The main subject of his thoughts is the combination women–money, and aspects of the scene before him which symbolize this—feminine garments, grooms, varnish, furs, sparkling equipment, coats of arms. The sequence of his thoughts already shows that deep down he knows the impossibility of achieving both love *and* money: he is forced to put Mme Arnoux into Mme Dambreuse's carriage to achieve the double even in his imagination. In the second description, there is a long enumeration of the various types of carriage making

---

[1] Durry, op. cit., pp. 17–19; cf. Castex, op. cit., pp. 26–7, and Tillett, op. cit., pp. 61–7, who quotes some of the same passages and makes similar points, although in very general terms.

[2] Cortland, op. cit., pp. 154 et seq.

up the scene: Frédéric has by now realized that one does not have to be immensely rich to ride down the Champs-Elysées—his own vehicle is hired for the occasion—and he is able to distinguish between the desirable and the ordinary with a connoisseur's eye. He is still preoccupied by money, but he is now looking at what it can achieve from the point of view of a 'have', rather than a 'have-not'; and he can see that there is considerable variation in degrees of 'have'. The same applies to the 'woman' half of his dream. He is only relatively speaking a 'have', for Rosanette constitutes an uneasy compromise, the nearest he has managed to get to the combination of Mme Arnoux's love and Mme Dambreuse's money which formed the goal of his first dream. (He does not yet know that even this modicum of 'have' will be withdrawn during the fateful dinner at the Café Anglais.) Yet in spite of his mental statement of disillusionment, quoted above—which was inspired at least as much by the knowledge that both Mme Arnoux and Mme Dambreuse had seen him at the races with Rosanette, as by any profound feeling—Frédéric believes he has achieved some worldly success, and various elements in the two descriptions reflect this. For one thing, although both are surrounded by sunset, they contrast strongly in atmosphere, and in each case are consistent with Frédéric's mood. In the first the physical atmosphere is unkind—cold winds and dust, the noise of the carriages on the roadway harsh; behind the Tuileries (where Frédéric has several times hoped for a chance meeting with Mme Arnoux (p. 33)), the sky 'prenait des teintes d'ardoise', recalling the sombre colours which nearly always surround Mme Arnoux; the Seine is 'verdâtre' and gives off sparks of light only where it 'se déchirait' against the bridges; and the trees are 'violacés', a colour with unpleasant connotations. In the second description the rain has just ceased, the sky is clearing; although pedestrians, such as Deslauriers, are likely to be splashed with mud, Frédéric is perfectly safe; the setting sun is shining brilliantly through the slight mist, the reflections from the carriages are a much softer colour—'roussâtre'—and the blue of the sky has 'des douceurs de satin'; the trees are 'reluisants' instead of being 'deux masses sombres'; and Frédéric is now no longer standing looking at

the unpleasant-seeming river (of life? of time?) from afar—by
his simile of the avenue being 'pareille à un fleuve où ondulaient
des crinières, des vêtements, des têtes humaines', Flaubert has
arranged for Frédéric to be *in* the river. No doubt this symbolic
stream still has the same unpleasant colour as the real one, with
only the occasional splash of silver—'Il le possédait, ce bonheur-
là, et n'en était pas plus joyeux'—but at least Frédéric *is* in it.[1]

Another group of Paris descriptions is formed by Frédéric's
walks through the city alone. We shall isolate four important
ones, all occurring in Part I of the novel, and all having direct
relevance to Frédéric's wavering fortunes. Three of them are
introduced by key 'mood' sentences, and the fourth terminates
with a similar sentence. In all cases, the details of the descriptions
reflect the moods, although not always in the same way. The four
key sentences are: 'Qu'importait d'ailleurs, puisqu'il pouvait maintenant la fréquenter tout à son aise, vivre dans son atmosphère'
(p. 70); 'Comme il n'avait aucun travail, son désœuvrement
renforçait sa tristesse' (pp. 91–2);[2] 'Une espèce de colère le
poussait' (p. 109); and 'Il n'apercevait, dans l'avenir, qu'une
interminable série d'années toutes pleines d'amour' (p. 126).

Two of these descriptions, then, reflect Frédéric's hope, and two
his despair. They are almost mechanical in their appearance: they
represent hope, despair, despair, hope, in that order, and are set
respectively in night, day, night, day. Thus we have a night and
a day scene of hope, and a night and a day scene of despair, with
all the obvious possibilities of inter-comparison which such an
arrangement allows. They are alike in that their mood is occasioned
by no more serious facts than Frédéric's impression of the figure

[1] Thibaudet, op. cit., p. 154, also points to the occurrence of the river symbol
here, but interprets it in a somewhat different way. Tillett, op. cit., pp. 62–3,
quotes the passage concerned, but does not venture beyond its literal meaning.
Cortland, op. cit., p. 35, also comments on its significance.

[2] The first part of this sentence is, incidentally, another good example of
Flaubert's increasingly subtle use of *style indirect libre*. It is not a fact that Frédéric
had no work to do, since he had just failed his August examinations and persuaded his mother that he must stay in Paris to work for the November ones,
'n'ayant pas de temps à perdre' (p. 89). It is only after he discovers that Mme
Arnoux has left Paris that the 'désœuvrement' comes upon him.

he cut in the preceding scene. The first passage (pp. 70–1) follows his first dinner with the Arnoux, which inspired unjustifiable optimism; the second (pp. 92–3) occurs during a period in which it becomes increasingly clear that he is not making the hoped-for progress with Mme Arnoux, in which she leaves Paris, Frédéric fails his examinations and makes a fool of himself before Arnoux; the third (pp. 109–10) when, although Mme Arnoux has returned, he has made no further progress, and after he has been to the Alhambra; and the fourth (pp. 125–6) follows the party at Saint-Cloud, where Frédéric experiences renewed optimism and passes his examinations. In the whole series, Frédéric's situation vis-à-vis Mme Arnoux has never changed, except in his own imagination: it is the imagined changes which set the mood of the descriptions. The passages are thus two steps removed from 'realism' in the sense which is often applied to Flaubert's descriptions. Yet at the same time they are extremely realistic, in that, like an impressionist painting, they record the appearance, rather than the nature, of things, while also faithfully reflecting the extremely low rational content in the average person's relationship to surrounding reality. Whether or not such a relationship is philosophically justifiable— and Flaubert would be the first to argue that it is not—is a different matter: it remains a fact that ordinary people are like that.

The two night scenes are similar in their general development: Frédéric wanders alone in a semi-trance, hardly knowing where he is going; there is a background of vague, continuous sound, the individual elements of which he cannot distinguish, given up as he is to his own thoughts; in both cases he is drawn as if by fate to the river, and the atmosphere is clouded by a light mist. The facts remain substantially the same; the emotions make them seem different. Frédéric's point of view, superimposed upon reality, gives the descriptions their colour.

It is interesting that the first of these Paris night scenes (the optimistic one) gives prominence to the Seine and its surroundings, in terms very similar indeed to the one on pp. 33–4 (v. *supra*, pp. 298–9), when Frédéric was in the depths of boredom and despair. Now we noted, in examining the descriptions of Mme

Arnoux, that even when Frédéric's optimism is reflected in symbols of light and gaiety, there nearly always remains some darkness as a restraining factor, so that the predominant atmosphere is consistently dark. I have argued that this serves as a continuous ironic reminder to the reader, above Frédéric's head, that his hopes are always illusory, that he will never succeed with Mme Arnoux; this is additional to the basic point of view technique, introduced because there is no other way of communicating this particular level of meaning. It does not, however, prevent the point of view technique from functioning normally in other circumstances: in periods of depression, Frédéric sees only depressing aspects of reality. So, too, with the Seine: that almost identical aspects should on one occasion appear to Frédéric to be a symbol of boredom and hopelessness, and later appear to him a sign of hope while remaining one of futility for the reader, merely emphasizes once more the illusory nature of Frédéric's attitudes to surrounding objects.

The first of the two daylight descriptions of Paris (pessimistic), brings us back to the river, which again forms part of a total picture of monotony and boredom, part of Frédéric's disconsolate view of smelly, unpleasant reality:

Il passait des heures à regarder, du haut de son balcon, la rivière qui coulait entre les quais grisâtres, noircis, de place en place, par la bavure des égouts, avec un ponton de blanchisseuses amarré contre le bord, où des gamins quelquefois s'amusaient, dans la vase, à faire baigner un caniche (p. 92).

The only bright point is the *colonne de Juillet*, which is in the opposite direction from where Mme Arnoux lives: on her side of the city he can see only the 'lourde masse bleue' of the Tuileries, which thus once more intrudes unpleasantly.[1]

The dreary atmosphere is intensified when Frédéric walks about the Latin Quarter, for this is August and there are very few students left. But although reality here both reinforces and

---

[1] Prefiguring the time—need one add?—when it will be ransacked by the populace, an event which coincides with the parallel vulgar destruction of Frédéric's ideal, with Rosanette in the rue Tronchet hotel.

expresses Frédéric's feeling of the emptiness of Paris (Mme Arnoux is in Chartres), it is still the feeling itself which predominates. After all, the Latin Quarter is deserted every August, but it is only this August that he notices the fact.

As if to stress this, the next paragraph takes Frédéric to the boulevards, where there remain any number of people—and now it is the crowds which he finds oppressive. His mood makes everyone seem ugly and stupid, just as it did at the Dambreuse mansion: '. . . il se sentait tout écœuré par la bassesse des figures, la niaiserie des propos, la satisfaction imbécile transpirant sur les fronts en sueur! Cependant, la conscience de mieux valoir que ces hommes atténuait la fatigue de les regarder' (p. 93). He himself would of course be one of the ugly ones for any other disgruntled passers-by.

What of the other, brighter description of Paris (pp. 125–6)? This one is set in August, too, and Mme Arnoux is again absent from Paris, and Frédéric is still no closer to realizing his ambition, and the Latin Quarter is still presumably dull and deserted, and the boulevards still crowded with the same unpleasant people— all the conditions which may have explained the previous description hold good. Only Frédéric's mood is different. The setting sun now has the same soft, feminine appearance as when he was in the carriage with Rosanette; the dust of earlier unhappy descriptions (pp. 33, 93) is being laid by water wagons, just as it will be laid by the rain when he is returning from the races; the dull Latin Quarter is not mentioned, although Frédéric still lives in that area; the cafés have a 'fraîcheur inattendue', and are full of silver and gold, flowers and mirrors; the passers-by have miraculously lost their stupid, sweaty self-satisfaction, and their conversation is no longer the subject of Frédéric's contempt; instead, 'des femmes passaient, avec une mollesse dans les yeux et ce teint de camélia que donne aux chairs féminines la lassitude des grandes chaleurs'—even the 'fronts en sueur' have disappeared! And finally, Frédéric's immense optimism is summed up in one incredibly silly sentence: 'Jamais Paris ne lui avait semblé si beau.' Paris, like Mme Arnoux, changes with Frédéric's humour.

Of the three occasions on which Frédéric returns to Paris, the first two form another pair. At the beginning of Part II, Frédéric's inheritance has saved him from the bourgeois life of Nogent and revived his hopes of being accepted by Mme Arnoux (pp. 145–9). His optimism, and hence his impatience, are based solely on the improbable assumption that his new-found wealth will make him more attractive to his idol, but this is sufficient to determine the description of the journey. Its very length is conditioned by the mood, for Frédéric's impatience makes him sensitive to distance and time. The witness technique is normal, with an impressionistic and symbolic picture created by the play of light and shade, and the buildings on the outskirts of Paris rushing by: Frédéric's excitement is reminiscent of Emma's as she approaches Rouen. True, the things Frédéric notices do not at first reflect his optimism by appearing attractive to him. The picture of Ivry varies from undeniably sordid to merely factual; but then, Ivry is not Paris— it is a last outpost of the hateful provinces. After the city toll-gate these distasteful sights miraculously disappear: the coach, with its fanfare, its cracking whip, and shouting driver, makes its triumphal entry in a flurry of passing pedestrians. Paris itself certainly looks beautiful to Frédéric, who is stubbornly persevering with his 'verres de couleur'. Even the river, which, faithful to its role, is here 'jaunâtre', is part of Frédéric's picture of beauty and hope:

> Une fraîcheur s'en exhalait. Frédéric l'aspira de toutes ses forces, savourant ce bon air de Paris qui semble contenir des effluves amoureux et des émanations intellectuelles; il eut un attendrissement en apercevant le premier fiacre. Et il aimait jusqu'au seuil des marchands de vin garni de paille, jusqu'aux décrotteurs avec leurs boîtes, jusqu'aux garçons épiciers secouant leur brûloir à café. Des femmes trottinaient sous des parapluies; il se penchait pour distinguer leur figure, un hasard pouvait avoir fait sortir Mme Arnoux.[1]

By contrast, Frédéric's other return from Nogent is much less auspicious. He had gone to Nogent to 'rest' after a particularly harrassing period in Paris, and precipitately left again when he

---

[1] p. 148. See also the remarks on this passage in Tillett, op. cit., pp. 61–2.

had no choice but to marry Louise if he stayed. Paris might after all be less harrowing than Nogent. As a result, 'Son retour à Paris ne lui causa point de plaisir' (p. 365). No long excited description of this journey—in fact, no description at all. And when he arrives, nothing but unpleasantness and emptiness. For it is August again, but this time it is the boulevards which seem empty; the houses are all closed up, his apartment is covered with dust, he is entirely alone. Not unexpectedly, the rare passers-by, with their 'mines renfrognées' have somehow become unsympathetic again.

Frédéric's third return to Paris—from Fontainebleau—is a little different (pp. 477–81). On a personal level, Frédéric is not for the moment immediately concerned with Paris. True, he is returning to look for a wounded friend, and one might well expect some anxiety to be reflected in the descriptions; yet the passage is strangely silent on feelings and motives. Reasons for this are not difficult to imagine. The novel makes it clear that Frédéric's friends are not very important to him. They come a bad third in an immutable hierarchy of people who interest him, after himself and his sexual possibilities. That he should have been willing to leave Rosanette for Dussardier is no doubt to be explained partly by the temporary satisfaction of his sexual appetites (for the first time in the eight years he has been in Paris), partly by a feeling of guilt (if he had had Dussardier's idealism he would never have left Paris at all), and partly because his behaviour is always inconsistent. In other words, this return to Paris has no intense motivation, is accompanied by no feelings of personal hope or despair. The main purpose of the description is to show not Frédéric, but Paris in revolution: the centre of interest is transferred from the character to the object. Now this was one of the main problems of presentation in *Salammbô*, and in that book Flaubert overcame it, where practicable, by introducing a 'combined' point of view, or at least having two witnesses with basically different outlooks to increase the possibility of objectivity; and where neither alternative was available, he tried to ensure that the witness viewed the scene as a stranger. The same basic conditions exist here. Frédéric's excursion to the capital

does not concern him so closely that he will automatically distort
what he sees; obviously anybody seeing Paris in such turmoil
would see it as a stranger; and for the whole period of Frédéric's
wandering through the city he is always accompanied by someone, even though his companions are nameless shadows. The
resulting description is no less impressionistic than one would
expect, with great insistence on light and darkness, on sounds
suddenly becoming audible and then disappearing, on progessive
description and purposeful confusion; but it contains no details
which could not have been seen equally well by anyone accompanying Frédéric, and his personal reactions are not mentioned.
Only his eyes are used.

Frédéric tells the truth

The statement that the reader can sometimes see objective facts
through Frédéric's eyes is important, for after all Flaubert remains
a nineteenth-century novelist, and in many ways a successor to
Balzac. Most of the descriptions of people's homes, and what goes
on there, demonstrate this. Naturally, Flaubert's normal concern
for integrating them with the rest of the novel (by using Frédéric
as his witness and by introducing them progressively and inter-
mingling them with the action) is still very much to the fore;[1]
the impressionism which is a basic part of Flaubert's descriptive
technique is usually obvious,[2] and these interiors are normally
described at such length because of their effect on Frédéric.[3] But

[1] For example, at Rosanette's ball, it is not until Arnoux's horseplay threatens
the chandelier and someone cries 'Gare au lustre!' that Frédéric looks at it, and
realizes he has seen it before—which was the point of mentioning it at all (p. 165).

[2] e.g. until Frédéric becomes accustomed to the bright light at Rosanette's
ball, he distinguishes nothing except 'de la soie, du velours, des épaules nues, une
masse de couleurs qui se balançait aux sons d'un orchestre caché par des ver-
dures . . .' (p. 164).

[3] e.g. Frédéric's explorations of Rosanette's apartment. Both the furnishings
and the women are part of his desire:

C'était bien là un milieu fait pour lui plaire. Dans une brusque révolte de sa
jeunesse, il se jura d'en jouir, s'enhardit; puis, revenu à l'entrée du salon, où il
y avait plus de monde maintenant (tout s'agitait dans une sorte de pulvérulence
lumineuse), il resta debout à contempler les quadrilles, clignant les yeux pour

when all this has been duly considered, it remains true that *l'Education* is a social novel as well, and Flaubert wanted to present an objective picture of material conditions at various social levels. Such matters have a certain interest in themselves, and in addition Flaubert adopted in principle Balzac's attitude to material surroundings: ' . . . toute sa personne explique la pension, comme la pension implique sa personne. Le bagne ne vas pas sans l'argousin, vous n'imagineriez pas l'un sans l'autre.'[1] He therefore goes to some trouble to show the interior of the Dambreuse household, the various abodes of the Arnoux and of Rosanette, and to present at least one soirée and one large formal meal in each—the latter series being completed by Cisy's aristocratic banquet and the dinner at the Café Anglais. These serve as a comprehensive series of social 'documents', presenting typical aspects of the life of all the people Frédéric frequents, and hence of the major sections of contemporary French society. It is possible to achieve this with reasonable objectivity by using Frédéric's point of view, in spite of its obvious selectivity. For one thing, the principle of the stranger's eye usually operates; for another, even in nineteenth-century breasts mere objects did not normally arouse the same emotions as did human beings, so that the scope for subjective distortion is considerably reduced. If the Dambreuse are extremely rich bourgeois, nothing will prevent their being surrounded by material signs of this, and nothing will prevent Frédéric from noticing at least some of them. No matter how selective he is, whatever he notices will remain typical. Even the order in which descriptions occur, and the relative speed with which Frédéric

---

mieux voir, et humant les molles senteurs de femmes, qui circulaient comme un immense baiser épandu (p. 168).

Frédéric later sees Rosanette's 'cabinet de toilette' in terms of similar preoccupations, for its description is introduced with the words: 'On voyait, tout de suite, que c'était l'endroit de la maison le plus hanté, et comme son vrai centre moral' (p. 188). In the same way, the details of Mme Arnoux's and Mme Dambreuse's homes reflect Frédéric's impression (pp. 66, 185). On occasions, this can cause complete distortion—the two presentations of Mme Arnoux's new home on pp. 155–6 and p. 192 hardly appear to refer to the same place, because Frédéric's mood has so thoroughly influenced what he chooses to notice.

[1] *le Père Goriot*, Garnier edition, p. 13.

is introduced into the more intimate sections of the dwelling, objectively reflect characteristic social attitudes. When Frédéric first visits the Dambreuse, he gets no further than the vestibule and M. Dambreuse's study (pp. 27–8); it is only by formal invitation that he is permitted to see more of the house (pp. 185–7), and it takes him a very long time indeed to penetrate as far as Mme Dambreuse's bedroom (p. 522). In Rosanette's household, on the other hand, a monumental bed is one of the first things he sees (p. 165); on his first visit he is free to explore the whole apartment (pp. 164 et seq.); when he next calls he is received in the 'cabinet de toilette' (pp. 185 et seq.); and he is soon allowed to talk to the mistress of the house while she is still in bed, even in mid-afternoon (pp. 211 et seq.). Material descriptions necessarily reveal some objective truth about the people they concern.

On the other hand, Flaubert did not believe that a prime purpose of the novel was to *explain* society in such terms—he did not, like Balzac, refer to himself in such grandiose terms as 'docteur ès sciences sociales', and usually preferred simply to point to the facts of such correspondences. His other artistic preoccupations ensure, moreover, that he is more fastidious about where and how and why his descriptions occur. Besides, Flaubert, as usual loth to accept any 'system', is not as thoroughgoing as Balzac in choosing only typical descriptive details, and pretending that they all explain their owner's character and social situation: some details are mentioned for entirely different reasons. The various objects (such as the silver casket and the chandelier, the dinner services and other gifts from Arnoux (p. 207)) which are to be found sometimes in Mme Arnoux's house, sometimes in Rosanette's, and sometimes in both at once, could hardly be typical of both women: they are included to give information about Frédéric and Arnoux, rather than about the women who own them, and also to help create one of the many symbolic patterns.[1] The yellow silk wall drapes in Rosanette's first apartment prepare for a subtle reminder, much later, of how much Frédéric

[1] See Cellier, op. cit., pp. 5–18 for some interesting comments on this and related questions.

had been impressed by her (compare pp. 164 and 202). The silver services mentioned at the dinners given by Cisy (p. 313) and the Dambreuse (p. 225) are intended not merely to be typical of the two milieux, but also to give ironic point to the mental remark made by Frédéric, when Deslauriers tried to persuade *him* to buy silver, instead of the fine china dictated by the influence of Mme Arnoux: 'Moi, à ta place, dit Deslauriers, je m'achèterais plutôt de l'argenterie, décelant, par cet amour du cossu, l'homme de mince origine.'[1]

Besides the desire to include atypical details for specific reasons, another factor influencing Flaubert's descriptions is his interest in change.[2] This is a novel concerned with life in time, and the changes wrought by time are at least as important as any given situation considered in itself. This fact would seem to constitute an important difference between the attitudes of Flaubert and Balzac. While Balzac frequently traces a character's history and development, this is usually introductory to the novel proper, a part of the scene-setting, and is presented in terms of the theory that the character's past explains both his present character and his present environment. This is true, for example, of père Goriot, père Grandet, la cousine Bette, M. Crevel, le cousin Pons and M. de Mortsauf. But having thus achieved a relatively stable material situation, Balzac develops his action while keeping the environment substantially the same. It is almost entirely the character's *past* which determines his physical milieu, while his present, what happens in the course of the novel proper, has relatively little effect.[3] Now while Flaubert adopted a basically similar method in *Bovary*, as can be seen in the development of both Charles and Emma's background, there are already signs that he is realizing its inherent illogicality. If a person's character, and the workings of fortune, have in the past affected his environment, then obviously they must continue to do so: neither

---

[1] p. 162. Another subtle use of *style indirect libre*: at first sight the last part of the sentence looks very much like a direct authorial comment.

[2] i.e. superficial change, which is part of the over-all irony. As Cellier (op. cit., pp. 11 et seq.) points out, the characters never really change at all, but invariably return to their starting-point.

[3] There are, of course, exceptions: Valérie in *la Cousine Bette* is one.

can be summarily traced through a series of vicissitudes to an arbitrary point which is to constitute the beginning of the novel proper, and then suddenly become invariable. Thus while Emma's home in Yonville remains basically the same, certain changes do take place—the re-designing of the garden, the gradual addition of various luxuries—which reflect her changing preoccupations. In *l'Education*, the necessity for change is recognized more fully. Frédéric himself changes his address more than once, and each new apartment reflects differing tastes, differing stages of development, and above all differing financial circumstances, as well as certain permanent characteristics. More important, the changing financial and social situation of Rosanette and Mme Arnoux can be seen in the details chosen to describe their homes. Rosanette's fortunes rise considerably between the time Frédéric inspects her original home (pp. 164 et seq.) and the time he returns to Paris and finds her living with a Russian count (pp. 368 et seq.), and then suffer a decline (p. 448); a comparison of the description of the Arnoux's house in the early part of the book (pp. 64 et seq.) with the one in which Frédéric finds them when he returns to Paris (p. 156) shows a distinct reversal of fortune, as does a comparison between their country house at Saint-Cloud (pp. 115 et seq.), the one at Creil (pp. 277 et seq.), and the one at Auteuil (pp. 388, 390–1); or a comparison between Arnoux's original art-shop (p. 29), with its luxurious salon above (pp. 47 et seq.), and his final establishment for the sale of 'religious art' (p. 566). (The Dambreuse household, needless to say, never changes: M. Dambreuse is more careful to change himself.)[1]

Finally, Flaubert did not go to the trouble of selecting at least one 'interior', one soirée and one banquet from each major social level just for the pleasure of writing a sociological essay. As with

---

[1] But he is not necessarily more wicked or hypocritical than the other characters because of this, as is usually assumed. The real difference between him and Frédéric, or Deslauriers, or Arnoux, or Rosanette, or Sénécal, or Pellerin, is that he is both luckier and cleverer in calculating in advance which side will best correspond with his personal interests. Like the others he is an adept at honest dishonesty—at any given moment, he is no doubt firmly convinced that what he is doing is morally right, as was Henry in the first *Education*. His rationalizations are similar to those of Frédéric, but in a different field.

several of the details contained within them, such as the silver casket,[1] recurrences of basically similar descriptions at different levels constantly impose upon the reader the necessity to make comparisons and contrasts. They are intended to provide an immensely complex network of cross-references, which help to tie the whole novel together: one of their most important functions is that they are an integral part of the novel's structure. In this they are of course considerably helped by the rest of the content of the scenes in which they occur. While this is not our immediate concern, it cannot go unnoticed that the manner in which both characters and ideas (especially artistic and political) keep recurring against the background of these descriptions, and like the descriptions remain similar in spirit in spite of their sometimes astounding changes on a superficial level, is a major contributing factor to both the complexity and the unity of this novel.

In many of his descriptions of people's material surroundings, then, Flaubert has superimposed sociological and structural considerations upon his basic point of view technique, so that on the whole they appear more objectively presented than descriptions of people. Such a course was probably the only one open to Flaubert. On the one hand he needed to maintain Frédéric's point of view, both for the reasons stated earlier and because in any case this point of view is a powerful unifying force. On the other hand, there is the difficulty of using for one's own purposes a point of view which one has taken great pains to teach the reader not to trust. The difficulty was temporarily overcome in *Bovary* by using *on* or the narrator, in *Salammbô* by the combined point of view, as a sort of archaeologically-orientated development of *on*. In *l'Education*, we have, as it were, two Frédéric's: one who lives and suffers and one who merely sees on behalf of the author.

[1] Another group of the same sort can be found in the *étagère* with its ornaments, the Bohemian glassware and the wall coverings of *cuir battu*, which Frédéric notices first at Arnoux's house (p. 66) and later at Rosanette's (p. 369). Several of these elements also form part of his own daydreams of the ideal apartment when he first hears of his inheritance (p. 139). These seem to constitute signs of a well-to-do bourgeois household, and to hint that all three tend towards precisely the same standards of domestic beauty when they can afford it.

There are occasions when Frédéric's mind registers nothing but facts, whether they be facts of décor, of behaviour, or of conversation. On such occasions, approximately the same conditions apply as when he was returning to Paris to look for Dussardier, or when Hamilcar returned to Carthage and attended the Council of the Ancients. The point of view is Frédéric's, but is restricted to what almost anyone, viewing the scene with a stranger's eye, would be likely to notice. This is usually achieved by arranging a situation in which Frédéric is not obliged to remain in one place, but for one reason or another has freedom to move about, to investigate several rooms, to view things from different angles, and so on— but only within the limits imposed by the situation.

This use of Frédéric as a pair of itinerant eyes is a part of Flaubert's technique which is called into service more particularly in the historical parts of the book. With the exception of a few more general explanatory passages, such as the historical background paragraph at the beginning of Part III (p. 410) and the statement about political clubs (p. 432), Flaubert uses Frédéric to maintain the advantages of impersonality (feigned at least), of unity, of immediacy, and of continual opportunities for impressionistic description; yet we are constantly aware that these passages are different from those where Frédéric looks at Mme Arnoux or Rosanette, for we are plainly expected to regard what Frédéric sees as facts, as real information which is simply dressed up for the occasion as his point of view. This seems sufficiently demonstrated by the fact that these descriptions have precisely the same tone, and are presented in the same way, whether Frédéric is alone or with someone else (Hussonnet, Dussardier, Arnoux, Rosanette).[1] In the Revolution scene, for example, there is little reference to Frédéric's feelings as he watches the fighting, except that he was enjoying himself, and there is no evidence that this feeling has affected the description in any way: he is simply

[1] Cortland, op. cit., pp. 42, 50–52, bases his comments on the inadequacies of the presentation of the Revolution, on the assumption that Frédéric's point of view is used. I believe he over-simplifies the situation, but his arguments should be considered.

walking about registering the scene. After he meets Hussonnet at the Tuileries, the only change is that more of Frédéric's feelings are now given expression, but only in direct speech, as if Flaubert wished to emphasize that here at least the descriptions are *not* being distorted by the interference of Frédéric's judgement. He is reduced almost to the status of the other characters, of cardboard people knowable only by their speech or by other externalized behaviour. Without the use of the combined point of view—or, rather, independently of it, for it is still sometimes used—Flaubert presents facts as well as unreliable impressions through Frédéric. For once, he avoids ascribing to his hero any interpretation of events (except in conversation, where it is harmless).

The same principle operates in the many artistic and political discussions, although these concern us only incidentally here. In these scenes Frédéric becomes a living tape-recorder instead of a self-adjusting optical instrument, registering only the facts of the various conversations. Again this is, in a sense, Flaubert the historian vying with Flaubert the novelist, and it is no doubt such scenes that Thorlby had in mind when he claimed that in several scenes Frédéric might as well not be present at all.[1] But the fact is that Frédéric *is* there, and that while his point of view is not the only one which could have done the recording—that is to say, the discussion scenes tell us no more about Frédéric than they do about the others—his presence is not without importance. For one thing, it is indicative of the society of the time that Frédéric and so many others are able to frequent members of all classes, from the aristocratic Cisy to the working-class Dussardier, to feel at home in their company and to take part in their most intimate discussions. In the nineteenth-century context, this testifies to a society which is unusually fluid because it is confused and dissatisfied, lacking strong direction and a stable class structure;[2] which is therefore moving towards a revolutionary state where a total reorganization will take place, where the

[1] Thorlby, op. cit., p. 27.
[2] Cf. p. 425: 'La France, ne sentant plus de maître, se mit à crier d'effarement comme un aveugle sans bâton, comme un marmot qui a perdu sa bonne.'

self-interest of individuals comes into the open, and where luck and cunning will be more important than birth or wealth in determining future status. Secondly, the point of view technique, even though applied with varying degrees of thoroughness, continues to be a unifying factor in the novel. If Frédéric were not present in the more factual, politico-historical scenes, if they did not form an important part of his personal education, if the stupid unthinking self-interest leading to the temporary collapse of an entire society did not symbolically parallel Frédéric's personal failure (and vice versa), then it would be difficult to see why Flaubert chose to lump together the two stories in one book. The fact is that they are not two stories but one, told on two different planes. Frédéric as an individual is the centre of one aspect, and Frédéric as a member of society—a society composed almost exclusively of Frédérics—is the centre of the other. The technical unity achieved by using Frédéric's point of view even where it is not indispensable, is an external indication of that deeper unity achieved by virtually equating Frédéric with France. France, in the novel, is composed of a large number of individuals, each representing a class, a theory, or a profession (suitably intermingled and overlapping, so that together they figure the complexity of a living society). Every one of these individuals demonstrates traits of character and attitudes to life which at one stage or another constitute a temptation for Frédéric, and which therefore draw him towards that individual, even when there is no sympathy on a superficial level; and each of these traits and attitudes finds some expression in Frédéric's own character or behaviour, whether at the time he feels the temptation or not. Each secondary character is a living symbol of one or more aspects of Frédéric's character, and in combination they represent Frédéric just as surely as they represent the French nation.

In the scenes concerned with theoretical arguments, the only way Flaubert can ensure that the reader's information should come through Frédéric, while at the same time holding to his self-imposed convention that Frédéric's mind will distort most things if given the chance, is by direct speech. Thus many scenes depend heavily on the spoken word, in a way which *Bovary* and

Salammbô do not:[1] all segments of society have the opportunity to state their views. Comment by the author is as usual kept to a strict minimum, Frédéric's personality is prevented from intervening, so that each scene is a factual representation of opinions. But the opinions change radically—if they had not, the history of the period would have been different—and the only method by which Flaubert can show these changes is by arranging a subsequent 'factual' scene of the same type, in which the same people express different views. One scene of direct speech therefore necessarily determines a series of others, which balance and contrast with the first. Flaubert must be continually arranging opportunities for these conversations to take place, and if unity is to be safeguarded, these opportunities must occur naturally within the context of Frédéric's personal search for success—a visit to Arnoux's *salon* or to a Dambreuse soirée must serve a dual purpose, both personal and social. This explains why so much of the novel is composed of scenes (dinners, dances, picnics, house-warmings, meetings) where people would naturally be expected to converse. It follows that a number of the important things Flaubert has to say are communicated by a technique other than the point of view method with which we are primarily concerned, even though it is just as impersonal. Most of the social and political message is conveyed by forcing the reader to compare passages of direct speech, in which the secondary characters show the instability and intellectual dishonesty which parallel Frédéric's. The two different techniques for the two aspects of the novel are bound together by the fact that both are expressions of the same story, and that Frédéric's point of view is always superficially present, even though it does not always bear the main weight of the message.

[1] In *Bovary* the characters' words are most frequently used to reveal character or to advance the action. Except in the *Conseiller's* speech and some of the discourses of Homais, they do not reflect social theories; and even when they do so, these are plainly caricatures, and do not need to be compared with others to reveal their futility. In *Salammbô*, direct speech is used more frequently to show social and religious theories (e.g. Salammbô's incantations, her conversation with Schahabarim, the dispute between Hamilcar and the Ancients); but the technique is neither as frequent nor as tightly interwoven as in *l'Education*.

The narrator retreats

Although passages which must necessarily be ascribed to the narrator amount to no more than 11 per cent of *l'Education*, their role must be carefully considered.

Direct commentaries by the author in person, claiming general validity in addition to their relevance to the immediate context, are easily disposed of. Apart from those already mentioned in connection with Frédéric's visits to the Dambreuse, which we have argued are Frédéric's own feelings elevated to the level of a general statement by him and not the author, such value judgements are very rare and usually very brief. Sometimes they are quite incidental, like the remark that Rosanette's riches 'seraient aujourd'hui des misères pour les pareilles de Rosanette' (p. 168) or that 'il échappe des fautes même aux plus sages' (p. 541). Sometimes they constitute a definite moral judgement on Frédéric, as in the remarks on his being incapable of action because of the strength of his passion (p. 245), on his self-delusion (pp. 261–2, p. 443), on his egotism (pp. 372, 407). Sometimes they are moral judgements on other characters or on humanity in general. Since none is more than six or seven lines long, they can scarcely be regarded as an important part of the technique of this novel. At best they can only briefly indicate the lines along which Flaubert is thinking, and as this is in any case clearly shown in other ways, the book would have been very little different without any of them.

The same cannot be said of some passages of direct political commentary, in which Flaubert could apparently not bring himself to allow the novel to speak for itself. In these passages, the factual portion of which is necessary to keep the reader abreast with developments, Flaubert unequivocally spits upon the behaviour and moral standards of the whole French nation (e.g. pp. 421–2, 424–5, 432, 482–3). That his most important authorial intrusions should come in the political section of the book underlines once more the fact that he is not able to use Frédéric's unreliable point of view to present his ideas fully, as in the rest of the novel. But even these outspoken comments do not add up to more than half a dozen pages altogether. It is undeniable that direct author's comment has now become a very minor element of Flaubert's novel-writing technique.

The 'bourgeois narrator' recurs in *l'Education*, but its importance is also reduced. It occurs largely where one would expect to find a hangover from *Bovary*: in the passages dealing with the provincial bourgeois of Nogent. The first signs of it appear during the explanation of Mme Moreau's situation, with statements such as: 'On la consultait sur le choix des domestiques, l'éducation des jeunes filles, l'art des confitures, et Monseigneur descendait chez elle dans ses tournées épiscopales' (p. 14). So, too, with her desires that Frédéric should become a minister, and her belief that he had the intellectual means to do so: 'Ses triomphes au collège de Sens légitimaient cet orgueil; il avait remporté le prix d'honneur'—as if this would automatically put him in the forefront of France's promising youth (compare Homais's statement that Emma 'ne serait pas déplacée dans une sous-préfecture'). So, too, with the following moral judgement: 'sa vertu s'exerçait sans étalage de pruderie, sans aigreur'. Yet almost immediately we see her indulging in an 'étalage de pruderie' as she prevents the discussion of the scandal-murder of the day (p. 14), while her behaviour towards Roque and his family, whom she ignores until (a) he 'legitimizes' his child by marriage and (b) he begins to be rich and influential, gives the statement about her virtue and her prudery its full flavour.

The bourgeois narrator rears his head again when Frédéric does not make a blinding success of his efforts to become a provincial lawyer (p. 132), he betrays his presence in the recital of M. Roque's domestic history (pp. 134–5), and in opinions on Louise's stormy puberty: 'Les bourgeois ne virent là-dedans qu'un pronostic défavorable pour ses mœurs. On disait que "le fils Moreau" voulait en faire plus tard une actrice' (p. 137; cf. p. 590). He is to be found occasionally in the other stronghold of the bourgeois, the *hôtel Dambreuse* (e.g. when the troubles of the Revolution have begun to subside, pp. 488 et seq.), although he is not called for very much here, since, as already noted, individual bourgeois are normally permitted to speak for themselves.

In spite of the overwhelming importance of the point of view technique, quite a large number of other short passages continue to show that Flaubert is not averse to letting his readers know that he exists to control the development of the action, that there is a superior intelligence standing behind Frédéric and organizing his experiences into a significant whole (which is just as well). Many of these passages are purely explanatory, intended to inform the reader, in a few simple words, of background facts which will help him understand the situation. None is of outstanding importance.[1]

The backgrounds of the various secondary characters are also briefly explained to the reader in terms which suggest an omniscient narrator, and yet which cannot be compared with the presentation often favoured by Balzac. It has already been noted that in general the reader learns about these characters progressively, as Frédéric himself finds out more about them. This is obviously true of Arnoux, M. Roque, Rosanette, Vatnaz, Hussonnet, and Dussardier. The same can be said of Martinon and Cisy, whom Frédéric already knew, but who are not presented to the reader until, tired of his solitary life in Paris, he begins to visit them; of Sénécal, whom he visits on the recommendation of Deslauriers, and without doubt armed with some basic information provided by the latter; and also of Regimbart and Pellerin, whom he first meets in Arnoux's *salon*. It is only after Frédéric begins to get to know them, and to visit Pellerin's studio, that we are given some explanation of their background. When the explanation comes, it is given in summary form, as if the narrator had collated and 'tidied up' Frédéric's gradual knowledge of them, and presented it in a single paragraph. This is an obvious necessity—there are so many characters in the novel that if all were presented strictly according to Frédéric's experiences, most of the book would be introductory. With several of the minor characters, then, a compromise is reached whereby their backgrounds are not presented until Frédéric is acquainted with them, but are then given in summary form by the narrator. In this way he plays the role of organizer, compressing certain of his hero's

[1] e.g. see pp. 44, 100, 114, 277, 410, 457.

less important experiences in the interests of brevity and perspective.[1]

The principle applies equally in the presentation of Deslauriers, with the exception that since he is Frédéric's best friend, the process is considerably expanded (pp. 17-20). An unusual feature is that Deslauriers's background is presented before he appears on the scene; but this is of course possible in this case, since Frédéric is on his way to meet Deslauriers. Thus, although the latter's past is fairly obviously a narrator's summary at the beginning, it does occupy Frédéric's thoughts quite naturally as he walks down to the rendez-vous; and some parts of it are clearly from the point of view of the two young boys at school. The whole passage presents the content of Frédéric's thoughts, if not their tone and development.

The practice of telling the reader in summary form what Frédéric already knows or has just found out about secondary characters occurs throughout the novel. Flaubert wishes to keep us abreast of how these people develop, thereby ensuring that his book remains a picture of a whole society, as well as increasing its irony. But he obviously cannot follow in detail the history of each, which would require several volumes. He therefore arranges that all the characters occasionally recross Frédéric's path, and when they do he devotes a short passage to summarizing what has been happening to them in the intervening period, and what sort of people they have become as a result. This bringing up to date usually occurs directly within the orbit of Frédéric's experience, even though he has had nothing to do with the way they have developed. As in the dialogue scenes, he is there simply to register the stories so that they are passed on to the reader. Such is the case, for example, on pp. 332-3, concerning Sénécal and Dussardier. The latter has just entered a period of closer friendship with Frédéric, having served as a witness in the duel with Cisy; and one day he reports to Frédéric that following his chance discovery that Sénécal was in prison, he had spent the whole day

---

[1] This is in contrast with a book like *la Cousine Bette*, where Balzac is continually introducing new characters, and then stopping to give a run-down on their personality and private history, providing in the process many details which most of the other characters could not possibly know.

finding out details. These details are then recounted, after which we are told some of Dussardier's own political opinions. Again it is the content, but not the tone or the actual words used, which is passed on to the reader. The passage cannot be regarded as *style indirect libre*: it is another example of the compromise mentioned above.[1]

Several of these passages have a distinct ironical tone, which can become quite fierce when Flaubert is dealing with those people with whom he personally would have least sympathy, in particular Sénécal and Vatnaz. It may be that the desire to pass on his opinion about the different brands of Socialism, for example, or the fight for women's rights, is an additional reason for his not always allowing his characters to give their own versions of their ideas, in direct speech. Sénécal would certainly not summarize Socialistic theories in anything approaching the way the narrator does on pp. 194–5 !

The omniscient narrator also breaks into the story in a minor way on several occasions to point out an immediate contrast between what a character is thinking and what another thinks he is thinking. This procedure also generates a type of irony, as when Rosanette makes a private vow never again to sleep with anyone but Frédéric, just at the time the latter returns fresh from his triumph with Mme Dambreuse, 'en s'applaudissant de sa perversité'.[2] He draws attention to his presence by such simple devices as putting an exclamation mark after the words 'le visage de Béranger !' (p. 376) or putting 'les princes de la science' in inverted commas (p. 538), or pointing out that he knew what was going on in two places at once (p. 536). Again, in the story of the duel (pp. 321–9) and the scene of the Dambreuse dinner party after the Revolution (pp. 487–506) there are so many changes in the point of view—sometimes Frédéric alone, sometimes other individuals, sometimes pairs or groups of people, and

---

[1] Other cases occur on pp. 75 (Sénécal), 173 (Delmar), 200 (Dussardier), 307–8 (Pellerin), etc.; there are at least a dozen more. On other occasions (e.g. pp. 158–9), such summaries occur before Frédéric has actually had the chance to discover their content, but as it is obvious that he is about to, the difference is not very important.

[2] p. 532; other examples pp. 111, 213, 315, 341, 430.

sometimes everbody together—that the normal technique is temporarily abandoned.

There remain to be considered three fairly long descriptive passages: the Seine and the countryside at Nogent (pp. 357-9), the *château* and forest at Fontainebleau (pp. 459 et seq.), and the Madeleine and Père Lachaise, on the occasion of M. Dambreuse's funeral (pp. 545-50). Like the Yonville description, all three contain several verbs in the present tense, as well as the device of the disinterested bystander, frequently used by Balzac and Stendhal. This draws attention to the narrator as a separate identity, who seems to be wanting to guarantee that what he is describing is true at this moment, as well as at the time of the novel. Of course we know that such descriptions are true, that Flaubert went there to verify them, but this is not really the point. While both Balzac and Stendhal usually had good reasons for this insistence on the veracity of their statements (the former wished to show that he was dealing with authentic contemporary social documents, and his statements were of the nature of footnotes in a sociological treatise; and the latter often needed to disguise the fact that some of his statements were not true at all and never had been), Flaubert had no such need. In general he was concerned only with ensuring that his statements were true, or likely to have been true, for the time in which the novel was set. Since he normally saw external reality only in relation to his characters and to the development of the action, this was all that was necessary. Had Fontainebleau castle and Père Lachaise cemetery disappeared the day after Frédéric visited them, this would not have made the slightest difference to his novel. Besides, this type of description does not stand out as something unusual in the novels of Stendhal or Balzac, who continually draw attention to themselves in other ways which Flaubert regarded as inadmissible. And even in the descriptions under discussion he is not always consistent in his use of the present tense, which makes his use of it even more puzzling.[1]

In spite of the obvious presence of the narrator, these passages

[1] See Thibaudet, op. cit., pp. 251-5, who says simply that the present, 'encadré

do not stand out as much as the Yonville description, for they are still integrated with the characters and the action. All occur naturally in the course of scenes of great importance for Frédéric (there is no hint of setting the stage first and proceeding with the action afterwards), and all have considerable psychological and symbolic significance. The Nogent description lays great emphasis on the Seine again, but it is a completely different sort of river from the one in Paris. One sees only the purity of nature, the tranquillity, the light, and the fertility of the river. More than this, 'l'horizon, en face, est borné par une courbe de la rivière' (p. 358). Now judging by the wording of the description, and the plans of the river in relation to Nogent published in *Les Amis de Flaubert* for May 1966, the horizon in question would be in the direction of Paris. Frédéric's view towards the capital, which so much attracts him, is shut off by the river itself, as if nature were telling him that it is in the despised provinces, beside Louise, who in this scene is perfectly willing to give herself to him, that his only chance of happiness lies. When he follows the river to Paris, he will find it smelly and dirty, with only the occasional flash of light.

The Fontainebleau passage is another instance of the tranquillity of the countryside, the more noticeable because Frédéric and Rosanette have left Paris at the height of the Revolution. Again it seems that Frédéric can be happy only outside Paris (the same idea occurs in his brief idyllic period with Mme Arnoux at Auteuil). Peace and solitude are emphasized, even in their hotel, and this is as true of the *château* itself as of the surrounding natural beauty. The description of the *château*, where the present tense begins to occur, shows both Frédéric's escapist feelings and Rosanette's indifference. Since nostalgia for the past frequently constitutes one element of the escapist's dreams, the tone of the description reflects the feelings a person like Frédéric would have. Thus even though the narrator makes no attempt to disguise the fact that he is responsible for the description, such emotions as are

---

dans des imparfaits, oppose un aspect permanent de la nature aux actes humains qui s'y développent'. This statement is only partly true, and does not take account of the rarity of the device in Flaubert's work.

expressed must be ascribed to Frédéric. When speaking of the paintings of Diane de Poitiers, for example, the author says: 'Tous ces symboles confirment sa gloire; et il reste là quelque chose d'elle, une voix indistincte, un rayonnement qui se prolonge' (p. 461). This sounds like a general authorial comment of the sort Balzac would make; but its value in the context is demonstrated by the next sentence—'Frédéric fut pris par une concupiscence rétrospective et inexprimable'. The comment was Frédéric's.[1]

Throughout the passage describing the park and the forest, a similar atmosphere of escape into natural and primitive conditions prevails. Nature even seems to be gaining a little on civilization, reclaiming its rights. Even in the courtyard of the dead palace— already a little decayed, 'couleur de rouille comme une vieille armure' (p. 459)—lichen was growing, and in the forest they notice a ruined abbey and grass growing where roads had been built. Flaubert's notes for this passage mention 'un fluide voluptueux'[2] and the final text clearly states the effects of this. The Seine also enters the picture again (pp. 468–9), in much the same way as in the Nogent scene.

The 'double witness' technique in this passage also necessitates some comment.[3] It is seldom used in *l'Education*, and there is no need here for the objectivity which justified its use in *Salammbô*: one imagines the purpose of having the description at all is to show the effects of nature on the couple.[4] A clue to Flaubert's

---

[1] Which is not to deny that such nostalgia was also one of Flaubert's personal tendencies, and that he was probably in sympathy with Frédéric's feelings here.

[2] Dumesnil, introduction to Belles Lettres edition of *l'Education*, vol. I, p. xciv. For other aspects of the symbolism of the forest, and contrasts with the river symbols, see Demorest, op. cit., p. 541.

[3] For further, and sometimes quite different, remarks on the use of point of view in the Fontainebleau episode, see Cortland, op. cit., pp. 67 et seq.

[4] The actual details presented are of course authentic. A glance at the comparison between the notes Flaubert took in Fontainebleau forest and the final version of his description (see Dumesnil, introduction to Belles Lettres edition, vol. I, pp. lxxxix–xcvi) will show that he included a very high proportion of the details he noted. But it does not follow, as La Varende maintains (op. cit., pp. 145–6) that this is an example of 'un abus certain dans la minutie du décor, dans sa réalisation trop souvent inutile et absolument gratuite'—even if this opinion *is* held by 'la plupart des lecteurs (gens de qualité)'.

intention is provided by Rosanette's obvious boredom with the
château, and a realization that we discover it by following Frédéric's
point of view alone: we are never told what Rosanette is thinking,
but deduce it, with Frédéric, from her behaviour and speech.
We have two witnesses, but access to only one mind. This is
contrary to Flaubert's practice in *Salammbô*. Obviously the point
he is making is that the two lovers have very little in common,
and he has found that he can easily do this without jumping from
one mind to the other.[1] During the description of the forest, we
continue to have access to some of Frédéric's thoughts and
feelings, while those of Rosanette are indicated by externalized
manifestations of them. Such emotions as are thus indicated,
moreover, are primitive and naïve: her reaction to Frédéric's
discourse on the age of the scenery is that 'ça la rendrait folle', so
she goes to pick flowers; her reaction to the deer is that she
would like to caress it; she is bad-tempered about having to walk
among the trees, and happier when she can drink lemonade and
look at a souvenir stall; she ignores the view, and is violently and
childishly afraid of the man with the snakes. Her reactions to the
other things they see are unlikely to be the same as Frédéric's:
she has very little of his brand of poetry in her soul. Yet in all
other parts of the description the emotions mentioned are
ostensibly common to both Frédéric and Rosanette: 'Debout,
l'un près de l'autre, sur quelque éminence du terrain, ils sentaient,
tout en humant le vent, leur entrer dans l'âme comme l'orgueil
d'une vie plus libre, avec une surabondance de forces, une joie
sans cause' (p. 466). The plural pronoun can only indicate that
what we have is Frédéric's emotion, which he wants to believe
is shared by Rosanette, but which in fact is not. We have two

---

[1] See also Castex, op. cit., p. 91 for a comment on the carp which Rosanette
finds so much more attractive than the *château*. Castex also points to the impressionism, the play of light, in the description; but whereas we would take this as
an indication of a continuing point of view presentation, he concludes that
Flaubert 'communique à son héros la pensée qu'il a eue et ainsi s'établit une con-
tinuité entre la réalité vécue et la fiction romanesque'. This does not take sufficient
account of the irony of the passage within its context—for example, Frédéric's
basking in the past glories of the nation, with a false and perverted patriotism,
while his friends are fighting for its future.

witnesses, but only one point of view: Frédéric is deluding himself about Rosanette's ability to respond to the things which affect him. When we are told: 'On pense aux hermites, compagnons des grands cerfs portant une croix de feu entre leurs cornes, et qui recevaient avec de paternels sourires les bons rois de France, agenouillés devant leur grotte' (pp. 463–4), we must see *on* as Frédéric, for Rosanette 'était désespérée, avait envie de pleurer'.

The funeral of M. Dambreuse is naturally important to Frédéric because it seems to mark the beginnings of worldly success. This is no doubt why he notices the fine, mild day and the flower market. But his interest in the service itself is minimal: the congregation and the interior embellishments of the church receive much more attention.[1] At Père Lachaise, too, the different designs of the tombs are recorded at such length because this is all Frédéric can find to interest him: 'Frédéric put admirer le paysage pendant qu'on prononçait les discours.'[2] The difference in tone and detail between this service and the one in *Bovary* measures the difference in attitude and emotion between the two witnesses, Charles who has lost his beloved wife, and Frédéric who is submitting to form as the price of an immense fortune—although both scenes contribute to the irony by so closely following the character's thoughts at a time when the reader knows how mistaken these are. Once more the passage containing the authorial present tense nevertheless seems adequately to reflect the state of mind of the witness, and its use remains a minor mystery.

The point of view of minor characters also occurs occasionally in *l'Education*. As in *Bovary*, this intrusion of another viewpoint

---

[1] Castex, op. cit., p. 43, remarks that Flaubert went to great pains to find and note details of the funeral service according to the Paris ritual, and then 'pour des raisons inconnues', failed to use most of them. If our argument is correct, one reason for it becomes clear.

[2] This is not to exclude another important reason for the description of the ridiculous tombs: when Flaubert was gathering details for this scene he comments: 'J'ai été pris, au Père-Lachaise, d'un dégoût de l'humanité profond et douloureux. Vous n'imaginez pas le fétichisme des tombeaux. Le vrai Parisien est plus idolâtre qu'un nègre! Ça m'a donné envie de me coucher dans une des fosses' (*Cor.*, VI, 9).

(usually achieved by simple juxtaposition, with no attempt to disguise the controlling hand of an omniscient narrator) is normally for a comic effect or for purposes of ironic comparison. It is not always possible clearly to distinguish such passages from conventional narration, except where *style indirect libre* is obviously being employed, but the point is academic since both techniques are relatively rare. The only really important passage is the one from Deslauriers's point of view, in which he tries to seduce Mme Arnoux, and this has already been discussed. For the rest, a few brief examples will suffice. Deslauriers's point of view occurs when he is annoyed or hurt by Frédéric's behaviour,[1] or when he is in the process of betraying his best friend. (It is an important part of the irony that in one way or another Deslauriers betrays Frédéric with all four women.) Rosanette's is used to recount her life story,[2] and to set out her financial difficulties, which must temporarily remain hidden from Frédéric—who, ironically, can get the money to save her only from Mme Dambreuse, but is already having difficulty obtaining money from this source to save the Arnoux, part of whose trouble is that they owe Rosanette money! The point of view of Mme Dambreuse shows her involvement in the complex money-lending affairs, and the jealousy which will lead to her forcing Frédéric to the sale of Mme Arnoux's possessions. That of Pellerin shows us the burlesque side of his search for artistic truth, and also his basic dishonesty where self-interest is involved (he thus resembles the other characters). While these and similar passages make useful contributions of detail, none is vital to the over-all concept of the book.

---

[1] e.g. p. 265, contrasting his anger directly with Frédéric's; but in spite of the different cause, the way his mind works is almost identical with that of Frédéric's, and the real purpose of the passage is doubtless to demonstrate this fact. The technique is very similar to the one used in the passage where Charles and Emma lie side by side in bed.

[2] pp. 471–3. This is a variation of the point of view technique, for it is in direct speech; but Rosanette's way of telling her story is exactly similar to Flaubert's normal narrative technique, as if he had literally placed her back in her childhood and made her re-live her experiences so that he could use her as his witness. Cf. the prostitute's life story in *Novembre*, also recounted to the hero, and our remarks on Henry's account of Mme Renaud's giving in to him, *supra*, p. 68.

The triumph of point of view

To summarize, then, by far the greatest part of *l'Education* is presented from Frédéric's point of view. For Flaubert, this has the advantage that several problems of unity in tone and structure are largely solved from the beginning, in spite of the complexity of the material he has to present. In choosing this solution, he would appear to have benefited from the experience gained in his two earlier works. To put the matter in its broadest terms, it can be said that *Bovary* is primarily the story of an individual, while *Salammbô* is the story of a society in crisis. *L'Education* tries to be more broadly-based than either, a combination of both, with neither aspect significantly more important than the other. Flaubert had used the technique of individual points of view with some success in his first novel, and added to it the method of combined point of view in his second. In *l'Education*, he was faced with the double problem of a more complex structure and a desire to tighten his method of presentation. This involved a certain modification of his earlier techniques.

His first important decision was to make individuals, rather than the society from which they had sprung, the centre of his new novel. In this he was greatly helped by the fact that the society with which he was dealing required less objectification than Carthage. In addition the crisis was internal, so that he had one and not two social structures to present. Thus he could more easily use a single witness to observe all aspects. His early plans show, moreover, that he had given considerable thought to selecting as his witness a central character whose social situation would permit him to observe a wide variety of social levels.

Having selected Frédéric as his witness, Flaubert had to consider ways of ensuring that his character represented typical aspects of the time and place: apart from his general theory of universality, he is concerned with 'l'histoire morale des hommes de ma génération'. This involved presenting the reader with the idea, scarcely imagined by the majority of literate people in the complacent Second Empire, that his generation had totally failed to meet the challenge of modern life (compare his lamentations about

the defeat of France in 1870); it also involved offering an explanation of this failure. Impersonality enters the picture, for Flaubert
felt he could not stand up and wave his arms in fury as a Victor
Hugo, or even a Balzac, did. He must *show* his hero failing, and
through him show everyone else failing as well—as in a Shakes-
pearian tragedy, the stage must finally be strewn with bodies, at
least morally. In *Bovary*, he had shown Emma's failure by two
main methods: by contrasting her point of view with that of
others, and by contrasting her point of view at one time with that
at other times. He has now realized that it is not necessary to use
both these methods. It is possible to achieve substantially the
same result with very little intervention of other points of view.
The development is based on the assumption that most people
damn themselves simply by being themselves. They usually have
such monumental egotism that they seldom see the rest of the
world except emotionally, in relationship to themselves ('voir
les choses comme elles sont'?), and at the same time have thought
so little about moral and other problems that they are convinced
all the answers are simple and straightforward ('ne pas conclure'?).
Since the concluding is based on observation and experience, it
follows that it is continually varying with emotional responses to
these experiences. It also follows that *all* conclusions are logically
false, even though there may be a 50–50 chance of their being
true in fact. Flaubert's method is to avoid deciding which ones
are true (he has sufficient humility to believe he is incapable of
this), and to restrict himself to demonstrating that all are logically
false. Frédéric's emotional responses inevitably result in conclusions
which show nothing but inconsistency and contradictions. This
is achieved without the assistance of contrasting points of view.

The chief danger of the method, especially in such a long and
complicated book, is that the reader will not make the comparisons
which are an essential part of it. This was already a danger in
Bovary, but it is much greater here. If the comparisons are not
made, a 'Frédéric Moreau, c'est moi' equation will be unavoidable, and indeed several critics accept this equation. But one of
the outstanding traits of Flaubert's character, as revealed in his
correspondence, is his constant self-examination; and this is what

Frédéric lacks most of all. There is no point in demonstrating that this or this theory or experience were common to Frédéric and Flaubert: such correspondences do not turn a novel into an autobiography. At best we could say that the novel *might* have been Flaubert's story, if he did not possess the critical faculties and single-mindedness so noticeably absent from Frédéric's character; but this is like saying a negro could pass for a European if it were not for the colour of his skin, and in any case it would mean that the novel could never have been written. Nor is the fact that Flaubert apparently identifies himself with Frédéric for most of the book particularly relevant. What Flaubert is trying to say about Frédéric is to be found not in the content of any particular scene (which is all Frédéric himself can see), but in the inconsistencies between scenes (which Frédéric is incapable of seeing). That is, Flaubert relies very heavily on the structure of the book to communicate his thoughts, so that within any given scene his apparent identification with the hero, while having several practical advantages which we have considered elsewhere, does not seriously affect his message—except for the unwary. Flaubert does not have to condemn Frédéric's behaviour, for it condemns itself. Beneath the apparently guileless factual record of Frédéric's experience there is a pattern of half-truths and delusions which can satisfy only a person like Frédéric. It is because he is satisfied with them that his whole life is consumed in running round in circles, with the result that at the end of the novel he is not more 'educated' than he was at the beginning.[1] And all this is achieved impersonally, for it comes through even though he has been allowed to argue his own case. The author almost never

[1] Which is my interpretation of the much-discussed final scene. There seems no valid reason for ascribing to Flaubert a sentiment about which Frédéric and Deslauriers agree. Surely these final words are exclusively the characters', just as the ending of *Salammbô* belongs to the Carthaginians and not to Flaubert. The only 'message' which can be extracted from them is that Frédéric and Deslauriers are morally exactly where they were in their adolescence, that their life has not been an education at all. This is independent of Flaubert's pessimism, or his desire to ' épater le bourgeois', and is simply a confirmation of the whole book: Frédéric is as silly now as he ever was. We would recall once more that for Flaubert, sighing over one's lost illusions is also a bourgeois trait, also an *idée reçue*—cf. *supra*, p. 223, note 1.

intervenes to let the reader know directly how false Frédéric's life has been.

We have argued, too, that if this is the case for the novel as a whole, there is no reason why it should not be so in the Mme Arnoux part of the story. Already in the early plans for the novel there was considerable evidence suggesting that the Schlésinger episode was neither the starting-point nor the main inspiration for this novel; and in the novel itself there are several reasons for arguing that Frédéric deluded himself about Mme Arnoux as much as about anything else. Idealization there undoubtedly is, but the idealization is self-centred and intermittent[1]—as false as any of his other attitudes. And it is Frédéric's idealization, not Flaubert's. The affair should be seen in perspective, as one aspect of a many-faceted book, and as an illustration of one side of Frédéric's character, revealing its true value only in comparison with other sides.

Changes in the point of view, then, do not have the same importance in *l'Education* as in either *Bovary* or *Salammbô*, but the communication of Frédéric's *Bovarysme* is perfectly adequate without them. The other task Flaubert had set himself was to show the *Bovarysme* of a whole nation. This is also achieved largely by using the same witness to register the actions and speech of others, and leaving the reader to effect the usual comparisons. Using the same witness preserves the external or mechanical unity of the work, while a deeper unity is achieved by making sure that nearly all the minor characters have at least some traits in common with one or more of the others, even of their enemies, and that all change their social or political position at least once, so that one can never be sure who will be on whose side at any given moment. The result is an immensely involved everchanging series of cross-relationships—Flaubert no doubt working on the assumption that something of this nature must have happened, or the royalists, the republicans, and the bonapartists could not possibly have been successively victorious in such a short period. The majority of Frenchmen, he argues, could not

---

[1] Cf. Durry, op. cit., p. 174: 'La passion de Fr. ... a des intermittences, elle le reprend quand son cœur est vide d'autres femmes.'

correctly be classified as any of these things, but as opportunists. These interrelationships, and the comparisons they invite, increase the unity not only in the sense that the removal of one of the characters would leave a gaping hole in the structure, which could be patched only by modifying many of the remaining actions, attitudes and scenes. They also provide a seemingly infinite variety of ironic contrasts behind which Flaubert can hide his personal attitudes, and each character exhibits attitudes having sufficient points of contact with Frédéric's for us to conclude that the weaknesses in his character which are responsible for his downfall (or, more precisely, his lack of progress) are the same as those which caused the social troubles in the French nation. The technique adopted therefore ensures several of what for Flaubert were the cardinal virtues of a work of art: unity, universality, irony, impersonality.

The technique of a double or combined point of view, relatively important in *Salammbô*, is hardly to be found in *l'Education*; although it is not uncommon to have several people witnessing a scene at once, this does not seem to have the effect of increasing the objectivity of presentation. This is no doubt partly because the concept of 'crowd' as a powerful monster with many bodies but only one tiny mind, is not so important to this novel, which is more concerned with the failure of individuals. Instead, Frédéric himself is credited with varying degrees of perspicacity, depending on what he is looking at and how nearly it concerns him. He is most unreliable in his judgements of people, and especially of women; a little more reliable when it comes to viewing material surroundings, which generally inspire fewer debilitating emotions; and most reliable when he is called upon to witness a street rising. In the last case he is completely uninvolved emotionally, and Flaubert is free to make him wander through the streets, viewing the most interesting events, wherever they may occur. His eyes are used to give a comprehensive view of the Revolution, such as Dussardier, for example, would be quite incapable of giving—he is too busy fighting. Because of his character, Frédéric can replace the narrator in these scenes, so that the apparent unity of viewpoint can be continued.

The methods so far summarized account for over 80 per cent of the total length of the book. The remainder is presented by direct speech, by the omniscient narrator, or from the point of view of various secondary characters. Generalized commentary by the author is rare, except that he does display his cynicism and disgust with the French nation in a few pages. Flaubert may have felt that his customary impassiveness was impossible here—since Frédéric has shown no real interest in the political events, and since in any case the whole book has so thoroughly demonstrated the unreliability and shallowness of both him and all the other characters, the reader could not be expected to recognize an author's mouthpiece if one suddenly appeared at this stage. Yet most of the authorial comments confirm, rather than add to, what an attentive reader would already have inferred from the development of the action, so these comments are rather difficult to explain. The other intrusions by the narrator or secondary characters are usually in the interests of efficiency, of a comic effect, or of irony. They are minor, but do show that even now Flaubert is not tied to any one means of presentation. He will always choose that which is most suited to his needs, provided that it does not clash with his basic artistic tenets.

Thus the point of view technique developed in *Bovary*, and used again with variations in *Salammbô*, has now become even more important to Flaubert: it is used more often, in a more thoroughgoing fashion. It is also used more subtly (which is partly a side-effect of its being more nearly restricted to a single character): indeed, even some critics who have recognized its presence in *Bovary*[1] have lamented its absence in *l'Education*. I have tried to show that it is indeed present, and that postulating its presence allows of an interpretation which differs from that which is most commonly accepted. It also permits the dismissal of one of the great 'problems' of the novel, the question of how Flaubert can talk so much about impersonality and yet apparently ignore his own principles in one of his two greatest works; and

---

[1] In particular Sarraute, loc. cit., p. 7; see also Thorlby, op. cit., p. 27; but the arguments developed by Cortland assume the constant use of Frédéric's point of view.

then the dismissal, too, of some of the uneasy compromises which have been offered to explain away this problem. If one tests the hypothesis by detailed examination of the text, it is found that it can be applied with considerable consistency. It is not difficult to advance theoretical reasons for accepting that such a technique would be attractive to Flaubert, because it allows him to put into practice most of his prized artistic dogma. And the application of it represents the culmination of efforts dating from at least the writing of *Novembre*, some twenty-seven years earlier, to express, in a manner consistent with these dogma, what Flaubert regarded as a fundamental psychological fact.

VI

THE DOUBLE ILLUSION

OUR survey of the *Correspondance* showed that Flaubert was convinced that the two traditional poles of a work of art—Truth and Beauty—were equally necessary. For him, this amounted to reporting facts of human behaviour and arranging them into a unified structure. The facts reported could come from any of the possible sources, including personal feelings and experiences. Whatever their origin, all had equal value as raw material: personal sources had no primacy over others. The facts which he used were so chosen that they illustrated what he took to be permanent, universal aspects of human behaviour: it is not entirely by chance that Flaubert's characters show family resemblances in spite of their widely differing cultures and historical periods.

Besides being chosen in terms of their relevance to human existence, the facts were also chosen for their relevance to the work of art. Each one of them must make a contribution to a pattern and a structure. Flaubert was among those who believe that life and art are intimately connected, but that they can never correspond: 'art' and 'artificial' contain the same root. Life is often not beautiful, but art must always be; and its beauty comes primarily from those elements which the artist has added to life: unity, pattern, rhythm, style. A work of art is self-sufficient, on the one hand complete, and on the other containing nothing extraneous. For both these reasons, the personality of the author is to be excluded. The author's personality, whether present in the form of autobiography or of 'preaching', would be superfluous, because a complete structure tells its own story, communicates its own message; it would also render the work incomplete, by the mere fact of making it relative, specifically applying it to one person instead of allowing it to be potentially applicable to all. The author's personality must of course be reflected in the facts he chooses, and in what he makes his structure say: this is inevitable, and quite sufficient.

Because life is the starting-point for art, because the facts used are chosen for their universality, the choice depends upon the author's individual views of what *are* permanent aspects of human behaviour. For Flaubert, such views could come only by an objective, non-emotional observation of the reactions of real people—including himself—to specific situations. In his case, the result of these observations was the belief that people are incapable of an objective, non-emotional observation, either of their own reactions or of those of others. Flaubert has come to believe that human errors and unhappiness result from 'concluding', from not making the effort to see things as they are, from allowing oneself (whether consciously or not, but usually not) to practise a permanent subjective deformation of reality. The process some-times results in 'right' views (i.e. those Flaubert holds himself), and sometimes in 'wrong' views: but all are wrong in that all are arrived at by using a wrong method. This is the message he would like to communicate in his works. But since he, too, is human, his own subjective deformations are probably responsible for this conclusion. After all, it *is* a conclusion, and therefore suspect. Hence he sees another reason for impersonality: if he as author makes a judgement, and this judgement is wrong or partial, the work may suffer. He also finds it necessary to develop a means of presentation which will separate him, as author, from his characters: the 'universal' characters he must present are, by the very fact of their universality, the opposite of what he believed people should be, of what he himself tried to be. He can have no real sympathy for them, except of a rather nostalgic type, in that they represent what he once was, but is no longer.[1] But he cannot

---

[1] Sympathy, that is, in the sense of sharing in and approving the emotions felt by the characters. That sympathy which consists of an ability to *understand* such emotions is a different matter: this Flaubert had in large measure, and tried hard to cultivate. For a fuller explanation, see Fairlie, op. cit., pp. 66–9, and Bollème, op. cit., p. 24.

openly separate himself, he cannot judge them and condemn them, even if he thinks they deserve it. This would be no more impersonal than showing sympathy for them, and after all they might be right when he thinks they are wrong, and vice versa. Besides, his observations had also shown him that 'right' and 'wrong' almost invariably co-exist in the same person or situation: 'La bêtise n'est pas d'un côté et l'esprit de l'autre.' Hence not one judgement but continual judgements would be required for every character; the novel would be nothing but judgements.

Such considerations do not preclude an ordinary, third-person omniscient narrator technique. Provided the narrator is perfectly detached and objective, provided he limits himself to reporting the situation, and does not take advantage of his privileged position to commentate or interpret or sermonize, impersonality is guaranteed. But art is also representation, illusion.[1] In order to interest the reader, to make him feel involved and to ensure that the work has a real effect on him, it is necessary to allow him to forget the presence of this too-perfect reporter. The narrator should efface himself, put the reader squarely before the matter of the work, allow him to perceive directly what is going on. Such effacement would also constitute a sort of guarantee of authenticity: the reader more readily 'believes' what he sees happening than what he is told happened. The analogy of drama—words and actions, externalized behaviour—springs to mind: it is well known that Flaubert's greatest literary hero was Shakespeare, and that throughout his life he was interested in the theatre. But it is well known that he was a monumental failure as a dramatist. One possible reason for this is that he found the theatre too limiting, in that it could present only one part of what he wanted. He was interested not only in externalized behaviour, but also in causes of it, not so much in human reactions alone, as in the

---

[1] Maupassant, in his preface to *Pierre et Jean* (where he acknowledges his debt to Flaubert), goes so far as to say that the illusion of art results from the careful arrangement, the harmony and structure of the work: 'Faire vrai consiste donc à donner l'illusion complète du vrai, suivant la logique ordinaire des faits, et non à les transcrire servilement dans le pêle-mêle de leur succession. / J'en conclus que les Réalistes de talent devraient s'appeler plutôt des Illusionnistes'.

relationship between a certain kind of human reaction and material reality: 'Il n'y a de vrai que les "rapports", c'est-à-dire la façon dont nous percevons les objets'. 'Il n'y a pas de Vrai ! il n'y a que des manières de voir.'[1]

When Flaubert made these statements, hc was applying them specifically to literature, to the various ways in which a writer can 'see' the material from which he has to make the work of art. But they could be equally well applied, in his view, to the people who are the subject of the work of art: 'il y a des peintres qui voient tout en bleu, d'autres tout en jaune ou tout en noir. Chacun de nous a un prisme à travers lequel il aperçoit le monde.' The illusion of art is two-fold: the artist has to arrange his work so that it gives the illusion of truth, of corresponding to life and to human experience; and he has to show his characters being the victims of their personal illusions, deforming reality as a result of their personality. On the stage, it is not difficult to externalize a mind, but externalizing what a mind perceives, when this perception has not necessarily a material reality of its own, and frequently not even a constant appearance of reality, is a different matter—at least on the scale on which Flaubert conceived it. *Saint Antoine* represented an attempt in this direction; and it is significant that it was a failure in its original form, that over the twenty-five years of its development it moved away from being a play to being a work intended only to be read. Flaubert's intentions just could not be expressed in the form of a play. Some of his plans for *féeries*—which also came to nothing—show a similar orientation. We find 'un homme à qui est donné le pouvoir de voir se réaliser tout ce qu'il pense', and a 'pauvre diable, artiste, penseur, tellement miserable et excedé de la vie qu'il desire en sortir', who takes drugs and sees his imaginings materialize before his eyes.[2] In another plan, Flaubert poses a person who has the ability to read people's thoughts, and here, too, the purpose was to objectify these thoughts, to show them to the spectator, in order to show the contrast between reality and appearance: 'Mais comment faire voir leur pensée?—par un

---

[1] *Cor.*, VIII, 135, 370.
[2] Durry, op. cit., pp. 58–60; see also pp. 62, 64, 66–7.

miroir, placé derrière eux, & où passeraient leurs rêves, à l'état d'ombre chinoise.'[1] Or we could consider the 'trois épiciers' who get drunk: 'Mais tout autour de moi se met à tourner — & effectivement tout tourne [bousin grotesque] — les deux battants du fond s'entr'ouvrent perspective splendide — chœur exquis — la toile du fond avance . . . ils sont dans leur rêve — & l'*Illusion* commence';[2] or the microscopic animals which 'grossissent peu à peu — peuplent la scène deviennent monstreuses & finissent par devorer le Savant.'[3] Certain aspects of *la Spirale* and of *le Château des cœurs*[4] reflect a similar preoccupation.

'Faire voir', 'représenter'; and 'faire voir' not merely material reality, but what a mind creates from material reality, what is often non-existent except in a mind. What Flaubert needed, of course, was the cinema, not the theatre. Perhaps only a lack of adequate technical resources prevented him from realizing some of these projects. If he had, the realist label under which he labours would look even more perverse and uncomprehending than it does already. In any case, the basic concept of these projects is remarkably similar in orientation to what Robbe–Grillet calls the *ciné-roman*. Consider, for example, this extract from the introduction to *l'Année dernière à Marienbad*:

La caractéristique essentielle de l'image est sa présence. . . . on peut dire que, sur l'image, les verbes sont toujours au présent . . .: de toute évidence, ce que l'on voit sur l'écran est *en train de se passer*, c'est le geste même qu'on nous donne, et non pas un rapport sur lui. . . .

Que sont, en somme, toutes ces images? Ce sont des *imaginations*; une imagination, si elle est assez vive, est toujours au présent. Les souvenirs que l'on 'revoit', les régions lointaines, les rencontres à venir, ou même les épisodes passés que chacun arrange dans sa tête en en modifiant le cours tout à loisir, il y a là comme un film intérieur qui se déroule continuellement en nous-mêmes, dès que nous cessons de

---

[1] Durry, op. cit., p. 69.   [2] Ibid., p. 71.
[3] Ibid., p. 73; see also p. 116.
[4] e.g. *Théâtre*, pp. 237 et seq., 247; see also the terms in which Dimoff, loc. cit., pp. 311, 313, 321, describes the plan of *la Spirale*, with its insistence on the intimate connection between real life and the hero's visions, the latter being brought about by the hero's imagination acting as a 'prism' which magnified the former.

prêter attention à ce qui se passe autour de nous. Mais, à d'autres moments, nous enregistrons au contraire, par tous nos sens, ce monde extérieur qui se trouve bel et bien sous nos yeux. Ainsi le film total de notre esprit admet à la fois tour à tour et au même titre les fragments réels proposés à l'instant par la vue et l'ouïe, et des fragments passés, ou lointains, ou futurs, ou totalement fantasmagoriques.[1]

The possibilities of today were hopeless dreams in Flaubert's time, and Robbe-Grillet goes much further along the road of non-logic than did Flaubert. But this extract helps us to see more clearly one of the directions of Flaubert's thought. He could not give it expression on the stage, but he transferred some of it—in a fairly timid fashion, it is true—to his novels. Robbe-Grillet has shown us that his *film intérieur* is equally applicable to the novel, and the two writers, for all their differences, do share a basic principle: in his own way, Flaubert is just as concerned in his novels with the 'presence' mentioned in the above extract. For both, it is two-fold: presence of the object (external reality), and presence of the mind perceiving the object.[2] For Flaubert, this double presence is the more readily attainable because it can be achieved by developing a tendency discernible in his works from the beginning: a preoccupation—almost a fascination—with material reality: 'Pour qu'une chose soit intéressante, il suffit de la regarder longtemps.'[3] A special kind of preoccupation, moreover, because he always had a tendency to note the fleeting, particular aspects of a scene, as well as the more permanent ones. There is here another good reason why theatre could never really have been his medium: it would not have allowed him to describe adequately what attracted him about objects. He would have had to content himself with naming them.

So much for the object. Flaubert also wanted to show the processes of a mind, by showing that mind looking at the object. As we have seen, the impressionistic elements of reality which

---

[1] Robbe-Grillet: *l'Année dernière à Marienbad* (Paris, les éditions de Minuit, 1961), pp. 15–16. Cf. Robbe-Grillet: *Pour un nouveau roman* (Paris, NRF-Gallimard, collection 'Idées', 1963), pp. 24, 147–9, 161, 177.

[2] And this in spite of Flaubert's consistent use of past tenses, which in fact does not affect the matter nearly as much as some modern writers appear to think.

[3] *Cor.*, I, 192; see also Bollème, op. cit., pp. 22 et seq.

attracted him presupposed the presence of a witness, and he usually took care to record that presence. He had only to develop this basic situation to its logical conclusion, to transfer his own preoccupation with reality to his characters, but without endowing them with his patiently-acquired knowledge that 'Il n'y a pas de Vrai ! Il n'y a que des manières de voir', in order to arrive at a point of view presentation. Like most mortals, they believe they are looking at reality (both material and spiritual) whenever they are looking at their personal version of it. Flaubert's own interests can thus be given a free rein, but only his characters can be held responsible for misinterpretations of what they see. By following the character's thoughts and perceptions, he can achieve that immediacy, that illusion, which the traditional omniscient narrator technique could rarely attain. The narrator, while not excluded automatically, is therefore used as little as possible.

It now remains for Flaubert to convey to his readers the critical level of which his characters are usually unaware, while at the same time following the characters' point of view. The two solutions he tried in the first *Education*—direct narrator intervention and the character's coming to self-realization—were both rejected, the first interfering with impersonality, the second with universality. In the projects for plays mentioned above, and in *Saint Antoine* and *Un Cœur simple*, there was no problem: the central delusion is so obviously a delusion that it suffices merely to depict it. In the novels, where the delusions concerned are more subtle, more ordinary and more complex, the problems are correspondingly greater. One part of Flaubert's thought required him to follow his characters closely, another required him to separate himself from them, but not explicitly and not totally. The two solutions he most commonly adopted were showing several points of view, and showing the same point of view in different circumstances. In this manner, he illustrates the idea that each isolated view is inadequate to represent the total situation, even though within each situation 'facts' are not lacking. The first method is more commonly used in *Madame Bovary*, and the second in *l'Education sentimentale*. Both depend upon active co-operation by the reader, and upon the assumption, seldom recognized, that very little of what appears in any given scene can be accepted at face value as being 'true', without first being compared and contrasted with details in other scenes, viewed by other people and/or in other circumstances. The general result is that the characters' views are to be found in the words of the book, while the author's views are most often in the spaces between the words. They are not pronounced, but are present in the arrangement, in the structure of the work, in the very large number of parallels which the method implies. It should be made clear, too, that they are negative views, in the sense that they merely show the author to be in disagreement with his characters. After the first *Education*, Flaubert seldom made a positive pronouncement on what should have been, but merely brought to light what he thought should not have been. His technique therefore corresponds with both his philosophical attitude—*Que sais-je?*—and his theory of impersonality.

It would, however, be quite wrong to give the impression that this was all Flaubert thought the novel was about. He was also very much of his time, and although he had some original contributions to make, he had no wish to break completely with tradition.[1] One immediate result of this is his desire for perfection of style, which frequently led him to express the thoughts of his characters in his own literary style. Another is that the individual in society was as important for him as the individual in isolation. In all his novels, he had to face the difficulty of presenting society as objectively as possible, while still underlining the subjectivity of the individual's attitude to it. This can be partly achieved by the methods outlined above, but other techniques were required to reinforce them. Among the commonest used by Flaubert were the narrator presentation (especially in *Bovary*), the combined point of view with which he experimented in *Salammbô*, and direct speech. The particular uses of each of these have already been examined, and there is no need to state them again here: it is important to recall, however, that whatever the method used,

---

[1] See, for example, *Cor.*, VII, 369: 'De même, interrogez notre ami Goncourt. S'il est franc, il vous avouera que la littérature française n'existait pas avant Balzac. Voilà où mènent l'abus de l'esprit et la peur de tomber dans les poncifs.'

good reasons can always be found for its use. Flaubert's methods of presentation were never an accident, he always chose that which seemed best suited to the situation in hand.

The use of a relatively wide range of differing techniques posed certain problems connected with unity and harmony. Flaubert had to find ways of linking them, so that the necessary changes would not force themselves upon the attention of the reader. He achieved this desirable unity of tone by various 'intermediate' techniques, especially *style indirect libre* and the bourgeois narrator (or its equivalent). The joints between two given methods of presentation are. thereby carefully plastered over. Each work could be compared with the colours of the spectrum: we can see that one end is violet and the other red, we can even see that red and orange occur side by side, but we cannot see at what exact point the colour ceases to be orange and begins to be red. In addition, the various techniques are completely interdependent, each contributes something necessary to the total picture: if one colour could be extracted, the sum of the remainder would no longer be white. Thus, although the point of view method may appear as the most important and the most original of Flaubert's techniques, it is impossible to argue that it alone presents the total message of any one of his works. Even in terms of the characters' subjectivity, it is usual for us to receive some of our information through point of view, but later to have the 'correcting' factor introduced by, say, direct speech. Neither method could stand without the other.

While *l'Education sentimentale*, like the other novels, contains all these different methods, and substantially the same devices for linking them, it differs in degree. Frédéric's point of view is followed to a greater extent than that of the previous 'heroes'. Even the objective representation of society is now achieved largely through him. This means a slight change in the normal orientation of the point of view method, as we have seen. But it also means that Flaubert has achieved in this novel even greater unity than before, between the individual and the social aspects on one hand, and between form and content on the other. Certainly this sort of unity is to be found in all his novels, and always as a result of conscious effort. But the structure of *l'Education sentimentale* is the culmination of all the preceding labour and experience: it is a monument of breath-taking proportions, which few others would have either the courage or the tenacity to design and build single-handed . . . *et ça reste dans le désert!*

BIBLIOGRAPHY

The following list is highly selective, and includes only those titles which have had a direct bearing on the present study.

ALBALAT, A., *Gustave Flaubert et ses amis* (Plon, Paris, 1927).

AMIC, H. (ed.), *Correspondance entre George Sand et Gustave Flaubert* (Calmann-Lévy, Paris, 1904).

AUERBACH, E., *Mimesis: the representation of reality in western literature*, tr. from German by Willard Trask (Doubleday Anchor, New York, 1957).

BART, B. F., *Flaubert's landscape descriptions* (University of Michigan Press, Ann Arbor, 1956).

—— 'Aesthetic distance in *Madame Bovary*', *PMLA* lxix (1954), 1112–1126.

BAUDELAIRE, C., *L'Art romantique* (Editions d'art Albert Skira, Genève, 1945).

BERSANI, L., 'The narrator and the bourgeois community in *Madame Bovary*', *French review*, xxxii, 6 (May 1959), 527–33.

BERTRAND, L., *Gustave Flaubert* (Ollendorff (Albin Michel), Paris, n.d.).

BEUCHAT, C., *Histoire du naturalisme français* (Corrêa, Paris, 1949).

BIELER, A., 'La couleur dans *Salammbô*', *French review*, xxxiii, 4 (Feb. 1960), 359–70.

BLIN, G., *Stendhal et les problèmes du roman* (Corti, Paris, 1954).

BOLLÈME, G., *La leçon de Flaubert* (Julliard, Paris, 1964).

BONWIT, M., *Gustave Flaubert et le principe d'impassibilité*, University of California publications in modern philology, xxxiii, 4 (1950), 263–420.

BOPP, L., *Commentaire sur 'Madame Bovary'* (La Baconnière, Neuchâtel-Paris, 1951).

BROMBERT, V., *The novels of Flaubert: a study of themes and techniques* (Princeton University Press, 1966).

BRUNEAU, J., *Les débuts littéraires de Gustave Flaubert, 1831–1845* (Armand Colin, Paris, 1962).

CASTEX, P.-G., *Flaubert: l'Education sentimentale* (Centre de documentation universitaire, Paris, 1959).

CELLIER, L., *Etudes de structure* (Archives des lettres modernes, Paris, 1964).

CENTO, A., *Bouvard et Pécuchet: édition critique, précédée des scénarios inédits* (Istituto universitario orientale, Napoli, and Nizet, Paris, 1964).

COLLING, A., *Gustave Flaubert* (Arthème Fayard, Paris, 1947).

COOK, A., 'Flaubert: the riches of detachment', *French review*, xxxii, 2 (Dec. 1958), 120–9.

CORMEAU, N., *Physiologie du roman* (la Renaissance du livre, Bruxelles, 1947).

CORTLAND, P., *The sentimental adventure: an examination of Flaubert's 'Education sentimentale'* (Mouton, The Hague, 1967).

DAICHES, D., *Critical approaches to literature* (Longmans, London, 1959).

DEMOREST, D. L., *L'Expression figurée et symbolique dans l'œuvre de Gustave Flaubert* (Conard, Paris, 1931).

DIGEON, C., *Le dernier visage de Flaubert* (Aubier, Paris, 1946).

DIMOFF, P., 'Autour d'un projet de roman de Flaubert: *la Spirale*', *RHL* (oct.–déc. 1948), 309–35.

DUMESNIL, R., '*Madame Bovary*' de Gustave Flaubert (SFELT, les grands événements littéraires, Paris, 1946).

—— *Gustave Flaubert: l'homme et l'œuvre* (Desclée de Brouwer, Paris, 1947).

       Introduction to *l'Education sentimentale* (Société les Belles Lettres, Paris, 1958).

—— *La vocation de Gustave Flaubert* (Gallimard, Paris, 1961).

—— '*l'Education sentimentale*' de Gustave Flaubert (Nizet, Paris, 1962).

DURRY, M.-J., *Flaubert et ses projets inédits* (Nizet, Paris, 1950).

ELIOT, T. S., 'The function of criticism', *Selected Essays* (Faber, London, 1949).

—— 'Tradition and the individual talent', *Selected Essays* (Faber, London, 1949).

FAGUET, E., *Flaubert* (Hachette, les grands écrivains français, Paris, 1913).

FAIRLIE, A., *Flaubert: 'Madame Bovary'* (Edward Arnold, Studies in French literature, London, 1962).

FERRÈRE, E.-L., *L'Esthétique de Gustave Flaubert* (Conard, Paris, 1913).

FREJLICH, H., *Flaubert d'après sa Correspondance* (SFELT, Paris, 1933).

FRIEDMAN, N., 'Point of view in fiction: the development of a critical concept', *PMLA* lxx (1955), 1160–84.

GERACE-DI VASTO, L., *Gustavo Flaubert nella vita e nell'arte* (Tipografia Mariano Ricci, Firenze, 1939).

GIRAUD, R., *The unheroic hero in the novels of Stendhal, Balzac and Flaubert* (Rutgers University Press, New Brunswick, 1957).

GOTHOT-MERSCH, C., *La genèse de 'Madame Bovary'* (Corti, Paris, 1966).

HEUZEY, J., 'Le costume de Salammbô', *Bulletin des amis de Flaubert*, ii (1951), 7–15.

JAMES, HENRY, 'Gustave Flaubert', *The house of fiction: essays on the novel*, ed. Leon Edel (Mercury Books, London, 1962).

LAPP, J. C., 'Art and hallucination in Flaubert', *French Studies*, x (Oct. 1956), 322–34.

LA VARENDE, J. DE, *Flaubert par lui-même* (Seuil, Paris, 1958).

LELEU, G., *'Madame Bovary': ébauches et fragments inédits* (Conard, Paris, 1936).

LEVIN, H., *The gates of horn: a study of five French realists* (Oxford University Press, New York, 1963).

LUBBOCK, P., *The craft of fiction* (Jonathan Cape, London, 1957).

MARANINI, L., *Visione e personnagio secondo Flaubert, ed altri studi francesi* (Biblioteca di cultura, Liviana, Padova, 1959).

MARTINO, P., *Le roman réaliste sous le Second Empire* (Hachette, Paris, 1913).

MASON, G., *Les écrits de jeunesse de Flaubert* (Nizet, Paris, 1961).

MAUPASSANT, G. DE, 'Le roman', preface to *Pierre et Jean* (Garnier, Paris, 1959).

MAYNIAL, E., *Flaubert* (Editions de la nouvelle revue critique, Paris, 1943).

MEIN, M., 'Flaubert, a precursor of Proust', *French Studies*, xvii (July 1963), 218–37.

MOREAU, P., *Flaubert: 'Madame Bovary'* (Centre de documentation universitaire, Paris, 1959).

—— 'L'art de la composition dans *Madame Bovary*', *Orbis litterarum*, xii (1957), 171–8.

MOSHER, H. F., *Point of view in the fiction of Gustave Flaubert and Ford Madox Ford* (University of Texas Ph.D. dissertation; University microfilms, Ann Arbor, 1967).

NAAMAN, A., *Les débuts de Gustave Flaubert et sa technique de la description* (Nizet, Paris, 1962).

POMMIER, J. and LELEU, G., *Madame Bovary: nouvelle version précédée des scénarios inédits* (Corti, Paris, 1949).

POMMIER, J., 'Durry: *Flaubert et ses projets inédits — compte rendu*', *RHL* (janv.–mars 1953), 108–12.

POPE, C., *The giant snakes: the natural history of the boa constrictor, the anaconda and the largest pythons* (Routledge and Kegan Paul, London, 1961).

POUILLON, J., *Temps et roman* (NRF–Gallimard, Paris, 1946).

POULET, G., 'La pensée circulaire de Flaubert', *NNRF* (juillet 1955), 30–52.

PRAZ, M., *The romantic agony*, tr. from Italian by Angus Davidson (Oxford University Press, London, 1933).

ROBBE-GRILLET, A., Introduction to *L'Année dernière à Marienbad* (Editions de Minuit, Paris, 1961).

—— *Pour un nouveau roman* (NRF–Gallimard, Paris, 1963).

ROUSSET, J., *Forme et signification* (Corti, Paris, 1964).

SAINTE-BEUVE, C.-A., '*Madame Bovary*' (4 mai 1857) and '*Salammbô*' (8, 15, and 22 décembre 1862), *Les grands écrivains français: études des 'Lundis' et des 'Portraits'*, ed. Maurice Allem; *XIXe siècle, Les Romanciers, II* (Garnier, Paris, 1927), 164–241.

SARRAUTE, N., 'Flaubert le précurseur', *Preuves* (fév. 1965), 3–11.

SHERRINGTON, R., 'Des dangers de la *Correspondance* de Flaubert', *Bulletin des amis de Flaubert*, xxiv (mai 1964), 27–37.

—— 'Illusion and reality in *La tentation de Saint Antoine*', *AUMLA* xxiv (Nov. 1965), 272–89.

THIBAUDET, A., *Gustave Flaubert* (NRF–Gallimard, Paris, 1935; reprinted 1963).

THORLBY, A., *Gustave Flaubert and the art of realism* (Bowes and Bowes, Studies in modern European literature and thought, London, 1956).

TILLETT, M., *On reading Flaubert* (Oxford University Press, London, 1961).

ULLMANN, S., *Style in the French novel* (Cambridge University Press, 1957).

VIAL, A., 'Flaubert émule et disciple émancipé de Balzac', *RHL* (juillet–sept. 1948), 233–63.

—— 'De *Volupté* à *l'Education sentimentale*', *RHL* (janviers–mars and avril–juin 1957), 45–65, 178–95.

WELLECK, R., and WARREN, A., *Theory of literature* (Jonathan Cape, London, 1961).

INDEX

References to works by authors other than Flaubert are included under the author's name; works by Flaubert are listed under their titles. Characters in *Madame Bovary, Salammbô,* and both versions of *l'Education sentimentale* are listed separately, while characters of other works by Flaubert are included in the entry for the work.